W9-DHI-910

ACTS OF HOPE

JAMES BOYD WHITE

# ACTS OF HOPE

## CREATING AUTHORITY IN
## LITERATURE, LAW, AND
## POLITICS

THE UNIVERSITY OF CHICAGO PRESS
CHICAGO & LONDON

JAMES BOYD WHITE is the Hart Wright Professor of Law, professor of English language and literature, and adjunct professor of Classics at the University of Michigan.

The University of Chicago Press, Chicago 60637
The University of Chicago Press, Ltd., London
© 1994 by The University of Chicago
All rights reserved. Published 1994
Printed in the United States of America
03 02 01 00 99 98 97 96 95 94  1 2 3 4 5

Published with the generous assistance of the John Simon Guggenheim Memorial Foundation.

ISBN: 0-226-89510-6 (cloth)

Library of Congress Cataloging-in-Publication Data

White, James Boyd, 1938–
Acts of hope : creating authority in literature, law, and politics
/ James Boyd White.
p.  cm.
Includes bibliographical references and index.
1. Authority. 2. Consensus (Social sciences) 3. Individualism.
4. Personalism. 5. Language and culture. I. Title.
JC328.2.W55 1994
303.3'6—dc20
94-8877
CIP

The paper used in this publication meets the minimum requirements of the American National Standard for Information Sciences—Permanence of Paper for Printed Library Materials, ANSI Z39.48-1984.

TO THE MONDAY NIGHT GROUP

*"A university bound in a lesser volume"*

# Contents

# PREFACE

This book is about what happens when authority becomes the subject of conscious thought and argument. For the most part we go through life yielding to the demands made upon us by the world, without thinking much about them: we stop at red lights, pay our taxes, show up on time for appointments, speak more or less grammatically, and so on. But sometimes a person will challenge the claims made upon him, either by interpreting them (or the facts) in his favor or, more deeply, by rejecting the authority of a regime entirely. This moment can be highly dramatic (as when Socrates' friend Crito tells him to escape from prison) but it is not always so. The management of the competing claims of the world on the self, the self on the world, is a primary human process; sometimes it is carried on instinctively, sometimes as the subject of conscious art. It is with performances of this art that this book is concerned.

From childhood on we are surrounded by directions to our conduct, or claims upon our lives, made by parents, friends, and children; by schools, churches, and synagogues; by policemen, judges, and legislators—by all the people and institutions that make up our private and public worlds. On the other side we have the exigencies or wishes of the self—our needs, or whims, or considered judgments—which sometimes harmonize, sometimes conflict, with these external demands. Thus it is across our lives that we face the question of the proper authority of particular people or institutions.

But the problem is deeper even than this, reaching every action of the

ix

mind, for even our languages are systems of authority. Think of learning one's native language, for example, as we all have done: to be understood at all we must speak it as it is spoken by other people, employing its terms and categories and gestures; yet our experience is never exactly the same as that of others, we have our own thoughts and feelings, and the question naturally arises, How adequate is our language to what we know, to what we have become? How far are we free, and able, to transform it? Huckleberry Finn, to take a clear and familiar example, grew up in a world in which the most important fact about any person was his or her race, and in which "nigger" was a standard term of description and address; then he found himself the friend of a runaway slave, without a language in which to describe that relation, which in turn meant without a way of imagining his life in his world. There was nothing to do at the end but "light out for the territories," which is not a possibility for any of us.

While the experience of Huck Finn might be thought extreme, we all have something like it. An ordinary part of growing up, for example, is that the young person finds the language she has inherited from her parents, with all its commitments to particular social practices and attitudes, most unsatisfactory; she feels she has to struggle, sometimes unsuccessfully, to find a language in which to express what she thinks and is, a language with which to make her future. What makes it even harder is that she has to do this as one who is partly made by what she wants to criticize, for we are all to a large degree shaped by the very institutions and practices whose authority we question. There is no clear line between inner and outer reality.

Sometimes a person experiences a similar collapse of confidence in the language of the larger culture too, suddenly seeing that it cannot say or do what he dimly feels it should. Such moments can be the occasion for great art or politics: Homer, in the *Iliad,* presents Achilles as coming to see as alien the language of honor upon which he has built his life, and in so doing makes a poem that is a great act of cultural and political criticism; Plato, in his dialogues, subverts and transforms the language of value by which his culture lived; Lincoln, in his public speeches, redefines our Constitution as rooted in the equality of all people. One aim of certain texts—in American literature the works of Emerson, Melville, and Dickinson stand out—is to induce such a collapse of language in the reader and by doing so to open up new possibilities for thought and life.

To say that the choice is either to resist or submit to the authorities we find in the world is too simple, partly because the authorities to which we respond often have a purchase in our own minds, partly because as we grow we find ourselves making authorities of our own: in reworking the languages we have inherited, from early childhood on, in making claims for the rightness of our conduct, or in arguing for the cogency of our reasons. Every speech act is a way of being and acting in the world that makes a claim for its own rightness, which we ask others to respect. Our life with language and each other involves the perpetual creation of authorities, good and bad, successful and unsuccessful.

IN THIS BOOK MY OBJECT IS to explore the way authority is thought about and constituted in a series of texts, chosen from different cultural contexts and different generic types. Each of them contains arguments that assert, or deny, that a person should submit to the authority of an institution or a set of social practices. In Plato's *Crito* the institution in question is the law of Athens, by which Socrates has been sentenced to death; in *Richard II*, it is the crown, which Richard claims by divine right and inheritance, but which Henry Bolingbroke takes from him on the grounds of misfeasance; in Hooker's *Lawes of Ecclesiasticall Politie*, it is the English church, which Hooker supports and the Puritans resist; in Hale's "Considerations Touching the Amendment or Alteration of Lawes" and in the modern Supreme Court case, *Planned Parenthood v. Casey* (1992), it is the existing state of the law, poised against desire for change; in Austen's *Mansfield Park*, it is the manners, and the master, of the family into which Fanny Price has been adopted; in Emily Dickinson's poems, it is the conventions that establish the forms of expression in which the poet, and especially the "poetess," must speak in order to be heard; in Mandela's speech from the dock, it is the law of South Africa that defines his conduct as criminal; in Lincoln's Second Inaugural Address, it is the Union, invoked to justify the awful war fought for its preservation.

In each case a speaker, or more than one, is confronted with claims that the institution in question has an authority that overrides his own wishes, judgment, or experience; he responds by acquiescing or by resisting, and in doing so, defines both himself and the institution in new ways. In doing this he participates in the creation of the very authorities he accepts or resists. In one sense at least his ultimate authority becomes the way of thinking and talking by which he does these things, the language by which he defines and adjudicates these competing claims. My interest is in the way this moment of conflict and tension—and creativity, too—is addressed in these texts, and in the possibilities for life they thus define.

ONE QUESTION FOR US AS READERS is whether we can understand and describe a text's claims to authority, including for the authority of its own performances. In this book I shall try to do that with the texts I read. But there is an evaluative question as well: What are we to think of the way of thinking and talking that a particular text performs and holds out as authoritative? How are we to judge it? The possible range of performances is after all enormous, from the worst to the best forms of thought and expression. This requires us to ask what those forms are. This is also a way of asking, To what modes of thinking and talking should authority be accorded?

This is not merely an intellectual but a political and ethical question. A claim for—or against—the authority of an institution or a set of practices is always, among other things, an invitation to create a community, both with one's interlocutor and with those others one speaks about, a community for which authority is claimed; and like other efforts to create community it can be analyzed and evaluated in political and ethical terms. Who are the actors here and how are they defined? What relation, of equality or subordination, exists among them? By what understandings or procedures is it regulated, by what aspirations motivated? What is this living tissue for which authority is claimed?

When we turn from reading texts such as these to our own lives as citizens and speakers we face a related set of questions: When and why should we grant authority to particular institutions or social practices, and when, by contrast, should we insist instead upon our own sense of what is right, or good, or necessary? If we are in doubt, how long should we defer making up our minds, with the aim of educating ourselves into what we are at first inclined to resist? Some such deferral is essential to all growing up, some such education a good thing; yet one ought not give up the right and duty to decide things for oneself in the end, and even a partial submission to an evil culture may have serious and enduring consequences. And as speakers ourselves: What kinds of authorities should we create in our own acts of thought and speech?

Every time we speak to an occasion at which the world makes claims upon the self, whether we do so in public or private, in the classroom, or on the pages of journals, with friends or with enemies, we respond to these questions and others like them. How are we to do this well? In a matter like this we need all the education we can get, and it is with the aim of learning from the performances of others, situated in other times and cultures, that I turn to the texts that follow.

. . .

*After reading this Preface and one of the chapters that follows, a friend wrote to ask: "I don't quite understand. Is authority in your view something to be combatted, or claimed (or both)?" She wrote from the world of literary criticism, where "authority" is usually not used in a good sense. There "subversion" or "transgression" are more common objects of praise; indeed they are sometimes seen as the central functions of literary art. Even in the law, which is built upon authority, there is a mistrust of this term, and of the idea that any person or institution has authority over another. I find helpful the distinction reflected in the title of my colleague Joseph Vining's book,* The Authoritative and the Authoritarian *(Chicago: University of Chicago Press, 1986). This is of course just to say that there are good and bad forms of this phenomenon and it raises the question, How are they to be distinguished? How can claims to authority be appropriately recognized and resisted, claimed and created? The art that this question defines is my subject here.*

# Acknowledgments

A GREAT MANY FRIENDS HAVE READ AND COMMENTED on portions of this book, or discussed with me its principal methods and ideas. Of these I want especially to thank Arthur Adkins, Milner Ball, A. L. Becker, Richard Bell, Lee Bollinger, John Comaroff, Conal Condren, Thomas Eisele, Thomas Andrew Green, Don Herzog, L. H. LaRue, Cristanne Miller, William Ian Miller, Martha Nussbaum, James Redfield, Terrance Sandalow, Teresa Scassa, Gerda Seligson, Debora Kuller Shuger, Philip Soper, Kent Syverud, Peter Teachout, Laura Wendorff, Robin West, Mary White, Nicholas White, and Christina Whitman. I want to make particular mention here of Joseph Vining, who first led me to think about some of these issues, and whose conversation has offered a continuing education. Robin West made the criticisms summarized at page 182, for which I am most grateful, as I am for her permission to reproduce them. Susan Prince was of great help with respect to the *Crito*, checking my translations and my arguments alike. I am especially grateful to Marcia Beach, whose patience and accuracy in putting this manuscript together for publication have been extraordinary.

I also want to express my gratitude for the financial support of the Guggenheim Foundation, the National Endowment for the Humanities, and the University of Michigan Law School. This book was begun at Clare Hall in Cambridge, which provided a perfect environment for work and life, and I wish also to thank those who maintain that extraordinary community.

My deepest thanks are to my wife, whose friendship and love exceed anything I could ever have imagined.

I

# The Claims of the World on the Self, the Self on the World

# ONE

# PLATO'S *CRITO:* THE AUTHORITY OF LAW AND PHILOSOPHY

THE *CRITO* IS ONE OF SEVERAL PLATONIC DIALOGUES about Socrates' last days: chronologically it follows the *Apology,* which consists of Socrates' speech at his trial, and it precedes the *Phaedo,* in which he considers the possibility of an afterlife. Like many of the dialogues it receives its name from a person, Crito, an old friend of Socrates who visits him in prison where he lies under sentence of death. Crito urges Socrates to escape, claiming that his conviction and penalty, however legal they may be, are unjust; that escape is perfectly practicable; and that Socrates therefore has a duty—to his friends, his family, and perhaps himself—to do it. Justice itself requires him to escape.

Socrates responds to these claims in many ways, but most famously in a passage in which he asks Crito to imagine what the laws (*nomoi*) and the common state of the city (*to koinon tes poleos*) might say to him about the justice of his proposed escape. They would say, Socrates tells him, that it would be unjust for him to escape against their commands, even if the sentence against him is unjust, for he owes them an absolute duty of obedience. There are several reasons for this. First, the laws are like his parents, for they regulated the marriage of his actual parents and his own conception, and they shaped his education too; he therefore owes them the obedience of a child to a parent or a slave to a master. Second, by continuing to live in Athens, when he could have left at any time, he has implicitly agreed to obey all its laws and decisions. His only legitimate way out would be to persuade the laws and the city that they are wrong, which he has tried but failed to do. He is therefore obliged to obey the judgment of the law and suffer death, even if the verdict compelling him to do so is unjust.

This summary of the speech of the Nomoi is imperfect, to say the least, but for present purposes it will do, for it suggests that this set of arguments, at least when stated in such a bald and unelaborated form, is very weak indeed. Why, for example, does it follow from the fact that Socrates has stayed in Athens that he has agreed to obey its laws and decrees, even when they are unjust? Why should we not read his actual conduct—particularly as it is summarized for us in the *Apology*—rather as agreeing to do what he can, at every stage and in every way, to advance the cause of justice? And why should this not mean correcting the city when it is wrong, including by disobedience when that is appropriate? For, as familiar Socratic doctrine tells us, the city can have no genuine interest in acting unjustly. Why, indeed, should an agreement to do, or suffer, something that is unjust be given any weight at all? And to turn to the even more problematic argument: For what reasons should we construe the relation between citizen and city as being like that of child and parent or slave and master? Even if we do take this step, why should these relations carry with them an obligation to do or suffer injustice?

Of course these questions might have answers, perhaps very good ones; no small part of Western political philosophy has been devoted to trying to work them out. But as the speech of the Nomoi is actually written, especially in its first version, it responds to virtually none of the questions we have about it, but consists instead of a series of conclusory declarations, with very little argument to support them, and that mostly, though not entirely, of low quality. We should not be misled by our familiarity with more recent and persuasive versions of these positions into misreading the way they are stated here.

The argument of the Nomoi is still more problematic when considered in light of the rest of Socrates' career, during which he has repeatedly argued that to live and act well is the supreme goal of life, and that "well" means, among other things, "justly." [1] The speech he imagines the Nomoi making, and which he invokes as authoritative, seems inconsistent with virtually everything else he has said and done, including in the *Apology*, where he boasts of his refusal to follow certain official orders and asserts an absolute commitment to leading the philosophic life. He says to the jury, for example, that he would not accept an acquittal that was condi-

---

1. In speaking of "Socrates" here and throughout I do not mean the historical person but the character created in this and the other Platonic dialogues, especially the early ones. I assume that one of Plato's goals is the definition of this complex person, or persona, and, therefore, that it is right to read these dialogues against each other.

tioned on his giving up philosophy but would persist in this course of life against their command. The only constraint he recognizes in the *Apology* is that of his own *daimonion,* the spiritual force that, he says, always tells him when he is considering doing something that he ought not do.

Various stratagems have been devised to reconcile the *Crito* with the rest of what the Platonic Socrates has said and done: for example, that the command he described himself in the *Apology* as disobeying (to arrest Leon of Salamis) was itself not really law but lawless; or that the Nomoi speak only presumptively, and thus recognize a host of unarticulated exceptions; or that the jury hasn't the power to make an acquittal conditional and that therefore his resolve, expressed in the *Apology,* to continue the philosophic life in violation of such conditions can be disregarded as merely hypothetical; or that the obligation "to do what the laws command or to persuade them otherwise" can be satisfied if one tries in good faith to persuade them, even if one fails; or, perhaps more sensibly than the others, that there is a crucial Socratic difference between doing and suffering injustice.[2] But these attempted reconciliations are dubious at best, both because the inconsistency with the rest of what the Platonic Socrates says simply will not go away, no matter how much we wish it to, and because the arguments of the Nomoi, as I shall try to show, are on the merits weak and conclusory. Although they happen to persuade Crito, I think that one cannot really imagine them persuading any criti-

2. See: (1) John Burnet, *Plato's Euthyphro, Apology of Socrates, and Crito* (Oxford: Oxford University Press, 1924), pages 253–54 (the order of the Thirty to arrest Leon of Salamis no law at all); (2) Terence Irwin, "Socratic Inquiry and Politics," *Ethics* 96 (1986): 400–15 (Nomoi's claims only presumptive); (3) Thomas C. Brickhouse and Nicholas Smith, *Socrates on Trial* (Princeton: Princeton University Press, 1989), pages 143–47 (the hypothetical character of his vow to continue to philosophize against a conditional verdict); (4) Richard Kraut, *Socrates and the State* (Princeton: Princeton University Press, 1984), pages 65–73 (on "persuade" as "try to persuade"); (5) A. D. Woozley, *Law and Obedience: The Arguments of Plato's Crito* (Chapel Hill: University of North Carolina Press, 1979), pages 30–31, 32, 44 (disobedience permissible if punishment accepted) ("try to persuade") (hypothetical character of vow in *Apology*); (6) Gerasimos Santas, *Socrates: Philosophy in Plato's Early Dialogues* (London: Routledge & Kegan Paul, 1979), pages 45–54 (distinction between *prima facie* and all-things-considered cases) (*Apology* and *Crito* involve different issues, the first conscientious disobedience, the other secret evasion); (7) R. E. Allen, *Socrates and Legal Obligation* (Minneapolis: University of Minnesota Press, 1980), page 109 (distinction between doing and suffering wrong).

On the distinction between doing and suffering injustice: while it is true that Socrates in the *Crito* suffers injustice, and that this is, as he says in the *Gorgias,* far less serious than doing it, the Nomoi themselves make no such distinction. They quite clearly say that the obligation is to do (*poiein*) whatever they command.

cally acute mind of the position they advance, that the Athenian citizen
has an absolute obligation to obey the laws even when they are unjust.

MANY OF THE DIFFICULTIES WE HAVE in reading the *Crito* are due, I
think, to a certain mistake commonly made not only in the reading of
Plato but in the reading of other philosophic texts too, namely, to think
that one can extract from a text a particular key passage—in this case the
speech of the Nomoi—and read it as though it stood alone, as a set of
arguments that could be abstracted from their context and assessed independently, rather than as a part of a larger text, with its own shape and
rhythm and texture. At a more general level the mistake is to assume that
the meaning of the text as a whole is propositional in kind, that is, that
it can be reduced to a set of claims each of which can be independently
tested for its truth or adequacy.[3] May it not be that at least the *Crito,* and
perhaps other Platonic dialogues, and indeed perhaps other texts we
think of as philosophic as well, have a meaning of a richer and more
problematic kind, one that cannot be reduced to the propositional? May
it even be that our modern aspiration to produce philosophic texts that
can be reduced to such forms is itself misguided, likely to fail, and perhaps
an evasion of philosophic responsibility?

I want to ask: What happens, especially to its argument about the
authority of law, if we read the *Crito* in a different way, as a composition
of which we assume all the parts have a place and meaning, no one of
which can be elevated above the others except in the terms, and on the
grounds, that the text itself affords?[4] To take one example: the dialogue
begins with Crito's visit to Socrates in jail, early in the morning, and with
talk about a dream Socrates has just had. Can we not take this part of the
text seriously, asking what it means, and not assume that it is just window
dressing, or "setting the stage," or otherwise marginal or irrelevant to the
matter at hand? We might even prepare ourselves to conclude, if the text

3. For an example of an approach to Plato of this kind, see Terence Irwin, *Gorgias*
(Oxford: Oxford University Press, 1979).

4. For a fine reading of the *Crito* on such premises, see Ernest J. Weinrib, "Obedience
to Law in Plato's Crito," 27 *American Journal of Jurisprudence* 85 (1982), discussed in a
note at page 310 infra.

so persuaded us, that this scene is more central to the text than the speech of the Nomoi itself.

The hope is that we may find a way to respect the text as it is composed, attending to its form, its methods, its various parts and their relations, and to discover the kind of coherence and meaning it then proves to have. We could put it, perhaps, that my object is to read this "philosophic" text not as a string of propositions but as "literature," that is, with an eye to possibilities of meaning richer and more complex than the propositional; but we would do this in part in the hope of being instructed in the falseness of the way we habitually distinguish between these two forms of thought and expression.[5] It may be that great philosophy is literary in many of its deepest commitments, great literature philosophic, and that what is called for is a way of reading both that attempts to recognize their full dimensions of meaning.

## ANXIETY AND REPOSE

We can begin with the opening scene: Crito has come, very early in the morning, to the cell of Socrates, whose wholly understandable question

5. Another way to put this would be to suggest that for Plato at least "philosophy" does not mean the creation of an intellectual system, supported by arguments—although that is how he has often been read—but rather an activity of mind that he at once exhibits in his dialogues and stimulates in his reader. After all, in his Seventh Letter—if that is indeed by him—Plato said that his real philosophy is not to be found in his writings but in his teaching, in the living engagement of mind with mind. One might read his writing, then, as attempting to replicate in his relation with the reader the dialectical activity that in its fullest form exists only in living conversation. In the terms suggested by the *Phaedrus*, where Socrates attacks writing, it may be Plato's object to create a text that, unlike most, does not simply say the same thing always but shifts its meaning as it is more deeply understood. *Phaedrus* 275d-e. This is possible because its meaning is not propositional in character but performative, residing in the activity in which it engages the reader.

For a development of this line of argument with respect to Plato's *Gorgias*, see my *When Words Lose Their Meaning: Constitutions and Reconstitutions of Language, Character, and Community* (Chicago: University of Chicago Press, 1984), chapter 4. For a similar argument with respect to Wittgenstein and Kierkegaard, see James Conant, "On Comparing Wittgenstein and Kierkegaard" (forthcoming). For a general approach to the relation between philosophy and literature, see Martha Nussbaum, *Love's Knowledge: Essays on Philosophy and Literature* (Oxford: Oxford University Press, 1990). On the other hand, it would hardly do simply to say that "philosophy" should be regarded as a kind of "literature," without more. Both of those terms require definition, at its best performative, in the text that says such a thing.

To put it the other way round and say that literature is, or can be, philosophic is not to

to him is the first line of the dialogue: "Why have you come at this time of the day, Crito—is it not still very early?" The first part of Socrates' question—"Why have you come?"—will receive an answer a few paragraphs later, when Crito says that he is coming to bring the "bad news" that the sacred ship, during whose voyage to Delos Socrates cannot be put to death, will arrive that very day. For the present, however, Socrates focuses upon the other and apparently more trivial question, about what time it is. When he is told that it is indeed very early, just first light, he expresses surprise that Crito was able to get into the jail at such an hour. Crito responds that he was allowed in because, through his earlier visits, he has come to know the jailer and, besides that, because he has done him a favor of some unspecified sort. Crito reveals that he has been sitting there quietly some time, beside the sleeping Socrates. When Socrates asks why he did not wake him, Crito says: "I did not wish you to be in such grief and wakefulness [as I am]."[6]

The dialogue thus has its origins in Crito's complex response to hearing the news about the ship. He cannot bear to carry it alone but needs to communicate it to Socrates, no doubt in the hopes that somehow this will make it tolerable. This is in fact the unstated answer to the second part of Socrates' question, namely, "Why did you come so early?" That Crito comes at all, is to tell the news; that he comes so early, rather than waiting till a more usual hour, manifests an anxiety or need, an incapacity to bear the news alone; this is in fact a rather appealing quality in him, attesting as it does to the depth and sincerity of his feeling for his friend.

But when he comes into the presence of Socrates, Crito does not wake him after all, in part no doubt out of a sense of consideration for him, lying peacefully asleep, but in part perhaps also because he discovers that merely to be in Socrates' presence gives him much of what he needs. For, he says, he has been sitting for some time beside him, full of wonder to perceive "how sweetly you sleep," and, as often before, "I have thought you happy in your character (tropos), and especially so in the present circumstance, [when I see] how easily and gently you bear it."

---

say that its experience can be translated into a set of propositions and arguments on philosophic themes. The point rather is that the activities and practices of literature can be seen to be of general, and not merely particular, value, as they instruct us about the conditions upon which life must be led, the nature and limits of language, the capacities of our minds, and so forth.

6. In summarizing portions of the *Crito* I have sometimes translated directly, in which case the extract is set off with quotation marks or in block paragraphs, sometimes paraphrased roughly, in which case there are no such marks.

The issue thus presented by the opening of the text is the contrast between anxiety and repose, sleeplessness and sleeping, between the capacity to bear this apparent misfortune gently and the incapacity to rest once one has received the evil news. I think that this contrast is in fact the central topic to which the rest of the dialogue is addressed, and that to it the "obligation to obey the laws" is something of a sidelight.

Two important points about the character of Crito emerge in this brief opening. First, as we have seen, Crito is shown to be a friend of Socrates, and in two ways: he both needs to be with him in his distress, and can let him sleep. There are thus in Crito qualities both of dependence and kindness, and they will play their roles in the dialogue as a whole. Second, when Socrates expresses surprise that the jailer let him in, Crito says: "He is accustomed to me, I have come so often, and besides he has received a benefit from me." Here we learn that Crito is the kind of person who can establish a friendly relationship with a jailer; this in turn suggests an element in him of human warmth, or perhaps just a general agreeableness. Moreover, the "benefit" of which Crito speaks—whether by this is meant a bribe or present, or some past act of generosity—has converted this acquaintance into a relation of positive reciprocity. This was the archaic form of public community among the Greeks (and among others too), and it gave rise to the dominant conception of justice as doing good to one's friends and harm to one's enemies.[7] It is this understanding of justice, deep in the culture, that Plato is most at pains to undermine in the *Republic* and elsewhere;[8] an understanding closely tied to the aggressive egotism of the heroic and classical worlds alike, which Plato wishes to replace with another vision of what is good for human beings, individually and collectively. It is thus hinted here, what later becomes apparent, both that Crito is a highly competent member of his culture, at home in his world and able to manage its relations with skill, and that the concep-

7. For further discussion see generally A. W. H. Adkins, *Merit and Responsibility: A Study in Greek Values* (Oxford: Oxford University Press, 1960); K. J. Dover, *Greek Popular Morality in the Time of Plato and Aristotle* (Berkeley: University of California Press, 1974), pages 180–84; and Mary Whitlock Blundell, *Helping Friends and Harming Enemies: A Study in Sophocles and Greek Ethics* (Cambridge: Cambridge University Press, 1989), especially chapter 2. Socrates of course questions this "ordinary Greek" morality.

8. The *locus classicus* is the position advanced by Polemarchus in Book I of the *Republic*. Compare also what Meno says in *Meno* 71e. Gregory Vlastos, *Socrates: Ironist and Moral Philosopher* (Ithaca: Cornell University Press, 1991), pages 179–99, argues that the *Crito* is a central text in Socrates' revolutionary rejection of the ethics of retaliation. The major issue is whether justice is to be thought of as a code of individual behavior, as a species of honor in fact, or as a quality of a whole human community and its life.

tion of human relations, and of justice, to which he instinctively resorts is that of reciprocity in the service of the self and of one's friends.

To Crito's comment about the ease with which he is facing death Socrates responds by saying that at his age it would be inappropriate [lit. "discordant"] to be vexed at such a thing. "But there are others," Crito says, "whom age does not release from such vexation." "That is true," says Socrates; "but tell me, why did you come, and so early?"

Here we have the first of a series of breaks or interruptions in the comfortable back and forth of question and answer between friends, an awkwardness of communication that will in fact become a major subject of the text. Here Crito suggests a point—it will be the main point of the dialogue in the end—that Socrates responds to age and death differently from other people, but Socrates turns away from it to something else, to his original question: "Why did you come?"

This repetition of the opening line marks not only its importance, which should be plain enough, but also the importance of the material that appears between its two occurrences—demonstrating Crito's emotional dependence, cultural competence, and fundamental kindness—for it invites the reader to ask why the dialogue does not begin here instead of with an apparent digression. This way of drawing attention to what seems at first unnecessary is a trope that will recur in the famous speech of the Nomoi, which goes on for several pages after the point at which it might naturally be said to conclude, namely, the point of Crito's first acquiescence in the conclusion it is urging. The text thus begins and ends with material that may seem otiose, but which I think is by this very fact marked as having a special significance; part of its meaning, indeed, lies in its apparent gratuitousness.

Crito's response to the question why he has come is to say that he is bringing news—"bad news, not bad to you I suppose, but to me and all your friends, bad and burdensome; and to me I think a heavier burden than to all the others." This sentence at once expresses Crito's own distress and predicts that Socrates will feel differently. It thus renders explicit the tension from which the dialogue as a whole proceeds, the difference in feeling between the two men. And from what Crito says here we can see that Socrates' later response is not a surprise but a coherent manifestation of his known character.

To the news about the ship from Delos, when Crito gives it, Socrates responds rather oddly, not by the direct expression of any feelings he may have about the meaning of this event but by saying that he doubts Crito's prediction that the ship will arrive that day. He explains that this is based upon a dream that he has just had, in which a woman clad in white appeared to him and said: "O Socrates, on the third day you may fertile Phthia reach."

> *Crito:* A strange dream, Socrates.
> *Socrates:* Yet clear in meaning, or so it seems to me.
> *Crito:* Too much so, I fear. But Socrates . . . [Here Crito launches into a lengthy and formal speech of persuasion, to be discussed below.]

What is the meaning of this dream, and, equally important, what is the meaning of the brief colloquy about it? At the most obvious level, the dream is read by Socrates as a prophecy that his death will happen in three days, not two. But what is the emotional significance of this fact, in this dream? The Greek reader would know that the words of the woman are a slightly modified quotation from a speech of Achilles in Book 9 of the *Iliad,* made when he is planning to quit the battle and go home to Phthia: "If the wind is fair," he says, "on the third day I may fertile Phthia reach." In the poem this is a moment of great poignancy, for it suddenly shows us how close is the homeland from which these warriors have been away so long, and which has seemed like another world; and it expresses a longing for home, and for peace, in the greatest and most violent warrior of them all.

As this dream defines it, then, the death that Socrates foresees is not an evil but a homecoming, a return to peace from the struggles of life. This is why he sleeps so soundly, why he is so calm in response to the anxiety of Crito. This is its bright meaning to him, which it will be the function of the rest of the dialogue to elaborate and make plain against the view of Crito that the imminence of the death is "bad news."

When, at the end of the passage, Socrates says that the meaning of the dream is clear, he in effect invites Crito to pursue with him the nature of that meaning, and with it the meaning of his impending death. But

Crito fails to respond to this clue, and instead rushes headlong into his speech of persuasion. This is the second rupture in the flow of their talk.[9]

## CRITO'S ARGUMENT

Crito's long speech, which follows next, has the earmarks of a prepared argument, like a lawyer's case. He begins with his thesis: "Still, even at this late date, be persuaded by me and save yourself." Then he gives his reasons.

### Reputation

First, he says, if you die I shall suffer not one but two disasters, for "in addition to the loss of such a friend as I shall never find again," I shall appear, to those who do not know us well, as one who had resources sufficient to save you but did not care enough to do it, and "what [reputation] could be more shameful than to seem to care more for money than for friends?" In his response Socrates wholly disregards the first point and seizes upon the second, correcting his old friend and student on the most familiar of grounds: Why, he asks, should we care about the opinion of those who do not know the truth? People of judgment will see these things correctly.

> Crito: But the present circumstances themselves show that the many are able to inflict not the least of evils, but nearly the greatest, if someone is falsely accused before them.[10]

9. Earlier it was Socrates who refused to follow up a line begun by Crito, who had remarked on Socrates' distinctive attitude towards his own death. Now Socrates seeks to pursue this very question. Why then did he not do so earlier? Perhaps the reason is that the dream provides a better context for thinking about this issue, for the dream is a direct expression of Socrates' own feeling rather than a comparison with others. We might read the text, indeed, as suggesting that Socrates brings up the dream deliberately, in order to present this issue in a more satisfactory way than Crito did.

10. In making this point Crito expressly identifies those "who do not know" or the "many"—whose opinions followers of Socrates have long known they need not respect—with the jurymen of Athens, who have just condemned Socrates to death and done so unjustly. What may seem in other contexts to be an abstract point about the "one who knows" and "the many who do not" is thus here given significance of another kind, for now the many have real power. The issue is no longer "mere knowledge," as Crito might put it, but "life and death," assuming—as Socrates would not—that the latter is far more important than the former.

Both speakers seem here to urge inconsistent attitudes: Crito that the verdict of the

*Socrates:* Would that they were able to inflict the greatest evils, Crito, for
then they would have the power to do the greatest good as well, and this
would be good for them. But they do not; for they cannot make a man
sensible or foolish, but act upon him without thought or care.

Socrates here seems to speak from a distance, out of an amused yet sadly
reflective state, with no apparent sense that he is involved in an emergency.
His reference at the end to the "greatest good" is at once a refusal to
accept Crito's sense of crisis and an invitation (his second) to explore their
differences of attitude. He tries to engage his friend in conversation, with
the apparent aim of leading him to a position from which the impending
death can be seen, if not as a good at least not as a serious evil; but Crito
will have none of it. He refuses this invitation too, and rushes on to the
rest of his case: "That is all true, Socrates, but answer me this . . ." This
is the third break in the conversation, another mark of its failure to get
going.

When one reads this text in this way, with an eye to all of its parts
and not merely to what seem to be its central speeches, it is full of difficulty and uncertainty, arising not least from the unsuccessful efforts of
the two friends to engage on a common question in a common way.
"How will Socrates respond to this man?" is the question we are invited
to ask, and to which the rest of the text, including the speech of the Nomoi, is a response.

Notice that so far Socrates has made no response whatever to Crito's
first claim, that he will lose an irreplaceable friend. How are we to read
this silence: As suggesting that this is a trivial loss? That Socrates has no
response to make to such a claim? If true, this would be a terrible defi-
ciency of feeling and indeed of character in him. The question raised here
and left unanswered is a thread waiting to be pulled that threatens to
unravel the entire text—indeed more than this text, the premises of dialectic and the philosophic life itself—by demonstrating their lack of a simple
element of humanity. It is one thing to greet one's own death with equa-

---

jurors be disregarded, but on the grounds of reputation, which itself grants authority to
"the many"; Socrates that only the opinion of the one who knows matters, but that the
verdict of the many, even though unjust, should be honored. This unmarked but real tension
gives the text much of its life and energy.

nimity, quite another to dismiss the feelings of bereavement that those who love you will naturally have. Is this whole dimension of life—awareness of the feelings of others, acknowledgement of grief and loss, caring for another—simply missing from the ideal life Plato offers us here and elsewhere? Crito's unanswered claim is a nagging question, defining a tension that will run to the very end of the text and prove at last, I think, to be an essential part of its subject.

## Competing Modes of Thought and Argument

The next piece of Crito's long set argument is rather endearingly inconsistent with what he has just said about the damage he fears that his reputation may suffer if Socrates refuses to escape: it is to tell Socrates to have no fear on his behalf, or that of their other friends, that if he escapes they will be accused by sycophants (roughly: informers) and forced to pay huge sums of money or suffer penalties beyond even that. "If you fear any thing of this sort, dismiss your fears; for we are right (*dikaioi*), I think, to run this risk in an attempt to save you, or if necessary an even greater one."[11] The inconsistency is plain: only a moment ago Crito was asking Socrates to escape on the grounds that his, Crito's, reputation might suffer; now he says that Socrates should pay no heed to the possibility of a much more dramatic kind of suffering on his part.

What unites the two arguments, as any lawyer could see at once, is that they support the same position. But one argument enacts a kind of timorousness for which Socrates gently reproaches him—why fear the opinion of the many?—the other a kind of bravery and generosity of spirit, springing from his sense of loyalty and friendship, from the same place indeed as his sense of grief, and one can only admire it. In this frame of mind Crito has no concern at all for the many or what they might do to him. The split between these two impulses is an instance of what Socrates elsewhere calls being divided against oneself, and which he says is just the condition from which dialectic and the philosophic life may release us.[12]

In the speech that follows, Crito first disposes of the practicalities, explaining how easy the escape will be—there is plenty of money, the sycophants can be bought, Socrates can live with friends abroad, etc.—

---

11. It is significant that Crito here speaks of himself and his friends as *dikaioi* ("right" or "just"), for in doing so—as in later calling Socrates' refusal to escape "unjust" (*oude dikaion*)—he strikes a theme that enables their talk to begin (though it will end on rather a different note).

12. See *Gorgias* 482b–c.

then makes his major claim: that it is not just (*oude dikaion*) for Socrates to allow himself to die. This as Crito knows is an argument that Socrates cannot let pass, for he has given much of his life to establishing the ethical centrality of justice and to giving it a meaning of his own. In raising the topic of justice, then, Crito is acting as a good student of Socrates; though perhaps there is an element of comedy here too, for the claim Crito makes—that justice requires Socrates to evade lawful punishment—is on the face of it bizarre.[13] And the particular conception of justice he invokes is exactly the one that Socrates has been trying most to repudiate and transform, namely, to do good to your friends and harm to your enemies. For Crito says that in refusing to escape Socrates will be doing to himself exactly what his enemies most wish to do to him, which is to bring about his death; while he will be abandoning not only his friends but his sons, to whom he owes a duty of care and education. He sums up his claim by invoking the standard language of value of his day and saying: "[W]hat a good and brave (*agathos* and *andreios*) man would choose, this you should choose, since all your life you have claimed to care for virtue (*aretē*)." Do not, he says, let us languish under the opprobrium or shame of having failed through cowardice of some sort (*anandreia*), you to escape, we to assist you.

Crito's argument is cast in the language of value characteristic of the world of Athens in which Socrates found himself, and indeed the earlier stages of that world as well. In terms that are deeply familiar, it embodies a kind of aggressive egotism, regulated by the principle of reciprocity, for it invokes both a conception of justice as retaliation—like the one that dominates the world of Aeschylus' *Oresteia*—and a related conception of positive reciprocity, which underlies the practices of hospitality that were so central to the ancient world. But as a statement of Socrates' idea of justice, or as an argument meant to appeal to him, Crito's argument is hopeless. Almost nothing could be worse.[14]

Crito closes his speech with a claim of emergency, an exhortation to

13. Maybe in this too Plato meant Crito to remind us of Socrates, who often argued for positions felt by his interlocutors to be impossibly paradoxical—for example that it was "better" to suffer injustice than to do it. See *Gorgias* 474b–79e.

14. Except to claim that justice itself has no meaning or value as Thrasymachus and Callicles do, as represented by Plato respectively in the *Republic* and the *Gorgias*. For more sympathetic treatment of these sophists, and the sophistic movement in general, see Eric Havelock, *The Liberal Temper in Greek Politics* (New Haven: Yale University Press, 1957) and G. B. Kerferd, *The Sophistic Movement* (Cambridge: Cambridge University Press, 1981).

act immediately or lose the chance forever; this is a pitch of the sort that one might find in the close of a lawyer's jury argument, or perhaps in a demagogue's speech to a crowd, a move made by a mind that is trying to overbear another. Its inappropriateness to the relation between Crito and Socrates could not be more marked.

In his distress, Crito has forgotten all he has presumably learned from Socrates about the opinion of the many, about the character of justice, and, what is of at least equal importance, about the kind of attitude and relation that is proper to a serious discussion between those who seek the truth, that is, to philosophic conversation.[15] In his definition of justice as helping your friends and hurting your enemies, in his concern for reputation, and in the kind of manipulative relation he tries to establish with his audience, this old friend of Socrates has collapsed from whatever education he may earlier have attained to the very position that Socrates has spent his life trying to refute and change. A depressing event for a teacher, to say the least, to see one's friend and student utterly fail to recall what you thought he had learned, and this precisely at the moment when it most matters, when the question of justice is presented as real and calls for action.

Socrates responds to Crito with great delicacy and accuracy. He, of course, refuses to reply to this speech with one like it—nothing could be less Socratic—and simply disregards for the moment the arguments and thesis it advances, focusing instead upon Crito's own emotional and intellectual condition: "Your eagerness is a fine thing," he says, "if it should prove to be rightly based; but if not, its very intensity makes it so much the worse." As for the merits:

> All my life I have obeyed, of all things available to me, only the reasoned argument (*logō*) that proves best to me as I think it out.[16] I cannot now toss out the reasoned arguments (*logous*) of an earlier time just because this [my death sentence] has come upon me, but to me they continue to seem nearly the same as they did. I honor and respect them just as before. Unless we should find that we have something better than them now, understand that I will not agree with you.

15. I base this assumption about their prior relationship partly on what we, and the original audience, can be assumed to know about their friendship and partly on the way in which Socrates later uses arguments that he explicitly assumes to be familiar to Crito.

16. Notice the connection here between persuasion (reasoned arguments) and obedience, and compare the discussion of this topic below, page 28.

And how are we best to determine whether we do have something better than our old arguments? Socrates suggests that they begin with the question Crito raised before, about opinions, namely, "Whether it is right to grant credence to some opinions and not to others."

The function of this brief speech is to transform the discourse, and the kind of community established by Crito's sincere yet overbearing and argumentative appeal, into another form, that of dialectic, in which two minds pursue a question together, seeking not to dominate each other but to discover the truth of it. This speech in fact begins to restore Crito to himself: it reduces the sense of urgency by dissipating it as irrelevant, and creates a sense of security in the very way the familiar and apparently detached investigation proceeds. In this sense it is a performance before our eyes of the way in which the philosophic life can lead one to disregard what others consider disasters.

## A New Start

Socrates next offers Crito what might be called a short course in Socratics, reminding him of what he already knows. The discussion is too long to summarize here in any detail, but one can say that its form is that of question and answer, apparently meant not to explore new ground but to recall what has been established many times before, especially that we should attend to and respect the opinion not of the "ignorant many" but of the "one who knows." This is true of the body, with respect to which we follow the advice of the doctor and the trainer: How much more true must it necessarily be of that nobler part of us that is improved by justice and damaged by injustice? As for the claim that the many have the power to kill us, we answer that our aim is not merely "to live but to live well," which, as we know, means "to live justly."[17] And we are to live justly always, not sometimes to do justice and sometimes not. To act unjustly is evil (*kakon*) and shameful (*aischron*), in every case and every way, even when we act this way in response to injustice being inflicted on us.

All this is of course not to define justice but only to assert its importance. But when Socrates accepts Crito's implicit challenge and agrees that if it is just for him to escape he will try it, otherwise not, he commits himself to the question, what justice is.

On this subject Socrates begins with the puzzling claim that to act

---

17. In Greek the phrase "to live well" has much less by way of moral connotation than it does in English; it might better be translated as "flourish" or "succeed." To say that to live "well" is to live "justly" is thus far more contestable in Greek than English.

unjustly is the same thing as to act badly towards (*kakós poiein*) another. This is puzzling because there is a deep ambiguity here: How do we determine whether we are acting "badly"? If by consulting the person upon whom we act, then Socrates is defining injustice as the equivalent of injury, with injury in turn defined as "doing to someone something they don't like or want." But this would be to define injustice and injury, and necessarily justice too, in terms of human will and preference. This would be unimaginably inconsistent both with Socrates' usual insistence that we cannot trust our culturally determined instincts and with his position that a kind of restraint or self-control is central to the ethical life.[18] It would entail an abdication of judgment precisely on those matters on which Socrates thinks it is most essential that we learn to judge rightly, namely, what counts as a true injury or true benefit. Yet if "badly" is to be determined not by the person we affect but by us in this very conversation, through dialectic, then the word is not very different, after all, from "unjustly": it marks an as yet unreached moral judgment. Thus we cannot say that the argument is much advanced by Socrates' definition; instead its function seems to be to introduce this very ambiguity concerning the proper role of the human will or preference in determining the meaning of justice—an ambiguity that will recur in the speech of the Nomoi.

Socrates takes Crito (and us) through two further very brief steps before he presents the famous speech of the Nomoi: first, he asks whether we ought not keep our agreements, if they are just. Upon receiving from Crito an affirmative answer to that, he asks: "If we go away [into exile], without persuading the city, shall we not be injuring (*kakós poiein*) others, and those whom we least should injure?" And in doing this "shall we be adhering to our just agreements or not?" To this Crito responds that he does not understand what Socrates means. This is hardly surprising. After all, the second issue, about "just agreements," is a wholly new topic and contains deep ambiguities. (Must the act agreed to be done itself be "just," or is it enough that the conditions under which the agreement is made are fair ones? In either form the argument is at best incomplete.) And the ambiguity about the meaning of *kakós poiein* discussed above—whether we see it from the point of view of the putatively injured, in which case it would be a revolution in Socrates' thinking, or see it from the point of view of "true harm," in which case it is nearly a tautology—

18. Socrates elsewhere speaks repeatedly in favor of the kind of restraint and control required to train horses or athletes, or to educate children, and he regards self-restraint as an essential element in mature life. See, for example, *Gorgias* 503c–7e.

is still with us and still confusing. This means that, despite what he will seem to say, Socrates introduces the speech of the Nomoi, not just to explicate what he has already said with adequate clearness but to do something else.

## THE SPEECH OF THE NOMOI

In turning—at last—to this speech it is important to recall, what we are perhaps too likely to forget, that Socrates is here speaking not to the world at large but to Crito, and not about the general issue of the obligation to obey the law, in any political state whatever, but about the propriety of his own contemplated escape. Crito has exhibited many things: an anxiety for himself, an impending sense of loss, tender concern for Socrates, a willing bravery to run great risks and to spend great sums, a collapse into the ordinary Greek morality of his day, and an amenability to Socrates' way of argument that has enabled him, for the moment at least, to be restored to some portion of his earlier attitudes and to his earlier relation with Socrates. He is a kind and brave man, concerned with what is right, but of limited intellectual power and thus unable to maintain a philosophic position with clarity and firmness.

The subject that has actually been established by the narrative and the conversation is the gap between the anxiety of Crito and the repose of Socrates in the face of the latter's impending death. The topic of justice, normally one of Socrates' favorites, has been introduced not by him but by Crito, as a ground of argument meant both to justify his own willingness to run risks on behalf of Socrates and to attack Socrates' unwillingness to escape. The question before them is stated as one of justice because Crito has put it that way, not because Socrates has done so; Socrates has for the moment accepted this definition of the issue and the related claim that if it is just for him to escape he will do so. But in what follows he will try to turn the dialogue to its true subject and to bring Crito to see at the end what he could not at the beginning, the ground upon which his own repose in the face of death actually rests.

As I suggested earlier, the form in which the question of justice arises is on the face of it odd, indeed slightly comic: Crito is arguing not that justice permits Socrates to escape, a position defensible on many grounds, but that justice affirmatively requires him to escape, a far stronger and less likely case—so little likely, on the face of it, as to be itself a kind of paradox, stated perhaps in unconscious imitation of the famous Socratic paradoxes. Socrates treats it solemnly, as a serious claim; but it is significant that he is about to address it not in his own voice but that of the Nomoi. This can be read as a way in which Socrates distances himself not only from what the Nomoi say but from the question as Crito has stated it.

The Nomoi in fact make not one speech but four (preceded by an introduction): at the end of the first, which is, in my view at least, wholly inadequate by any measure, almost a parody of bad argument, Crito announces that he is persuaded by it. This response defines by performance part of the problem that Socrates faces throughout, namely, Crito's limited intellectual capacity and consequent pliability in the face of any argument whatever. When Socrates then goes on to say more, this movement is not prompted by Crito's disagreement, as is usual in dialectic, but has another origin, the desire to move Crito from one set of understandings, from one way of talking, to another. What we see in the second stage of the speech, and even more in the third and fourth, is a gradual rewriting of it to bring Crito, and the reader, away from the false issue raised by the first stage of the speech to the question at the center of the dialogue.

### Prelude

When Crito tells him that he does not understand what he has said about "injuring those he ought least to injure" and "violating his just agreements," Socrates says:

> If as we were about to run away from here (or however our escape should be called) the laws and the common state of the city might come and stand before us and say: "Tell me, Socrates, what are you intending to do? By this deed which you undertake, do you intend anything other than to destroy the laws—that is, us—and the whole city too, so far as you are able? Or does it seem to you that the city can continue to exist, and not be overturned, in which legal judgments (*dikai*), once made, have no strength, but are rendered powerless at the hands of private parties, and so destroyed?"[19]

Notice that in this brief argument the Nomoi assume that all acts of disobedience to the laws are morally the same, and all a kind of injury to them. They employ a non-Socratic definition of "injury" or "destruc-

---

19. It is important to notice that Socrates speaks not of what the Nomoi "did say" or "do say," nor even, for the most part what they "would say," but of what they "might say." He uses, that is, the optative mood, rather than the indicative and this is a way of marking the speech as hypothetical, tentative, or imagined.

tion," for they assert as unquestioned their own view of what is harmful and what is not, including their right to carry on in their own career of assumed injustice. They build, that is, on the version of *kakós poiein* that means "to do something to someone that he does not like" rather than "to do someone an injustice." One could well imagine Socrates in another context responding that if the laws or other actions of the city are unjust, the city is not injured but helped by disobedience. This is in fact the kind of correction that human beings and human institutions often need, for an example of which one need look no farther than Socrates' own behavior, described in the *Apology*, when he refused the order of the Thirty to arrest Leon of Salamis. It fits with what else we know of Plato's Socrates that he would believe that no one has the right to compel another to do what is unjust.[20]

The Nomoi here speak of submission to the judgments of a court, and of the law that requires such submission, rather than of obedience to the laws more generally. This could be important, because a much stronger case can be made that judicial judgments ought not to be disturbed, at least if they have been reached in a fair way, than that positive laws requiring unjust action ought to be obeyed. In the former case one would argue that the person has had a chance to explain to the court why it should decide his way, and has failed. He must be bound by it, notwithstanding his disagreement with the outcome, or judicial judgments will have almost no weight: after all, the loser almost always thinks the judgment bad, and there would be no way to determine the rightness of his claim except by another proceeding, which would in the usual case be just as liable to error as the first one was. But all of this is of no avail to the case actually made by the Nomoi, for they will soon make plain that they are speaking of the duty to obey every law of the city, not just the one respecting the finality of judgments.

Moreover, the argument that one is bound by fair procedures even when a particular result is wrong, so familiar to us as almost to amount to second nature, rests on a kind of skepticism that it would be surprising to see either Socrates or Plato affirm. At least in its modern form, the argument claims that we are bound by the determinations of others largely because no one can really know the truth, or know what justice

---

20. It is true that here Socrates is asked to suffer rather than to do injustice. This is plainly the lesser evil, but it is still an evil; moreover, there is nothing in the speech to suggest that it does not apply to affirmative conduct and much, including the repeated use of the verb "to make" or "to do" (*poiein*), to suggest that it does.

requires. This argument defines justice not substantively, in terms of ends or relations, but in terms of procedures and arrangements. On this view whatever the properly elected legislature or properly informed judge or jury do is by definition just; not in the sense that we must agree with it but in the sense that we must grant it authority, at least until it passes all bounds of acceptability. But, as I say, the Nomoi do not in fact develop this argument, and, equally important, the moral skepticism on which it rests is deeply inconsistent with the main thrust of Socrates' work here and elsewhere, which is that it is our deepest duty to discover the just and to do it.

Socrates himself does function out of a skepticism of a kind, his sense that we do not yet know what justice is. But his usual procedure for living with ignorance is not acquiescence in the judgments reached by the city— which is, after all, nothing but the opinion of the many "who do not know"—but dialectic, the heart of which is that the two parties to the conversation disown all loyalties except to each other and to the discovery of truth. Our ignorance is a ground not for refusing to make judgments about justice but for the imperative that we try to discover what it is and follow its commands; if the goal of moral knowledge eludes us, as perhaps it eludes both Socrates and Plato, we shall still have spent our lives in a way worthy of human beings. What is called for, then, as Socrates makes plain by performance in the *Apology,* is not simple obedience to the city but a kind of intellectual and ethical engagement with it.

### The First Version of the Nomoi's Speech

About these opening remarks of the Nomoi, Socrates asks: "What shall we say, Crito, to these things and others like them? Someone—and especially a rhetorician at a lawsuit—might have a great deal to say, especially on behalf of that law (*nomos*) now being destroyed [by us], which establishes that legal judgments once reached shall be authoritative.—Or shall we say against the Nomoi: 'The city has treated us unjustly and reached its judgment wrongly?' "—To this Crito agrees.[21]

---

21. In suggesting that they might say to the city that it "has acted unjustly towards us," Socrates temporarily invokes the conception of justice that Crito has earlier articulated, namely, that it is right to repay injustice with injustice, and at least in this way to "harm one's enemies." Socrates will later reject this view of justice, as he has done before; his use of it here can then be read as meeting Crito on his own ground.

Notice that this line of argument assumes that Socrates' escape would be "unjust" on the grounds that it would "harm" the city, which is the very question at issue.

This is the point at which Socrates presents the first full version of the speech of the Nomoi. The passage reads like this:

"O Socrates, is this [i.e., that our injustice entitles you to act unjustly against us] what is agreed between you and us, or [is our agreement rather] to stick by whatever judgments the city reaches?"—If we wondered at what they said, perhaps they might go on: "Do not be amazed at what is said, Socrates, but answer us, especially since you habitually employ question and answer yourself. Come now, what accusation have you to make against us and the city that you undertake to destroy us? Is it not true, first off, that we brought you into existence and that it was through us that your father took your mother and begot you? Tell us, have you any complaint to make about those of us [i.e., the laws] who regulate marriage, that all is not well with us?"—I have no complaint, I would say.—"But do you have any complaint against those laws concerning the nourishment and education of a child once he is born, in which you yourself were brought up? Or did those of us appointed to govern such things not provide well when we ordered your father to educate you in music and gymnastics?"—You did well, I would say.—"Well then. Since you were brought into existence and nourished and educated by us, can you possibly claim that you were not ours, both our child and slave, you and also your ancestors? And if this is so, do you think that you stand on an equal footing with us with respect to justice, so that whatever we might undertake to do to you, you think it right for you to do such things back to us?[22] For surely justice is not equal between you and your father, or your master if you have one, so that, whatever you might suffer, this you do back to them: being slandered you do no slander, being hit you do not hit back, and so forth. Shall you then be on an equal footing with the laws and the city with respect to justice, so that if we should undertake to destroy you, thinking it just, you might undertake so far as you are able to destroy us, the laws and the whole country? And do you say that in doing these things you would be acting justly, you who have cared so much about the truth of virtue? Or are you so wise that you forget that the country is more to be honored than your mother and father and all your ancestors, and more holy and sacred and of greater importance, both among the gods and many right-minded people? And do you forget

---

22. The Nomoi here take Socrates' imagined response—"My conduct is justified by your injustice"—as a version of the conception of justice Crito invoked, namely, "hurting your enemies." "The verdict made the city our enemy, hence retaliation is justified"; such is the argument that the Nomoi are answering.

that it is more necessary to honor, and yield to, and serve the country when it maltreats you than your father, and either to persuade it [otherwise] or to do what it commands, and to suffer, if it should order you to suffer something, bearing yourself peacefully, whether it is to be struck, or bound, or if it should lead you into war, possibly to be wounded or killed, that these things are to be done, and justice is to be found here? Do you forget that one is not to withdraw or run away or leave one's position, but in war and in the courts and everywhere else one is to do what the city and the country should command, or persuade it which way justice lies? And that while it is a sacrilege to use force against either one's father or one's mother, a still greater sacrilege it is to use force against the country?"—What shall we say to this, Crito? Do the laws speak the truth or not?

—The truth, it seems to me, says Crito.

This speech, though expanding on the opening remarks discussed above, still does not, in its present form at least, withstand much critical examination. It assumes throughout that to disobey the laws is to injure them and the city, when it may well be argued that to disobey an unjust law is to do the city, and the laws themselves, a service. Indeed in such a case obedience itself may be an injury. And in drawing an analogy to the duties owed by children to parents, and slaves to masters, the speech assumes that the obligation of obedience in those cases is both absolute and just, when in fact here too it might be that to disobey an unjust order is to serve, to obey to injure, and, more generally, that the obligation, whatever it is, should be conditioned on many exceptions, based on other standards of justice. And upon what does the domestic obligation rest in the first place? Not consent, for one does not choose a parent or a master, and obviously either might be vicious. The speech assumes that the duty to obey is self-evident; it thus works as an unreasoned appeal to the culture, to the way things are, of exactly the sort that Socrates' interlocutors often make and that he is normally at pains to expose as both intellectually and ethically inadequate.[23]

---

23. Notice also that to concede that one has no complaint to make about certain laws—here those relating to marriage or education—is no argument at all on the question whether one is obliged to obey other laws that are unjust.

Part of the puzzle of this text arises from the circumstance that Crito and the Nomoi, imagined by Socrates as speaking against each other, are in fact both representatives of the culture to be refuted by Socrates. Crito and the Nomoi agree on more than they differ, and it is with this area of agreement that Socrates will mainly concern himself, refuting both at once. But it will not look much like refutation, for in transforming the speech of the Nomoi into another mode Socrates' aim is not so much to defeat Crito as to instruct him.

At the center of the argument of the Nomoi is the implicit claim that the city is like a person and that you are for it or against it in all things; whether you "help" or "hurt" is to be measured not by any external understanding of what justice requires but by the city's will or preference. The city is either your friend or your enemy, and this in all respects; if the former, the Nomoi implicitly argue, as our help to you in the past demonstrates to be the case, you must help us; this means that you must do whatever we want, however unjust it may be to you or to others, for if you do not you will be hurting us. This is an implied invocation of the sense of justice as "helping your friends and hurting your enemies," which Crito has affirmed and Socrates always resists. The speech as a whole is thus as far from Socrates' own views, and methods of thought, as one could well imagine; exactly the sort of jumble of unreasoned analogies and conclusory assertions, reaffirmations of cultural assumptions, of which it is his habit to make mincemeat.[24]

WHY THEN IS IT HERE? It is, I believe, a performance by Socrates of the sort of argument that Crito's own earlier argument seemed to invite, a way, that is, of meeting Crito on his own terms. You will remember Crito's set speech, full of arguments why Socrates should escape; it was a kind of lawyer's speech, invoking the common sense of morality and justice, and this is a response in kind. (Socrates as much as tells us so when he speaks of what "a rhetorician might say"; and he speaks throughout not in his own voice but that of the Nomoi, who are dogmatic and authoritarian in manner.) This speech actually mirrors the speech it is responding to, both in its underlying conception of justice as helping friends and hurting enemies, and in its conception of "harm" or "injury" described above. It would not persuade you or me, or perhaps anyone else, but it persuades Crito. It is a way of speaking to Crito in his own terms and at his intellectual level. As his acquiescence suggests, it "works"; yet in another sense its evident defects call for further treatment. It is here not as a serious

---

24. I speak here of the speech as it is composed in the text. Of course one could say a great deal as a general matter about the bearing of status and contract upon the obligation to obey the law, and these topics are deep in our own thought. But the Nomoi say virtually nothing beyond the assertion of bald conclusions; this is in fact a large part of Plato's point in composing the speech as he does.

statement of Socrates' own views—quite the opposite—but as a text that catches Crito's modes of thought and argument, so that they may be changed. It is not meant to stand as it is, but to be rewritten, transformed into something else, and in such a way as to carry Crito with it; and this process of rewriting is the center of life in this text.

### Rewriting (I): The Citizen's Agreement

How do the rewritings of this speech work the transformations to which I allude, and where exactly do they bring Crito and the reader at the end?

In its next version—the second—the speech of the Nomoi develops the idea that there is an agreement between Socrates and the laws which obliges him to obey them. In the form in which we have already seen it this argument is wholly conclusory, for who is to say that an agreement exists or what its terms are? And to judge by Socrates' remarks in the *Apology*, his own conception of the agreement he has in fact made, with himself if not with the city, is that he should continue to lead the philosophic and dialectical life he there describes, wherever it takes him and whatever should happen to him. And even if we assume that an agreement to obey all the laws was made, explicitly or by conduct, why should any respect at all be accorded an agreement which purports to require one to do or to suffer something unjust?

What the Nomoi now say gives some content to the idea of agreement: since the laws permit any adult to leave the city at any time, taking their goods with them,

> whoever of you remains, observing the manner in which we decide cases and manage the rest of the city, we say he has already agreed with us by this conduct to do whatever we might command. And one who does not obey, we say acts unjustly in three ways, that he disobeys us who are his parents, that he disobeys those who nourished him, and that having agreed to obey us he neither obeys nor persuades us [that we are wrong]. . . . We give him two alternatives, either to persuade us [that we are wrong] or to do [what we order], of which he does neither.

This is a much more interesting and persuasive version of the argument, resting as it does not upon the authority of an *ipse dixit* but on the conduct of the citizen who has chosen to remain. But as an interpretation of this conduct it remains conclusory: Why should one, simply by remaining, be held to have agreed to obey all the laws of the city, including the unjust ones? The theory of the Nomoi, after all, would oblige anyone who stayed in the city to obey any imaginable law, say one prohibiting public speech or requiring one to carry out genocidal murders.[25] The relative importance of the city compared to parents and friends, referred to earlier, would only make more important the obligation to keep whatever agreement one did make, not in any way define its terms. And, more simply, why does past acquiescence commit one to future obedience? If the claim rests on simple consent, one should be able to withdraw it whenever one wants. And on what basis does this supposed agreement really rest? It is not as though the citizen has in practical fact the sorts of options the argument supposes, for all kinds of forces may keep a person in an Athens of which one deeply disapproves. This kind of argument has a vulgar twentieth-century version, expressed in the bumper stickers that say: "America: Love It or Leave It."

There is perhaps a qualification implicit in the remark that one has to do what the city orders "or persuade it," meaning persuade it that it is wrong. This has been read as meaning that one need only *try* to persuade the city of its error, but such a construction is both (in my view) linguistically incorrect as a matter of Greek and philosophically out of tune with the main thrust of the speech.[26] In fact it destroys the whole case that the Nomoi are making, for it would always be an out that one had argued seriously and honestly for the justice of one's conduct;[27] besides, in this case Socrates himself has tried to do exactly that and should, under this reasoning, be free of the very obligation the Nomoi are claiming he is bound by.

One might more plausibly modify the "persuasion" qualification by arguing that a city that failed to allow for regular processes of persuasion would not be entitled to obedience, for it would have violated a central term of the agreement itself. But this would not work to excuse Socrates'

---

25. There is also perhaps the qualification that the city must think that what it is doing is just. But this would apply to almost all laws, perhaps all laws, for as Plato has shown us more than once, it is virtually impossible for a person to admit that what he is doing is truly unjust.

26. See Kraut, *Socrates and the State,* pages 65–73, for the best statement of the argument I am resisting. It is true that the present tense "may express an action begun, attempted, or intended" (Herbert Weir Smyth, *Greek Grammar,* rev. ed. [Cambridge, Mass.: Harvard University Press, 1956], par. 1878), but it does so only when the context requires it, and whether that is so is the question in issue here. As Smyth puts it, "The idea of attempt or intention is an inference from the context and lies in the present only insofar as the present does not denote completion." For Kraut's contrary view, see pages 72–73 of *Socrates and the State.*

27. This is true, of course, only if one's conduct is indeed just; but the whole argument assumes that. The subject of argument here is the duty to obey laws and decrees that are concededly unjust.

escape, for Athens has provided just such a process. And in any event there can be little support for reading such a qualification into this language, for it would really be just a sophisticated version of the claim that the Nomoi have already rejected, namely, that Socrates is not obliged to suffer the penalty because the city has decided it unjustly. The very idea that the obligation to obey is dependent upon the justice of the conduct of the city, whether "justice" is defined substantively or procedurally, is antithetical to the main thrust of the Nomoi's argument. If taken seriously it would wholly undermine their claims, for it would invite us to ask what should be taken as the proper conditions of the obligation to obey the law, which might include a great many things: full participation as an equal in the making of laws, a fair distribution of resources and opportunities for political action, adequate procedures for speaking to the legislature or the judiciary, and so on. This is a line of thought natural to us in the twentieth century, and it can carry one very far in limiting the obligation to obey the law; but it is not how Socrates represents the Nomoi as thinking, nor indeed how he thinks himself.[28]

One more point about the repeated remark that the citizen is to do what the Nomoi command or to "persuade" them that they are wrong: the same word that in its active and transitive form is usually translated as "persuade" (*peithein*), in its middle or passive form means "obey" (*peithesthai*). There is no etymological connection between the two English words, and they would normally be thought of as having different complements: "persuade" and "agree" (or "yield," or simply "be persuaded"); "obey" and "command." This point is especially important in legal thought, where it has long been customary to think of a rule of law

---

28. As I suggested above, it would be in principle possible to distinguish between two kinds of injustice, and say that injustice in the particular result is no ground for disobedience of the laws in general, but that injustice in the process by which laws are made or applied is such a ground. This would appeal to those who want to distinguish between an unjust system and unjust results, and to say that allegiance to an essentially just system requires toleration of results that seem unjust, either because they are inevitable in an imperfect world or because the judgment as to whether they are truly just can never be confidently made; in this sense whatever the reasonably fair system does is as "just" as anything human can be.

But this line of argument is not I think present in the speech of the Nomoi; and if it were it would remain very far from the position normally advanced by Socrates, for the argument of the Nomoi requires the citizen (at least of a state which has permitted him to depart) to comply with all its laws, however unjust they might be, including laws requiring him to commit affirmative injustice. Crito may be swung over to such a position by this speech, but that should not be said either of Socrates or of the reader.

as a "command," and of what it demands of its audience as "obedience." But the Greek term suggests that there is a deep connection between persuasion and obedience: that there is no obedience without persuasion of some kind, if only a threat, and no persuasion without something like obedience, or submission. *Peithein* might then best be translated as "to subject to verbal and intellectual force," *peithesthai* as "to yield to verbal and intellectual force." What this suggests about authority is that it is always created in part by those who are subject to it, that it is never total, and that it is present whenever we recognize the force of an argument or text. When the Nomoi say that Socrates has agreed "to obey us" but in fact neither "obeys" nor "persuades," all three verbs are from the same root, and the argument thus has a kind of punning or tautological form, which has in addition the effect of eliminating the possibilities for education and community otherwise suggested by the idea of persuasion. The view of the Nomoi thus boils down to a conflict of wills: either you must obey us or we you.

**Rewriting (II): Socrates' Own Agreement**
The third version of the speech of the Nomoi achieves a further transformation, in which it sheds at once the highly generalized sorts of arguments described above and many of the difficulties that they present. For the speech now moves from an argument based on the kind of agreement that any citizen makes with his city, by remaining there when the city permits him to depart, to the agreement that Socrates himself has made, not with any city but with Athens.

For Socrates, the Nomoi's imagined argument runs, more than any other Athenian has made such an agreement by his conduct. He has lived at Athens more exclusively than almost anyone else, never going out of the city to see the sights, "nor ever for any other reasons, except on military duty," nor has he taken voyages as other men do, nor shown any interest in the laws of other cities.

> Still more: in this very lawsuit, it was possible for you to propose the penalty of exile, if you had wished, and then you could have done with the consent of the city what you now undertake to do against its will. [At trial] you preened yourself on the fact that you were not troubled if it were to become necessary for you to die, but chose, as you put it, death over exile. Now you are not ashamed (*aischunesthai*) of these words, nor do you have regard for us, the laws, whom you undertake to destroy, but you do what the most wretched slave might do, trying to run away against your under-

taking and agreements, by which you agreed to live as a citizen under us.— But answer us this straight off, whether we speak the truth when we say that you have agreed, not in words but in your conduct, to live as a citizen subject to us, or not.

When the question is put to him, Crito once more says that he agrees with what the Nomoi are saying. But what he assents to here is vastly different from the earlier formulations, for now the ground of the argument is the agreement Socrates himself has allegedly made with the city to which he has devoted much of his life. The question is no longer abstract or theoretical but particular; it is not about the meaning of residence in the city as a general matter but about the meaning of Socrates' own life, which might be—indeed it is suggested here it is—different in significant respects from the meaning of that of others. This is not abstract or legalistic talk—from these predicates, these conclusions—but highly personal.

The speech really asks Socrates a question: "Isn't this the meaning of what you have done, and agreed to?" In doing so it necessarily concedes that on this point Socrates himself is the ultimate witness. In framing this part of the speech Socrates thus shifts his subject, from the forfeitures his conduct has arguably entailed to what its meaning is, both to him and to his audience. This is the ground upon which he will ultimately rest his case that his impending death is not the "bad news" that Crito sees it to be but an event that can be accepted with repose, even satisfaction, not only by Socrates himself but by his friends.

An even more particular ground for the duty not to escape is suggested by the closing reference to Socrates' behavior in this very proceeding, where his own choice of a proposed penalty in effect made it impossible for the city to order his exile. For under the procedures of Athenian law, the jury could not set its own penalty but had to choose between the two proposed by the parties: death, by Socrates' accuser; by Socrates, at first the "penalty" of a lifetime of free dinners, in recognition of his services to the city, then, upon prompting, a small fine. By failing to ask for exile, the argument would run, Socrates has waived his right to it, and in this sense agreed to his punishment. He cannot now take against the city's will what he might have had with its acquiescence; or, to put it slightly differently, the city should at least be given the chance to offer him, through the channels of the law, what he now claims the right to take on his own. This argument is a specification of the earlier ones—by remaining you agreed; you must submit or persuade—but with radically different force, for it is now grounded in a particular act, a strategic choice, to which he is being held. To speak of it as a species of agreement hardly stretches things at all. If the thrust of Socrates' own position were legalistic, it could perhaps rest on this waiver, without more.[29]

But his position is not legalistic. What matters to Socrates far more than the "waiver" he might be said to have made is the meaning of that gesture as part of the meaning of his life as a whole. He thus brings us back to the reasons why he did not ask for exile in the first place, which for him are still in force and render irrelevant the whole conversation in which Crito has involved him when he claimed that it would be unjust for him not to try to escape.

### Rewriting (III): The Meaning of This Life, This Death

In the final version of the speech, the Nomoi first sum up the argument from agreement (making plain that they are referring to Socrates' particular undertakings rather than to a general obligation of citizenship), then go on to argue in terms that remind us of Crito's initial concern with the opinions of others: they say that if Socrates obeys them (or: is persuaded by them) he will "not make himself ridiculous" in his escape from the city as he otherwise will. This theme is an odd one, for in its explicit form it is a direct appeal to the opinions not of the "one who knows" but of the many, an appeal in fact of just the sort that Socrates has rejected earlier in this dialogue and earlier in his life as well. But, as we shall soon see, this speech works at the same time in another way, to address the question Socrates has been pursuing from the beginning, namely how to explain to Crito—how to get him to see and feel—that what Crito now regards as a dreadful event is in fact not one, that the coming death is not to be deplored or feared but accepted as a fitting end to Socrates' life.

This is what the Nomoi say: If you escape, Socrates, "what good shall you do yourself or your friends? Your friends are likely to become exiles themselves, and deprived of the city and all their goods." And as for you, "if you go to a well-run neighboring state, Thebes or Megara, for both are well-governed . . . you will come as an enemy to their constitution; those who care for their own cities will be suspicious of you, considering

---

29. But the merits of this argument should not be overstated: to ask for exile would mean foregoing asking for what justice requires. And why should the city be able to compel such a waiver? As Socrates puts it in the *Apology*, to propose such a penalty would be to accuse himself of a crime, when he is guilty of none. *Apology* 37b. For a vivid account of the evils of exile, see Lysias 7.41 ("On the Olive Stump").

you a destroyer of laws; and this will confirm the judges here in the rightness of their verdict, for whoever destroys the laws may very likely corrupt the young and unthinking" (which was the offense of which Socrates was convicted). Yet if you avoid well-regulated cities and orderly men, "will you have a life worth living? Shall you approach these men and speak shamelessly to them—saying what? Making the arguments you have given here, that justice and virtue are of the greatest value to human beings, and so are the established customs and the laws? Do you not think that the whole Socratic enterprise will then seem incoherent?" If you go to Thessaly, where Crito has his friends, which is the most disorderly place of all, perhaps you will enjoy hearing pleasant tales of your ridiculous escape from prison, dressed in disguise. And where will your arguments about justice and virtue be then?

And as for your children, the Nomoi go on, will you raise them in such barbarity? Or leave them to be raised by friends in Athens? But that of course you can do also if you die.

> —"So be persuaded by (or: obey) us, Socrates, who are your nurses, and do not put children, or staying alive, or anything else, before justice, so that when you get to the lower world you have all these things to say in your own defense to the rulers of that place.[30] It is plain that if you do these things it will not be better or more just or more sacred for you here, or for those who belong to you, nor will it be better for you when you get there. As things are, you will depart [for Hades], if you should do so, as one treated unjustly not by the laws but by men. But if you should escape, shamefully repaying injustice with injustice and wrong with wrong, breaking your agreements with us, and doing harm to those whom you should least hurt—yourself and your friends and your country and us—we shall treat you harshly while you live, and our brothers, who rule in Hades, will not receive you benignly, knowing that you tried to destroy us, so far as you could do so. So let not Crito, rather than us, persuade you what to do.

The point of this last rewriting is to demonstrate to Crito not why escape would be "unjust" in the sense Crito supposes, but why it is that Socrates does not and cannot want the life that escape would give him. The claim in the end is a simple one, and the same now as it was when

---

30. Compare *Gorgias* 523–27, where Socrates imagines himself addressing his judges in the afterlife, saying that this is the court he cares about, and *Apology* 40e4–41a5, to much the same effect.

he spoke in the *Apology*, namely, that for him to die now, in this effort to speak the truth to the city, is a fitting end for him; not so comfortable, and perhaps not so fitting, as to be maintained by the city at their expense for life, in recognition of his services, but fitting nonetheless. Socrates cannot wish to escape; and, in this conversation equally important, his friends cannot properly wish it for him either.[31] Perhaps, indeed, once they recognize that this is the way things are for him, they may come to feel the same essential repose that he does.

What the Nomoi say about his past does not establish that he has entered into an agreement, in character like a legal contract, that obliges him to stay in the city against his will, but that he has established a relationship with the city which it would be an abandonment of self to abandon now. For he has not merely resided in Athens, as the Nomoi say, he has made his relationship with Athens a central social concern of his life. He has tried to establish a dialectical relationship with the city—insofar as one can have such a relationship with a city—in which he seeks to say the truth, to refute and to be refuted, and this perhaps nowhere so clearly as in the *Apology*, where he argues for his acquittal, but in terms that make it impossible for the jury to grant it without granting at the same time the truth and value of the goal to which he has directed his life.

## A FITTING END

Why is this a fitting end? Not because it is of itself a good thing to suffer unjustly at the hands of Athens; but because this end, unlike escape, does

---

31. It is true, however, that he said that he would attempt it if he were persuaded that justice so required: Is the dialogue then necessarily about the justice of escape or submission after all? Surely Socrates would not remain if he thought it unjust to do so, and we can therefore take it that he genuinely does not think that "justice requires him to escape." But this is actually a rather unlikely position; as I said above, it is part of the comic tone of the dialogue that Crito should urge it upon him. It is to be distinguished from the much stronger argument that justice *permits* him to escape; but the latter argument is irrelevant since Socrates prefers, for very good reasons, not to do so.

The whole argument about the requirements of justice presupposes, in an unstated way, a conflict between the will and the right, affirming the claims of the latter over the former. But Socrates is saying that he does not experience this conflict and therefore—except in the unlikely form in which Crito presents it to him—the issue of the justice of his proposed conduct is simply not before him. The question whether justice forces him to stay, like the question whether it forces him to leave, just doesn't come up. Compulsion is not his topic, but choice and meaning.

not require Socrates to give up the major purpose of his life. Indeed, it is a way of fulfilling a major part of that purpose, which is to establish the value of thinking and talking about what we ought to be and do collectively, as a polity, and not merely as individuals: to establish, that is, the legitimacy of discourse about the nature of the just community. His success in doing this is in fact the foundation of our own political thinking ever since, which depends upon our being able to imagine ourselves not merely as individuals who happen to be found together, our interests in temporary conflict or harmony, like rats in the maze of life, but as a larger polity, as a city or nation or society that has a moral life and career of its own of which we can ask the question, Is it just?

There are now, as there have always been, currents of opinion that wish to deny the value and coherence of that question, and the legitimacy of the discourse based upon it. Yet this question is what has enabled us to think about ourselves as we have in the West, from Plato through Cicero and Aquinas and Machiavelli to the present time. If all were reducible to the individual (or to the family), to a calculation of individual costs and benefits, it would be impossible to talk, as Socrates did and as we have ever since, of a city or nation as having a character and moral life, which could be analyzed and judged by comparison to an ideal.[32] Socrates' death expresses his commitment to that possibility; to turn away would be to deny it. If he escaped to Megara or Thessaly, he could pursue questions of justice, if at all, merely as a theoretical matter, without the engagement with the actual that can make the pursuit real. For in his life Socrates has constituted Athens as an idealized dialogic partner, a moral actor for whom justice can be as central a concern as it is for an individual. It is this fictive creation partly of his own making that he would rather die than deny; especially when the death, like this one, would do so much to make this fiction real.

Athens is his city: both the actual polis and, equally important, the vision of what it could become if it were to define itself by a concern for justice, if it were to ask the question Socrates taught individuals to

---

32. Plato is of course building on earlier visions of the city as having a moral life. Think of the beginning of *Oedipus Tyrannos,* for example, where all of Thebes suffers from the moral pollution brought upon it by one man, or of Thucydides' *History,* which imagines the cities as moral actors in another way, as capable of making and breaking treaties, of mass murder, of supreme folly, and so on. Plato's achievement is to see the city as a moral actor from the inside, as he sees the human soul as well; justice becomes a term for its essential health, including the proper distribution of role and competence to its various parts.

ask—How are we to lead our lives in a just way?—and mean it.[33] This is what he cannot leave without abandoning himself. To walk away would not be to break an agreement to which he is held against his will but a commitment to a sense of himself and the possibilities of human life to which he has devoted his existence; it would indeed "injure those whom he ought least to injure," as the Nomoi claimed, but in a very different sense from theirs. To abandon his commitment to this conversation with this partner would be to destroy the meaning of his life.

Socrates thus dies in order to establish the value and coherence and meaning of a certain sort of conversation, in which we still participate and from which we still benefit. This is what he wants Crito to see. But it is not admiration for the Athens that actually exists, or for "the many" that run it, that motivates him. He is profoundly separated, in attitude and value, from those who dominate his culture. In speaking to Crito, for example, he said that between those who think as he does, that one should never act unjustly, and those who think otherwise, there is such a difference that there can be no common deliberation but only mutual contempt. And his perpetually reiterated scorn for "the many," who do not think and do not know, as opposed to the few who do, expresses much the same feeling. In the *Apology* he acknowledges this sense of distance, explaining why he has never been politically active by saying that it would certainly have led to his death. The *Apology* can in fact be read as a kind of heroic attempt to do the impossible, to represent his life in ways that make it acceptable to the public, when in fact nearly everything he says seems likely to infuriate the jury all the more. It is not surprising that the vote goes against him, especially in a proceeding guided by standards so vague as to amount to a kind of ostracism; it is surprising instead, as Socrates said, that so many voted for him.

It would be a great mistake, then, to think of Socrates as operating out of a comfortable view of his city and its people. He is their most severe and troubling critic. Yet it has been a central part of his lifework to turn them in a certain direction, towards thinking of justice as their

---

33. In the *Apology* 29d he said: "As long as I am alive and able, I will not stop doing philosophy and advising you and pointing out errors to whomever of you I happen to meet, saying, as I usually do, 'Oh, my most excellent friend, you are an Athenian, a member of the city greatest and most well known in wisdom and power: do you not take shame at caring about money, seeing to it that you might have the most you could, and about reputation and honor, but you neither care about nor plan your life being mindful of self-discipline or the truth or your soul, how it might be in the best state it could be?'" (Translation by Susan Prince.)

ultimate collective concern, and, though he is never optimistic about the prospect, it is the imagined possibility that he might succeed upon which he will not turn his back. He starts a certain kind of conversation with his city and will not give it up. This is not a conversation that can be translated to another city, another world; his engagement is with this particular city, just as it is with this particular Crito.

## THE AUTHORITY OF PERFORMANCE

What, then, according to this text, *is* entitled to respect and authority? For, at least on the reading I have suggested, the laws are not, or not to absolute authority of the sort the Nomoi claim for them. Beyond that we can say rather little about the kind of authority Plato or Socrates regard them as having, and subject to what exceptions, for that question is not the one pursued here. In this dialogue, despite appearances, no very clear position is taken with respect to the authority of law.

But this is not to say that there are no claims to authority made here. In a sense any text makes a claim to authority, in that it makes a claim to attention and thus asserts the value of its own arguments and processes of thought, and this one is no exception. When we ask what kind of claims this one makes, we find that some of them are quite explicit. Socrates says early on, for example, that he will not now give up the "reasoned arguments" (*logous*) that have proved best in the past just because he faces imminent death, unless of course they are now shown to be defective. This is to invoke the authority of reason itself, and in two ways: the old arguments are entitled to respect because they are reasoned; but it is also true that he will now abandon them if he is persuaded that better reasons call for that. What one is properly to obey is reason, he seems necessarily to be saying, but this of course only suggests the question that his own performance must answer: "What is a good reason, and thus entitled to obedience?" That of which one is properly persuaded, he impliedly says, thus uniting the two meanings—persuade and obey—of the Greek verb *peitho,* and suggesting that here, as throughout the Socratic corpus, it is the process of philosophy itself, or what he usually calls dialectic, that is ultimately authoritative.

This is hardly a surprise, for elsewhere in the dialogues Socrates repeatedly tells us that he puts the authority of dialectic first, as the only thing we can, in our ignorance of the truth, rely upon. In the *Gorgias,* for example, he defines dialectic, opposing it to rhetoric, this way: in the dialectical conversation, unlike the rhetorical one, there are only the two parties to the process; they proceed by question and answer, not by making speeches; each promises to tell the truth as he sees it; each, knowing that his own knowledge is defective, actively seeks refutation from the other; and each, for the moment, is loyal only to that relation, calling in no others as witnesses, asking what they think, but calling only on the other party to the dialectic as his witness. Each speaker is to accept as authority, for the moment at least, only the relation so established with another and the activity it makes possible, the conversation itself, in the course of which, as Socrates practices it, our language, the very material of our thought and the ground of our connection to others, is broken down and remade.[34] A dialectic that sought to establish the superior authority of the laws, or of anything external to itself, would be a contradiction in terms. On this view, the true authority invoked here, that of dialectic, would be directly opposed to the one purportedly invoked, that of the laws of Athens.

But this view of dialectic will not work here, for in his relations both with Athens and with Crito Socrates modifies what he usually means by "dialectic": because Athens is a constructed entity, with whom question and answer are impossible, and because Crito is simply not up to the demands of that kind of conversation and of life. With Athens it is a dialectic of a career, the performance of a way of life, which reaches its clearest and most challenging expression in the *Apology*, where for once the fictive construction of Athens has something like a real and momentarily united form in the jury, whom Socrates can address as a surrogate for the city as a whole. The essential thing is for Socrates to state as truly as possible what he has done and why, and to shift to the city the responsibility for dealing with it. He will seek not to please the jurors but to refute them, yet he will do all this out of a recognition of the incompleteness of his own knowledge. To ask for exile in that context would be to destroy his commitment to speak the truth in this relationship, upon which the meaning and coherence of his life depends; to seize exile now would do the same, only even more markedly so.

With respect to Crito—who is in some respects also a surrogate for the city more generally—Socrates cannot engage in dialectic in the usual sense, for Crito is not capable of it. Socrates is therefore not so much

---

34. For further accounts of dialectic, see Vlastos, "The Socratic Elenchus," *Oxford Studies in Ancient Philosophy* 1 (1983): 27–58 and Richard Robinson, *Plato's Earlier Dialectic*, 2d ed. (Oxford: Clarendon Press, 1953).

refutational as anagogic, leading Crito as it were by the hand from one position to another. He seeks not to mortify or humiliate, not in this sense to "hurt" dialectically and beneficially, and thus to correct, as he describes dialectic doing in the *Gorgias* and elsewhere, but to instruct in a softer way. He demonstrates the kind of friendship it is possible for Socrates to have with Crito, and thus addresses a central difficulty with the Socratic corpus, namely, what kind of relationship the dialectician can establish with one who is not himself fully capable of dialectic. This is itself a performance of kindness, and it respects the kindness of another; this enactment of kindness, reciprocal to Crito's own, works in the end as a response to the first claim that Crito made, which, as you remember, was not that it is unjust for Socrates to refuse to escape, but that it would mean for him, Crito, the loss of such a friend as he should never find again.

Socrates made no response to that claim when it was made and has still not given it a formal answer. But, on the reading of the dialogue I have suggested, everything that follows, every question and speech, is meant as a response to it, both as an acknowledgment of the reality of Crito's sense of loss and as an attempt, in an act of friendship, to reduce that pain by bringing Crito to see the meaning of the event in different terms. What we see here is kindness responding to kindness, respect for what is worthy of respect in a person of limited capacity, and the exercise of an art at once intellectual and social, whose function is to teach by transforming his interlocutor's perceptions and understandings of the truth. Thus it is that the text has the form it does, leading Crito from one position to another: respecting his sense that he will lose a friend he loves and bringing him in the end to see that the continued existence of that friend, as the person he loves, is now impossible. He is not to grieve for Socrates, nor even for himself, at this verdict and its consequences, for it is not the verdict that deprives him of his friend but that friend's character, which is what he loves in him.

So what then is actually invoked as authority here? Not the laws; not the reasons for obeying the laws, for that topic is dropped when the argument is in a most unsatisfactory state indeed and transformed into another one; not even dialectic in its pure form; but another sort of conversation, another sort of philosophy, created by another sort of text, the

*Crito* itself, defining its own idea of reason, its own way of being with language and with others.

What is this kind of reason? To start with the negative, the dialogue obviously rejects the mode of discourse offered by the Nomoi in their first speech, which is abstract, propositional, conclusory, and unreasoned in character—as authoritarian in performance as it is in its message—just as it rejects the methods of Crito's first speech too. These two speeches make a pair that capture much of the contemporary state of Athenian discourse, Crito invoking the "ordinary Greek" conception of justice (helping your friends and hurting your enemies), the Nomoi marshalling another set of appeals that would also seem compelling in "ordinary Greek," based upon one's self-evident duty to one's city.[35] In this way these two speeches define the kinds of argument that it would be second nature for an educated Athenian to make. And by kinds of argument I mean not only the particular positions taken but the way they are explained and justified, the reasons offered as persuasive, including the tone of voice, the attitude towards one's audience and towards countering arguments, in short, the whole intellectual and ethical performance of the text. Imagine trying to engage the Nomoi in philosophic conversation, and I think you will see how impossible it would be, and perhaps something as well of Socrates' difficulty in addressing Crito himself.

The dialogue works with these two voices in different ways, using one—that of the Nomoi—to answer the other, then rewriting it to make a very different case indeed. The mode of thought performed in the dialogue as a whole is thus dramatic and literary, in contrast to Crito and the Nomoi alike, both of whom seek to argue from the top down, from general principle to particular conclusion, in a standard rationalist way.

---

35. Owing partly to its small size, partly to its inherent susceptibility to civil war, the polis was perceptibly fragile. This perhaps gave a kind of self-evidence to the duty not to impair its capacity to survive as a functioning unit, even at the cost of doing or suffering injustice. Think of the practice of ostracism, by which a person would be exiled by a special vote (apparently without any claim that this action needed to be based on any principles of justice), or the way in which Thucydides presents as treasonable Alcibiades' claims to have a right to retaliate against the city that harmed him.

I am grateful to Arthur W. H. Adkins for this point. He has also suggested in correspondence that one purpose of the *Crito* may have been to defend Socrates against the charge that he was responsible, as Alcibiades' teacher and lover, for this conduct and its justification. One can read the speech of the Nomoi as responding directly to the claims of Alcibiades, in Thucydides VI.92. On civil war, see especially Thucydides' account of the civil war in Corcyra—his image of the chaos with which every city was in principle threatened—and recall that Athens itself was torn by internal war more than once during the last years of Socrates' life.

The kind of reason for which authority is claimed in the dialogue as a whole is very different in quality: its idea is not to make arguments good for all time, in all contexts and languages, but to carry on a conversation that is appropriate to this relation, with this person—or city—and this language, under these conditions of ignorance and uncertainty. This is true at once of Socrates' conversation with Crito and of Plato's with us, his readers. Both place at their center not abstract propositions of fact or value but the enactment of character and relations; both make the difficulty of thought and speech itself a central issue; both insist upon the primacy of the related questions, "What kind of person should I be?" and "What kind of city should Athens be?"

The movement is corrective, from the authoritarian and the propositional to the authoritative and enacted. The life of the text is in this movement, in its transformations of one way of thinking and being into another, like music. In a sense the ultimate ground of this dialogue is narrative, for it all depends upon one's acquiescence in Socrates' claim that this is a fitting end to such a life. Its ultimate value, like the value of Socrates' own career, lies not in any theoretical scheme or system but in the kind of life it invites and makes possible.[36]

In its relation to us as readers the text is challenging, for it presents us with a real puzzle: a set of pieces that do not fit together, though we may try again and again to force them, until we see it not as an intellectual structure but as a piece of social and political action. It offers us no firm place to stand—certainly not in the first speech of the Nomoi—but a difficulty, in the working out of which we must assert our own mind against the incompleteness and defectiveness, not of the text as a whole, but of certain arguments within it.

The effect of this dialogue, like many, is not to offer the reader a system, a structure of propositions, but to disturb and upset him in a certain way, to leave him in a kind of radical distress—even while leading Crito to greater repose. For what is the right attitude, after all, to take towards laws that require us to suffer what is unjust? That require us to do it? Can we fashion arguments, better than those of the Nomoi, out of their materials of status and agreement? In a sense, Socrates is refuting a

---

36. Indeed it makes doubtful whether any conversation that is as abstracted from experience and particularity as that proposed by the Nomoi (and readily pursued by philosophers ever since), say on the question whether "the citizen has a duty to obey the law" and if so "whether that duty is absolute or qualified," could meet the standards of thought and discourse established by the *Crito*.

version of himself when he refutes Crito's claim that justice requires escape, for this is just the sort of paradoxical thing he likes to urge, and he certainly thinks that the claims of justice are paramount—or are they, when the law requires its opposite?[37]

Such tensions are not a peculiarity but a standard feature of the Platonic dialogues. Think of Socrates' perpetual insistence upon proceeding by question and answer, for example, rather than by long speeches, a principle violated as often as followed; or his apparent assumption that the questions he asks, say about the nature of justice or courage, can be satisfactorily answered in their own terms, which is countered by his repeated resort to myth and fable as ways of talking; or his claim that he "knows nothing," contradicted constantly by his certainty on many questions, substantive as well as procedural; or his obvious love for poetry, against his rejection of it; his respect for inspiration, answered by his insistence on reason; or, of special relevance to the *Crito*, his claim for the exclusive authority of dialectic and philosophy, answered by his repeated engagement in traditional religious and civic observances; or, again of relevance here, his unremitting contempt for "the many," who rule Athens and dominate its culture, and his equally unremitting loyalty to, and love for, his city.

Despite what is sometimes claimed for the *Crito*, this kind of writing grants authority to no proposition, to no institution—not even to dialectic—but to the life of thought and imagination enacted here by which the questions of rightness and wrongness, authority and no authority, are addressed. It does not precipitate out into system or doctrine but is always a fresh demand upon the particular moment, the particular mind.

The dialogue at once stimulates and frustrates the reader's own desire for an authority external to himself. We want Plato (or Socrates) to tell us what authority the law has, and a part of us wants this to be very great indeed; but he will not do that and offers us instead contradictory and paradoxical movements of the mind, with respect to which we can locate ourselves only by becoming active, affirming and rejecting the various

---

37. Compare here the *Euthyphro,* where Socrates' interlocutor similarly engages his attention by claiming that what he is doing—prosecuting his father for causing the death of a slave—is just and holy, even though unpopular, a classic Socratic position. In the *Euthydemus,* the effort is to distinguish Socrates from others who are similar to him in a different respect, namely the teachers of eristic argument, who succeed in confusing their auditors, as Socrates also does, but by logical tricks rather than dialectic. See Thomas H. Chance, *Plato's* Euthydemus: *Analysis of What Is and Is Not Philosophy* (Berkeley: University of California Press, 1992), especially pages 13–21.

claims from our own point of view; as we do this, we find our affirmations and rejections are themselves subject to challenge. Instead of an authority out there in the world—the law—and instead of an intellectual authority, a mode of reasoning that will proceed ineluctably from general principles to particular conclusions, this text offers us a mode of thought that is inherently inconclusive and puzzling, and thus transfers the problem to us. Like Crito, we look for arguments that will constrain like iron bands; we are naturally susceptible to voices like those of the Nomoi, telling us how things are; it is the great art of this dialogue both to bring these aspects of the reader to life and to challenge them. The ultimate meaning of this text lies in the way it constitutes its reader: more deeply puzzled, more fully alert, more wholly alone.

This text offers us the experience of incoherence partly resolved, then, but resolved only by our seeing that our own desires for certainty in argument, for authority in the laws—or in reason, or in persuasion— are self-misleading; that we cannot rest upon schemes or formulae, either in life or in reading, but must accept the responsibility of living, which is ultimately one of establishing a narrative, a character, a set of relations with others, which have the kinds of coherence and meaning it is given us to have, replete with tension and uncertainty. This is what Plato means by philosophy.

WHAT IS TROUBLING ABOUT THE Crito in the end is not its absolutism, or its elevation of the institutional, but the reverse: that in its claim to make the dialectical conversation the only authority it tends to erase the value of every formal institution, every other aspect of culture. Quite the opposite of a treatise in favor of an authoritarian view of law, then, its tendency is to erode respect for everything outside the present conversation, including law itself, as law is usually conceived. Another way to put this point is to say that the kind of conversation it enacts and celebrates has no, or almost no, place in the world outside itself.

But suppose that the law we saw in the world, or imagined, was not the authoritarian, unreasoned, conclusory voice of the Nomoi, but a conversation that met the standards of the Crito? Would it then be possible to write a text in favor of the authority of law which enacted, and thus claimed authority for, a conversation that continued in the public places of the community, a conversation in which the law itself mirrored the processes of thought here enacted and held out as authoritative? The claims for the authority of the present conversation and that of the larger conversation, the larger institution, would then cohere, not split apart. This would require a different sort of law from any imagined by Socrates, and perhaps a different kind of dialectic too. The movement would be from "You should grant authority to the commands of the law if there are good reasons to support it," to "You should grant authority to the law, because it is itself reasoned in a proper way." And by this we would not mean merely logical coherence but that its conversational processes met the requirements of comprehension, openness, respect for the other, kindness, and devotedness to truth that characterize the performance of Socrates here.

Can this be? It is one of the questions of the chapters that follow.


. . .


*In this chapter I report on my reading of the* Crito, *telling you what the structure and meaning of the dialogue is. Who am I to do this? you may ask. Or, to relate the question to the theme of this book, What kind of authority do I claim for my reading?*

*I like to think of reading as being like travel, and of this kind of criticism like travel writing. In either case the authority upon which one relies is simply one's own experience of the place or text. Of course my Plato is somewhat different, perhaps very different, from yours, just as my New York or Athens is different. In talking about either I do not assume that you must see just what I have seen and nothing else; of course what you observe is different, and its meaning is different too, as it is placed in a context of other experiences, other texts, read and imagined differently. This does not mean, however, that we should not talk about what we see. Just the reverse, it is the ground upon which we can hope to learn from each other: to learn different questions, different ways of directing our attention, different connections with the rest of life. I do not think of myself as telling you how things are so much as reporting on my experience, which you can check against your own.*

*In doing this I talk for the most part as if what Plato wrote were directly accessible to me, and as if I make it so to you. Yet this text is deeply foreign, composed in a different language millennia ago. Why do I not draw attention to the opacities and difficulties that reading Plato presents, to the essential foreignness of this text?*

*This is a matter of emphasis. Sometimes one is right to stress what is strange, sometimes what is familiar. My own experience of Plato has involved a struggle of almost forty years with the intractable language in which, and about which, he wrote. He may be in the "Western Canon" but that does not mean that he is easy to understand or widely understood. For me the starting point is his alienness, which does not need emphasis; I am trying to overcome it at least a little, by showing one way in which he can be made sense of in our language. I am trying, that is, to make an old text present in our world, to connect its life with our own.*

# II

# CREATING A PUBLIC WORLD

# Two

# SHAKESPEARE'S *RICHARD II:* IMAGINING THE MODERN WORLD

I N TURNING NOW TO A PLAY WRITTEN IN ENGLAND in the 1590s, we make a dramatic shift in time and culture, and in genre as well, but our subject, at a certain level of generality at least, remains the same, for this is a play about authority. Not the authority of the law so much as the authority of the crown: the story it tells is the deposition of Richard by Henry Bolingbroke, later Henry IV.

The play can be read as taking a clear-cut position for Richard (or against him), just as the *Crito* can be read to take a position in favor of the absolute authority of law. But, as we have seen, the *Crito* is not reducible to the single speech of the Nomoi (especially in its first and most authoritarian version), but should be read as a text composed of several voices, answering each other in the shifting contexts that the conversation defines as it proceeds; likewise *Richard II* should not be read as supporting royal absolutism, or denying it, but rather as offering a way of thinking about it. Like the *Crito,* it is not reducible to a single position but consists of countering and contrasting voices, speaking to each other out of specific situations. Its meaning is not to be found in any one of them standing alone: not in Richard's great speeches on kingship, not in John of Gaunt's poem of praise and lament for England, not in Henry's speech justifying his return, not in the Gardener's invocation of the great chain of being, but in the ways in which these voices answer one another, across the line of the narrative that they at once clarify and motivate. What makes the play especially useful for our purposes is that so much of it is about authority—the authority of the crown, the authority of inheritance, the authority of public need or private opportunity, and so on. As it argues about these questions of external authority each of the speeches also performs its own methods of thought and expression, for which it

47

necessarily claims a kind of authority as well, as indeed Shakespeare does for the play itself.

The movement of the play involves the transfer of royal power and authority not only from one man to another but from one kind of man to another, one kind of world to another. We begin the play in an imagined version of the Late Middle Ages, in which it is possible to talk about the divine right of a man to be king, and end in something like the modern world, Shakespeare's and our own, in which is most unclear what should count as a title to govern, and why.[1] In this sense Shakespeare in this play invents, or brings to the surface where it can be seen and felt, the problem of authority to which constitutional theory has ever after been addressed.

As readers of the play we naturally want to know how these two men, and the two ways of imagining the world and claiming authority within it that each exemplifies, are represented and defined; how the transition from one to the other is achieved; what attitudes the play seems to invite towards the two elements that it thus puts in contrast, and what understanding of them it makes possible; and, finally, what kind of authority the play claims for itself, as a way of thinking and imagining the world.

## QUESTIONS OF AUTHORITY

In *Richard II* an indubitably lawful king, Richard Plantagenet, is deposed by his cousin, Henry Bolingbroke, who, as Henry IV, then takes his place on the throne. For a constitutional lawyer or political philosopher at least—and perhaps for any American, imbued as we are from birth with doctrines of legitimacy—such a plot naturally suggests a series of fundamental questions about the political authority of the crown, which we expect the play to address. Upon what principle or theory does the king's authority rest? Is his right to the crown absolute or is it subject to defea-

---

1. This is how the play presents it, but historically the situation is more complex. The doctrine of divine right of kings was urged in a more extreme and radical form in Shakespeare's time, and for a period thereafter, than it was in the Middle Ages itself. While on medieval terms the king was touched with divinity, he was also conceived of as having a place in a larger structure, marked by reciprocal obligations, with power limited as well as granted. The extreme seventeenth-century version of the doctrine knew far less constraint. The classic work on the medieval kingship is Ernst H. Kantorowicz, *The King's Two Bodies: A Study in Medieval Political Theology* (Princeton: Princeton University Press, 1957), of which the second chapter deals with *Richard II*.

sance or forfeiture on certain conditions? Or is it simply a form of raw power, garbed in a flimsy cloak of ideology? What limitations, if any, are there on the power of the crown? Is Henry right or wrong to seize the crown, and why? And when a king is deposed, whether rightly or wrongly, what should happen next: ought the crown go to the next in line of inheritance, to the one who did the deposing (or to him only if the deposition was rightly or lawfully done), or to whom? By whom, and how, is all this to be decided? Since, as we shall see, Richard's deposition is a ceremony in which he participates in some sense voluntarily, additional questions are raised: What place and effect has the consensual transfer of the crown? Is the crown the sort of personal effect that can be given away, under any circumstances, to anybody? Or is it in fact not alienable at all? Or is it some third thing, subject to different rules?

But these are mostly modern questions of a lawyer's sort, appropriate to the way we think today, not to the way the play was written. They invite responses, in terms of political theory or constitutional law, of a kind that in fact work against the life of this text, which lies not in abstract and conceptual thought but in the way the drama works: in what people in imagined situations can be imagined to say to each other as their stories develop. The voice of the general theorist is nowhere present; the voices here are rather those of particular characters, as Shakespeare presents them—Richard, or John of Gaunt, or the duke of York, or the bishop of Carlisle, and so on—each speaking from a particular position to a particular moment, and in his speaking engaged in action with others: urging on, calming down, consoling, lamenting, threatening, insulting, teasing, and so forth.

It is not an abstract or universal question, then, that Shakespeare pursues here but a series of particular ones. What can be said by such a one as this or that, so situated, in favor of the crown's authority or against it? How can the deposed king talk about his right to the crown, his right to rule? What can his deposers say? The imagination at work here is in this sense a rhetorical one; and the subject of the play is less the "crown" abstractly regarded than the various languages by which the crown is given meaning of one kind or another, as these characters organize themselves in relation to it.

Shakespeare's questions are particular in another sense as well, for they are particular to a cultural and historical moment: in one way, to the fourteenth century, when the events here represented—or something like them—actually occurred, but more significantly to the sixteenth century, when the play was composed and performed. For in Shakespeare's time the authority of the crown was itself a troubled question. Elizabeth, who came to the throne after the great reversals achieved first by Henry VIII, then by Mary, held her title, after all, in a sense from the usurping Henry Bolingbroke; she had no children; and where was the crown to go on her death? She was to experience at least one direct rebellion, by the earl of Essex. In religion too authority was uncertain: the crown was shifting from one religion to another, imperiled and imperiling. The Church of England, of which she was the head, had declared its separation from Rome only in the 1530s, and its legitimacy was challenged from both sides, by the Romans who denied it the authority of tradition and by the Presbyterians who denied it the authority of scripture. In this era of challenged and collapsing authorities there emerged, perhaps in response, a strain of high authoritarianism, in church and state alike, one form of which was an elaborated version of the divine right of kings, a note heard both at home and abroad; this was ultimately to lead to autocracies like those attempted by Charles I in England and achieved by Louis XIV in France.

For centuries readers of the play have found themselves asking which side Shakespeare is on: Does his play affirm the authority, perhaps the divine authority, of the crown? Or does it assert the right of energy and competence to seize power from the weak or ill-advised? Elizabeth herself saw it this way, saying, it is reported, "I am Richard II, know ye not that?"[2] But I think Shakespeare is on neither side, or both; and that this play—like his sonnets, like his other plays—works on the principle that the truth cannot be said in any single speech or language, but lies in the recognition that against one speech or claim or language is always another one. In this sense its life is that of voice speaking against voice; this life is what it ultimately holds out as authoritative: not the crown or the usurper, but its own performances.

But it is nonetheless the case that the play has a movement, the transfer of royal power and authority, and it is hard not to ask whether this is represented as progress or a decline. What does this play invite us to think and feel about the transformation it achieves; about the two main figures, about the ways of imagining the world and claiming authority within it that each represents, and about the transition from one to another?

---

2. For the story see William Shakespeare, *King Richard II*, edited by John Dover Wilson (Cambridge: Cambridge University Press, 1939), page xxxii.

## TRIAL BY CEREMONY

It would be tempting to begin with one of Richard's great speeches setting forth the claims of the crown, and we shall in fact look at some of these below. But much of their meaning lies not in what they say but in what precedes them, in the context against which they are heard. It is best therefore to begin, as we did with the *Crito*, with the opening scene.

The play starts with the initiation of a formal proceeding (the technical word is "appeal"), which is brought before Richard, as king, by Henry Bolingbroke against Thomas Mowbray, duke of Norfolk, charging him among other things with the recent murder of the duke of Gloucester, one of Richard's uncles. The audience may already know, but will in any event soon learn, that Richard is himself suspected of having ordered Gloucester's death, so this is a challenge in fact, whether in intention or not, to Richard himself. But this is nowhere made plain, or intelligibly suggested, in the ceremonious speeches of attack and defense with which the play begins.[3]

This proceeding, which results in the scheduling of a trial by battle between Bolingbroke and Mowbray, would have been nearly as strange to Shakespeare's audience as it is to us, and for the play to begin with it is to draw our attention explicitly to this social form. As an audience we are a bit like anthropologists dropped into a village just as a ritual begins; our task is to make sense of what we see, to understand the story as it unfolds before us, and in order to do that we need to understand what these people are doing and what it means.

The play at first gives rather little help: we know that Richard is to hear the charge and is thus in some sense superior to it. These men, that is, do not simply fight to kill each other but come before him, as a kind of umpire or judge, and this to some degree confirms, and helps create, his authority. Richard's first speech is in his official role: he asks his uncle, John of Gaunt, Henry's father, whether he has "sounded" Henry to deter-

---

3. Another piece of background that the play only gradually reveals is that the crown jumped a generation in going to Richard, whose own father died before he could assume the throne. Richard has thus been surrounded since childhood by powerful uncles—Gloucester, York, Lancaster (John of Gaunt)—who did much to try to control him. Indeed, as Holinshed tells the story, Gloucester, who was killed in Calais on Richard's order, had organized a rebellion against Richard and meant to seize his Crown; if so, his killing, even if not proper, was in the service of the Crown and its legitimacy and certainly not treason. See William Shakespeare, *Richard II*, edited by David Bevington (New York: Bantam Books, 1988), page 120.

mine whether he proceeds "on ancient malice" against Mowbray, or "worthily, as a good subject should, On some known ground of treachery in him."[4] This is a question not only about Henry's motives but about the form of the charge, to ensure that it claims that Henry acts not for himself but for the crown, that is, that this is a case of treason and not a private matter. When John of Gaunt gives him his (somewhat qualified) assurances, Richard calls the two men before him.

The litigants then engage in the ceremonial exchange of highly conclusory charges: Henry accuses Mowbray of "treason"—"Thou art a traitor and a miscreant, / Too good to be so, and too bad to live"—to which Mowbray responds in kind: "I do defy him, and I spit at him, / Call him a slanderous coward, and a villain." These speeches have something of the character of legal pleadings, formulaic and conclusory, yet they are poetic displays as well, performances in a highly verbal ceremony of mutual attack. Henry throws down his gage, with taunts: "Pale trembling coward, there I throw my gage"; Mowbray picks it up, saying:

> I'll answer thee in any fair degree
> Or chivalrous design of knightly trial;
> And when I mount, alive may I not light,
> If I be traitor or unjustly fight! [I.i.80–84.]

As we listen to the opening challenges of Bolingbroke and Mowbray, we have no way of knowing which is right or even of forming a tentative opinion on the matter, no way of orienting ourselves confidently with respect to this fatal struggle. All we have is a set of rather empty claims of treachery, on both sides, and a willingness to fight to settle them. As observers of the play we naturally wish to have the narrative make sense, we want to know "what really happened" to produce Gloucester's death; but the play satisfies our need for clarification rather poorly, as we shall see below, and the procedure of trial by battle satisfies it not at all.

It is true that Richard asks Henry to make his charges more specific, but the speech in which Henry responds, by modern standards of legal pleading at least, is an odd one indeed. While it does make certain factual allegations, they are all subsumed under a general charge of treason, cast in terms some of which cannot possibly be true:

---

4. Quotations throughout are from William Shakespeare, *King Richard II*, edited by Peter Ure (London and New York: Methuen, 1956) (Arden edition), with the kind permission of Methuen and Co.

Look what I speak, my life shall prove it true:
That Mowbray hath receiv'd eight thousand nobles
In name of lendings for your Highness' soldiers,
The which he hath detain'd for lewd imployments,
Like a false traitor, and injurious villain;
Besides I say, and will in battle prove,
. . . . . . . . . . . . . . . . . . . . . . . .
That all the treasons for these eighteen years
Complotted and contrived in this land
Fetch from false Mowbray their first head and spring;
Further I say, and further will maintain
Upon his bad life to make all this good,
That he did plot the Duke of Gloucester's death. . . . [I.i.87–100.]

In his response Mowbray denies the charge of embezzlement, admits—what was never charged—that he once did conspire to kill John of Gaunt (but says that that has been forgiven him), and with respect to Gloucester says only: "I slew him not, but to my own disgrace / Neglected my sworn duty in that case."[5] Does Mowbray mean that he failed to prevent the murder, or that he failed to carry it out? The very question whether the murder of Gloucester should count as treason in the first place is thus rendered uncertain. (If Gloucester himself was a "traitor," that is, Richard and Mowbray may have been in some sense right to kill him.) What then could the battle, if it were to take place, be thought to settle? No question of fact, no principle of law or morals; only the struggle of will and power between these two actors, and this only tentatively, for the question of its meaning would always be open, subject to yet another challenge and battle.

The effect of these speeches is not what today we hope of legal pleadings, to define an issue of fact or law that can be resolved by trial, but to cast the dispute in absolute terms as one of loyalty or treachery, honor or villainy. One person must be wholly right, the other wholly wrong. The idea of the speeches, and hence of the trial by battle itself, cannot be so much to prove who killed Gloucester, or did other particular things, as to establish an altogether different kind of claim, which is ultimately

5. He rather understandably says nothing about having been the source of "all the treasons for these eighteen years."
This speech follows Holinshed quite closely. Is Shakespeare just not thinking when he composes it? Or is the lack of fit between charge and answer part of the meaning of the play?

about the character of the individuals involved, namely, whether they are false or true, to which the facts alleged are really only evidentiary or exemplary.

Nothing that the king or the disputants can do will clarify the crucial questions, Who killed Gloucester? at whose instance? and why? In this sense the play presents us with a set of social practices that establish a dimension of meaning and a field of action that are ceremonial in character in the special sense that their significance is not dependent upon what happens, or has happened, elsewhere in the world. In this domain, it does not matter who actually killed Gloucester; it only matters who charges whom, and how, and how the defendant responds, and ultimately who wins the battle. The drama accepts this mode of proceeding by never telling us what the truth is, thus showing us how it is possible to proceed without even asking that question.

Thus far it has seemed that this dispute is regulated by the king much as a modern law suit is regulated by the court. But it quickly appears that the king's power here is limited, not by law but by the parties themselves. For when, after hearing them, Richard orders each of the men to put down the gage he has taken up, each explicitly refuses to obey his command. Mowbray explains why in terms that neither Richard nor anyone else can deny:

> Myself I throw, dread sovereign, at thy foot;
> My life thou shalt command, but not my shame:
> The one my duty owes, but my fair name,
> Despite of death, that lives upon my grave,
> To dark dishonour's use thou shalt not have.
> I am disgrac'd, impeach'd, and baffl'd here,
> Pierc'd to the soul with slander's venom'd spear,
> The which no balm can cure but his heart-blood
> Which breath'd this poison.
> . . . . . . . . . . . . . . . . . . .
>
>                         Take but my shame,
> And I resign my gage. My dear dear lord,
> The purest treasure mortal times afford
> Is spotless reputation—that away,
> Men are but gilded loam, or painted clay.
> A jewel in a ten-times barr'd-up chest
> Is a bold spirit in a loyal breast.

Mine honour is my life, both grow in one,
Take honour from me, and my life is done. [I.i.165–83.]

In a similar speech Henry also refuses to give back the gage he has taken up; as a result Richard orders a trial by battle to take place between them. This means that the power of the crown, seemingly so great, is in fact threatened or qualified by another set of practices or institutions, based upon the individual assertion of honor, which the crown cannot control. Two ways of imagining this conflict are thus poised against each other: the first sees it as a trial, in which two subjects submit themselves to their king; the second sees it as a kind of combat, in which there are only the two equal knights challenging each other's honor. Here the second way preempts the first. Loyalty to the crown may be the greatest of virtues, but it can never be at the expense of honor.

## FEUD AND CROWN

We learn more about the second way of organizing life described above, and its relation to the crown, in the brief scene that follows, in which Gloucester's widow demands of John of Gaunt that he take revenge for her husband's murder. Here is part of what she says, in a great rhetorical and ceremonial display:

Ah, Gaunt, his blood was thine! that bed, that womb,
That mettle, that self mould, that fashioned thee
Made him a man; and though thou livest and breathest,
Yet art thou slain in him; thou dost consent
In some large measure to thy father's death
In that thou seest thy wretched brother die,
Who was the model of thy father's life. [I.ii.22–28.]

The duchess here speaks out of a way of organizing life and exercising power that is inconsistent with the idea of kingship, against which kingship is poised and which indeed it is a way of regulating. This kind of ethics and politics is chivalric or feudal: its central value is that of individual and family honor, which is to be maintained at any cost; its central form of action is revenge. The king is not a judge, let alone a sacred figure, but is just another actor in the drama of the feud. The speech of the duchess, seeking to inspire her husband's brother to revenge her husband's death, is in fact a specimen of a well-established genre, with its own forms of speech, images, and iconography.[6] In it she invokes the culture of the feud that is historically prior to kingship in the European world; in this play it is represented as the cultural basis upon which kingship rests.[7] Kingship is in fact a kind of solution to the problems it presents, for one of the emerging functions of the crown is to restrain and control the feud, to civilize it as it were, thus making possible a kind of peace and order that it perpetually threatens. We see the crown having this effect, for example, in Gaunt's response to the duchess:

> God's is the quarrel—for God's substitute,
> His deputy anointed in His sight,
> Hath caus'd his death; the which if wrongfully,
> Let heaven revenge, for I may never lift
> An angry arm against His minister. [I.ii.37–41.]

This helps explain one of the great puzzles of the play, which is why it begins with the challenge thrown down by Henry to Mowbray, accusing him among other things of the murder of Gloucester. This opening scene is an enactment at once of the chivalric culture and of its imperfect regal regulation. The challenge defines the relation between the two opponents as primary; the battle as the essential act by which that relation will be determined; and the crown as regulating that process, but always incompletely.

As THE AUDIENCE WE ARE PLACED IN A position like that of an actor in this world, unable to know the truth about the facts of Gloucester's death and told that the issue will be resolved by death. But, as I say above, the issue that would be so resolved is not really an "issue" in our sense at all, not a question of fact or law but the struggle of hatred between these two, whatever its origin; whoever wins the battle, we shall know no more

---

6. See William Ian Miller, "Choosing the Avenger: Some Aspects of Bloodfeud in Medieval Iceland and England,"1 *Law and History Review* 159 (1983). J. M. Wallace-Hadrill, *The Long-Haired Kings and Other Studies in Frankish History* (London: Methuen, 1962), pages 121–47, describes the coexistence of the feud and crown among the Franks.

7. For the story of the evolution of kingship in one part of Europe, see Snorri Sturluson, *Heimskringla: History of the Kings of Norway*, translated by L. M. Hollander (Austin: University of Texas Press, 1964), which portrays a feudal world so bloody and uncontrolled that the autocratic rule of the strongman seems by comparison a step towards civilization.

about the circumstances of Gloucester's death. And any resolution would be tentative at best, for it might well give rise to a reciprocal obligation, on the part of the loser's son or brothers, to avenge his honor with still another battle. The meaning of the battle, like that of the crown, lies in the gesture, the object, the act, the person, not in any secondary explanations, or reasons, or justifications. The king speaks; the gage is thrown or picked up; the appellant is killed or kills. Here, in the ceremonial action or object, is where meaning and authority lie.

In this way the opening scenes show us that Richard's language of kingship, his way of imagining himself and the world of which he is a part, is threatened and undermined by the language and practices of the feud of honor, even though these are for the moment regulated by and accommodated within the kingship. They provide a place to stand outside the kingship, a way of thinking and feeling which naturally resists it, and in this way contribute to our sense that the loss of the crown, when it comes, is a comprehensible, even inevitable, event. But more than that. The very intensity and force of the honor-based imperatives help explain the absolute character of the claims made the other way, on behalf of the crown, for example by Gaunt in the speech quoted above. Such force as this could be resisted and regulated only by an equivalent force on the other side. Our exposure to these motives makes intelligible, that is, not only the collapse of the crown but the rigid and absolute attitudes of its adherents.

## CEREMONY, ENGLAND, AND INHERITED RIGHT

The tensions between the feud of honor and rule of the crown provide much of the energy by which the play moves, as the next scene, that of the battle itself, makes plain. Here the opponents appear, repeat their charges in elaborate and conclusory declamations, and prepare to fight. But Richard halts the proceedings, consults with his council, and announces his decision: there shall be no battle; both men shall be exiled, Bolingbroke for ten years, Mowbray for life. Richard explains the decision to stop the battle by reference to the public interest, seeing in bloodshed not resolution but further bloodshed, in this way at once acknowledging the force of the feudal motive, which will not accept defeat, and seeking to impose his will upon it. For the disparity in the terms of exile, he gives no reason at all. Once Mowbray has left, Richard, apparently out

of pity for Gaunt's sorrow, cuts Bolingbroke's exile to six years. Bolingbroke chafes, Gaunt consoles him, but in the end Bolingbroke goes.

How is one to read Richard's conduct here? His stopping the battle
is the assertion of the monarchy over the feud, his own power over that
of the combatants, though as I say his decision also recognizes the force
of the feud it controls. The double exile is perhaps an artful compromise,
by which he rids himself of a dangerous rival at the price of half-admitting
his complicity in the murder of Gloucester. (Think what his situation
would have been had Bolingbroke won the battle!) But there is a sense in
which these questions of motive are all wrong: the nature of Richard's
claim to power is that it is beyond question, beyond interpretation, existing as significant in its own realm of ceremony or law. And in any event,
and whether we see Richard's action as skillful or as whimsical, there is
no resolution yet but at best a deferral.

In the next brief scene Richard is seen at ease and as it were offstage,
with his cousin Aumerle, the son of the duke of York, and the two royal
favorites, Bagot and Greene. He now speaks in an entirely different way,
not as king but as the person who holds that office. First he describes
Bolingbroke's triumphant procession to the sea, hailed by the common
people and seeking their favor; he sees in this a threat to his crown. But
the Irish wars require attention; Richard says that he will go himself, supporting his army by tax farming and direct impositions.[8] Then he hears
that Gaunt is taken ill and sees in this the possibility of a solution to more
than one problem:

> Now put it, God, in the physician's mind
> To help him to his grave immediately!
> The lining of his coffers shall make coats
> To deck our soldiers for these Irish wars.
> Come, gentlemen, let's all go visit him,
> Pray God we may make haste and come too late! [I.iv.59–64.]

The ugliness of these sentiments sounds a note of which we shall hear
variations throughout the play: for while Richard is a king he is a bad
one, not only in his imperiousness of manner but in his failure to respect
the rights of his subjects and his tyrannical whimsicality; here, in this
cheapness of mind and feeling, he is shown to be a bad king in another

---

8. Tax farming was the sale, for cash, of the right to collect the king's taxes.

sense, a bad person.[9] All this means that Bolingbroke's challenge, which up to now we have had no way to judge—is it based on the wrongful murder of a kingsman, or is it just an assertion of ambitious will?—now has the after-the-fact support of Richard's visible wrongdoing.

This theme is sounded expansively in Gaunt's famous death-bed speech:

> This land of such dear souls, this dear dear land,
> Dear for her reputation through the world,
> Is now leas'd out—I die pronouncing it—
> Like to a tenement or pelting farm.
> England, bound in with the triumphant sea,
> Whose rocky shore beats back the envious siege
> Of wat'ry Neptune, is now bound in with shame,
> With inky blots and rotten parchment bonds;
> That England, that was wont to conquer others,
> Hath made a shameful conquest of itself.[10] [II.i.57–66.]

The force of this speech is that of a poetic denunciation; it creates in language a sense not of honor or the crown but of England itself, damaged by its ruler. It is a continuation of the mode of ceremonious declamation with which the play begins, but this time not in the service of a charge of treason or defending against it; rather it makes a claim that there is something beyond the crown and feud alike, the nation itself. This nation has a constitution, as every organism does, and is subject to health and illness. It has a moral existence and career, and its welfare is the ultimate source of political authority. Gaunt's speech is thus the invention of a third discourse, as it were, in addition to those of feud and crown, that of England as a whole.

When York hears what Richard plans to do he resists him too, but in a different way, in a speech that sets forth still another way of imagining the king and his authority:

---

9. His position in popular esteem is summed up in the charges made by Ross:
> The commons hath he pill'd with grievous taxes,
> And quite lost their hearts. The nobles hath he fin'd
> For ancient quarrels and quite lost their hearts. [II.i.246–48.]
The use Richard will make of Gloucester's wealth, however, is not to waste it in luxury but to support the Irish wars. He makes no distinction between himself and his realm, between his public role and private self, and thus does not expose himself to charges that he exploits his power in one capacity to benefit himself in the other.

10. "Pelting" means "paltry."

Seek you to seize and gripe into your hands
The royalties and rights of banish'd Herford?
Is not Gaunt dead? and doth not Herford live?
Was not Gaunt just? and is not Harry true?
Did not the one deserve to have an heir?
Is not his heir a well-deserving son?
Take Herford's rights away, and take from time
His charters, and his customary rights;
Let not to-morrow then ensue to-day:
Be not thyself. For how art thou a king
But by fair sequence and succession? [II.i.189–99.]

The claim made here (out of which Edmund Burke two centuries later will make a whole philosophy of law and the constitution)[11] is that the rights and powers of the crown are not absolute, not immanent or independent of the claims of others, as Gaunt has suggested and Richard will claim; rather, they rest upon the practice of inheritance, and so conceived they are powerfully constrained, for the king cannot in any way impair the inherited rights of others without impairing his own. His authority is seen, that is, as a special instance of a larger principle which also creates rights, and hence authorities, in others.

This speech of York has powerful resonances later in the play, for it is upon the ground of inherited rights that Bolingbroke, speaking in fact to York, first justifies his return against the orders of the king:

If that my cousin king be King in England,
It must be granted that I am Duke of Lancaster.
You have a son, Aumerle, my noble cousin;
Had you first died, and he been thus trod down,
He should have found his uncle Gaunt a father
To rouse his wrongs and chase them to the bay.

. . . . . . . . . . . . . . . . . . . . . . . . . . .

What would you have me do? I am a subject,
And I challenge law; attorneys are denied me,

---

11. Edmund Burke's *Reflections on the Revolution in France* (edited by C. C. O'Brien [London: Penguin Books, 1969]) seems in fact to have been influenced by this play, most of all in this image of inheritance, which is the central metaphor of Burke's philosophy. But other images also recur: the idea that in one case England, in the other France, has made a "conquest of itself," for example, and the distinction, at the center of *Richard II*, between a "bad king" and a "usurper." (Burke, *Reflections*, pages 297–98, 108.)

And therefore personally I lay my claim
To my inheritance of free descent. [II.iii.122–35.]

According to this pair of speeches, then, what is primary is not the king
and his crown, or the feud, or England, but the principle upon which the
king's authority depends, which is inheritance; and that principle justifies
Bolingbroke, or so he claims, in resisting the royal decree. As he later says:
"I come but for mine own" (III.iii.196.).

## IMAGINATION AND REALITY

What does it mean, then, to Richard and those who think like him, that
he is king? As he repeatedly states it, the idea seems to be the simplest
imaginable, that by birth and nature he is The King, as inherently and
uniquely and unarguably as he is the person in his body, or male rather
than female. Kingship is his essence; whatever military force another
might command, such a one could never become king, except as Richard
did, by birth.

Listen to him speak to Aumerle, on his return from Ireland, when he
has just learned that Bolingbroke has landed against him:

> Discomfortable cousin! know'st thou not
> That when the searching eye of heaven is hid
> Behind the globe and lights the lower world,
> Then thieves and robbers range abroad unseen
> In murthers and in outrage boldly here;
> But when from under this terrestrial ball
> He fires the proud tops of the eastern pines,
> And darts his light through every guilty hole,
> Then murthers, treasons, and detested sins,
> The cloak of night being pluck'd from off their backs,
> Stand bare and naked, trembling at themselves?
> So when this thief, this traitor, Bolingbroke,
> Who all this while hath revell'd in the night,
> Whilst we were wand'ring with the Antipodes,
> Shall see us rising in our throne the east,
> His treasons will sit blushing in his face,
> Not able to endure the sight of day,
> But self-affrighted tremble at his sin.
> Not all the water in the rough rude sea

Can wash the balm off from an anointed king;
The breath of worldly men cannot depose
The deputy elected by the Lord;
For every man that Bolingbroke hath press'd
To lift shrewd steel against our golden crown,
God for his Richard hath in heavenly pay
A glorious angel: then, if angels fight,
Weak men must fall, for heaven still guards the right. [III.ii.36–62.]

As king, Richard imagines that he will command loyalty in the people, that enemies will quail before him, indeed that angels will fight on his side. But even if these expectations prove wrong, even if he loses the military struggle, and no matter what else might happen, he is the king and is so till he dies, just as the sun is the sun in heaven. Like that sun he has powers that no other being can claim.

This is a vision of authority far simpler, and in a sense far more crude than anything suggested in the *Crito,* for it is, in the usual sense of the term, wholly unreasoned. Richard has authority because he is the king, and he is the king not by any process of political selection but by birth, that is, by a bare genetic fact—the eldest son of the eldest son—coupled with a sacramental and irreversible act, anointment and coronation. From the authority of king and crown there can be no appeal to the world of reason and debate and justification; his authority is present in his person and needs no further words. Indeed, it would be diminished by any attempt to justify or explain it; the authority of argument and reason is no authority at all, nothing but human talk and chatter, compared to the authority of the king. The person of the king is in this way made a fetish, an object of immanent meaning and authority, dependent on nothing but itself.

It is of course not Richard alone who thinks this way—it would be a species of insanity if he did so without being widely supported by others—for he expresses a thread of understanding that runs through the whole culture, as we saw in the speech of Gaunt quoted above. And the bishop of Carlisle, in the scene just referred to, tells Richard:

Fear not, my lord. That Power that made you king
Hath power to keep you king in spite of all. [III.ii.27–28.]

And much later, when Henry announces his intention to take the throne, Carlisle says to those around him:

My Lord of Herford here, whom you call king,
Is foul traitor to proud Herford's king,
And if you crown him, let me prophesy—
The blood of English shall manure the ground,
And future ages groan for this foul act,
Peace shall go sleep with Turks and infidels,
And, in this seat of peace, tumultuous wars
Shall kin with kin, and kind with kind, confound.
Disorder, horror, fear, and mutiny,
Shall here inhabit, and this land be call'd
The field of Golgotha and dead men's skulls. [IV.i.134–44.]

The king is the king, Carlisle is saying; to depose him is to violate the order of the divine and natural world, and this will have its revenge. The king is not the king because we say so, or believe so, or so consent, or because we choose to arrange our collective lives in this way, all of which are modern ways of thinking of it; he is the king because he is the king. This is an argument from self-evidence, the strongest kind of all, at least until the ground of self-evidence is successfully thrown into doubt.

But in the play it has already been thrown into doubt: by the language and practice of feudal honor, by the principle of inheritance, and by the idea of England itself. This means that for the audience defined by the experience of this play Richard's speech is not the simple assertion of un-questioned truths, as it seems, but an act of self-definition and self-creation and language in poetry, continuous not only with the "scepter'd isle" speech of Gaunt, to which it is a kind of answer, but with those other acts of heroic (or romantic) self-definition against the world that lie at the center of English Renaissance drama: think of Romeo and Juliet, of Doctor Faustus, of Lear, of Hamlet, even of Caliban, and of Coriolanus too. In Richard's speech we see a version of the self-creative mind at work, the mind of the Renaissance hero, making itself something against the force of a world that denies it. It offers us a claim of meaning in a torn and perhaps chaotic world. Much of its appeal lies in this very fact, not in its tone of apparent security but in the sense we have that it is uttered against the odds.[12]

This means that we should read Richard's kingship speeches in a

---

12. On this type of self-assertion see Stephen Greenblatt, *Renaissance Self-Fashioning: From More to Shakespeare* (Chicago: University of Chicago Press, 1980).

somewhat different way from any suggested so far. It is not true that his image of the crown is self-evident to all, unthreatened; it is threatened on every side. Yet to argue for the authority of the crown would to a large degree destroy it, for, as I suggested earlier, this would render it subordinate to the very processes of argument itself, to reason, policy, and judgment. The crown by its nature cannot have an apologist or advocate. But it can have a poet; and this is the role of Richard in this play, to create a poetry of kingship.

The meaning of Richard's speech thus comes in large part from the context in which it is found and to which it is a response, in which it is not merely a restatement of what everyone believes but an act of heroic assertion. It is one of a series of scenes or panels: Bolingbroke's challenge, Mowbray's response, the refusal to pick up the gages, the appeal by the duchess to John of Gaunt and his refusal to act, the scheduling of the battle and its disruption, the exile of the parties, the speech of the dying Gaunt, the seizure of his lands, the return of Henry. It speaks with sublime confidence, but this is not natural or easy, as one might think; it is achieved by an effort of mind and imagination. The crown for which authority is here claimed is not merely invoked but created in the speech, and created in a poetry whose formality and ceremoniousness enact and reinforce the authority of the king. It is a claim to create an order of reality that has independent force and vitality. In this sense it is a form of constitutional thought.

In character this claim is similar to that made by the feudal ceremonies of trial by battle: one does not pierce their forms to discover what really happened or why the appeal was really brought. The ceremony *is* the relevant reality. (So Richard, when he lands, picks up the soil of England in his hands as if it were England.) This speech is likewise a performance of the power of mind and language to create a new kind of reality, or to make an old one new, that of the crown. This is the same power that is performed in the theater itself, where for a moment we inhabit another world made by human imagination, as Shakespeare himself repeatedly—above all in *The Tempest*—makes us see.

The power of the imagination to make real is a deep theme of the play. We see it in Gaunt, not only in his "scepter'd isle" speech but in his advice to Henry in Act I, where he tells him to redefine his exile in such a way as to make it more tolerable:

> Go, say I sent thee forth to purchase honour,
> And not the king exil'd thee; or suppose

Devouring pestilence hangs in our air,
And thou art flying to a fresher clime.
Look what thy soul holds dear, imagine it
To lie that way thou goest, not whence thou com'st.
Suppose the singing birds musicians,
The grass whereon thou tread'st the presence strew'd,
The flowers fair ladies, and thy steps no more
Than a delightful measure or a dance;
For gnarling sorrow hath less power to bite
The man that mocks at it and sets it light. [I.iii.282–93.][13]

But Bolingbroke responds:

O, who can hold a fire in his hand
By thinking on the frosty Caucasus?
Or cloy the hungry edge of appetite
By bare imagination of a feast?
Or wallow naked in December snow
By thinking on fantastic summer's heat?
O no, the apprehension of the good
Gives but the greater feeling to the worse.
Fell sorrow's tooth doth never rankle more
Than when he bites, but lanceth not the sore. [I.iii.294–303.]

Here, as we shall see him do in the deposition scene as well, Henry stands with "reality" and against the "imagination." But he will soon find that meaning lies not only in material things, as he thinks, but in imagination too, and in particular that the loss of the language of kingship is one he cannot remedy; similarly Richard, first in the deposition scene and later in prison, will find that the power of his imagination to make and remake the world in language has its limits too.

Once Bolingbroke has landed, the play moves quickly and inexorably to the deposition of Richard and Henry's assumption of the crown. It then turns in on itself and becomes reflective, working out what that event means, both for Richard, the poet stripped of his crown, and for Henry, who now has a crown that means something new and different. In this way we are gradually brought to see something of what the world has lost in losing the idea and reality of a king.

---

13. "Presence" means "royal presence chamber."

## The Deposition

At the deposition scene our uncertainty as to Henry's motivation becomes increasingly problematic. He claims, both on arriving in England and when he first meets Richard, that he comes only for the lands of which he has been illegally deprived. But it is also true that immediately upon landing in England he orders the execution of Bushy and Green, an act of royal power (or treason); that he brought the initial challenge against Mowbray, which was necessarily a challenge to Richard; that he is no upstart but almost as well-born as Richard and therefore a credible candidate for the crown; and that his present offering of arms to his sovereign is hardly a peaceable proceeding.

What are Henry's motives then? In particular, when does he aim at the crown? These questions may be thought inappropriately psychological in character—after all, there is no real Henry here to ask them about—but they retain their force if they are recast as questions about directing the play, and they are then inevitable, for the director has to decide how the role of Henry should be acted. To them, central though they are, the play does not give clear answers, but I hope here to propose a reading that will suggest a possible line of thought on the issue of motive and at the same time show something of what Henry's conduct comes to mean, to him within the play, to the world of which he is a part, and to us in our world.

When Henry at last confronts Richard, with the armies all on his side, the crown alone on the other, he tells Northumberland, his emissary, what to say to Richard:

> Noble lord,
> Go to the rude ribs of that ancient castle,
> Through brazen trumpet send the breath of parle
> Into his ruin'd ears, and thus deliver:
> Henry Bolingbroke
> On both his knees doth kiss King Richard's hand,
> And sends allegiance and true faith of heart
> To his most royal person; hither come
> Even at his feet to lay my arms and power,
> Provided that my banishment repeal'd
> And lands restor'd again be freely granted;
> If not, I'll use the advantage of my power
> And lay the summer's dust with showers of blood

Rain'd from the wounds of slaughtered Englishmen—
The which, how far off from the mind of Bolingbroke
It is such crimson tempest should bedrench
The fresh green lap of fair King Richard's land,
My stooping duty tenderly shall show. [III.iii.31–48.]

This is an utterly impossible speech: the proviso in the middle and the threat of war at the end are completely inconsistent both with the obeisance performed in the opening gesture and with any credible idea of "allegiance and true faith." In this speech Henry makes a move and at the same time undoes it wholly.[14] If Richard is king, Henry owes him fealty without condition and cannot threaten him without committing treason. To say, as he does at the end, that the function of his obeisance is to show how peaceful-minded he is, is to redefine obeisance itself as a stage in a negotiation. Richard could not accept this offer, on these terms, and remain, in any sense that he could recognize, the king of England.

Richard realizes this, knowing that the only terms on which the crown can exist are those of automatic and unquestioned awe and reverence. In one final display of his poetic power on behalf of the meaning of the crown, he says this to Northumberland:

We are amaz'd, and thus long have we stood
To watch the fearful bending of thy knee,
Because we thought ourself thy lawful king;
And if we be, how dare thy joints forget
To pay their awful duty to our presence?
If we be not, show us the hand of God
That hath dismiss'd us from our stewardship;
For well we know no hand of blood and bone
Can gripe the sacred handle of our sceptre,
Unless he do profane, steal, or usurp.

. . . . . . . . . . . . . . . . . . . . . . .

Tell Bolingbroke, for yon methinks he stands,
That every stride he makes upon my land
Is dangerous treason. He is come to open
The purple testament of bleeding war.

---

14. Notice that Henry's best claim, that he comes only for his inheritance, implies a limit on his action which he does not observe, for he takes the crown that by inheritance belongs to another. He not only violates the language of kingship, then, but the language upon which his own claim depends, that of rightful inheritance.

But ere the crown he looks for live in peace,
Ten thousand bloody crowns of mothers' sons
Shall ill become the flower of England's face,
Change the complexion of her maid-pale peace
To scarlet indignation and bedew
Her pastures' grass with faithful English blood. [III.iii.72–100.]

This is one last claim of regal authority and power, a last attempt to speak as king. Northumberland responds, in a highly sanitized version of Henry's speech to him, that Bolingbroke comes only:

for his lineal royalties, and to beg
Infranchisement immediate on his knees,
Which on thy royal party granted once,
His glittering arms he will commend to rust,
His barbed steeds to stables, and his heart
To faithful service of your Majesty. [III.iii.113–18.]

What comes now is a stunning reversal. Richard simply grants all of Bolingbroke's demands, without reservation:

Northumberland, say thus the king returns:
His noble cousin is right welcome hither,
And all the number of his fair demands
Shall be accomplish'd without contradiction. [III.iii.121–24.]

The question the play here presents, and requires us as readers—or actors or directors—to address, is why Richard does this, and what meaning he gives it. I think that we should take it that Richard sees what Bolingbroke does not, that once the crown has become the subject of effective threat and negotiation it is no longer the crown at all. From the moment his imperious display is disregarded by Bolingbroke, kingship, as he has known it, becomes impossible and therefore valueless. There is nothing except unconditional submission that Bolingbroke can give him.[15] If Bolingbroke is not going to give him that, Richard will not keep the crown—not be part of that kind of degradation of himself and it—but will resign it.

---

15. Some sense of this is expressed in his peroration to Aumerle:
    What must the king do now? Must he submit?
    The king shall do it. Must he be depos'd?
    The king shall be contented. Must he lose
    The name of king? a God's name, let it go. [III.iii.143–46.]

Indeed, to return to the question of Henry's motive, I think that the impetus for him to take the crown really comes not from him but from Richard, who suddenly yields everything in a way that Henry, the master of domination, simply cannot resist. It is a kind of judo trick, by which Richard tosses Henry suddenly into the position of a usurper, into possessing a crown the meaning and value of which he has himself destroyed. This is to think of Henry as a man without imagination, a kind of bull who sees what he wants at the moment and gets it, a force of nature. He lacks the capacity to see what else he might want, to understand the meaning of what he does, or to recognize that this meaning is made, by himself and others, in the language in which it is talked about, described, and judged. As he rather proudly stated in his speech about the "frosty Caucasus," he sees what he sees and that is all. And what he sees, here, is that the force of arms can prevail over mere words, and symbols too, like the crown; what he doesn't see is that arms need words to give them place and meaning. The symbol he seizes has no meaning apart from the ways of talking that define and support it.

## THE GARDENER'S SPEECH

The fall of Richard is the context in which we are given the famous speech of the gardener that compares the commonwealth to a garden and the duties of the king to those of a gardener. This speech is often referred to as an expression of the Great Chain of Being, the sense that the universe mirrors at one level of social or natural reality the structure of another and that all levels are connected.[16] This view is often associated with the divine right of kings, for every order—whether the family, the garden, the church, the universe, or the nation—must have its head. But the actual thrust of the speech is quite different:

> Go, bind thou up young dangling apricocks,
> Which like unruly children make their sire
> Stoop with oppression of their prodigal weight,
> Give some supportance to the bending twigs.
> Go thou, and like an executioner
> Cut off the heads of too fast growing sprays,

16. The classic statement of this idea is Arthur O. Lovejoy, *The Great Chain of Being: A Study of the History of an Idea* (Cambridge, Mass.: Harvard University Press, 1936).

That look too lofty in our commonwealth:
All must be even in our government.
You thus employed, I will go root away
The noisome weeds which without profit suck
The soil's fertility from wholesome flowers.

. . . . . . . . . . . . . . . . . . . . . . . . . . . . . .

O, what pity is it
That he hath not so trimm'd and dress'd his land
As we this garden! We at time of year
Do wound the bark, the skin of our fruit-trees,
Lest, being over-proud in sap and blood,
With too much riches it confound itself;
Had he done so to great and growing men,
They might have liv'd to bear, and he to taste
Their fruits of duty. Superfluous branches
We lop away, that bearing boughs may live;
Had he done so, himself had borne the crown,
Which waste of idle hours hath quite thrown down. [III.iv.29–66.]

What this imagery really says is that however a person becomes king he must exercise his powers competently or lose them; and this not through any rule of morals or politics or right, not as a result of theory but through the operation of ineluctable forces in the world. The gardener and the king each begin by holding a position, itself unexplained and unjustified; but each also has a set of duties and functions to perform, and if they perform them ill the nature of the world is such that they will lose their power. This in effect means that each person ultimately holds his position not by birth or right but by virtue of his competence; incompetence loses the crown and garden alike. Richard was an ineffective king and, therefore, by a process as natural and inevitable as the growth of weeds in an unkept garden is replaced by another. In modern terms, we would call this an empirical not a normative statement, but it carries a normative consequence: we should not be surprised when for such reasons kings fall from power, nor indeed lament them much, for this is the way of the world. This is a way of talking very different from the royal ceremony, the feudal challenge, the patriotic appeal, or the claim of right by inheritance, whether to land or crown. It emerges from the conflicts among those discourses, and is itself removed, scientific, cold.

OUR OWN EXPERIENCE AS AUDIENCE in fact confirms the claim of this speech, for we have presumably watched the events of the play unfold, as readers of narrative in our culture regularly do, by testing the degree to which the story moves by, and thus confirms, a shared sense of what is natural and probable. To the extent that we have acquiesced in the narrative as a likely one we have acquiesced as well in the understandings, here expressed by the gardener, by which it works. In seeing how natural it is that Richard should suffer deposition we have affirmed it not only as natural but in a sense as right.

When I speak of testing the narrative by our sense of the natural and probable I mean nothing out of our immediate experience, for this is something we do whenever we read or hear a story. What might be called the material premises of a particular narrative—that stuffed bears can talk, that the king has divided his kingdom in three parts, that beings on the planet Zolcon have no gender—need not meet this test; within a very wide range our conventions permit the author to choose them as she will. But once given them, the narrative works, if it does, only by the invocation of the audience's sense of how the people are likely to act and speak on the conditions they have been given. If we find the movement improbable, we will lose interest in it; if we find it probable, we find ourselves committed, without knowing it, to the sense of human nature and of the world by which it works. This is why narrative is so effective a means of argument, and why it can usually be met only by a competing narrative, activating a different sense of things. The function of the gardener's speech is to make explicit the understandings by which the movement of the first part of the play, the collapse of Richard's reign, can be at once explained and justified as natural.

## THE MODERN WORLD

In the rest of the play we, and Henry, begin to see what it means that he has seized the crown yet become no king. He faces rebellions of his own, some of which he puts down with a mixture of ferocity and generosity, others of which will continue to plague him. In the last act, successive messengers come on stage to tell of the defeat of rebels, whose heads have been sent to London set on pikes. This is the bloody beginning of the wars that Carlisle and Richard both predicted and that the audience knows are certain to come, the Wars of the Roses.

Even more telling than this is what happens to the language of "rebellion," "traitor," "treason," the language with which the play began. Henry cannot use this language in a satisfactory way, because it accuses him— he is, as Carlisle says, himself a traitor—yet he cannot do without it either, for it is essential to the coherence of his rule that he have some such way of talking. Upon what ground can he call upon the loyalty of anyone?

York demonstrates the impossibility of his own situation and of everyone's, for he is one to whom loyalty is the first principle. When Henry arrives in England to reclaim his lands, York at first rejects him: "Tut, tut! grace me no grace, nor uncle me no uncle, / I am no traitor's uncle. . . ." (II.iii.86–87.) But after Henry's seizure of the crown he undergoes a complete reversal and affixes his loyalty to Henry. When he then discovers that his own son Aumerle is engaged in a plot against Henry, he exposes him—"Treason, foul treason! Traitor! Slave!"—and begs Henry to kill him. York is a man who cannot live without the language of loyalty and treason, yet this language, under these circumstances, leads him to impossible positions. Did he not raise his son to be loyal to the king? Only Carlisle, who insists that Richard still is king, can speak this language coherently, and he is instantly arrested (for "capital treason") and very nearly killed.[17]

Earlier, in the scene in which the crown is physically transferred, Richard makes wholly clear the impossible situation of everyone in the play: "God save the King!" he cries out to the assembled nobles, all of whom are, of necessity, silent, but with a shouting significance. For who is the king? Richard forces it upon them: "Will no man say amen?" (IV.i.172.)

He goes on, in this scene, to force Bolingbroke to "seize" the crown (a pun on the legal term "seisin") and to perform his own dissolution of identity: "God pardon all oaths that are broke to me, God keep all vows unbroke are made to thee!" (IV.i.214–15.) This dissolution is personal as well as official, as he makes clear in the famous looking-glass scene: Richard is showing us that he actually *was* the king, in his essence and not by accident alone, and that when kingship is stripped away nothing is left, or nothing but the power of poetry to lament, to redefine the prison as the world populated with his imagining. This is a reduction of the self to an irreducible core that can maintain a kind of integrity in the face of its own dissolution, the same movement that we see in *Lear* or the *Oedipus*

---

17. Compare Richard's speech to Northumberland, in which he says that Henry will not be able to trust him. (V.i.55–68.) This claims, in a way that would please Plato, that the unjust man can have no friends.

plays or *Prometheus Bound,* and it entitles the play to the name of tragedy.[18]

HENRY IS A MAN OF POWERFUL WILL, clear decision, some generosity, and a capacity to arouse feelings of friendship and loyalty, and in all of this is more "competent" than Richard. But he is not—and in some sense cannot be—king and cannot call upon the resources and language of that office. When at the chaotic ending of the play Henry learns that Richard has been murdered—as he had to be, as Henry perhaps implicitly commanded—he has no way of talking about his situation at all, except to undertake a crusade to the Holy Land by way of expiation. But England is full of "rebels," and, as we shall see in the next play in the series (*Henry IV, Part One*), they are well able to tell the events of this play over to themselves and others in such a way as to make plain that Henry is not and cannot be king as Richard was.[19] That resource is gone forever.

Shakespeare marks this for us by the way in which Henry, immedi-

18. See Kantorowicz, *The King's Two Bodies,* chapter 2; Michelle Gellrich, *Tragedy and Theory: The Problem of Conflict since Aristotle* (Princeton: Princeton University Press, 1988).

19. See, for example, *Henry IV, Part One,* I.iii. Hotspur has won some prisoners in fighting the rebels but refuses to turn them over to Henry, unless the king agrees to ransom Mortimer, Hotspur's brother-in-law (and arguably the rightful heir to Richard's throne). Henry, knowing as Richard did that the crown is not the crown if successfully challenged, responds with peremptory demands. Worcester, Hotspur's brother, claims that the king should treat his family generously since he owes his power in part to them, and Henry orders him from his presence. Hotspur admits that he did, as he has been accused, abuse the king's messenger (a dandified royal favorite whose manners he could not bear); yet he still insists on the ransom of Mortimer.

When Hotspur, Worcester, and Northumberland—the last of whom played such a brutal role in the deposition of Richard—are alone, they remind themselves of Richard's declaration of Mortimer's legitimacy and the memory of Richard himself, "that sweet lovely rose." As Worcester sees it, they really have to rebel: the king will "always think him in our debt, / And think we think ourselves unsatisfied, / Till he hath found a time to pay us home." The very fact of his indebtedness to them, that is, will be intolerable to him; having been his friends at the time of making him king, they are of necessity his enemies now.

Later, in III.ii, Henry, speaking to Hal, says that he himself would never have got the crown had he behaved like his son, here talking as if the crown were a prize to be won by valor. He compares Hal unfavorably with Hotspur, going so far as to say that the latter has a better claim, through his conduct, to the crown than Hal has by inheritance. "Even as I

ately upon becoming king, revives the inquiry into the death of Gloucester. In one sense this is essential for him: if he can establish that this killing
was done by Mowbray, at Richard's instigation, this will tend to justify
his rebellion and usurpation. To leave the matter unresolved, on the other
hand, would leave a cloud over what he has done, for the people of England would ask the question Shakespeare has invited his audience to ask,
whether Henry's initial challenge was not motivated by a desire to unseat
Richard. But Henry's attempts to deal with it are disastrous: to begin
with, he relies upon information provided by Bagot, one of Richard's favorites who, according to Henry, misled the former king; Bagot accuses
Aumerle, the son of the duke of York, and a confidant of Richard, but we
have no reason to think correctly so; Aumerle denies it and is challenged
by three other lords in succession, and defended by a fourth; all this
presents Henry with the possibility of an even more divisive and threatening trial than the first one was, and offers, like that one, no possibility of clarifying the underlying facts and no prospect of settlement
either. Here we have the invocation of a ceremonial mode of discourse
and dispute, but without the conditions, delicate and unstable, that once
supported it.

At the end of the play we are left in the modern world, in which it is
most unclear what can count as a ground upon which one person can
have power over another, and why. In this sense *Richard II* can be read as
having invented—or brought to the surface where it can be seen—the
problem of authority to which our constitutional discourse has ever after
been directed.

---

was then, is Percy now." All of this is a view of the crown which makes it impossible for
him to invoke the languages of loyalty, trust, and right. He cannot tell his own story in a
satisfactory way.

At the beginning of Act III of *King Henry IV, Part Two,* Henry shows that he knows all
this, in the famous speech that concludes, "Uneasy lies the head that wears the crown." He
recalls Richard's prediction that Northumberland, having been traitor once, will be such
again. The best claim he can make for himself is that "then, God knows, I had no such
intent, / But that necessity so bow'd the state / That I and greatness were compelled to kiss."
And in speaking to Hal just before his death, in Act IV.v.181, he says: "God knows, my
son, / By what by-paths and indirect crook'd ways I met this crown; and I myself know
well / How troublesome it sat upon my head: / To thee it shall descend with better quiet, /
Better opinion, better confirmation."

His life has been ruined by his usurpation. The most he can hope for at the end is that
with his death the crown can return to its basis in inheritance, the very principle he violated.

## The Authority of the Play

In such a universe, in which the language of kingship falls apart, leaving nothing to take its place—not even raw power, for, as the play makes plain, all power ultimately depends upon a language in which claims to its justice and coherence can be made—how are we to think and talk about our shared experience, especially our political experience? According to this play, what forms of talk and life about the public world are entitled to our respect and use, and in this sense to authority? Certainly the play does not regard the crown and kingship (as Richard does) as the unquestionable and supreme authority, for it is all about how that way of talking is eroded and destroyed. Nor does it ask us to think that majesty is meaningless because fictional or that the desire for a just and proper authority, or for coherence in the public world, is pointless or stupid. We are left at a loss, except for this: that the play itself offers us a set of experiences which we can, for the moment at least, take as the ground from which to see the world. Like the conversation of Socrates, which claims for itself an authority higher than that of the laws it seems to celebrate, the play is itself a way of thinking and talking for which it claims a value and authority, for the moment at least, higher than that of kingship. We should ask, then, of this play, as we did of the *Crito,* what kind of thinking, what way of talking, it exemplifies and constitutes as authoritative.

Let us think of it this way. In the first half of the play the audience is led to see how impossible a king Richard is, and thus to understand and sympathize with the forces that lead to his overthrow. Richard is capricious, unjust, and perhaps murderous; of necessity we ally ourselves with his defeat as we watch it happen, if only to the extent of seeing it as natural and probable. The second half of the play shows us something of what this revolution means, and creates in us new understandings both of the premises upon which Richard's rule rested and of the possibilities for social meaning it established, which are now gone forever. For after the deposition there is no king, but only a man in power. There is no language in which he (or we) can satisfactorily describe his situation, or explain or justify his power. And without such a language there can be no adequate institutions either, for institutions are themselves nothing but practices of language set up on a permanent basis. Rather like Satan in *Paradise Lost,* then, Henry is unable to find or make any way of talking to create a new world that does not affirm the old, that does not condemn his rebellion and deny him the right to speak and act at all. He lives on modern terms, familiar to us, but without the benefit of the languages we have since put together to define and shape and limit power, without, that is, the resources of constitutional discourse. There is a sense in which the play does not end, as we think of plays as ending, with a closure, but, like *Troilus and Cressida* say, simply stops in the midst of incoherence.

It is true that we, as the audience, are complicitous in the deposition, as I suggest above, and that our complicity is corrected; but not to a firm and stable position that could be cast in one set of propositions or another—certainly not to an affirmation of the divine right of kings—but to an understanding of the way language, this language anyway, falls apart under the pressure of events, leaving nothing to take its place. And the force of the play reaches beyond this particular language: if this can happen to the language of kingship, of all languages, it can happen to any language whatever.

IN THIS WAY *Richard II* brings to the surface of our attention the problem of political (and especially royal) authority, and works out a way of addressing it by including the possibilities for speech on either side and by showing what is likely to happen when these possibilities are poised against each other. This is art, of course, and of a high kind, but it is also a kind of thought, a mode of analysis and contemplation, different from our own but from which we might well learn when we come to speak on such matters. For in the world defined by this play—and it is our world too, though the conventions of our talk deny it—maturity of thought and writing lie not in the attempt to reach statements of firm conclusion; not in conclusiveness at all, not in propositions asserted through the elaboration of system, but in tentativeness and inclusion, in the capacity to hold in the mind at once, or in rapid sequence, a variety of incompatible ways of talking, none of which can be a master language. To think that we could articulate general premises of political authority, establish their truth, and from them by inexorable logic infer a set of subsidiary propositions, of which we could say, this is the truth, would in this world be a form of insanity. The most we can hope to do is what Shakespeare does, to develop one way of talking as far as we can, then poise it against another; that is where the truth lies, in the relation between languages (and the practices of life they entail), not in anything that can be said in any single language. The virtue to which we should aspire, then, is not conclusiveness, but inclusiveness within an order.

This means (if the play so persuades us) that every claim of authority we can make, on any subject and in any language, should be regarded as marked by a kind of structural tentativeness, for every claim implies its counter within its language, and every language implies a host of others answering it. To see things this way is to make active a sense of limit, not only of language but of mind. Here is where we are, in this brightly lit and circumscribed place, the theater; we are offered a set of possibilities for speech, utterances that it is imaginable that people situated thus and so might say, cast in contrasting languages. They fit together, not in a logical but in a poetic or rhetorical order, to tell a story. One voice answers another; none offers a firm ground upon which any can be excluded. Beyond this circle of speech and light is the dark and chaotic night.

THERE IS NO POINT IN ASKING whose side Shakespeare is on, as I said earlier, for here, as always, Shakespeare is on both, or all, sides. As his plays and sonnets both show, he seems incapable of articulating a position, or expressing a feeling, without instantly, or at the same time, expressing its counter or contrary. His is a mind that comprises human reality by imagining the widest range of possibilities for human speech and thought, and doing so with sympathetic recognition: think for example of Caliban's speeches on Prospero's island, or of Claudius's great speech of remorse in *Hamlet,* both of which upset our expectations as to what can be included within the human and appealing. Or think of a famous sonnet, such as "Shall I compare thee to a summer's day?" which starts out praising the beloved by comparison to summer; but then it makes summer itself less than wholly desirable; and it concludes by praising the poem itself, which will supposedly make the beloved immortal—but not in a very meaningful way, since the sonnet has in fact told us nothing of this person at all. Or think of "That time of year thou mayst in me behold," which laments aging but at the same time makes it beautiful; or of "When to the sessions of sweet silent thought," which seems to deplore the painful memories of the past, which the present love promises to erase, but in fact also values them.

To use the sonnet for a moment as an example of a general tendency I mean to describe, one might say that this form, for Shakespeare, is like a little drama, in which he starts with a moment, a phrase, a situation, and then explores by contrast and transformation the possibilities for human speech that it occasions. The sonnet in a sense rewrites itself and in doing so transforms itself; the same is true of the plays, which are also a series of transformations through rewriting, the object of which is to carry us through a range of possibilities for human sentiment and expression. This is not the kind of thinking that proceeds by logical steps from premise to conclusion but, as I suggest above, by resistance, by inclusion or comprehension of the possibilities for speech and thought. Similarly, it is governed not by the principle of noncontradiction, the ruling doctrine of modern exposition, but an opposite one, the principle of controlled and progressive countersaying. The meaning lies in the music the voices make, the spaces and tensions and silences among them, as much as in any of its formulations in words.

Compare *Coriolanus,* where we are told that the greatest warrior of Rome cannot bear to be subject to the newly established tribunes, the voices of the people, and is banished for his insolence. He joins the enemy and brings Rome to its knees; yet he cannot continue in this course against the pleas of his mother, who in arguing with him invokes not pity for her, or his wife, child, or his friends, but his honor, saying that if he destroys Rome his good name will be destroyed in the only community he cares about. Coriolanus tries to make a life of pure honor for himself in a "world elsewhere," but he cannot: the honor he seeks is not an abstraction, nor a kind of self-knowledge, but a mark of respect that can only be conferred by the community of which he is a part. He, like Henry, is dependent upon a language which he cannot destroy or disregard with impunity. From a larger point of view, the play shows us that neither he, nor the tribunes, can survive without the other: that in the field of constitutional politics, as in the theater itself, the great virtue is the integration of contrasting and opposing voices.

Shakespeare's work throughout has affinities with Chaucer's *Canterbury Tales,* which could be described in similar terms, and indeed with the structure of the great gothic cathedrals, similarly inclusive in their aim, comprehending at once the sublime and the grotesque, the immense and the minuscule.[20] This way of writing, by poetic comprehension, unites

20. This is part of what leads Russell Fraser to say that Shakespeare is the last and greatest of the medieval artists. Russell Fraser, *The Dark Ages and the Age of Gold* (Princeton: Princeton University Press, 1973), pages 43–45, 223–24, 264–65.

the concerns of beauty and truth alike, because beauty can be thought of, as Coleridge suggested, as the comprehension of contradictions within an order and because on these understandings the truth of any utterance lies not in itself but in its relation to another; and the concerns of justice too, for justice can be seen to be a way of giving each voice, each possibility for speech, its widest and fullest range.

This kind of work has obvious similarities to law, for, like law, it is a way of seeing what can be said on both sides; but not only both sides of an existing question, the very statement of which defines the language that can be used to respond to it, but "both sides" in a deeper way: seeing how competing languages can be framed and put to work, entailing as they do competing ways of imagining and acting in the world. Here these possibilities are arranged not at haphazard but in such a way as to lead us to accept first one, then the other, and in the process to undo ourselves.

The effect of the whole is rather like a Socratic *elenchus* at work on the main terms of the discourse—treason, loyalty, crown, etc.—which are so deeply undermined that they can never be used again by the attentive reader, or at least not with the old naive confidence they once enjoyed. The effect of the play is to leave us in a position of greater uncertainty than ever about our languages, with an increasing sense that we can have nothing to say upon which we can lean without question. Its movement is one of intellectual and moral affliction, as we are brought to the limits of our imaginations and understandings; like the characters in the play we come at the end to a kind of silence, but a silence that is itself a way of facing our situation in the world.

This suggests that the ethics and politics of the play is Socratic too, for it locates us in a position of increased responsibility and decreased certainty, expanding our knowledge of the way in which valid forms of thought and speech erode each other. The position Shakespeare brings us to share is in a deep way paradoxical, for in one sense it is all icy objectivity and detachment—this is the way the world is, the play is saying, this is how people talk, one poised against the other; I am the analyst or surgeon who can see one, then another, each in its fullness; sympathy would blur the picture—yet, in another, it is the grandest affirmation of our common humanity, of the multiplicity of languages that define us; it is work belonging in the same class, and for the same reason, as the great poems of Homer.

I HAVE SPOKEN BOTH OF *Richard II* and the *Crito* as claiming authority for the forms of thought and speech they exemplify. In what sense do I use the word "authority" here? Obviously neither the play nor the *Crito*, nor Socrates in the *Crito*, conceives of itself as issuing a command that one is obliged to obey. But this is not the only kind of authority. The play's claim is that it presents a way of thinking and imagining that is intellectually and ethically superior to the language of kingship, just as the *Crito* claims that its mode of discourse is superior to that of the Nomoi. This kind of authority works by persuasion, and as the Greek word *peitho* reminds us, persuasion and obedience are different aspects of the same practice.

Could one imagine a polity built upon this kind of discourse? It was Plato's life work to try to show how that could be done; Shakespeare, I think, simply does not care to address that question. It may, after all, be the case that the possibilities for life and language in the realm of public power simply do not rise to those of the theater, as he defines them. In such a case one does better to affiliate oneself with these, and live in that way closer to the truth, than to claim for public discourse what it cannot deliver. As Socrates claims predominance for the community of philosophers, so Shakespeare may make a similar claim for those who think and talk his way. But I think one can still read the play as leaving us with the question, analogous to that asked of the *Crito:* Is it imaginable that there should be a "crown," an institution of government that would meet the standards of thought and expression defined by this play? Is it imaginable that law itself should do so?

· · ·

*Having read this book in manuscript a friend said to me in effect: "From Plato to Shakespeare and on to Austen and Dickinson! With the partial exception of Mandela, your book treats works that are all drawn exclusively from the humanistic tradition of Western high culture. Whether you mean to or not, you are necessarily claiming that Western culture has a unique value, and that you and your readers all belong to it and affirm its premises. To make matters worse, you use 'we' all the time, claiming a false cultural commonality with your reader. You speak throughout in a version of the Western liberal voice, as if it could not be questioned. This you simply cannot do."*

*Of course in making this book in this way I define myself as belong-*

*ing to a certain culture. I make no claim for the priority of this culture, however, or for these texts, but I do for their value, including in the increasingly pluralistic world we inhabit. This book is in fact an argument for their value.*

*More controversially, I believe that part of this value lies in the fact that this tradition is in some sense "ours." American culture is made from many sources, but predominantly those of Western Europe. This is where the languages most of us speak come from, and most of our political ideas and institutions too. Different people, and different groups, will naturally locate themselves differently with respect to it, but it remains an important—and to me valuable—fact that the high culture of the West is part of our shared life.*

*Yet this talk about "culture" or "tradition" at such a degree of generality is not quite right. I am not simply the product of a finite number of texts all promoting the same social or cultural values, nor are you. Each of us is an individual as well as a member of a group or profession, and I write in part to affirm the element of individuality in intellectual and imaginative life. The various traditions we emerge from are redefined, in a sense recreated, in each generation, by each person. It is one of my objects in this book—both in the readings I propose and in the connections I hope to establish among them—to make a partial reconstitution of the tradition in which I grew up. Not everyone raised as I was would read these texts as I do, after all, or even see them as having special interest and importance.*

*As for my "we": I mean it not to express an assumption that you already think as I do, nor as an authoritarian claim of what must be so—"I think this way, therefore you must too"—but as a gesture in the optative, an expression of hope: "I think this way, and hope you will try it out, at least for the moment." It is meant as an invitation to join an activity, which it is the reader's task to accept or decline.*

# Three

# Hooker's Preface to the *Lawes of Ecclesiasticall Politie*: Constituting Authority in Argument

At nearly the same time that Shakespeare was confronting the
problem of authority in his play *Richard II*, Richard Hooker was
trying to find a way to live in another part of the culture, the
church, in which an old authority had recently been lost. For when he
was writing, in the late 1580s, only a half-century had passed since Henry
VIII first separated the Church of England from Rome, setting it up on
its own basis. This separation had itself been rather quickly reversed, during the reign of Mary, and it was not until 1559, under Elizabeth, that
the Church of England was finally established as the only lawful church.
It was still most uncertain what kind of authority it could have: it no
longer had the authority of Rome and the pope, rooted in hundreds of
years of institutional tradition, yet it did not have the authority claimed
by the Reformed churches either, namely, a form of governance in confor-
mity to scripture. For the episcopacy was said, by some at least, to be
inconsistent with the form of the church in apostolic times, as this was
described in the New Testament. The task Hooker set himself, and it was
not an enviable one, was to defend the constitution of this church, and its
authority, against its critics on both sides, but especially those for whom
its reformation was incomplete.

The text in which he did so, *Of the Lawes of Ecclesiasticall Politie*,
was enormously influential not only in its own time but during the great
constitutional debates of the seventeenth century, for its argument was
seen to reach the governance not only of the church but of the state.
People of very different persuasions called upon it as authority, from
Archbishop Laud and Charles I to John Locke, who made repeated refer-

82

ence to it.[1] There being no one in England of comparable range and quality before Hooker, he can I think fairly be called the father of British constitutional thought.

While the question of proper authority in the government of a church may seem strange or even trivial to some modern readers, to Hooker's contemporaries it was neither of these things but of the first importance.

1. The *Preface* and first four books of the *Lawes* were published in 1593. "The much longer fifth book was not printed until 1597, the sixth and eighth books posthumously in 1648, and the seventh in 1662." Richard Hooker, *Of the Laws of Ecclesiastical Polity: Preface: Books I to IV*, edited by Georges Edelen (Cambridge, Mass.: Harvard University Press, 1977), page xxix. This is volume 1 of the Folger Library Edition of *The Works of Richard Hooker*, edited by W. Speed Hill, used here for all quotations. Since the notes to this edition are not complete, one should consult as well the hitherto standard edition, *The Works of Mr. Richard Hooker*, edited by John Keble and published by Oxford in various editions from 1836.

Hooker's eighth book, on the authority of the crown, was absolutist in tone, hence invoked by the supporters of the monarchy in the late seventeenth century. But he also uses language supporting a social contract theory of government, especially in Book I, chapter 10, which Locke invoked extensively, using the conservatives' main authority against them. Locke's use of Hooker, however, gives a somewhat misleading impression, for in everything else they differed. Hooker, one of the last medieval minds, has a view of the world entirely different from Locke's; he builds on hierarchy and natural law, and ultimately argues to a different end, not the right of revolution but the duty of submission. Equally important, they belong to different traditions in intellectual style: Locke rationalist, dogmatic, and helping to create what we now think of as political philosophy; Hooker literary and rhetorical, part of a far less fully studied tradition including Swift, Blackstone, Burke, and American constitutional thought from Chief Justice Marshall through Justice Harlan.

The most useful single recent volume on Hooker is *Studies in Richard Hooker: Essays Preliminary to an Edition of His Works*, edited by W. Speed Hill (Cleveland: Case Western Reserve University Press, 1972). The Keble edition referred to above is indispensable. Also valuable for background are Patrick Collinson, *The Elizabethan Puritan Movement* (Berkeley: University of California Press, 1967); John S. Coolidge, *The Pauline Renaissance in England: Puritanism and the Bible* (Oxford: Clarendon Press, 1970); Horton Davies, *Worship and Theology in England: From Cranmer to Hooker, 1534–1603* (Princeton: Princeton University Press, 1970); William Haller, *The Rise of Puritanism* (New York: Columbia University Press, 1938); Peter Lake, *Anglicans and Puritans? Presbyterianism and English Conformist Thought from Whitgift to Hooker* (London: Unwin Hyman, 1988); Peter Lake, *Moderate Puritans and the Elizabethan Church* (Cambridge: Cambridge University Press, 1982); Peter Munz, *The Place of Hooker in the History of Thought* (London: Routledge & Kegan Paul, 1952); Debora Kuller Shuger, *Habits of Thought in the English Renaissance: Religion, Politics, and the Dominant Culture* (Berkeley: University of California Press, 1990); and Quentin Skinner, *The Foundations of Modern Political Thought*, volume 2 (Cambridge: Cambridge University Press, 1978). See also Sheldon Wolin, "Richard Hooker and English Conservatism," *Western Political Quarterly* 6 (1953): 28–47.

On the development of Hooker's reputation, see Conal Condren, "The Creation of Hooker's Public Authority: Rhetoric, Reputation, and Reassessment" (copy on file with the author).

At a certain level of generality, indeed, the central question he addresses is of obvious significance in any era: in the absence, or at the demise, of a plainly established institution of unquestionable, or unquestioned, authority—the pope, the crown—who shall have the power to rule, and why, and how far? The question of legitimacy in church government, that is, is simply one version of the question of legitimacy in government more generally, which is perhaps the most unsettling and universal of all social and political questions. It is not too much to say that this issue has dominated our thought about public life ever since.

For us in America the answer, worked out over the past two centuries and more, has been to create another such authority, namely, "the People," to whom we attribute the adoption of our Constitution and even the framing of the constitutional text itself. We take care that this sovereign should never be confused with the sum of the actual human beings alive in our country at any one time—for we do not conceive of this authority simply as a form of majority rule—but think of "the People" in a different way, as a kind of fictive entity constituted over time, in the life of the nation as a whole and in our institutions.[2] This is a complex and artificial construction of authority indeed, one that owes its debts both

2. I have elsewhere tried to show how Chief Justice Marshall helped create the idea that "the People" were united at the moment of making the Constitution as they never have been since. Once that document was established, creating the institutions and defining the rules by which political life should be led, the people collapsed into their natural state, as individuals and groups with antagonistic interests. In this way Marshall gives the Constitution the character of a sacred text, written by an Author no longer present among us and requiring a trained interpreter, a role to be filled by the Supreme Court. James Boyd White, *When Words Lose Their Meaning* (Chicago: University of Chicago Press, 1984), pages 255–56, 262–63. This sounds antidemocratic, and in some sense it is; but so is the idea of a Constitution itself, insofar as it limits or retards the wishes of momentary majorities.

For an argument that there are two other "framing moments" in our history, responsible respectively for the Civil War Amendments and the New Deal, see Bruce A. Ackerman, *We the People* (Cambridge, Mass.: Harvard University Press, 1991).

It is perhaps worth saying in this connection that our conception of our own sovereign, the People, is a highly artificial construct, insofar as we do not mean by it what a majority desire on any given day, but rather imagine the People as constituted in our institutions and defined by our collective history. Sometimes indeed we incline towards a view of the People as consisting of our traditions and our culture, in this not very different perhaps from the medieval crown. But the idea that the framers of the Constitution, and the Constitution itself, are fictive is no argument against them. All thought about collective life requires simplification; all such thought is constitutive; and this "fiction," one of the roots of which we perhaps see in Socrates' way of imagining Athens, has been at times a source of enormous good.

to Protestant and Catholic conceptions of government,³ and it has served us rather well.

But for Hooker no such apparatus of thought and imagination existed. The question that he faced—and with him the church, and beyond the church the polity as a whole—was thus a stark one: Once the church has broken from Rome, by what authority should it—could it—be governed? To the Roman church the English church was illegitimate because it denied the authority of Rome; to the Protestant reformers it was illegitimate both because it did not follow Calvin and Knox in reorganizing itself along presbyterian lines and because its rituals, ornately Catholic in number and style, were not simplified to accord with apostolic practice. Upon what—other than a simple power grab by a determined king— could its authority then rest?

## THE POLITICS OF PROTESTANTISM

To begin to understand Hooker's response to that question, it is important to see that the loss of authority was an issue not only for the English church but for all the Reformed churches in Europe. This was in fact the natural result of the central change effected by the Reformation, namely, to locate authority in scripture—"sola scriptura" was one of Luther's watchwords—rather than in the mixture of tradition and scripture that the Roman church had worked out. For it was the reformers' view that God spoke to man primarily through the sacred texts, not through the history of human institutions (certainly not through the Roman church). The church derives its authority from scripture, said Calvin, and not scripture from the church. And the church they saw described in the scripture (by which is mainly meant the *Epistles* of Paul and *The Acts of the Apostles*) was not episcopal in form, nor given to elaborate ceremony and fine music and art like the Roman, but simple in organization and in style alike.⁴ For this reason the reformers thought that the contemporary

---

3. Protestant in its elevation of the founding text, read across time to apply to new circumstances, Catholic in its respect for the tradition so created. For brief discussion of this polarity in American constitutional law, see Levinson, "'The Constitution' in American Civil Religion," *Supreme Court Review* (1979): 123.

4. Others saw it differently. See Keble's introduction to his edition of the *Works*, page lxii (1888 ed.).

church should be restructured along the same lines: congregations should participate in the choice of their leaders, sacraments should be reduced to two (baptism and holy communion), the altar should be replaced with a table at which communicants sat, rather than kneeling in the Roman way, and vestments, statuary, and stained glass windows should be destroyed. The history of the Roman Church, so far from being an alternative source of authority, was seen as a story of progressive and complete corruption. The pope was Antichrist.

The reformers conceived of the relation between God and man in stark and simple terms, with apparently little role for mediating institutions. The central text was St. Paul's statement that justification comes by faith alone: in Luther's reading this means that salvation is not a matter of good conduct or merit nor in any way an achievement of the self; not a matter of good citizenship in the church or of compliance with its rules, customs, or practices; not the result of good works or even of repentance. It is the result of faith, and faith is conceived of not as a human attainment but as granted by grace, for God's own reasons, to some few people, or perhaps many, none of whom, by their radical sinfulness, can be said to deserve it. At its most extreme this is an image of man as an individual, without a corporate history, facing a God who can be known directly, either through the scriptures or through the operation of the Holy Spirit. Yet at such an extreme there would be no role for the church itself, and the Protestants did insist upon the centrality of the community of the godly in the Christian life. For them, indeed, the church became the central place in the culture, a manifestation of the spirit of God active in human community, a sense captured in the Puritan idea of the "edification," or educational building, of the spiritual temple that was the church.[5] This was not a mediating institution, as they saw the Roman church, but a direct expression of God's spirit, in which all the godly participated directly.

But still the text was primary; and once everything is said to rest upon a text, it will rather quickly be seen to have embarrassing silences, uncertainties, multiple and even inconsistent meanings. There are two central questions: How is its meaning to be determined? And, when there is a difference of interpretation, Whose reading is to prevail, and why?

5. On "edification" see Coolidge, *The Pauline Renaissance in England: Puritanism and the Bible*, especially chapter 2; Lake, *Anglicans and Puritans?* pages 29–31, 45–49, 122–26, 164–69; and, more generally, Shuger, *Habits of Thought in the English Renaissance*.

When the Protestant movement locates authority in the text alone, and salvation in faith alone, it at the same time suggests a rather problematic answer to these questions of authority in interpretation, for if God speaks to us all through the sacred text, it follows that the text should be available to all. Is everyone then to be an equal judge of its meaning? What is to be done when differences arise? Two natural tendencies of Protestantism were the spread of literacy and the translation of the Bible into the vernacular, for to keep the text in a foreign tongue, or the Christian unlettered, would be to stand between God and his people.[6] But one result, and in retrospect at least a rather obvious one, was to multiply both the forms of the text itself and the number of its interpreters, for if it is available to all, it is hard to deny the conclusion that all are entitled— or obliged—to judge its meaning for themselves, especially in a movement that spoke of "the priesthood of all believers." The control that the Roman church had attained by the use of a Latin text, fixed in form and available only to the educated priesthood, was gone; in its place was a doctrine, the priority of the text, which turned out to have democratizing and schismatic consequences very far indeed from the intentions of those originally promulgating it.

Such pressures towards radical individualism would be a problem, of course, for any organization, and the several Reformed churches found various ways of addressing it. Perhaps the most common was to say that the text can be rightly read only with the aid of the Holy Spirit; it is therefore the "spirit," in another more ordinary sense, in which the text is read that determines the rightness of a reading.[7] But this of course just changes the question: Who has the right spirit, and how do we know? To this question no fixed and reliable response was ever

6. Luther was quick to separate civil from church government, acquiescing in the authority of the state. This concession meant that debates about the right governance of the church were less threatening to civil regimes than might have been the case. From a psychological point of view it may indeed have been motivated by the desire to deny the revolutionary tendencies of his doctrines.

7. Thus the Protestant turn to the text becomes a turn away from it as well: not towards tradition but towards inner experience and knowledge. Rules and canons of interpretation can have little force on the person who believes that God is present in the text, speaking directly to his soul. The text is not to be reduced to legalisms or literalism but read as a response to the Person who is present in it. Reading the text thus merges with the kind of preaching that is meant to work directly on the soul of the listener. This Protestant tendency towards the spiritual reaches perhaps its greatest expression in the Quakers, who gave up texts and ceremonies entirely, living by the "inner light" alone.

found.[8] From the beginning Protestantism has accordingly been marked by a tendency towards the multiplication of sects. Once the believer reads and judges, who is there to tell him he is wrong? There is no Pope or council to interpret the text, and not much force to the argument that you ought not to secede, since the church itself was secessionist. Like Shakespeare's Henry IV, the Protestants discovered that they could not invoke in the same old way a language of authority they had disregarded. The hermeneutics of protestantism is the hermeneutics of proliferation.[9]

In our country we seem to tolerate quite happily the enormous variety of churches that arise from such premises, either through indifference to religion and its purported truths or because, although we value religion, we have insulated it from the realm of governmental power and discourse. On these questions, we say, the state cannot speak; only private associations and institutions, ultimately only the individual, can speak, because her adherence to one church or another is a matter of her individual choice. Religion is finally a personal not a social matter, a question of the relation between the individual and her God. In such a way we have as it were constitutionalized an extreme form of the protestant idea.

But for Hooker and most of his audience it would have been unthinkable to hive off religion to the private sector, or relegate it to the zone of individual consumer choice, removed from matters of state: it was itself an aspect of government and among its most important. The objects of the church and the objects of the state were inextricably intertwined, in a conception of the commonwealth that was at once material and spiritual. The church owned vast wealth; it was supported by taxes; it had judicial power; attendance at its services was mandatory; and the power of the state was often justified, as we have seen, in religious terms.[10] However we may happen to feel on such matters, neither in England nor on the continent was there a substantial body of opinion that this was anything but right. The true religion was the true religion and an essential part of

8. Max Weber's *The Protestant Ethic and the Spirit of Capitalism* (New York: Scribner, 1930) is in large part about the outer consequences of the inner turmoil that was produced by radical uncertainty on this and the parallel question, whether one was saved or not.

9. For an argument defending Protestantism against this charge, see John T. McNeill, *Unitive Protestantism: The Ecumenical Spirit and Its Persistent Expression* (Richmond, Va.: John Knox Press, 1963).

10. The Act of Uniformity (1559) required all ministers to use the same form of worship, and attendance at church services was compelled by An Act to Retain the Queen's Subjects in Obedience. See G. R. Elton, ed., *The Tudor Constitution: Documents and Commentary,* 2d ed. (Cambridge: Cambridge University Press, 1982), pages 410, 458.

the fabric of public as well as private life; to maintain it was a proper object of the state; difference of religion was accordingly a proper ground of war, among the most common both in this century and the next, and in England itself people had recently been burned to death for their Protestant or Catholic beliefs. To make the choice of religion, or no religion, optional, as we do, would have been nearly impossible to imagine.

There were of course extreme Protestants who favored separation from any official church, and toleration for themselves, but when they established their own regimes, as in Geneva or Massachusetts, they tended to enforce an establishment upon others as readily as others had done to them. And Hooker's own concern was not with such extremists, but with those who wanted to reform and maintain the Church of England. This was not a small or insignificant group but perhaps a majority of the priesthood. The Church of England was by now largely Calvinist in its theology and many of its leading clergy had spent the years of Mary's rule in exile on the continent, in Geneva or the Netherlands, and were acquainted with what reform could achieve. And, in a more general sense, almost everyone agreed that some reform was necessary: churches all over England had fallen into physical disrepair, and the clergy were to a distressing degree incompetent to do anything other than go through the motions of the sacraments and the reading of lessons; many of them were certainly not capable of instilling a sense of Christian urgency and meaning through their preaching.

The people Hooker addressed were at work within the church, then, not outside it; they were committed to its reform, not only in the sense just mentioned but by the abolition of the episcopacy and the establishment of a presbyterian form of government. To this group the separatists were a kind of embarrassment, arguably representing the extreme tendencies of their own views, and from them they felt they had to distance themselves.

During the years leading up to Hooker's work there were great controversies over reform, both in Parliament, where the Admonitions of 1572 called for immediate restructuring of the church, and in the pulpit, especially in London, where the case was argued on both sides with energy and intelligence. Perhaps the leading spokesman for the church was Archbishop Whitgift, for reform Thomas Cartwright; indeed, much of the body of Hooker's text is directed specifically at Cartwright himself as well as at Walter Travers, with whom Hooker had for some time engaged in theological controversy through an exchange of sermons.

By the time Hooker's book was actually published, in the 1590s, the Anglican establishment had for the moment prevailed; but after the accession of James I in 1603, and still more after Charles came to the throne in 1625, the issues were revived. After a period of regal and episcopal supremacy, reform swept the board, both before and during the Protectorate, until the compromises of the Restoration and the Revolution of 1688 were reached. The forces with which Hooker contended were thus not marginal, but central to the life of the church and nation, and they would soon prove dominant.

For our purposes the central point is this, that Protestantism almost accidentally brought to the surface of consciousness and made real the question that has occupied political philosophy and constitutional discourse ever since: What person, or institution, or set of practices, should have authority over others, and why? This issue had been debated in the Middle Ages, of course, but largely as a theoretical, not a practical, matter. That it first arose in connection with the government of the church does not much disguise the fact to us, nor did it to contemporaries, that it reached the state as well.

## THE AUTHORITY OF THE RHETORICAL COMMUNITY

In thinking about Hooker's text it will be useful to distinguish, as we did with the *Crito* and *Richard II* as well, between (1) those institutions or practices in the real world to which it argues that authority should or should not be given—in the *Crito* the "Nomoi," in *Richard II* the "crown," and, here, the "lawes of ecclesiasticall politie"—and (2) those modes of thought and expression by which the text works, and for which it claims an authority of another kind.

To begin with the first issue, Hooker believes with the reformers that the scripture is the central source of authority. It is both supreme and adequately plain in all matters essential to our salvation. Scripture tells us all that it is necessary for us to know and does so in terms that are accessible to any of us. On such matters, the individual's own reading, his own conscience, is the ultimate umpire and guide. No man should do that which he is persuaded in his heart is against the will of God. To yield one's conscience to the commands of an institution is to give up one's humanity and responsibility. In all of this he stands squarely in the tradition of reform.

But all this is true only as to "matters essential"; many questions relating to Christian life, including most of those bearing on the organization of the church and the details of the liturgy, are of another kind, important enough in their own right but on the great question of salvation indifferent. With respect to these, one should yield one's judgment to established authority, even when one disagrees. Hooker's ground for this position is in part pragmatic, for without such a principle we should have no common church at all but an unlimited fragmentation. And on such matters scripture itself often speaks ambiguously, or not at all, and can thus itself be read to define a field in which human learning and judgment have a place, and respect for learning too; a field in which not just the text, that is, but institutions too should have authority.

Following Aquinas, Hooker imagines not one thing called "law" but a hierarchy of laws: the laws of God regulating himself; the laws of God governing angels; the laws of nature governing natural processes; the laws of nature in another sense, namely, those moral laws, discoverable by reason, that regulate all human beings; and last—and lowest—laws merely human, such as the laws of the church and state. These last are authoritative, entitled to respect and obedience, only insofar as they are not inconsistent with those of a higher species of law. Unlike the Nomoi in the *Crito*, that is, Hooker says that one is not obliged to respect or obey all laws of church or state but only those that do not conflict with higher laws, either those laws of nature that are available to all rational beings or those rules of revelation that are made plain in the scripture.[11]

Such, roughly, is the pattern of authority Hooker sees in the world and recommends to his reader. But in this chapter I shall be less concerned with analyzing this pattern than with matters of the second kind identified above, namely, the modes of thought and forms of expression by which Hooker seeks to reach his reader, the kind of conversation and community he seeks to establish with one who disagrees. To this end I will draw attention especially to what Hooker says in the *Preface*, where he speaks directly to those with whom he is arguing about the nature of the dispute in which he is engaged and how he hopes it can proceed. For

---

11. The role of reason is crucial for Hooker: "[T]hat authority of men should prevaile with men either against or above reason, is no part of our beliefe." (II.7.6.)Compare:

> Howbeit when scripture doth yeelde us precedents, how far forth they are to bee followed; when it giveth naturall lawes, what particular order is thereunto most agreeable; when positive, which waye to make lawes unrepugnant unto them; yea though all these shoulde want, yet what kind of ordinances woulde be moste for that good of the Church which is aimed at, al this must be by reason founde out. [III.9.1.]

Human laws, being shaped by reason, can be changed by reason too. (III.10.2.) Scripture cannot authoritatively identify itself (I.14.1) or interpret itself, so its laws too require reason. Hooker's best definition of reason is of course his own intellectual performance.

Hooker of course knows that there are those who are unpersuaded by his views on the merits, especially those who think that scripture enjoins a presbyterian form of government and a puritan style of worship. His aim is not to dismiss these people, but to establish the grounds upon which his differences with them can be argued out. Like Henry at the end of *Richard II*, Hooker addresses a situation in which one authority has dissolved, leaving nothing that can automatically take its place. He faces, that is, the problem of justice and politics in the modern world.

Under the circumstances as he understands them, all we really have is our differences of view and the opportunity to discuss them; in some sense, then, what must be regarded as authoritative is the discussion itself. This means that Hooker is himself directly engaged in the rhetorical creation of authority, and he knows it. For him, as for Socrates in the *Crito,* the authority he recommends will be the authority of a certain kind of thought, speech, and argument, in which he himself engages. This, as we have also seen, is the authority of a community as well, the community he seeks to create in his text. He is trying to create a rhetorical community, a community of people thinking and talking certain ways, and to do this not only with people disposed to be like-minded but with those disposed to disagree with him on fundamental substantive matters.[12] This community, established first in his text and then, if his text succeeds, in the world, is the true source of authority he offers his reader.

But what kind of conversation is entitled to respect and authority across our lines of difference? What kind of community should we be, constituted by what understandings of argument and talk? These are Hooker's questions, as well as the "substantive" ones outlined above, and they are the questions of modern pluralism as well, at the center of much controversy in our own world. It is Hooker's response to them, both in what he says and in what he does by way of performance, that I wish to trace out here.

We can read the *Preface* as an invitation to talk on certain terms, then, and we can evaluate it that way too, asking how Hooker addresses his various audiences: the committed reformers; those in the church likely

---

12. A rhetorical community, not a dialectical one, for it involves more than two people, works by speeches rather than question and answer, and seeks inclusion of a variety of views. Perhaps equally important is the attitude towards language: dialectic, at least of the Socratic kind, seems to dissolve the language upon which the interlocutors rely, while rhetoric builds upon it. (For a fuller statement of this function of rhetoric with particular reference to law, see "Plato's 'Gorgias' and the Modern Lawyer," in my *Heracles' Bow* [Madison: University of Wisconsin Press, 1985], chapter 9.)

to be persuaded by them; those inclined to favor the established church but perhaps with little intellectual basis or political fervor; and those deeply committed to episcopal government too, for whom the text will redefine the object of their common commitment, creating, in its own modes of thought and writing, a version of the church for which it argues. Hooker's aim is to create a text that so far as possible can be read by people in all these groups with respect and attention, can in fact be passed from one to the other, and thus help to establish the terms on which these groups and their spokesmen might speak to each other.[13] How does he do these things?

## READING THE OPENING SENTENCE

Hooker's *Preface* begins with its title, which has its own significance:

*A PREFACE.*

To them that seeke (as they tearme
it) the reformation of Lawes, and
orders Ecclesiasticall, in the Church
of ENGLAND.[14]

Hooker is telling us here that he is speaking to those with whom he disagrees, that he understands the language in which they term themselves and their concerns, and that he regards that language as arguable. He will not accept without question their denomination of themselves as "reformers," but to say this necessarily opens him to having his own language challenged too. To realize that terms of description are terms of argument, and that they can be questioned, puts into the realm of the contestable the very language in which we talk, and of necessity does this on both sides.

13. Hooker has not written an abstract or merely philosophic text, that is, but means to engage his readers about an actual issue confronting them. He wants it to be read and acted on by those who are concerned with the issue of church government. In this it provides a precedent for Edmund Burke's *Reflections on the Revolution in France*, which is likewise a work of practical argument.

14. I use the Folger edition throughout, as I explain above. But I omit typographical indicators of original foliation, and for the sake of readability have transposed the *Preface* from italic to roman type. The references to chapter and paragraph, following Keble, have become standard.

He begins to speak to them as follows, in a complex and significant sentence to which I shall pay close attention:

Though for no other cause, yet for this; that posteritie may know we have not loosely through silence permitted things to passe away as in a dreame, there shall be for mens information extant thus much concerning the present state of the Church of God established amongst us, and their carefull endevour which woulde have upheld the same. [1.1.]

We can think of this sentence as attempting in its small compass to do what the *Preface* as a whole is meant to do: to establish Hooker as a voice and mind; to create a relationship with his readers, opponents and friends alike, that will work as the ground upon which a conversation can proceed; to define the topics and methods of his proposed conversation in such a way as to entitle it to the kind of authority he claims for it; and in doing these things to define, in performance, the institution for which he argues. How does this sentence work, and how well does it succeed?

The first and perhaps most important feature of the sentence is the language in which it is composed, vernacular English rather than Latin, which was the language of international scholarship, theology, and diplomacy. This is itself to define both the audience and speaker as English and implicitly as part of the reform movement as well, which systematically affirmed the vernacular against Latin. In affirming that the truth can be said as well in English as in any tongue it works as a slightly covert appeal to nationalism, as it also does in the way Hooker defines the issue upon which he and his opponents differ: it is not simply the abstract question, how a Christian church ought to be organized, but the far more culturally particular and located question, how the English church should be organized. This focus on the nation suggests that the answer to the problem of church government might be different elsewhere, in other countries,[15] and thereby begins to commit Hooker and his reader to his essential position, that certain matters are of first importance, others secondary. For how can a national church exist, except on a view that respects local

15. For Hooker's somewhat complaisant attitude towards French and Scottish presbyterianism, see Book III, 11.16. In distinguishing the law of the Old Testament from modern conditions he says the following, which in its terms reaches very much farther, to an acceptance of real difference in church government and style: "A more dutifull and religious way for us were to admire the wisedome of God, which shineth in the bewtifull varietie of all things, but most in the manifold and yet harmonious dissimilitude of those wayes, whereby his Church upon earth is guided from age to age, thoughout all generations of men." (III.11.8.)

arrangements and customs and thus recognizes the nonuniversality of certain truths? This is exactly the view that Hooker is trying to lead the reformers to accept.

How about the shape of the opening sentence? Sentence structure is in fact a large issue throughout Hooker's text, for to him the sentence is a form, like a poetic form, and much of his meaning lies in his use of it. But to understand what he is doing requires a little background, for we are differently situated and do not naturally think of the sentence as he does.

Hooker wrote at a time when the proper shape of the English sentence was a topic of public concern and controversy. Until the Reformation and indeed during much of it as well, as I said above, the language of disputation was Latin. But the Reformation validated the vernacular: the Bible had been translated into English; the Book of Common Prayer, itself originally a translation of the Mass, was composed in English; and now serious prose literature was for the first time being written on large scale in English rather than in Latin. But in what kind of English? For the most part English had been the unselfconscious language of ordinary life, Latin (or French) the language of state and diplomacy and the university. Rather little attention had accordingly been given questions of English diction or grammar or spelling or to the forms of the English sentence. In Latin, by contrast, the humanists of Italy, and later of the North, had found a literary and linguistic model in Cicero, whose Latin established in their eyes a norm of purity for them to emulate in diction and form alike. In English there was no such model, and as a glance, say, at Malory's *Morte Darthur* will show, there was very little shared sense of the shape of the English sentence.

One question for the time therefore was, What should the English sentence be like? One school of thought considered Cicero an appropriate model for English as well as Latin. But this to some degree went against the genius of our uninflected tongue, for Cicero's style depended upon the power of Latin to suspend closure by the deferral of grammatically necessary elements to the end of the sentence. The feeling of this kind of sentence was that of a whole, closing of its own force, in a circle or period. (Cicero said that no good writer needed punctuation of any sort.) In English, by contrast, then and now, we depend mainly upon word order to shape our utterances—John hit the ball; the ball hit John—and cannot place the various items of a sentence wherever we wish in order to suspend closure. Yet some, Hooker among them, nonetheless thought that Cicero's Latin model could serve for writers of English; others tried other forms, from the balancing act of Lyly's *Euphues* to the relative linearity of Bacon. The shape of English prose was unresolved until Dryden, nearly a century later, established the style that has prevailed ever since.[16]

Hooker's first sentence has some of the periodic character we associate with Cicero and other Latin writers, especially in beginning with a subordinate clause, which defers both the main subject and its verb. The effect of this, here and elsewhere, is to perform the value of subordination itself, through the creation of a structure which has more and less important parts. The deferral of the main verb, and with it the grammatical completion of the sentence, similarly works to enact the value of deferral, of postponing conclusion until all the parts are present. At its strongest, as Georges Edelen has argued in an important article on the subject, this kind of writing requires, and thus values, the suspension of judgment while argument is completed.[17]

Our sentence begins with the phrase, "Though for no other cause,

16. For the history of English prose see, for example, Janel M. Mueller, *The Native Tongue and the Word: Developments in English Prose Style, 1380–1580* (Chicago: University of Chicago Press, 1984); Morris W. Croll, *"Attic" and Baroque Style: The Anti-Ciceronian Movement* (Princeton: Princeton University Press, 1966); George Saintsbury, *A History of English Prose Rhythm* (London: Macmillan and Co., 1922). Samuel Johnson speaks of Dryden's style, particularly in the prefaces to his plays, in a way that imitates what he describes: "They have not the formality of a settled style, in which the first half of the sentence betrays the other. The clauses are never balanced, nor the periods modelled; every word seems to drop by chance, though it falls into its proper place." Samuel Johnson, "Life of Dryden," in *Rasselas, Poems, and Selected Prose*, 3d ed., edited by B. H. Bronson (New York: Holt, Rinehart, and Winston, 1971), page 372.

17. "Hooker's Style," in *Studies in Richard Hooker: Essays Preliminary to an Edition of his Works*, edited by W. Speed Hill. Hooker makes this value explicit, for example, here: "In the meane while it may be, that suspence of judgement and exercise of charitie were safer and seemelier for Christian men, then the whot pursute of these controversies, wherein they that are most fervent to dispute, bee not always the most able to determine." (IV.14.7.) Here is an example of a complex sentence that suspends grammatical closure nearly to the end:

Wherein seeing that no more is by us mainteyned, then onely that scripture must needes teach the Church whatsoever is in such sort necessarie, as hath beene set downe, and that it is no more disgrace for scripture to have left a number of other things free to be ordered at the discretion of the Church, then for nature to have left it unto the wit of man to devise his owne attyre, and not to looke for it as the beastes of the field have theirs: if neyther this can import, nor any other proofe sufficient bee brought foorth that wee eyther will at any time or ever did affirme the sacred Scripture to comprehende no more then onely those bare necessaries; if we acknowledge that as well for particular application to speciall occasions, as also in other manifolde respectes infinite treasures of wisedome are over and besides aboundantly to be found in the holy scripture; yea that scarcely there is anye noble parte of knowledge, woorthy the minde of man, but from thence it may have some

yet for this": what does it mean that it takes this form rather than, what would be more familiar to us, something like: "For the following reasons"? To start with the word "though" is to locate us immediately in a conditional and uncertain world (much as if he began with the word "if"), and this expresses a tentativeness, an acknowledgment that there may be other reasons, other truths. Hooker is here insisting that proper speech is not simply declarative—not the plain speech of the Puritans—but modal, conditioned, qualified.

Next: What is the "cause"? "that posteritie may know." This is to invoke a sense of future as well as present time, and hence the movement of time itself, including the past. The kind of time invoked is not only a physical but a cultural process, which of necessity involves characterization and selection. To imagine posterity is to imagine someone else, looking back across a gulf, engaged in the process of describing and evaluating what he sees. Hooker thus incorporates into the text at the very beginning the idea of another person, different from the disputants, representing a different point of view; and just not any point of view but a more knowledgeable one, from which the present disturbances can be seen in proper light and proportion, that is to say, with appropriate discrimination of the important and the trivial, of things essential and things indifferent.[18] This phrase thus contributes to the relativism that is so much a part of Hooker's case, and to its idealism as well, for when we think of posterity we imagine the good judge, who knows what we do not, making as it were a final judgment of a kind that cannot be made yet.

---

direction and light; yea, that although there be no necessitie it should of purpose prescribe any one particular forme of Church-governement, yet touching the manner of governing in generall the precepts that scripture setteth downe are not fewe, and the examples manie which it proposeth for all Church-governors, even in particularities to followe; yea, that those thinges finally which are of principall waight in the verie particular forme of Church-politie (although not that forme which they imagine, but that which we against them upholde) are in the selfe same scriptures conteyned: if all this be willingly graunted by us which are accused to pinne the worde of God in so narrowe roome, as that it should be able to direct us but in principall poyntes of our religion, or as though the substance of religion or some rude and unfashioned matter of building the Church were uttered in them, and those thinges left out, that should pertaine to the forme and fashion of it; let the cause of the accused bee referred to the accusors owne conscience, and let that judge whether this accusation be deserved where it hath beene layd. [III.4.1.]

18. Is there a connection between this idea of posterity as judge, looking back on what we say or do with knowledge we do not have, and the idea of judicial review of legislative acts? An important part of the justification of this power depends on the fact that the Court is situated differently from the legislature, both in time and in culture.

What is posterity to know? That "we have not loosely through silence permitted things to passe away as in a dreame." The "we" is in some sense of course Hooker himself, for he is here explaining and justifying his own act of composing the *Lawes;* but beyond Hooker it includes those for whom he speaks, and perhaps—a hint of it anyway—those with whom he disputes, his whole generation, at least if they will now respond to him in the way that he means to invite. He here speaks out of a sense of occasion, of impending loss, and with an express acknowledgement that what he says may have no effect at all in the immediate world. This is to perform a kind of humility, a recognition of his own limits; and it reinforces the idea of posterity, of some other judge who sees all, knows all, and judges rightly. And notice here how the phrase, "loosely through silence permitted things to passe away as in a dreame," in its own fluidity and extension mirrors or performs its meaning. The sentence itself becomes syntactically loose and dreamy; it loses its bearings for a moment then regains them.

The main clause of the sentence is this: "there shall be for mens information extant thus much concerning the present state of the Church of God established amongst us." This clause complicates the social world yet another degree, in speaking as it does of the "men" who are its audience and the "us" amongst whom the church has been established (here pretty plainly meaning all Englishmen). This phrase defines the church not as a supranational or universal entity but as a local institution, "established amongst us." Like the use of English itself, this commits him, and his reader too if he does not find himself objecting, to a conception of the church as varying from place to place and, therefore, to the distinction between matters essential and those indifferent.

The sentence seems to close hard here, since it for the first time completes a grammatical structure; but in fact it goes on, with what follows marked by that fact as an addendum, hence stressed: "and their carefull endevour which woulde have upheld the same." Here the pronoun is unclear: does "their" mean "our," or refer to those "men" who have not endeavored to uphold the church but to reform it, or is it a kind of demonstrative, really meaning "that" sort of endeavor? My own sense is that the language means: "the careful endeavor of those who wished to uphold the church." But in any event this phase shifts the promise made about the text; it will not be merely "information" but contain judgment too.

HOOKER GOES ON TO SAY THAT "the wonderfull zeale and fervour wherewith ye have withstood the received orders of this Church" led him to consider whether or not they were right in their position that the church should be transformed as they desire. "But when once, as neere as my slender abilitie woulde serve, I had with travaile and care performed that part of the Apostles advise and counsell in such cases whereby he willeth to try *all things*," he concluded this, as his "finall resolute persuasion":

> Surely the present forme of Churchgovernment which the lawes of this land have established, is such, as no lawe of God, nor reason of man hath hitherto bene alleaged of force sufficient to prove they do ill, who to the uttermost of their power withstand the alteration thereof." Contrariwise, "The other which in stead of it we are required to accept, is only by error and misconceipt named the ordinance of Jesus Christ, no one proofe as yet brought forth whereby it may cleerely appeare to be so in very deede." [1.2.]

Hooker has, like a good lawyer, defined the question in such a way as to place the burden of proof on the other side. But this is not merely a trick, one that could be played back on him, but a part of his central case; for his thesis of matters essential and matters indifferent, and the duty of yielding in the latter case, supports this allocation of the burden. This statement of burden of proof is in fact another way of stating his main claim.

It is "the explication of which two things" for which he has written his treatise. He asks that his readers relax any hostility they may have towards him and

> regard not who it is which speaketh, but waigh only what is spoken. Thinke not that ye reade the words of one, who bendeth him selfe as an adversarie against the truth which ye have alreadie embraced; but the words of one, who desireth even to embrace together with you the selfe same truth, if it be the truth. . . . [1.3.]

In other words: though I have my position, and you yours, both firmly taken, let us talk to each other in the hope of finding a common truth. But this does not mean that he relaxes his vigor, as his diction here makes plain: "For the plainer accesse whereunto, let it be lawfull for me to rip up to the verie bottome, how and by whome your Discipline was planted." Hooker in this way establishes a central tension, between the idea of inclusion implicit in the very practice of argument, which he has so far been stressing, and the insistence on his own judgment, for which he will argue on the merits.

## The Story of Calvin

Hooker begins the next stage of his argument rather surprisingly, with a history of the career of John Calvin, who was the founder of the discipline the reformers wished to impose. The Lutheran church, temperamentally conservative, had for the most part maintained episcopacy as its mode of government, and it was Calvin who transformed Lutheran principles into his radical vision of theology and church government. The story of Calvin has great prominence in the *Preface* and accordingly in the *Lawes* as a whole, and we are thus invited to ask: Why does Hooker begin this way? How, that is, does this story serve to persuade the reformers (and others) of his position, and how does it begin to establish the ground of authority upon which Hooker's case will ultimately rest?

Hooker commences the story in Geneva, just at the moment when the bishops of that city had given up the Roman church. The civil government of the city was "popular, as it continueth at this day: neither King, nor Duke, nor noble man of any authoritie or power over them, but officers chosen by the people yerely out of themselves, to order all things with publique consent. For spirituall government, they had no lawes at all agreed upon, but did what the Pastors of their soules by persuasion could win them unto." (2.1.) For us, as modern democrats and perhaps agnostics, this may seem like a fine state of affairs; but to Hooker, and indeed to Calvin, it seemed an utterly impossible chaos, fraught with the greatest dangers. Calvin quickly saw "how dangerous it was that the whole estate of that Church should hang still on so slender a thred, as the liking of an ignorant multitude is, if it have power to change whatsoever it selfe listeth." (2.1.) For that reason, Calvin, together with some of the other ministers, persuaded the people "to binde themselves by solemne oath" not to admit papacy amongst them and "to live in obedience unto such orders concerning the exercise of their religion, and the forme of their ecclesiasticall government" as their ministers should set down.

The churches of Geneva, which were independently self-governing, now in effect competed with each other to see who could be the furthest removed from Rome: "whereupon grewe marvelous great dissimilitudes, and by reason thereof, jealousies, hartburnings, jarres and discords amongst them." (2.2.) These might have been readily resolved, except that each church thought that its own particular arrangements were "everlastinglie required by the lawe of that Lord of Lords, against whose statutes there is no exception to be taken." The churches, that is, rooted everything in the commands of scripture, as they variously read it, and, refusing to distinguish between the essential and the indifferent, created irremediable differences amongst themselves, and this despite the fact that they shared the same fundamental attitudes and interests.[19] As Hooker gently puts it, a "smal, common conference before hand might have eased them of much aftertrouble." (2.2.)

Calvin and his two associates refused communion to those who would not be governed by them in accordance with the oath, and were in response banished from the town. But a few years later, the Genevans wanted Calvin back again and passed a resolution of the senate for his recall. One reason they wanted him was his increase of fame abroad. Another was that in negotiations with them he had shown flexibility over certain matters of indifference, especially in his willingness to use unleavened bread in the sacrament notwithstanding his own preference for common bread. They thought "his yeelding unto them in one thing" might lead to a general condescension of his will to theirs.

In that they could not have been more wrong:

> He ripely considered how grosse a thing it were for men of his qualitie, wise and grave men, to live with such a multitude, and to be tenants at will under them, as their ministers, both himselfe and others, had bene. For the remedy of which inconvenience he gave them plainly to understande, that if he did become their teacher againe, they must be content to admit a complet forme of discipline, which both they, and also their pastors should now be solemnely sworn to observe for ever after. Of which discipline the main and principall partes were these: A standing ecclesiasticall Court to be established;

19. "For by this meane it came to passe, that one Church could not but accuse and condemne another of disobedience to the will of Christ, in those things where manifest difference was betweene them: whereas the selfe same orders allowed, but yet established in more warie and suspense maner, as being to stand in force till God should give the opportunitie of some generall conference what might be best for everie of them afterwards to doe; this I saie had both prevented all occasion of just dislike which others might take, and reserved a greater libertie unto the authors themselves of entring into farder consultation afterwards. Which though never so necessarie they could not easilie now admit, without some feare of derogation from their credit: and therefore that which once they had done, they became for ever after resolute to maintaine." (2.2.)

perpetuall Judges in that Court to be their ministers, others of the people annually chosen twice so many in number as they to be judges together with them in the same Court: these two sorts to have the care of all mens manners, power of determining all kind of Ecclesiasticall causes, and authoritie to convent, to controll, to punish, as farre as with excommunication, whom soever they should thinke worthy, none eyther small or great excepted. [2.4.]

Although Geneva at first assented, a few years later the town rebelled again. The senate admitted to the town a man, Bertelier, whom the eldership had excommunicated, and claimed as a general matter the power of excommunication for itself, "cleane contrarie to their owne former deedes and othes." (2.5.) Calvin left the city; the city wanted him back and, suspending their decree, submitted the case to the judgment of four other Swiss cities. Calvin wrote to the ministers in those cities, saying that "God and all good men were now inevitably certaine to be trampled under foot" unless those four cities should give sentence for Calvin and the other ministers of Geneva, in a judgment that must contain the following two things: "the one an absolute approbation of the discipline of Geneva as consonant unto the word of God without any cautions, qualifications, ifs or ands; the other an earnest admonition not to innovate or change the same." (2.6.) But the four cities, acting as a court, held only that the consistorial laws of Geneva were "godly *ordinances* drawing towards *the prescript of the word of God, for which cause . . . they did not thinke it good for* the Church of Geneva *by innovation to change the same, but rather to keepe them as they were.*" (2.6.)

SEE HOW THIS WORKS: it is Calvin, the Reformers' founder and hero, who sees that a city with no government is impossible and seeks to impose one; it is Calvin who distinguishes between the indifferent and the necessary (when he agrees to administer communion with unleavened bread); it is Calvin who, when the Genevan churches break into fragments by insisting that every point of difference among them is a matter of everlasting sacred law, imposes a common regime upon them all; it is Calvin who, when his differences with Geneva cannot be resolved by argument alone, submits to the judgment of an arbitrator; and it is thus in a sense with Calvin's own authority, for he has submitted to the process that produced it, that the arbitrator says what has just been quoted, that Calvin's laws are good ones, but not the only possibilities, and that they should be maintained not because they uniquely conform to the word of God but because the burden of showing that they should be discarded has not been carried by his opponents. This is exactly the position Hooker seeks to establish with respect to the laws of the Church of England. In this way Hooker makes Calvin, the central authority of the reformers, his own witness on the most essential points of his argument.

More than that, he makes his reader his witness too, for a reason I suggested in connection with the reading of *Richard II:* as we read this story, and find it filling our minds, we either affirm that these events are natural and probable, given our sense of the nature of human beings and the conditions on which they live, or not; if the latter, we stop, and hem and haw, and resist; if the former, we read on, the continuous dream of the narrative uninterrupted.[20] If this happens, we find that we have unknowingly affirmed the premises on which it works, that people are like this, that the world is like this. We have joined Hooker's rhetorical community.

And what are people like in this narrative world? They are given to claim more knowledge, with greater certainty, than they should; to value their own notions far above the peace and order of their communities; and to struggle for power under cover of a struggle for ideas. They are especially likely to assert that they know what in fact cannot be known, and to claim divine inspiration for this knowledge. They are in need of the intellectual and ethical discipline provided by a culture and its institutions. When they are seen from a distant point by a person who does not take sides over the matters that exercise them—by "posterity" in fact, for it is into a version of posterity that Hooker here transforms his audience—the intensity and tenacity of their disputes make them seem foolish and unpeaceable, and this on both sides. All this works as a call for discussion, for hesitation in affirming certainties, and for compliance with the judgments of others. The acquiescing reader is led to affirm the practical necessity of distinguishing the indifferent from the essential and, in the former case, of yielding to communal authority. The view of life on which the narrative works, as a natural and probable story, is also the view on which Hooker's arguments on the merits make most sense. To the extent we read through the story of Calvin, nodding our head in

20. This is a modified version of John Gardner's language, used in *The Art of Fiction: Notes on Craft for Young Writers* (New York: Knopf, 1984), pages 30–31.

agreement, we thus affirm, below the level of consciousness, the attitudes that underlie his positions.

This is at its heart a rhetorical view of life, founded on uncertainty of knowledge and difference of opinion, and the way Hooker proposes to live on such conditions is rhetorical too: not by conclusive logical or factual demonstration but by argumentative conference, by distinguishing between what matters essentially and what matters little, and by constant recognition of the fact that we need some way to live together or we shall split into tiny fragments. This means granting authority both to the decisions regularly reached by the community's regular officials and, more important, to judgments reached in conference, after deliberation and argument. It makes discussion of a certain sort its highest authority (saving always the plain commands of scripture); and the question, what kind of discussion this should be, Hooker is answering by performance.

Here is a single long sentence, from this section of the *Preface*, which catches much of the way Hooker's narrative works. You will remember that Calvin established a system of government of the city by a council, made up of laymen and ministers, with the former outnumbering the latter two to one (though the appointment of the ministers was perpetual, of the laymen for a term). Hooker says some of the laity saw this as "little better than a popish tyranny disguised and tendered unto them under a new forme."

> This sort, it may be, had some feare that the filling up of the seates in the Consistorie with so great a number of lay men, was but to please the mindes of the people, to the ende they might thinke their owne swaye somewhat; but when thinges came to tryall of practise their Pastors learning woulde be at all times of force to overperswade simple men, who knowing the time of their owne Presidentship to be but short, would alwayes stande in feare of their Ministers perpetuall authoritie: and among the Ministers themselves, one being so farre in estimation above the rest, the voyces of the rest were likely to be given for the most part respectively with a kinde of secret dependencie and awe: so that in shewe a marvelous indifferently composed Senate Ecclesiasticall was to governe, but in effect one onely man shoulde, as the Spirite and soule of the residue, doe all in all. [2.4.]

This sentence has the structure of a complex argument, based upon an estimation of the way in which people are likely in fact to behave beneath the surface of formal claims and pretenses. It works only as we acquiesce in this estimation. Thus when we are told that the people may be misled into thinking they have power, when in practice they will naturally be ruled by the clergy, who will themselves be ruled by Calvin, the sentence depends upon the reader's sharing an implicit sense of these probabilities. Yet we may not be conscious of this. Like the *Preface* more generally, this sentence thus works by activating and clarifying our own implicit sense of human nature.

Notice that once again the form of the sentence enacts its meaning, as it first constructs complexity of structure and diction and thought, and then reduces it to utter simplicity: "doe all in all." The complex intellectual constitution of the sentence is converted to the tyranny of a single person, a single thought. The text in this way brings to life the reader's own sense of the reality of those conditions of life that make it essential to engage in discussion, argument, and conference and that also entitle the results of those processes to respect, both as a moral and as a political matter.

If Hooker elevates a kind of conversation to his central authority, how is this kind of conversation defined? It is too early to try to respond to this question in full, but we can already see that the processes of mind and speech that Hooker enacts, and by enacting authorizes, include those of superordination and subordination: the subordination of the less to the more important; of the individual to the community; and of the community to the processes of judgment over time for which his word is "posteritie." In most things one's judgments should be tentative, and always given with an eye to their accommodation—perhaps a better word than subordination—to the views of others. He rests his case ultimately on his view of human nature, including himself, as fallible, vain, self-centered and self-glorifying, and he sees collective life, in the church and in this debate, as a mode of collective self-correction. He thus leaves himself open to those who can persuasively argue that this or that particular truth is settled beyond discussion and to those who can answer his story, based upon his view of the way human beings work, with a story of their own.

### Two Versions of the Reformers' Case

If such is our nature, and such the condition of our lives, how are we to address the divisions that have arisen within the church? The reformers are persuaded that they have the truth; "we being as fully perswaded otherwise, it resteth that some kinde of triall be used to finde out which part is in error." (2.10.) The purpose of the present work is to be a stage in such a trial, in such a conversation.

Hooker begins with that part of his case that he shares with the reformers: "The first meane whereby nature teacheth men to judge good from evil as well in lawes as in other things, is the force of their owne discretion. . . . [W]hatsoever we doe, if our owne secret judgement consent not unto it as fit and good to be done; the doing of it to us is sinne, although the thing it selfe be allowable." (3.1.) He thus starts with the experience and responsibility of the individual person, not with the institution of the church or a retelling of the sacred story. In this he leaves himself perpetually open to the claim, by any individual, that his conscience compels another view; Hooker thus recognizes his audience as one who has the capacity and the responsibility to make up his own mind, and who must therefore face, in a serious way, the question how that is to be done. Simply to rest upon a party position would be sinful.

Next: "Some things are so familier and plaine, that truth from falshood, and good from evil is most easily discerned in them, even by men of no deepe capacitie." (3.2.) This is true, Hooker says, for the most part at least, of all things necessary to salvation, "eyther to be held or denied, eyther to be done or avoyded." And these are "not onely set downe, but also plainely set downe in Scripture." So far Hooker is with the reformers. But he then goes on to say that with respect to other matters—all those that divide us in fact—the case is otherwise: we can never be sure we are right, for the questions are complex and difficult, and we are liable to error. We should therefore recognize the proper role of knowledge and discipline, in religious no less than civil law. Since we have no sure guides to knowledge, our situation is what I called rhetorical: we must accept at once the limits of our own minds and the responsibility of judgment, and be ready to find our own position flawed.

### The Multitude

Our limits are not only intellectual but what Hooker would call "spiritual," we today perhaps "psychological." Hooker makes this plain in his next long section, where he explains how it is that the reformers' case has been so widely accepted by "the multitude," those whose acceptance cannot rest on an intellectual understanding of the merits of the points of debate. Here Hooker once again tells a narrative, as he did about Calvin, and this one too works as a manifestation of his understanding of the nature of our minds and the conditions on which we live.

Here, Hooker tells us, is the way the reformers' case is made: "First in the hearing of the multitude, the faults especially of higher callings are ripped up with mervelous exceeding severity and sharpnes of reproofe; which being oftentimes done begetteth a great good opinion of integritie, zeale and holines, to such constant reproovers of sinne." (3.6.) The next thing is "to impute all faults and corruptions wherewith the worlde aboundeth, unto the kind of Ecclesiasticall governement established." (3.7.) Next they propose "their owne forme of Church governement, as the only soveraigne remedy of all evils; and . . . adorne it with all the glorious titles that may be." (3.8.) The "fourth degree of inducement is by fashioning the very notions and conceipts of mens minds in such sort, that when they read the Scripture, they may thinke that every thing soundeth towards the advancement of that discipline, and to the utter disgrace of the contrary." (3.9.)

This of course requires them to find, plainly set down in the scriptures, what other people do not see; hence the next step, "which is the perswading of men credulous and over capable of such pleasing errors, that it is the speciall illumination of the holy Ghost, whereby they discerne those things in the word, which others reading yet discerne them not." (3.10.) Then it is "instilled into their hearts, that the same Spirit leading men into this opinion, doth thereby seale them to be Gods children," and as such to be distinguished from all those who are in error, "whereby the one sort are named *The* brethren, *The* godlie, and so forth, the other wordlings, timeservers, pleasers of men not of God, with such like." (3.11.) The result is that "if once they have tasted of that cup, let any man of contrarie opinion open his mouth to perswade them, they close up their eares, his reasons they waigh not, all is answered with the rehearsall of the words of John, *We are of God, he that knoweth God, heareth us.*" The result is this: "Shew these egerlie affected men their inhabilitie to judge of such matters; their answere is, *God hath chosen the simple.* Convince them of follie, and that so plainely, that verie children upbraid them with it; they have their bucklers of like defence. *Christs owne Apostle was accompted mad. The best men evermore by the sentence of the world have bene judged to be out of their right minds.*" (3.14.)

This is the story of the progressive loss of the capacity for rational thought and discourse; as an account of fanaticism it belongs with Swift's great work, *A Tale of a Tub,* which it may well have influenced. There is much to condemn in what is described here, but, for present purposes at least, nothing more than the way in which people of this disposition refuse to engage in reasoned discourse with those who think otherwise.

What is represented by Hooker's imagined actors as a theological position, and thus above argument, is shown to be a refusal to participate in the essential practices by which community and culture are maintained and transformed across lines of difference. This is the heart of Hooker's effort: to show that the essential thing, in our common human situation, is the capacity and willingness to engage in conversation, of the kind he is attempting to begin, with those who disagree; but against the mind that is closed, nothing can be done.[21]

## The Learned

Hooker next turns to the more learned of the reformers, on whose "shoulders is laide the burthen of upholding the cause by argument," and addresses their central claim, that the church should be governed by their discipline because that is the discipline established by the apostles. (4.1.) But is it not odd "that such a discipline as ye speake of should be taught by Christ and his Apostles in the word of God, and no Church ever have found it out, nor receyved it till this present time"? (4.1.) Of their central position, that the form of church discipline should be brought "unto the state which then it was at," he says that this is "a thing neither possible, nor certaine, nor absolutely convenient," for the church is incompletely described in the scripture, the passages are open to conflicting readings, and with respect to certain of the matters that are known, we would be right not to follow them (as with respect to the sacred kiss with which early Christians greeted one another). (4.4.) The reformers' invocation of the opinions of like-minded people abroad is of little persuasive effect, because naturally those people who share the commitment of the reformers will share their judgments too. And, while many of the people whose opinions are invoked are themselves highly honorable, we cannot infer from their mutual agreement a shared perception of what rational people

---

21. Hooker puts the point this way:
   Most sure it is, that when mens affections doe frame their opinions, they are in defense of error more earnest a great deale, then (for the most part) sound believers in the maintenance of truth apprehended according to the nature of that evidence which scripture yeeldeth: which being in some things plaine, as in the principles of Christian doctrine; in some things, as in these matters of discipline, more darke and doubtfull, frameth correspondentlie that inward assent which Gods most gracious Spirit worketh by it as by his effectuall instrument. It is not therefore the fervent earnestnes of their perswasion, but the soundnes of those reasons whereupon the same is built, which must declare their opinions in these things to have bene wrought by the holie Ghost, and not by the *fraud* of that evill Spirit which is even in his illusions strong. [3.10.]

would see, as the reformers claim, because their opinions derive so much from one another.

The effect of this section is not so much to refute the reformers' case as to show that it is open to real argument. For Hooker's purposes this is enough, for once it is open to argument the matter falls out of the category of the essential into that of the indifferent, where opinion may rationally vary and where, therefore, respect should be accorded the judgments reached by authoritative institutions.

## How to Think and Talk

Next Hooker responds to the reformers' call for a conference to decide these things. This would be a good thing, in his view, but only on certain understandings. The passage in which he spells these out is crucial to the whole text, for here he makes explicit what he otherwise expresses by performance, namely, what he thinks the conditions for proper argument are, and what principles and understandings ought to govern the rhetorical community whose task it is to address the divisions between the reformers and others that cannot be decided by conclusive demonstration. The first condition is that the reformers cannot expect the existing law to be suspended until "in the hearing of thousands ye all did acknowledge your error and renounce the further prosecution of your cause." (5.2.) You cannot, that is, claim the right to have your way until you are persuaded otherwise. A community cannot be built upon the premise that participation is voluntary or optional at every stage; you must rather live with what we are until you can persuade the rest to change.

From this follows the first of his proposed rules of debate, that the burden of proof be on the reformers because they seek "to destroy a thing which is in force, and to draw in that which hath not as yet bin received." (5.3.) The other proposals are that they agree to proceed issue by issue, beginning with the most general, and to reach conclusion on one before going on to the others; that both sides agree to be represented by a speaker and to be bound by his representations; that a journal of the proceedings be published and that no other publications of what transpires should be made. Finally, the council or other authority before whom the argument be made must have the power to determine the dispute with finality. This has, after all, been the practice within Christendom from apostolic times to the present. "Are ye able to alleage any just and sufficient cause wherefore absolutely ye should not condescend in this controversie to have your judgements overruled by some such definitive sentence, whether it fall out to be given with or against you, that so these tedious contentions may cease?" (6.2.)

This is the upshot of what I have called Hooker's rhetorical view of life, the sense that on a very wide range of matters indeed human reason can reach no fixed and certain resolution, both because it cannot know what needs to be known and because the human personality is always in danger of becoming swollen with a false assurance of its own righteousness, and thus unbalanced and unreliable. In this field, which includes all matters of church government—and civil government too, for that matter—the test has to be that of reasoned argument, both ways; and always with the recognition that the two sides may fail to persuade each other, in which event there must either be a final decision of some sort, or chaos.

BUT THERE IS A POSSIBLE RESPONSE to all this, which Hooker imagines thus:

> Ye will perhaps make answere, that being perswaded alreadie as touching the truth of your cause, ye are not to harken unto any sentence, no not though Angels should define otherwise, as the blessed Apostles owne example teacheth; againe that men, yea, Councels may erre; and that, unlesse the judgement given do satisfie your minds, unlesse it be such as ye can by no further argument oppugne; in a word, unlesse you perceive and acknowledge it your selves consonant with Gods word, to stand unto it not allowing it, were to sinne against your own consciences. [6.3.]

The vice of excessive self-reliance, of self-insistence, is one to which reform, and protestantism more generally, naturally tend, for the location of all teaching in the sacred text tends to free the self from the bonds of shared reason and culture that bind us together into a community and to justify whatever the individual happens to find there. It is Hooker's central claim that this right of self-judgment be given up, in favor of the community. To support this claim he invokes God's establishment of judges in the Old Testament:

> God was not ignorant that the Priests and Judges, whose sentence in matters of controversie he ordained should stand, both might and oftentimes would be deceived in their judgement. Howbeit, better it was in the eye of his understanding, that sometime an erroneous sentence definitive should

prevaile, till the same authoritie perceiving such oversight, might after-
wardes correct or reverse it, then that strifes should have respit to growe,
and not come speedily unto some ende. [6.3.]

What of the central principle, invoked by Hooker himself at an earlier
stage, that men ought not "do any thing which in their hearts they are
perswaded they ought not to doe"? First, he tells us, the persuasion must
be "fully setled in their hearts," and it must take into account the desir-
ability of finality: "For if God be not the author of confusion but of peace,
then can he not be the author of our refusall, but of our contentment, to
stand unto some definitive sentence, without which almost impossible it
is that eyther we should avoyd confusion, or ever hope to attaine peace."
(6.3.) In this context at least, where one seeks to disobey an established
tribunal, it must also be based upon reasons "demonstrative" and not
"meere probabilities." "Any one such reason dischargeth, I graunt the
conscience, and setteth it at full libertie." (6.6.) But as to probabilities,
where men may differ, we are in the zone of the uncertain—of the rhetorical—and of the necessity for the acceptance of communal judgment.

All this is a way of saying that when the parties enter into their dispute they should make the process a real one, in which each side advances
what arguments it can and prepares to live with the consequences. The
only alternative is a fragmentation of the community and the self, a descent into the sort of insanity that many of the followers of reform have
been shown to exhibit.

It is in the context so established that Hooker briefly summarizes the
larger work of which this is a preface, implicitly characterizing it as a
contribution to just such a dispute as he has described. The first topic,
necessary to understanding the kinds of duties he has been describing,
will be the nature of law itself, "declaring therein what lawe is, how different kindes of lawes there are, and what force they are of according
unto each kind." (7.2.) In the second book he will speak to the question
whether the reformers' discipline can be found in the scripture or not,
and how far, by contrast, the scripture supports the established polity.
The following books address the questions whether it is right in the first
place to expect scripture to establish a form of church government, good
for all time; whether the rituals of the established church are "popish rites
and ceremonies," and hence not entitled to authority; the character of
sacraments and prayers; the proper jurisdiction of bishops and other ministers; and finally the power of the sovereign in the English polity as a
whole. All this can be read as his own effort at making good on the under-

taking he proposes that they share, for full argument on the issues that divide them.

## Insanity and Fanaticism

Hooker now returns to his narrative mode, this time to develop a sharpened sense of the dangers inherent in the methods of reform. He begins with the Barrowists, who have separated themselves entirely and unlawfully from the church. They are a real embarrassment to the reformers, who do not want to take that step, but, as Hooker puts the statement in the mouth of an imaginary Barrowist, they cannot escape so easily: "From your breasts it is that we have sucked those things which when ye delivered unto us ye tearmed that heavenly, sincere, and wholesome milke of Gods worde, howsoever ye now abhorre as poison that which the vertue thereof hath wrought and brought forth in us." (8.1.) If the structure and rites of the established church are those of the Antichrist, as you say, and the one thing needful is their reform according to scripture, how are we wrong to separate ourselves in order to make the church you call for?

> For adventuring to erect the discipline of Christ without the leave of the Christian Magistrate, happily ye may condemne us as fooles, in that we hazard thereby our estates and persons, further then you which are that way more wise thinke necessarie: but of any offence or sinne therin committed against God, with what conscience can you accuse us, when your owne positions are, that the thinges we observe should every of them be dearer unto us then ten thousand lives; that they are the peremptory commaundements of God; that no mortall man can dispence with them, and that the Magistrate grievously sinneth in not constraining thereunto? [8.1.]

This speech, and others like it, demonstrate that the natural disposition of the doctrines being advanced by the reformers (at least unless there be an agreed submission to an arbitrator or judge) is that each person or group shall judge for himself, separating himself and his friends off into a new church of the godly, all without control beyond that of the individual conscience. This would recreate the very circumstances that Calvin himself thought so intolerable in Geneva.

The tendency of these principles, explicit in the Barrowist, implicit in the reformers, is to challenge not only the church but the crown, the nobility, and all established government. They in fact challenge all other learning, for they derive all truth from a reading of the text, beyond which they say there is nothing needful; and they tend to the destruction of the law itself, "your opinion" of which "is that the knowledge thereof might be spared, as a thing which this land doth not neede." (8.4.) For the "reasons wherewith ye would perswade that Scripture is the onely rule to frame all our actions by, are in every respect as effectuall for proofe that the same is the onely law whereby to determine all our Civill controversies." (8.4.)[22] This is to make explicit what the reformers had from the beginning tried to cover, that their doctrines have the potential for the subversion of all established government, with nothing to take its place but an anarchy of conflicting readings of the sacred text, unless this be supplanted by an authoritarian rule by a fixed interpreter. For Hooker, as for Shakespeare, there is no language of constitutional democracy to fill the vacuum.

To make even more plain the tendencies of the reformers' principles, Hooker now gives an account of the intellectual and spiritual history of the Anabaptists. These were extremist Protestants disowned by Luther and Calvin themselves as well as by the English reformers. The point, of course, is that their excesses flow naturally from the principles of reform, a point that depends, as the earlier narrative did too, upon the reader's acquiescence in the sense of human nature and the conditions of human life out of which the story functions. What characterizes these people— and this would characterize many of us, if we shared their methods of thought and action—Hooker argues, is a kind of insane delusion of grandiosity, and of just the sort we earlier saw adumbrated in the account of the way the reform appeals to the "multitude."

The Anabaptists "were sollicitors of men to fasts, to often meditations of heavenly things, and as it were conferences in secret with God by prayers, not framed according to the frosen maner of the world, but expressing such fervent desires as might even force God to hearken unto them." (8.6.) They reproved all who lived differently from them; they asserted that with respect to church government, they "only had the truth, which thing upon perill of their lives they would at all times defend; and that since the Apostles lived, the same was never before in all points sincerely taught." (8.7.) "When they and their Bibles were alone together,

---

22. Here it is worth repeating that one of the main points of Hooker's treatise itself will be to establish that in the world there are many different kinds of law, with different subjects, different kinds of authority, and that any sensible way of thinking about the question of church government will require attention to the issue, what sort of law should govern the question.

what strange phantasticall opinion soever at any time entred into their heads, their use was to thinke the Spirit taught it them." (8.7.)

All this is offered as a set of reasons why "there is . . . most just cause to feare least our hastines to embrace a thing of so perilous consequence should cause posteritie to feele those evils, which as yet are more easie for us to prevent then they would be for them to remedy." (8.14.)

## A Call to Argument

Hooker closes with a call to his adversaries:

> The best and safest waie for you therefore my deere brethren is, to call your deedes past to a newe reckoning, to reexamine the cause yee have taken in hand, and to trie it even point by point, argument by argument, with all the diligent exactnes yee can; to lay aside the gall of that bitternes wherein your mindes have hitherto overabounded, and with meekenes to search the truth. Thinke yee are men, deeme it not impossible for you to erre: sift unpartiallie your owne hearts, whether it be force of reason, or vehemencie of affection, which hath bread, and still doth feede these opinions in you. [9.1.]

Whether or not his opponents follow this advice (given not without bitterness of its own), this is an undertaking by him to do exactly these things; he is here establishing the standard by which he holds out his own text to be judged. Having said this, he cannot disown it.

And the same can be said as well for his claim to be motivated by charity, his wish to be of one mind with his adversaries and the like.

> Far more comfort it were for us (so small is the joy we take in these strifes) to labour under the same yoke, as men that looke for the same eternall reward of their labours, to be joyned with you in bands of indissoluble love and amitie, to live as if our persons being manie our soules were but one, rather then in such dismembred sort to spend our fewe and wretched dayes in a tedious prosecuting of wearisome contentions: the ende whereof, if they have not some speedie ende, will be heavie even on both sides. [9.3.]

We have as a community fallen into strife of an unseemly and destructive kind; as Gregory of Naziansen said, Hooker goes on, "The only godlines we glory in, is to find out somewhat whereby we may judge others to be ungodly."

But our trust in the almightie is, that with us contentions are now at their highest floate, and that the day will come (for what cause of despaire is there) when the passions of former enmitie being allaied, we shal with ten times redoubled tokens of our unfainedlie reconciled love, shewe our selves each towards other the same which Joseph and the brethren of Joseph were at the time of their enterview in Aegypt. Our comfortable expectation and most thirstie desire whereof what man soever amongst you shall anie waie helpe to satisfie (as we trulie hope there is no one amongst you but some way or other will) the blessings of the God of peace both in this world and in the world to come, be upon him moe then the starres of the firmament in number. [9.4.]

The structure of the last sentence, like so many of Hooker's, enacts the values of complexity and inclusiveness of thought. It creates a world, as a poem does, and one that cannot be represented as a string of ideas but has the quality rather of a circle or a globe, and thus calls, literally, for circumspection. It includes and includes, yet suspends judgment to the end; when judgment falls, as it does in one way here, in another way in the great sentence about the new constitution of Geneva, it falls with a force beyond mere assertion, with the finality of something concluded. In this way Hooker enacts in his prose the kind of thought he recommends, the kind of mind reasoning with others. Talk as I talk, he says, and see what happens to your confidence in your slogans. Any single phrase or clause, any rallying cry, must be combined with others in a sentence of this kind, and this will transform it beyond recognition. This is a style in which it would be impossible to advocate revolution or to insist upon the rightness of a few plain truths plainly spoken.

Likewise the narratives—of Calvin, of the conversion of the multitudes, of the Barrowists and the Anabaptists—all work as an invitation and a challenge. If you accept the naturalness and probability of these stories you accept as well—you must—the understandings by which they work: that human beings need the discipline of government or they will be overcome by their self-grandiosity; that government can only work if it has authority to resolve matters with finality; that one must distinguish between matters essential, on which scripture and your conscience speak, and the vast range of matters indifferent, where we cannot simply know the truth but must live with our ignorance and our differences of mind, our awareness that all of us can have our judgment clouded by grandiosity, and so on. And these stories work directly on the reader's desire: as one works through the text one finds oneself wanting government to exist in Geneva, wanting the churches to distinguish essential from indifferent, wanting them to lead a communal life less crazed than that of the fanatics, and these desires bear equally upon one's own life.

To the extent any of this is doubted, Hooker says to his reader: persuade me in such a fashion, writing prose that equally combines and suspends, that in its narratives calls equally upon human experience. Can you do it?

In this way, by performance as well as by doctrine, this *Preface* works as an invitation to the establishment of an argument of a certain sort, and hence of a community, to which should be accorded, in all matters not governed by the plain letter of the scripture or the plain voice of the spirit, the only kind of authority it is possible for human institutions to attain. Hooker finds a way, in the process of argument itself, to live communally in a world in which old authorities are gone; and in so doing to establish a new authority, that of the conversation in which he is engaged.

## HOOKER'S CONSTITUTION

Hooker's text was of course not actually composed in response to *Richard II*—it was written a few years earlier and was far too grave in its tone and concerns alike to permit allusion to such a piece of popular entertainment—but it might be helpful to think of it that way. *Richard II* begins with a richly imagined version of medieval kingship, qualified by other forces, the whole making up a complex and comprehensible world but not an especially stable one. Like all real worlds, it is marked by tensions that threaten to undo it. But it is manageable, at least in the sense that one can see what people in different situations might say to themselves and to others. One could even imagine oneself speaking in these different roles, which is perhaps the only kind of order it is given human societies to have.[23]

At the end of this play the rhetorical coherence of that world has been destroyed, and we, like the characters in the drama, inhabit a universe in

---

23. We are trained by our own language of political organization, perhaps by our own Constitution, to think otherwise, to conceive of a social and political order as a structure, with power flowing from one institution to another in ways that can be recorded on an organization chart, as though it were a machine that worked by hydraulic mechanics. But this is never true; power is always in question; and although Shakespeare's picture of kingship may seem to be frail and unstable, such is the nature of all human organizations.

which the language of kingship and treason and loyalty and property are all unworkable. In a sense no one knows what to say now; no one has an adequate language. The effect of this ending is to present us with a strikingly modern version of the problem of political authority: in a world in which there is no inherited authority to call upon, no established title to rule, who should have the power to govern and why? As I said above, our own answer, worked out over centuries, has been to say that political authority derives from the consent of "the People," expressed through elections based upon universal adult suffrage, but this was not an available resource for Shakespeare and his audience.[24] He leaves us in an intellectual and political vacuum, with an ending that is no ending and with no way to imagine the future. His own way of thinking of it, as worked out in the later plays in the sequence, is to see the modern English crown as rooted in a kind of original sin, from which it is redeemed partly by time, partly by the good qualities of the ruler—such as the sporadic generosity of Henry IV and the heroics of Henry V—and partly by the great need for a central government if the nation is to be free from civil war.

The vacuum with which Shakespeare left his audience pointed to a genuine contemporary problem, but one that was more vivid with respect to the church than the crown. Although Elizabeth faced revolt, and Charles was to be deposed only fifty years later, the authority of the Tudor Crown was not a matter of overt public debate, while the authority of the church as then constituted was very much in question. If *Richard II* can be read as bringing to the surface of its audience's attention, with clarity and force, the problem of authority to which constitutional discourse has ever after been directed, Hooker can be read as the first major work in such a discourse. He is the father of English, and hence of American, constitutional thought. In a sense it is an accident of no great significance that he happened to write about the church rather than the state, for the central question of Protestantism is the central question of free government. When the legitimacy of the crown is eventually thrown into doubt, as happens in the next century, the fundamental questions will be exactly the same: in a world in which authority is questioned, Who should have the power to govern, on what conditions, and why?

It is Hooker's achievement to answer that question in two ways, first

---

24. The theory of medieval kingship, as opposed to the more absolute doctrine of absolute monarchy that was evolving as Shakespeare wrote, also included an element of consent of the governed, but this was a highly artificial and constructed consent, never so far as I know even in imagination taking the form of election based on universal suffrage.

by setting forth a set of arguments justifying respect for the odd hybrid that was the English church—Calvinist in theology, Roman in governance, nationalist in everything—and, of equal importance, by defining in his own practice the modes of thought and argument to which he thought authority should be given. It is "the church" to which one should grant authority; but to the church as defined in this text. In the *Preface* Hooker both describes and enacts the way in which he thinks the conversation should proceed; in this he creates a kind of polity with the reader, which is at once the authority upon which his arguments most depend and an exemplification of what they mean in practice, a definition in fact of the church for which he argues.

Hooker is not dialectical: he does not proceed by question and answer, he does not lead his reader into the sort of aporia or distress that Socrates and Plato believe essential to thought, and he does not place first the welfare of those whom he addresses but instead the welfare of the community of which both are a part. In this sense he is rhetorical—though not in the negative sense, of saying whatever will persuade, seeking to flatter his audience, making the weaker argument the stronger, and so on, for one never has the sense that he is making arguments in which he does not believe. In a way that dialectic properly speaking cannot do, his kind of rhetoric is a way of focusing upon the ways in which a community larger than two, a polis or a church, can be created and maintained through practices of language.

Hooker's text, then, offers its reader the experience not of education by confusion, as the *Crito* does, nor of the breakdown of a language, as *Richard II* does, but of persuasion. The movement in these three texts is from philosophy, an essentially private activity, at its best in groups of two, to the drama, a public activity but both physically and imaginatively separated from the world of power, to the creation of public authority in an institution that works by argument. Hooker seeks to constitute his reader as one who, like him, has views, arguments in support of his views, disagreements with others that he does not expect to be resolved by eventual concurrence of minds, and the wish to resolve these differences by something other than war or separation. Hooker's version of this wish is for a certain kind of argument in which each side, while not giving up its commitment to its own views and arguing for them strenuously, recognizes that the larger goal of unity and peace may require the subordination of judgment, on some kinds of matters at least. His narratives, if they work, lead the reader to make active his own sense of the nature of humankind and the way things work in the world; to support Hooker's essential distinction, between the necessary and the indifferent; and to accept his position that submission, not to established authority simply, but to a process of argument and judgment, is necessary to the continued existence of any form of government whatever.

All this could be read as a wonderful elaboration of what is so crudely put by the Nomoi, when they say that Socrates must persuade or obey. It is also a performed response to the question left us by *Richard II,* for it says that we can address the vacuum created by that play by speaking to each other in a certain way—rational, respectful, invoking common human experiences, and subject to certain procedural forms. His proposal is that the opposing forces constitute a new community, formed by their understandings as to the way in which their differences should be addressed and resolved. This is in fact a proposal for a kind of constitution, in essence like the American one in fact, which could also be defined as a set of understandings about the ways in which differences should be defined and addressed. In both cases, of course, these understandings require the affirmation of what is agreed to as well, for only by such affirmations can difference be defined. In this sense Hooker's is a proposal for rhetorical cohesion through the prosecution of difference. This conversation, if you will engage in it on my terms, he says, is the way that we will remake and reform the institution of government and life we call the church.

The mode of thought and life that Hooker's prose offers its readers is in one sense integrative, combinatory, pluralistic, for it makes room for diversity of view and experience; yet it creates structure through subordination and superordination, that is, through hierarchy of value and desire alike. To speak this way, in sentences like his, requires balance and comprehension of mind, a capacity to put many things together into one, and a sense of shape and order. To speak in narratives like his one must be able to invoke the ways in which human beings actually live and act, for these stories work only upon shared understandings on those matters. The immensity of the labor involved in the production of this enormous text displays a kind of seriousness of mind, earnestness of engagement, that calls for the same from the reader. This is a text that calls upon the whole mind to say what it believes in light of everything else it thinks and knows, including the fact that there are others, of good will, who think otherwise. Although Hooker argues for an established authority against proposals for reform, as he defines them it is the reformers who are authoritarian, sure that they are right and eager to impose their will, the church that is open to doubt and argument and that seeks resolution by conference rather than fiat. Hooker is indeed judicious, as Locke repeatedly called him, for his work has many of the merits of judicial work at its best.

One danger for the modern lawyer is that the essential structure of Hooker's position will seem so familiar as to be unchallengeable, especially the premise that one should distinguish clearly between matters fundamental, as to which we should reach basic agreement, and other matters, where we can expect and should tolerate widespread disagreement. For him the two categories are the matters essential to salvation, as to which scripture speaks plainly and as to which no one should yield his judgment, and all the rest, with respect to which one should be prepared to yield one's judgment and to accept that of established authorities, of custom, and of learning. For modern lawyers, the categories are constitutional law and all the rest: in talking about the former, we carefully distinguish the latter, leaving this or that policy to the judgment of the states, knowing that they will in all likelihood differ from each other. These are not necessarily small matters, either: they include modes of taxation, kinds of education, whether or not to punish with death, and the like, and one may care deeply about them. The point is rather a jurisdictional one: these are not within the ambit of constitutional discourse. Likewise, for Hooker, the matters that exercise the reformers are not within the jurisdiction scripture has defined for itself: it either does not speak to these items, or speaks unclearly and, therefore, leaves such questions to the realm of human wisdom and learning.

WHAT DOES HOOKER'S WAY OF THINKING MISS? Or: Why were the reformers not all instantly persuaded by him? The reason has partly to do with the way in which scripture was itself conceived: if you think of it as a set of commands, what Hooker says makes good sense. If you think of it, however, as God speaking to humanity, not simply as a set of rules for one's conduct but as a way of affecting the heart and spirit, the situation changes. It may be true that the language is unclear, the reformer would say, but we can still use it as our guide, analogically, trying to divine what He would want; even where the scripture does not command, that is, it speaks and we can try to hear it. A similar difference of view exists on the nature of the church: for the reformer this was not just a branch of government to be regulated by law and human wisdom, it was the redemptive presence of Christ in the world, the community in whose life God lived. As St. Paul put it, the essential function of the Christian life is the "edification" of the church, by which he meant not the material structure but the spiritual community, the function of which is to bring people to faith and in that sense to edify them too. Such a community is not constructed in a legalistic manner, around the topics of clarity and ambiguity; it is a world of the spirit in which broken hearts are healed, faith brought to life, and it is to be lived in the spirit too. The scripture is to be read not literally but with an eye always to its deepest meanings.[25]

This vision has its own appeal and its own dangers. I mention it simply to say that Hooker's way of thinking and talking is not the only possibility. From our own perspective what is likely to be more troubling than Hooker's legalism, which we in fact tend to share, is his treatment of the outsiders, the Barrowists and Anabaptists, whom he ridicules as insane fanatics. It will not be lost on us that these people were mainly poor or working class, without the advantages of education, and Hooker comparatively powerful and wealthy; these are the terms in which we think, and our democratic allegiance will be with those he condemns, who included after all our own Pilgrims. And, for reasons suggested earlier, we tend to resist the very idea of authority in religious matters—everyone should be free to have his own religion, however kooky it might be, and what is the Church of England to insist otherwise? These people were sincerely pursuing the truth, after all.

But one virtue of Hooker's text for us may be that it stimulates such responses in a context that calls for their evaluation. We too use stereotypes to place whole classes of people beyond the pale of discussion. Think of the contempt that modern intellectuals have for "fundamentalists" of every stripe—Christian, Jewish, or Islamic. These people are not often spoken of as sincere seekers of the truth whose views are entitled to respect, though no doubt many of them should be. On the other hand,

---

25. There are modern analogues to this view. Justice Douglas, for example, is often seen by lawyers as one who disregarded the text and decided on the basis of his "values," but he could be seen as part of legitimate interpretive tradition too, of a different kind from Hooker. He could thus claim that in a case like *Griswold v. Connecticut*, 381 U. S. 479 (1965), which found a right to "privacy" in a Constitution that used no such word, he does not disregard the text, as is usually charged against him, but reads it; though he does this not for its words but for their meaning—that is, for their spirit. This can be discerned only by a person qualified by the spirit; hence Douglas's tone of confident righteousness, his dismissive attitude towards the arguments—to him merely legalistic—of his fellow justices. It is perhaps not an accident that he was the son of a Protestant preacher.

we may be right to think fanaticism an evil, whether it is religious or political in kind, and might well envy Hooker's skill in exposing it.

The question that Hooker at once raises and by performance answers is how one might best think about an issue such as this. Out of the materials available to him he creates a mode of thought and offers it to his reader: one that distinguishes between the way things look now, to those of us engaged in a conflict, and the way they will look to "posterity," namely, those who have come to know what we do not and to see more accurately who we are; one that correspondingly recognizes the limitation of any human claim to knowledge or virtue and at the same time holds out the possibility of improvement by experience; one that speaks to the reader as a person of independent judgment and conscience, whose fundamental commitments must be respected even in the midst of disagreement, and one whose judgment is sought in the matter in dispute; one that respects the individual conscience, yet recognizes deep human capacities for grandiosity and self-righteousness; one that both distinguishes between the essential and the inessential and gives this distinction institutional form, reserving one to the individual mind and to scripture, allocating the other to the processes of institutional life; one that in its own movements, in the very sentences in which it is cast, enacts the values of distinction and comprehension, of inclusion and suspension. The mode of thought he performs and recommends, and to which he seeks to accord authority, is not a technique of thinking merely but a way of being and living, alone and with others. Suppose we were to try to engage in it, and to write sentences like his: What would be the consequences for our minds and characters?

. . .

*The disagreements addressed by the writers discussed in this book can be seen for the most part not as differences within a single language but as differences between languages. Thus to speak about the crown in the language of Richard, or the law in the language of the Nomoi, or the church in the language of the Puritans precludes the possibility of thinking what Henry Bolingbroke, and Plato, and Hooker by contrast actually think; and the reverse is true as well. In a situation like this there is no point in urging people to be "reasonable" in the usual way, because what we have is a competition between different forms of reason, each leading to a different set of results: to a different community, with a different way* of living. What makes Shakespeare's achievement so remarkable is that he can include several opposing modes of thought; but even he does not achieve a resolution. He can go no farther. Hooker reaches out as far as he can in that direction.

There are similar incompatibilities among our own discourses today, especially I think between the ways of using language and the mind characteristic of the humanities and the forms of language and thought cast in the model made by natural science—those of economists, public choice theorists, and analytic philosophers. I think of this difference as an opposition between literary and theoretical ways of thinking. One mode works on the idea that a text has a thesis, stateable in the form of a proposition and supported by arguments and data; the other on the idea that a text offers an experience of mind and language that is not reducible to outline form. Its words acquire their meaning not by stipulative definition but through the transformation of the language itself. The gap between these two modes of expression cannot, so far as I know, be bridged by the use of any other language. One speaks one way or the other. The choice of language ends up being the choice of result, since what is most deeply at issue is how we should think and talk and who we should therefore be. There is in my view no "superdiscourse" that can control all the others. All that can be done in this kind of conflict is to work out your position, in your language, as well as you can, hoping that it will appeal to others. This is what the writers discussed in this book seem to me to do, and do well; in that sense I offer them as models for all of us.

FOUR

# HALE'S "CONSIDERATIONS TOUCHING THE AMENDMENT OR ALTERATION OF LAWES": DETERMINING THE AUTHORITY OF THE PAST

IN THIS CHAPTER AND THE NEXT I turn from the crown and the church to the law, asking how its authority is, and ought to be, defined and created. To this end I shall examine two texts drawn from very different periods of our tradition. The first is an essay on law reform by Sir Matthew Hale, a distinguished seventeenth-century judge; the other is a recent Supreme Court opinion, *Planned Parenthood v. Casey* (1992), dealing with the constitutionality of state laws prohibiting or regulating abortion. Each text addresses the question how far the existing law should be regarded as fixed, how far it should be regarded as open to change.

In doing so each raises an issue central to the working of law in our culture, perhaps in any culture, for an essential subject of legal thinking is the role of the past. The lawyer's main work, after all, is with texts written by others in a past, recent or remote, for which a claim of authority is made. Of course, opposing lawyers will argue about which texts should count as authoritative as well as about their meaning, but both will normally agree that the case is spoken to with authority by some array of texts from the past. Thus one lawyer will argue that a case is governed by a particular statute—or judicial opinion or contract or regulation—the other will argue that it is not, but is subject rather to another set of texts. With respect to each text chosen, the two sides will of course offer competing interpretations, though there are limits to the degree they can reasonably differ.[1]

---

1. In any particular case, that is, there will be issues so clear that they are not worth arguing: one lawyer will have to concede that this statute, however apparently helpful to him, really has no bearing on the case, the other that this judicial opinion, even though

Lawyers naturally work by disagreement, as they argue for contrary results; but in doing this they work by agreement as well, reaffirming the terms in which their conversation can proceed at all. Everything that is not arguable is for the moment affirmed. The law is in this sense a rhetorical system that prosecutes disagreement by affirming agreement; in this respect, indeed, it is coercive, for a court will not listen to someone who fails to make the concessions it requires. To be heard in the places of the law you must speak the language of the law. Yet at the same time the law is a system in the process of its own transformation, for at every stage it is an open question, what must be conceded, what can be challenged.

Among us at least the law in this way always gives some weight to the past—to the way things are, to judgments made by others in other circumstances. The lawyer and judge must not only ask themselves how this case should be decided as a matter of abstract justice, but how it should be decided in light of this or that array of texts, reflecting decisions made by others. Their own authority in fact depends upon that of the texts they interpret. Which decisions are entitled to respect, and how much, and what they mean, are of course all open questions; but they are real questions too, and cannot be simply ignored, without erasing what is distinctive, and distinctively valuable, in the law. They are the central issues of legal thought. It is by insisting on these questions, and making them the subject of public thought and argument, that the law creates a world in which powers are distributed among different actors, public and private, each with his own set of capacities and competences, and with corresponding duties to respect those of others. For in our system of government no legal actor has plenary power, except perhaps a constitutional convention. This fact is an essential part of what is meant by government under law, by the idea of a constitution, and, among us, by the sovereignty of the people.

A central part of the activity of law is thus the identification and interpretation of texts, composed by others in other times, to which fidelity is due. But it would be a mistake to assume from this that the decision of particular cases is always rigidly determined by the particular array of

---

apparently damaging, does govern his case. Likewise on issues of interpretation some arguments simply are not worth making. Not that the ingenious lawyer can think of no argument at all for the favorable application of a particular text—for example, that the "thirty-five years of age" requirement for election to the Senate in the Constitution really means "age of maturity," which is now twenty-one—but that it would be a waste of his time and damaging both to his client and to his professional standing to make such an argument to his actual audience.

texts that bear upon it.[2] The nature of the world, and of our minds, makes that impossible, as the whole structure of legal thought and argument makes plain. It is equally foolish, however, to say that the texts of the past have no constraining effect: everyone who has cast aside certain arguments as not worth making, or advised a client that he cannot win on this or that issue—that is, every lawyer—knows the opposite is true.

In our legal culture, however, there are forces that would override or occlude this structure. There is a tendency in legal education today to focus less on the questions I have identified than on what I would call issues of pure policy: What ought the rule be by which this case, or, more usually, this class of case, is decided? The assumption is that this is the only important question; after all, why should one care what other people have thought, except to the extent one is persuaded by them on the merits? The whole field of law and economics, which has no way of recognizing the distribution of power of the sort I describe, is built on such a view, as is modern analytic philosophy, which proceeds on the assumption that a certain form of abstract reasoning on abstract topics ought to dominate every other discourse.[3] But the true question for the lawyer is not simply by what rule this case should be decided, but how the case should be decided given a particular array of arguably authoritative texts that speak to it, expressing the judgments of others.[4]

2. This is a view sometimes attributed to our predecessors of the late nineteenth and early twentieth century under the name of "formalism," but I myself doubt whether anyone ever really believed it, the experience of law is so strongly to the contrary.

3. On the assumptions upon which modern philosophy of this kind proceeds, the case can be put even more strongly: "It would be unethical or wrong to decide a case unjustly simply because prior judges had decided similar cases in such a way." That assumes, however, the very question in issue, which is whether one's own perception of what justice requires ought to be conclusive, or whether, by contrast, it would be better and wiser, indeed more just, to defer to the views of others. Suppose the argument shifted only one element, for example, to read this way: "It is unethical and wrong to decide a case unjustly simply because a legislature"—or constitutional convention—"has so decreed."

For an interesting exchange on this issue, see Frederick Schauer, "Precedent," 39 *Stanford Law Review* 571 (1987); Anthony T. Kronman, "Precedent and Tradition," 99 *Yale Law Journal* 1029 (1990); and David Luban, "Legal Traditionalism," 43 *Stanford Law Review* 1035 (1991).

4. I speak of the case because the lawyer's life is shaped by this social and intellectual form. She is called into play when a client perceives a problem, usually particular in kind; from this problem she looks to the law, to see what materials of thought and argument it affords. The texts of the law come to life for her as she faces, or if she is a planner, as she imagines, particular problems. The perspective of the policymaker, and often of the law professor, is different: imagining himself for the moment supreme, he asks what rule would be best for society. Of course the lawyer will address questions of policy too, and she must

This is I think mainly a matter of emphasis. Nearly everyone would agree that some respect has to be paid to at least some prior texts. To deny that would be to arrogate all power to the present decider, the present moment—a version of just the sort of despotism it is the point of government under law to make impossible. And it is inherent in the judicial situation that to ask others to respect your decisions requires you to respect those of others.

More deeply even than this, it is impossible to think or speak without according respect to the past, for our language, and in particular the language of the law, is a complex system of meaning made by others, inherited and perhaps transformed by us, which we cannot do without and cannot use without respecting. It has a kind of authority that we at once acknowledge and employ. We are embedded in practices and processes that enable and restrain us, that do much to shape the way we imagine and live in the world. There is no place beyond culture from which to describe a pure utopia. This is inescapable both in the law and out of it. As users of language and inhabitants of culture we must and do respect the past, which has made us what we are and affords the materials of our thought. The questions are, When? and Why? and How far? and on them one should not expect answers that can be clearly articulated in the form of rules or criteria. Such questions do not state alternatives so much as define topics or fields of thought, with respect to which we can hope from a writer not final resolution but the demonstration of method. It will not surprise the reader of this book to be told that the way of thinking a writer recommends by performance is in a sense his real authority. In turning to Sir Matthew Hale's work on this subject, our question will accordingly be, What is the way of thinking and speaking, the mode of life and being, that he enacts and recommends to us?


## SIR MATTHEW HALE

Sir Matthew Hale was chief judge of the court of the King's Bench after the Restoration in 1660. By common consent he was the most distinguished judge between Coke and Mansfield, with an extraordinary career. Born in 1609 and orphaned at five years of age, he was educated by a guardian and sent to Oxford, where for some years he prepared himself

---

be able to do that, but always from a particular position, defined by the interests and desires of her client on the one hand, and by the state of the law on the other.

for the clergy. But he became abruptly taken with another sort of life and set out to be a soldier in the Netherlands. Before departing, however, he was the object of a lawsuit which threatened his inheritance; in working with his lawyer, the famous Serjeant Glanville, he became fascinated with the law, and in 1629 joined Lincoln's Inn. Called to the bar in 1637, he was enormously successful, involved in the defense of Archbishop Laud and perhaps Strafford as well, and he was prepared to act for King Charles, if Charles had submitted to the Court. He was not so much of the king's party, however, as a constitutionalist, resisting extremes on both sides. After the king was deposed and killed in 1649, Hale became a judge of the court of Common Pleas under the new government and served as a member of Parliament as well.[5]

For our purposes most important, he was chair of the Law Reform Commission of 1652, often called the Hale Commission. While he himself believed deeply in the need for law reform, he was in this position under pressure from the radicals to make more sweeping changes in the substance and administration of the law than he thought wise. The proposals before him included, among other things, the establishment of a new county court system with wide jurisdiction, to be staffed by elected laymen; the abolition of imprisonment for debt; and the reform of the land law. Thanks partly to the composition of the commission, which had radical representation but was not dominated by it, partly to Hale's committed but balanced leadership, many of these provisions were accepted but with moderating qualifications. For example, the county court system was adopted, but without the proposed provisions for the election of its members and for its independence from central government control. More extreme positions urged by the radicals—such as the abolition of the central courts and chancery, even the abolition of the legal profession—were never considered at all.[6] Hale was a force for moderation, but

5. For Hale's life see Edmund Heward, *Matthew Hale* (London: Robert Hale, 1972) and William Holdsworth, *A History of English Law,* volume 6, 2d ed. (London: Methuen, 1937), pages 574–95. A striking feature of his career is that he was chosen for important positions by the new government, notwithstanding his ties to the Crown; then, after the Restoration, he was once more given significant power, notwithstanding his service to the Protectorate. He was evidently a person deeply respected by people of very different political persuasions, in part for his learning and in part for his character, including the sincerity with which he held his essentially moderate views.

6. My account is mainly based upon Mary Cotterell, "Interregnum Law Reform: The Hale Commission of 1652," *English Historical Review* 83 (1968): 689–704, and Donald Veall, *The Popular Movement for Law Reform 1640–1660* (Oxford: Clarendon Press, 1970), especially pages 79–86.

not a conservative drag on the engine of reform: he himself believed strongly in the necessity of many of the changes, especially relating to the courts and the land law.

With the Restoration of Charles II in 1660, Hale was made chief baron of the exchequer and, in 1671, chief justice of the King's Bench, a position he held until 1676, the year of his death. During this time he wrote several important books, none of which was published in his lifetime. The most significant were *The History of the Common Law*, composed in part as an answer to Coke; *The Analysis of the Law*, in which he attempted to reduce English law to a comprehensible intellectual structure, on its own principles; and a treatise, *Historia Placitorum Coronae*, usually called *The Pleas of the Crown*. This last has been enormously influential, still affecting how we think about criminal law and the related fields of arrest, search, and seizure, in constitutional and common law alike. It was equally significant as representing a new kind of legal thought, for in this work Hale meant not simply to arrange cases and rules under headings, as his predecessors had done, but to understand them in terms of their reasons, indeed to see them as properly shaped by reason.[7] Similarly, in the essay discussed below, "Considerations Touching the Amendment or Alteration of Lawes," he conceives of the law not as a series of particular rules or decisions but as a cultural process, with its own modes and standards of transformation.

In these respects he can be compared with his Jacobean predecessor, Sir Edward Coke, who was also a great exponent and defender of the common law but whose conception of the law was rather different: as a fixed and unchanging body of principles of enormous antiquity—reaching back, in fact, to the Trojans supposed to have founded Britain—which were obscured by history, and especially by Norman accretions. According to him, the task of the lawyer and judge is to uncover what is and always has been there. Coke said that the life of the law is "reason." By

---

7. See Holdsworth, *A History of English Law*, pages 590–91. Hale's *The Analysis of the Law* was an attempt to schematize English law, on modified versions of civil law principles, in which Hale was well educated. His system, though sketchy and incomplete, became the basis for Blackstone's *Commentaries*. See Holdsworth, page 591. A fine account of Hale's historical work can be found in the editor's introduction to Sir Matthew Hale, *The History of the Common Law of England*, ed. Charles M. Gray (Chicago: University of Chicago Press, 1971), pages xi–xxxviii.

A real puzzle is Hale's reluctance to publish his work while he lived. Whether this was due to perfectionism, to an incapacity to finish things, or to a sense of privacy, it is impossible now to know. For valuable speculation, see Gray's introduction to *The History of the Common Law of England*, pages xvii–xviii.

that he meant not the kind of reasoning from purpose that is second nature to us but a kind of antiquarian research coupled with reasoning by
analogy, a process that in fact enabled him to work reforms in the law,
under cover of venerating its established principles.[8]

The essay discussed below, "Considerations Touching the Amendment or Alteration of Lawes," exists in a manuscript dated 1665, just five
years after the Restoration.[9] Of course it may have been first written a bit
earlier, but for our purposes the exact date is not important; what matters
is that this is not a speculative or abstract piece, pursued for purely intellectual reasons, but a response to his own actual experience of law reform
and its difficulties, both during the interregnum and after the Restoration,
when the work of the Hale Commission was largely undone by the Parliament.[10] Hale's effort is to try to think through the attitudes proper to the
process of law reform and to recognize the dangers that inhere in it. He

8. See Gray's introduction to *The History of the Common Law of England*, page xxvi;
Veall, *The Popular Movement for Law Reform 1640–1660*, pages 66–67.

Coke stood up to James I on behalf of the common law, famously declaring that the law
worked by an "artificial reason" that had its own authority, in which the king was not
competent. For the story, and its basis, see Richard Helgerson, *Forms of Nationhood: The
Elizabethan Writing of England* (Chicago: University of Chicago Press, 1992), pages 98–99.
His central position was that the crown was subject to law, and that this law was to be determined by Parliament and the courts, not the crown itself. Towards the end of his career he
became a member of Parliament and a spokesman for the idea of constitutional restraints on
the crown, to be enforced by Parliament, an idea that has been enormously important, especially in American constitutional thought. In England, this kind of thinking was rendered to
some extent irrelevant by the Revolution of 1688, which did much to establish the sovereignty
of Parliament. Pressure for limitations on the sovereign naturally dissipated, that is, when the
sovereignty shifted from the crown to the Parliament, where in England it still remains.

For further discussion of Coke, see J. G. A. Pocock, *The Ancient Constitution and the
Feudal Law: A Study of English Historical Thought in the Seventeenth Century* (Cambridge: Cambridge University Press, 1957), especially pages 37–55, 170–81, 242–43. For a
general history of constitutional thought during this century, see J. W. Gough, *Fundamental
Law in English Constitutional History* (Oxford: Clarendon Press, 1955).

9. It has been published, so far as I can learn, only in Francis Hargrave, *A Collection
of Legal Tracts Relating to the Law of England*, volume 1 (London, 1787), pages 253–89,
to which all page references here are made. For summary and discussion, see Heward, *Matthew Hale*, pages 156–66.

10. It was at least revised, if not wholly composed, after the Restoration, as the reference to "the King's return" on page 274 makes plain. In this section Hale argues that the
time is now ripe for the process of revision and reform, as it was not during "the late
troubles." "But now things are settled upon their right basis, and the parliament returned
to its original constitution, the season, for aught I know, may be well enough for such an
enterprize." (Page 275.)

Hale's treatment of the considerations touching the reform of law as a general matter,
to which my attention will mainly be given, seems to be polished and complete work. His

does this both in general and in connection with specific proposals. I have chosen it rather than, say, a passage by Coke both because the position it takes is more deeply related to the way we think and because it seems to me to exemplify so well the attitudes it recommends. Since it has been published only once, in 1797, and is not widely available, I shall summarize and quote from it much more freely than I would otherwise do.

IN THIS ESSAY HALE SPEAKS ABOUT the restrictions proper not to judicial but legislative change, which may strike us as odd, for we normally speak as though the legislature can properly modify the law whenever it thinks the prior law unwise, unless—in the United States—prohibited by the Constitution. It is the judiciary, not the legislature, who for us is bound by the doctrine of precedent, and it is with respect to the judiciary that what Hale says will be most directly relevant to us. Yet our legislatures too are in a sense bound by the past, and more fully than our normal talk allows. Think of what is involved in the change of a rule of property, for example, or a rule governing the making of wills, upon which many may have relied; or of the quasi-constitutional status that attaches to certain of our statutes, often passed after great controversy, such as the Sherman Act, the Wagner and Taft-Hartley Acts, the Civil Rights Acts of the 1960s, and so forth. And we are repeatedly faced with an analogous problem in the constitutional field, whenever someone proposes a new constitutional amendment: Is the Constitution a fabric we should touch rarely, and only upon lengthy deliberation, or should the people feel free to make it express their shifting views of things? This was an issue, for example, in the debates on the Equal Rights Amendment, which may have failed in part because of the feeling that it was not necessary to take the drastic step of amendment to achieve the protections it promised. They could have been afforded, it was argued, by the courts under existing doctrine.

Yet, whatever the role of the past may be in legislation and constitutional amendment, it is still true that in America it is mainly the judicial branch that regularly faces the question of proper "alteration and amendment" of the laws. When should judges feel free to change that part of

---

analysis of specific proposals, however, is plainly unfinished, for he does not get to most of the matters he mentions in his introduction to this section, at page 275.

the law, constitutional or common, that lies within their jurisdiction? Or, to frame it slightly differently, when should they feel bound, against their own judgment on the merits, by what a prior court has done, and why? In our day such questions tend to be the subject of political slogans, claiming that judges should "find the law, not make it," or applauding (or condemning) "judicial activism," on the right or the left, and they have been the subject of considerable professional debate as well, especially with respect to the career of the Warren Court.

What can be said, in general terms, about the authority of the legal past and about the conditions under which, and the reasons for which, it is right to alter and amend it? And: How, in what forms of expression and by what modes of thought, should we proceed to think about this question? For however we do this we shall of necessity be claiming for our own way of thinking and talking an authority of its own; in doing this we shall in turn define, in our own performance, our conception of the law whose authority is in question.

These are Hale's questions, and my first aim here is to give an account of his response.

## HALE'S *CONSIDERATIONS*

The form in which Hale works is suggested by his title, *Considerations,* which he describes as the development of all that can sensibly be said, first on one side, then another, of the question:

> The business of amendment or alteration of lawes is a choice and tender business, neither wholly to be omitted when the necessity requires, and yet very cautiously and warily to be undertaken, though the necessity may, or, at least, may seem to require it.
>
> And that I may the more evenly guide myself in this discourse, I shall begin with the consideration of both those extreames, viz.
>
> I. The error in the excess, the over-busy and hasty and violent attempt in mutation of lawes under pretence of reformation.
>
> And, II. the error in the defect, a wilfull and over-strict adhering in every particular to the continuance of the lawes in the state we find them, though the reformation of them be never so necessary, safe and easy. [Page 253.]

Hale's starting point is the recognition that neither of the two "extreames" is possible; that sensible thinking and writing must find a way to incorporate something of both tendencies; and that an attitude of caution is proper throughout. He is thus committed from the beginning to the composition of the text on rhetorical or literary principles, to a text, that is, whose merit, and whose modes of coherence, lie in the inclusion of contraries and contradictories, not in logical purity or consistency.

How is this to be done? Hale proceeds in a lawyer's way—as we would think of it—by considering first one, then the other extreme. But he does not put the affirmative case for inaction, then the case for action, as lawyers would do, but rather proceeds negatively, or critically: he first puts the case against too much readiness to act, then against too much reluctance to do so. His speaking stance is thus always from the center, about the extremes, rather than from the extreme positions themselves.

In this way the text works, as its title suggests, as a mode of considering a situation, or as what I have called a way of thinking and talking. It proceeds from the middle, and self-correctively, focusing on the tendencies to foolishness that it is human nature to exhibit. In this respect Hale's text is a species of a genre to be found quite outside the law—in Jeremy Taylor's enormously popular *Holy Living* and *Holy Dying*, for example, or the *Rambler* essays of Samuel Johnson a century later. Like these texts, and like the legal hearing and the judicial opinion too—though these as I say usually take the form of paired affirmative positions—it works by inclusion, by canvassing the possibilities for thought or speech that a situation presents, trying to bring them all into mind at once. In Hale's case it is not surprising that he thinks this way, for while he himself was a committed law reformer, he was, during his time on the commission, subject to pressures to be far more radical than he would have wished, and, after the Restoration, he was witness to the undoing of what had been achieved by the commission, in what was to him no doubt an exhibition of destructive and mindless conservatism.

### Against Change

Hale begins with the considerations that render "very dangerous" the "over much hastiness in changing of old lawes and introducing of new." The first is that every old law has the advantage over every new one "that it is better known already to the people who are concerned in it, than any new law possibly can be without some length of time." This single consideration, he says, should weigh heavily indeed and should "make people very shy and careful in changes."

We may think that this consideration has melted away with our new technologies of communication, but to say so would miss an important part of Hale's point, namely, that the law has much of its existence, in a sense its only real existence, in the minds of human beings. This is of course still true. Most lawyers will tell you that the plethora of computers and databases, like the phone and the photocopier, produce an "information overload," which in one sense does make lots of new things readily available; but this will mean little except confusion, unless the new information can be integrated into the way people, and in this case especially lawyers, think. The very excess of information may in fact make change harder to achieve, since on the face of it people are likely to fall back on old habits rather than try to master the unmasterable. To change a way of thought takes a great deal of time, as those who struggle with new regulatory statutes, or revisions of old ones, will often attest.[11]

Then:

> It is most certain, that time and long experience is much more ingenious subtile and judicious, than all the wisest and accutest wits in the world co-existing can be. It discovers such varieties of emergencies and cases, that no man could ever otherwise have imagined. It discovers such inconveniencies in things, that no man would otherwise have imagined. And on the other side, in every thing that is new, or at least in most things, especially relating to lawes, there are thousands of new occurrences and intanglements and coincidencies and complications, that would not possibly be at first foreseen. And the reason is apparent; because lawes concern such multitudes, and those of various dispositions, passions, wits, interests, concerns, that it is not possible for any human foresight to discover at once, or to provide expedients against, in the first constitution of a law. Now a law, that hath abidden the test of time, hath met with most of these varieties and complications; and experience hath in all that process of time discovered these complications and emergencies, and so has applied suitable remedies and cures for these various emergencies. So that in truth antient lawes, especially, that have a common concern, are not the issues of the prudence of this or that council or senate, but they are the production of the various experiences and applications of the wisest thing in the inferior world; to wit, time, which as it discovers day after day new inconveniencies, so it doth successively apply new remedies: and indeed it is a kind of aggregation of

---

11. My own taxation teacher, in 1963, regularly thought and spoke of the income tax in terms of the 1938 Code, not its 1954 recodification. Similarly, in applying the 1976 revision of the Copyright Act, meant to be a complete recodification and a new start, the courts have to some degree persisted in reading it as if it were the earlier act it was intended to supplant. For a description see Jessica Litman, "Copyright, Compromise, and Legislative History," 72 *Cornell Law Journal* 857, especially at 859–62, 896–904 (1987).

the discoveries results and applications of ages and events; so that it is a great adventure to go about to alter it, without very great necessity, and under the greatest demonstration of safety and convenience imaginable. [Page 254.]

As the law is by the former paragraph located in the minds of men, by this one the minds of men themselves are located in "time," a process of collective experience that to some degree remedies the inherent limitations of any particular mind, working from any particular point of view.[12] Whenever human beings act, we do so with hopes or expectations as to what our conduct will mean; but the conditions on which we live are such that we can never know enough to be wisely confident in any of our predictions. As all lawyers know—for they spend much of their time with cases that were not and cannot have been contemplated by the legislature—the world perpetually outstrips our imagination, throwing up patterns and contradictions that no one could foresee. "Time"—closely related to Hooker's "posterity"—is Hale's word for our collective experience, the testing of a rule or practice in many contexts, from many points of view; it almost amounts to a collective mind. Whatever has this kind of experience as its author is more firmly grounded than anything we could invent today. This is what makes Hale's attitude towards the past a matter of true respect for authority rather than simple prudence: for him "Time"—by which he means the community and culture over time—knows better than we do. "Time" has knowledge, and judgment, that we lack; its works should therefore be respected and deferred to, even when our own knowledge and judgment go the other way. Nothing could be farther from this than the modern presumption in favor of our own judgments. For Hale we should change the law as if changing a building made by others: "as long as the foundations or principals of the house be sound, they must not be tampered with." (Page 272.)

This conception of time is at work when we contemplate the future as well as the past:

An overbusy meddling with the alteration of lawes, though under the plausible name and pretence of reformation, doth necessarily introduce a

---

12. Compare J. Duncan M. Derrett, "The Trial of Sir Thomas More," *English Historical Review* 79 (1964): 449, especially 470–71, where More says that a common human opinion over time is significant evidence of congruence with God's will. Or, as Hooker more pithily puts it, "The generall and perpetuall voyce of men is as the sentence of God him selfe." (I.8.3.)

great fluidness lubricity and unsteadiness in the lawes, and renders it upon every little occasion subject to perpetual fluxes vicissitudes and mutations. When once this law is changed, why may not that which is introduced be changed, and so onwards in perpetual motion? So that possibly in the period of an age or two, the law of a kingdom, and with it it's [sic] government, may have as many shapes as a silkworm hath in the period of a year; so that they that now live, cannot project under what laws their children shall live, nor the child or grandchild understand by what laws the kingdom was governed in the time of the father or grandfather; and thereby the constitution of the government, the rules of property, and all things that are concerned to have the greatest fixedness that may be, shall become as lax and unstable, as if every age underwent a new conquest from a foreign state. [Page 255.]

This passage defines further the character of human life: it imagines the present as the future's past, as the past's future, and thus sees each of us as having commitments and interests in both directions. Essential to the process of life, for the individual as well as for the polity, is a sense of coherence between past and future, which is always put at risk by change.[13]

13. This passage has resonances in *Richard II*, especially where Gaunt says: "That England that was wont to conquer others / Hath made a shameful conquest of itself." (II.i.65–66.) And in Burke as well: "It is impossible not to observe, that in the spirit of this geometrical distribution and arithmetical arrangement, these pretended citizens treat France exactly like a country of conquest. Acting as conquerors, they have imitated the policy of the harshest of that harsh race." Edmund Burke, *Reflections on the Revolution in France*, edited by C. C. O'Brien (London: Penguin Books, 1969), pages 297–98.

And compare:

And first of all the science of jurisprudence, the pride of the human intellect, which, with all its defects, redundancies, and errors, is the collected reason of ages, combining the principles of original justice with the infinite variety of human concerns, as a heap of old exploded errors, would be no longer studied. Personal self-sufficiency and arrogance (the certain attendants upon all those who have never experienced a wisdom greater than their own) would usurp the tribunal. Of course, no certain laws, establishing invariably grounds of hope and fear, would keep the actions of men in a certain course, or direct them to a certain end. Nothing stable in the modes of holding property, or exercising function, could form a solid ground on which any parent could speculate in the education of his offspring, or in a choice for their future establishment in the world. No principles would be early worked into the habits. As soon as the most able instructor had completed his laborious course of institution, instead of sending forth his pupil, accomplished in a virtuous discipline, fitted to procure him attention and respect, in his place in society, he would find every thing altered; and that he had turned out a poor creature to the contempt and derision of the world, ignorant of the true grounds of estimation. Who would insure a tender and delicate sense of honour to beat almost with the first pulses of

Hale goes on to say: "Overmuch tampering with and changing of lawes, which have obtained by long use and custome, is commonly very ungrateful and unacceptable to the people, into whom their ancient laws and customes are twisted and woven as a part of their nature." That is, we are not only situated, as the earlier paragraph suggests, in a process from which we benefit but the workings of which we cannot wholly understand, we are ourselves in large part made by that process—call it time, call it culture—which creates in us what Burke, perhaps recalling this very passage, would later call "a second nature."[14]

Upon such considerations as these, "the wisest men in all times have been very tender and jealous of changes of lawes." Even William the Conqueror restored the laws of Edward the Confessor; and when the clergy proposed in the time of Henry III that the ecclesiastical law with respect to bastardy be adopted, they were told *"nolumus leges Angliae mutari."* In citing these authorities Hale is himself exemplifying the respect for the past he means to recommend: they did it, and we should too.

In a few paragraphs, reaching over little more than two pages, Hale has sketched out not only an attitude towards law but a conception of individual and cultural life which supports that attitude, and has done so

---

the heart, when no man could know what would be the test of honour in a nation, continually varying the standard of its coin? No part of life would retain its acquisitions. Barbarism with regard to science and literature, unskilfulness with regard to arts and manufactures, would infallibly succeed to the want of a steady education and settled principle; and thus the commonwealth itself would, in a few generations, crumble away, be disconnected into the dust and powder of individuality, and at length dispersed to all the winds of heaven. [Pages 193–94.]

14. Burke, *Reflections on the Revolution in France,* page 299. Compare his famous remarks on "prejudice," the internal effects of living in a coherent culture:
Many of our men of speculation, instead of exploding general prejudices, employ their sagacity to discover the latent wisdom which prevails in them. If they find what they seek, and they seldom fail, they think it more wise to continue the prejudice, with the reason involved, than to cast away the coat of prejudice, and to leave nothing but the naked reason; because prejudice, with its reason, has a motive to give action to that reason, and an affection which will give it permanence. Prejudice is of ready application in the emergency; it previously engages the mind in a steady course of wisdom and virtue, and does not leave the man hesitating in the moment of decision, sceptical, puzzled, and unresolved. Prejudice renders a man's virtue his habit; and not a series of unconnected acts. Through just prejudice, his duty becomes a part of his nature. [Page 183.]
Hale also says that when laws are proposed, they may "possibly please the multitude with wonderful expectations of good and benefit thereby" and all may seem well; but our imaginations and understandings being what they are, the people are likely in the event to "find themselves disappointed" and their mouths will be "opened against innovation," often with consequences most dangerous to the public order. (Page 255.)

in such terms that it is hard to see what else he can say. It has much of the diversity, richness, and completeness of a poem: What remains to be said?

## Human Nature

Hale's first addition to what he has said is the conversion of these "considerations" into principles, as follows:

> Therefore it is of great importance upon any alteration of the lawes to be sure,
>
> 1. That the change be demonstrable to be for the better, and such as cannot introduce any considerable inconvenience in the other end of the wallet.
>
> 2. That the change, though most clearly for the better, be not in foundations or principles, but in such things as may consist with the general frame and basis of the government or law.
>
> 3. That the changes be gradual, and not too much at once, or at least more than the exigence of things requires. [Page 256.]

Of these, the second is the most interesting, for it has not been expressly argued for in the paragraphs that precede it. The idea seems to be that since the changing of ordinary laws is so fraught with danger and difficulty, it naturally follows that fundamental laws ought to be untouched. This is to produce a rough equation between the principles of the constitution and natural law, which, according to Hooker and others in that tradition, is not subject to modification or supersession by merely human preferences. Of course this kind of "natural law" is not universal, for other countries are governed differently. It is rather that people working over time have concurred in the laws they have; and in Hooker's phrase, "The generall and perpetuall voyce of men is as the sentence of God him selfe." [15] (I.8.3.)

There next follows a new chapter, which does not so much add to the first as explain it in terms of moral psychology: "I shall now examine,

---

15. Burke will later build on this, in the passages quoted above and others like them, claiming that the constitution not only works according to the principles of nature—"Our political system is placed in a just correspondence and symmetry with the order of the world. . . ." (page 120)—but shapes our nature:

> We fear God; we look up with awe to kings; with affection to parliaments; with duty to magistrates; with reverence to priests; and with respect to nobility. Why? Because when such ideas are brought before our minds, it is *natural* to be affected. [Page 182.]

what are those humours in men, that commonly breed this disease and instability in men in relation to the change of lawes." Rather than set forth more reasons to be slow in making changes, that is, he will turn our attention to those aspects of human nature, in ourselves and others, that give rise to the disposition to change, that we may "gather thereby a prudent jealousy, when we see changes ushered in by such persons or dispositions or at such seasons or times, though the pretensions may be plausible." He is giving us, that is, a list of characters and occasions that, when we meet them, should trigger our caution—no doubt the benefit of his own experience on the Hale Commission. As Chapter 1 rested on the value of the cultural process at work over time, this one will expand on those weaknesses in the nature of human beings that make cautiousness to change sensible. Again, this is not merely a lesson in prudence: it is a reason to trust the judgments of others—of "Time"—more than our own and thus to grant them authority. His catalogue of human error, as you will see, bears a certain resemblance to Hooker's treatment of the Protestant fanatics. Both of these writers share the sense that our own susceptibility to distortion is itself a ground for respecting the culture and its institutions, which are imagined as being more wise and more stable than we are.

First, some "persons and dispositions" are simply in love with change for its own sake. "The very same itch of novelty and innovation" that leads some to new fashions in gestures or clothes carries such people to innovations in laws as well: "a certain restlessness and nauseousness in what they have, and a giddy humour after somewhat which is new, and possibly upon no other account but because it is new."

A second ground of it is possibly some personal mischief, that they in their own particular have received by the present constitution of lawes. For there is in mankind a passionate self-law, which makes men think, that whatsoever crosseth them in their interest or concern is unjust and fit to be altered. And upon this account it will be impossible for any law to be stable; for laws are not fitted for persons, but for things, and must of necessity displease or prejudice the interest of one partie. That, which may be preserves the right and property of one man, may and must of necessity cross and thwart that which another man mistakenly thinks or calls his right: and if upon a peevish, discontented humour, every man that is crossed by a law must be studying of alterations, there must be no law at all; for possibly that very new law, that such a discontented person would introduce, will one time or other do him a mischief; or if it do not, yet it may do another man a mischief in his concern, and will as much justify him in a new innovation as it could the other in the last.[16] [Page 257.]

An error of another kind is to think that a system of laws can, and therefore should, be perfect. "And hence if there once occur any inconvenience in a law, presently away with it, and a new frame or model must be excogitated and introduced, and then all will be well. But this is a great error; for it is most certain, that when all the wisdom and prudence and forecast in the world is used, all human things will still be imperfect."

And the reason is apparent; because it concerns the manners of many men, which are so various, uncertain and complicated, both in themselves and the circumstances adhering to them, that they are not possibly to be exactly fitted. We see in the concerns of one man, how various his actions, his passions, his concerns are; how they change every moment; what new circumstances adhere to them to-day that did not yesterday: and if the state of things be so various and complicated in one man, how various, intricated and perplexed will they be with a multitude of men! And if they are various in respect of a multitude of men, how various will they be with a multitude in various successions of ages, and the occurrences or emergencies thereof! [Page 258.]

Here Hale pauses to anticipate an objection, natural to anticipate in his time, that surely the law given by God to Moses was perfect? Perfect, yes, says Hale, "according to the use and end for which it was designed." While the moral law of the two tables was and is universal,

yet the judicial lawes, as likewise the ritual or ceremonial, were never in the design of Almighty God intended farther than that people to whom they were given, and no longer possibly to that people than the state of that republic continued. It was indeed exactly accommodate to the state of that people to which it was given; and therein the wisdom of God is not only justified, but manifested and exalted; for it was exactly suitable to the end it was designed. But we cannot say it was fitted, or that there was any need

16. Notice that the basic move by which Hale proposes that one person's claim be tested is by asking what someone else, with different and perhaps opposed interests, would say. This is the heart of the ethical teaching of our law, at work in its central institution, the legal hearing. For this to work, however, the parties must argue: it would not be enough simply to utter conclusory declamations of attack and defense, as Mowbray and Bolingbroke do in *Richard II*.

it should be fitted for another people; for that was not within the design of Almighty God. . . . [I]nasmuch as there be things peculiar and proper to the state and condition of one people, that are not common to the state of another, nay not of the same people at another time; . . . it is scarce possible to frame one judicial law for all people; or if it were possible, yet it were not prudent, because inconvenient.[17] [Page 259.]

This is of a piece with Hale's opening chapter, defining something very much like what in connection with Hooker I called a rhetorical view of life. Hale's effort here is not to identify absolutes or universals or certainties but to find a way to think and talk where there are no such things: where the imagination of man is weak, and the multiplicity of his interests and desires very great; where circumstances vary from person to person, place to place, age to age; where culture and personality take many different forms; where the human world consists of innumerable points of view and observations, oscillating in unseen ways between conflict and harmony.

Thus even among the Hebrews it was part of the wisdom of God to provide for the modification and supplementation of law through the "great council of that people" called the Sanhedrin. Hale concludes "that that law was contrived with most perfect wisdom for that people, and during that state; and therein constituted in a great measure the wisdom of it in that accommodation. But to translate that law to another people, to whom it was not accommodate, were a wrong to the divine wisdom."[18]

The fourth ground of overhasty change is ignorance, since a failure

---

17. Compare Hooker's view that the plain commands of conscience and the scripture, along with those natural laws that are accessible to all people by the exercise of their reason, are immutable, while other laws, merely human, are open to wide variation. Like Hooker, Hale was faced with people who claimed divine blessing for a rather wider range of laws than he himself was willing to believe.

18. Compare:
"It is most certain, the specifical natural law that is given to birds is most wisely accommodate to them by the divine wisdom. But for any man to say, because it is a most wise law, therefore it were fit to be used by beasts or fishes, were to distort and wrong the divine wisdom, by misapplying it to such a use and such animals, for whom it was never intended to be a rule or law. And though the specifical nature of Jews and Gentiles and all nations be the same, yet it is certain, that there ever were, and ever will be, great variety in the states dispositions and concerns of several people; so that that law, which would be a most wise apt and suitable constitution to one people, would be utterly improper and inconvenient for another." [Page 260.]

to understand the reasons of a law makes it harder to bear its pains and discomfitures:

> They think the lawes are foolish; because if they were reasonable things, they must understand them without study, as they do the force of an argument, or the fallacy or strength of a syllogism or a mathematical demonstration, or other: and they think their reason is much undervalued, if it be told them, the law is reason, and the law is thus; and they are presently apt to say, they understand reason, and blame the law, because they understand it not, when they think it is below them to be ignorant of any thing. And upon this account they will become Solons and Lycurgi, and legislators, and frame a law, that they themselves may know and approve because they make it; and as the Israelites in the wilderness they would have Gods that they may see, that may go before them.[19] [Page 261.]

More reasonably, ignorance leads people to attribute to a law defects that belong to its administration, not its substance, or to seek its reform on the ground of an inconvenience that is real enough, yet without understanding what mischiefs this law avoided. "As he that will for every small matter be altering of his house, as he will ever be medling and never be at rest, so he may before he is aware endanger the whole fabrick, while out of an over-curious nicety he is impatient of every little defect." Once people have thought of a new solution to an old problem, they are likely to be "in love with the product of their own heads," and "seldom discover the inconveniencies till they feel them; like boys, that blow a bubble out of a walnut shell, which when it is up run after it with their eyes fixed only upon their bubble, and never consider what ditches they fall into or what breaches they run into in their pursuit, till they feel the damage which they had not prudence or patience to foresee."

Finally, the temptation to change the laws may be fed by the passions, especially vain glory, ambition, fear, envy, and malice "at the professors and profession of the law."

HALE HAS HERE NOT SO MUCH SET OUT "REASONS" why one ought to hesitate to change the laws as involved the reader in a view of the nature

---

19. Again like Hooker, and with Coke, Hale here believes that "reason" in the law is not simply the human faculty used to discover natural laws, available to any person, but a

of humanity and culture—of our knowledge and passions and self-delusions, of our embeddedness in cultural processes from which we benefit but which we cannot fully understand—in such a way as to invite us to have a different set of attitudes and sentiments from those we brought to our reading. Hale in this way seeks to make his reader aware of and alive to circumstances that we normally would pass over without attending to them. At the very least, this text offers the person who takes it seriously a kind of checklist of topics (or "considerations") that he can run through in his mind whenever he is tempted to respond affirmatively to the suggestion of another, or indeed of himself, that the law should be changed. The text can thus be used as a self-corrective meditation, offered to the reader for his own improvement; and not merely of his intellect, for once we start speaking in this way of time, of culture, of human nature, and of the laws, it will be hard for us to fall into the more obvious forms of enthusiastic mistake. In this, the form of the "considerations" is analogous to the form of Hooker's sentences: it cannot be used for the most extreme forms of fanatic or radical change, but it rather commits the writer to a view that life is complex and that his own mind is limited. Like Hooker's own account of fanaticism, it is meant to help the reader protect himself against self-grandiosity, the kind of pride that leads one to pit the certainty of one's own moral rightness against the experience of the community and its culture.

## Against Refusal to Change

But our account of this form is still incomplete, for we have looked only as it were in one direction from the position it defines, and there are dangers in the other as well. Hale brings the reader up short with the following opening to his chapter 3:

> By what hath been said in the two preceding chapters, a man would suppose, that all alterations, amendments, or reformations, of municipal lawes, were wholly to be interdicted; and no room left for it with safety or prudence; but what hath been once settled for law must stand everlastingly without any reformation or alteration; and that men were better to live under the inconveniencies of an old law, than undergo that hazard and inconvenience, which may incurr by any amendment or superinduction of any new lawes. [Page 264.]

---

specialized art or craft, based upon its own particular knowledge, or what Coke called "artificial reason."

Indeed, he goes on, many people are actually of this view. The "motives reasons or temptations" include first of all a disposition, especially in those who have long practiced the law, to "contract a kind of superstitious veneration of it beyond what is just and reasonable."[20]

> They tenaciously and rigorously maintain these very forms and proceedings and practices, which, tho' possibly at first they were seasonable and usefull, yet by the very change of matters they become not only useless and impertinent, but burthensome and inconvenient and prejudicial to the common justice and the common good of mankind: not considering that forms and prescripts of lawes were not introduced for their own sakes, but for the use of publick justice; and therefore, when they become insipid useless impertinent and possibly derogatory to the end, they may and must be removed. [Page 264.]

Similarly, there is in some an excess of timidity, "an over-jealous fear" that inconveniences may result, and "this lion in the way choaks all industrious application to this most necessary business." Added to this is the fear of displeasing those who benefit from the present arrangements, especially great officials whose positions are at risk; and the apprehension that one change may lead to others, "like a little wedge put into a great piece of timber." ("But this may be with care and vigilance prevented.") Finally, the name of reform itself has so suffered in recent years "that men are as fearful to be under the imputation of a reformer of the law, as they would be of the name of knave or fool or hypocrite."

But "good and wise men may and ought to make some prudent essay even in this great business," to support which he propounds another set of considerations, the first of which is that "we are not without excellent and happy examples" of reform: for one, Roman codification under Justinian, which reduced two thousand volumes of the laws to three; for another the success of King Edward I, and others, in reforming English law. Here is a sample of what Edward did:

> By the statute of Glocester he gave an action of wast, where none before lay; and he fixed the jurisdiction of great courts to 40s. and upwards. By the statute of Westminster the 2d, he altered the nature of estates of fee

---

20. As we can imagine Hale in the prior chapters resisting the claims of his more radical colleagues on the Hale Commission in the 1650s, here we can imagine him resisting the views of the conservatives who, after the Restoration in 1660, wanted to return the law to its pristine earlier form in every jot and tittle.

conditional at common law, which bred a great change. He settled the proceeding in ward, *quare impedit,* replevins, writs of mesne; gave *scire facias* and *elegit* where none was before; took away age *in cui in vita;* gave a *quod ei deforceat* where none lay before; took away the effect of a collateral warranty in some cases without assets; gave receipt to the wife and him in reversion upon default; took away essoins in many cases; and made divers other notable alterations, which turned about a considerable part of the administration of lawes; and by the 24th chapter gave an outlet to supplemental remedies upon new emergencies, *ne contingat, quod curia regis deficiat conquerentibus in justitia.* Again, he prohibited the alienation of lands in mortmain; made the country liable to answer for robberies committed; prohibited the new creating of tenures; and limited the jurisdiction of the ecclesiastical courts, and of the Marshalsea and other courts. These and many more acts made a very great alteration in the law, and to very good purpose. [Page 267.]

These invocations of experience (and they go on, down to the reign of Elizabeth) are a transformation of his original image of time: we can now see that the past experience from which we should draw includes not only the system or structure entitled to authority, but a process of change which is likewise, by the same test of success over time, also entitled to authority. He thinks of tradition as containing principles of change as well as of constancy, thus capturing in one image the whole habit of his mind to think in terms of contrary tensions.

The transformation of his image of time is made explicit in the following passage, where, in a remarkable reversal, "Time" is suddenly seen not only as the builder of culture and wisdom but as a destroyer too, a force against which human skill and effort should be directed:

The second consideration is this, that, as all sublunary things are subject to corruption and putrefaction, to diseases and rust, so even lawes themselves by long tract of time gather certain diseases and excrescences; certain abuses and corruptions grow into the law, as close as the ivy unto the tree or the rust to the iron, and in a little tract of time gain the reputation of being part of the law. [Page 268.]

It is not only "abuses and corruptions" that need reform: "there are some things, that are really and truly parts of the law, as necessary to be reformed as the errors or abuses of it."

[T]he stream of things have as it were left that channell, and taken a new one; and he, that thinks a state can be exactly steered by the same lawes in every kind, as it was two or three hundred years since, may as well imagine, that the cloaths that fitted him when he was a child should serve him when he is grown a man. The matter changeth the custom; the contracts the commerce; the dispositions educations and tempers of men and societies change in a long tract of time; and so must their lawes in some measure be changed, or they will not be usefull for their state and condition. . . . All that, which I contend for in the first and second chapter, is, not to render lawes of men like lawes of nature fixed and unalterable, but that it be done with great prudence, advice, care, and upon a full and clear prospect of the whole business.[21] [Page 269.]

## Conclusions

Hale next sets forth, as you remember he did (rather oddly) at the end of Chapter 1, a set of principles which for him emerge from these considerations. They do not surprise us and need not detain us long: there are two extremes, both to be avoided; "if there must be an error, let it be rather in the defect than the excess"; no reform should "tend to the alteration of the government in any measure," and "nothing [should] be altered that is a foundation or principal integral of the law; for these are very sound and ought not to be touched, lest the whole fabrick should be endangered"; reform should be done deliberately, at leisure, on full debate, and, so far as possible, by another of the courts rather than parliament; when parliament does speak let it be with finality and clarity but never retrospectively.[22] The drafting of the bills should be left to the judges, who after all have more of the relevant knowledge, and they should be asked to speak in Parliament too, to explain what they have done. (This is a precursor of our modern law reform commissions, law institutes, and the like.) Finally, this should be undertaken only in times of stability and peace.

Most of this is unexceptionable enough (though there is some special pleading on behalf of his own profession, indeed of himself, in urging such a role for the courts), but it is not especially striking or interesting, except in relation to the three chapters that precede it. It would have been

21. Hale, whose mind had a practical and modern cast, was even more open than Hooker to the idea that laws should and do change with human experience and needs.

22. The American system presents another version of the doubleness reflected here, attributing to constitutional law a very different status from the laws of the states or federal legislation: the former controls the latter, and it is the judiciary that has the main task of seeing that it does.

possible for him to start here, and no one would have felt anything missing; just as it would have been possible for Plato to start the *Crito* at the second point at which Socrates asks his friend "why he has come." As in that case, in this one too I think the importance of the opening material is marked by its seeming gratuitousness. Here Hale is defining himself, and us, and the conversation of which we are part, in such a way as to create a set of understandings, a method of thought and a mode of expression, which can have an authority superior to the existing body of laws— for it is the mode of thought that determines which laws may be changed and how—even in an era far less given to change than our own. Not superior to "the law itself," however, for he defines the law as including the process of its reformation, which, in its ideal form at least, proceeds in the manner he here exemplifies.

The last point, a central one, requires some expansion. It is an apparent premise of most of our talk about law, perhaps built into the nominalizing and labeling tendencies of our language, that law exists outside of us, as the speaker and hearer, in the world, as a social phenomenon. And of course in some sense it does, but only insofar as we define ourselves as external to the community and discourse it defines. Once we recognize that this is our law, either because we are lawyers or because it speaks to us, things change. Law has its meanings in the readings we give it; I believe it has its continued life and authority, indeed its continued shape, through our understanding and acquiescence, and through the texts we make as well. For what is granted authority is not only the set of prior texts themselves but the processes by which they are both interpreted and rewritten (or "reformed"), and our participation is essential to both.

Thus it is that Hale in his context makes plain what we also saw in the *Crito,* that the authority of the laws he discusses is secondary to the authority of the discussion itself, and not merely to its intellectual aspect: to the community he establishes in his text, with the past and its texts, with his inherited languages, and with his readers, actual and potential. Here, in the performance of the text, is where its claim to authority rests; and this performance works as a definition of the "law" it speaks about, just as Hooker's performance defined the "church" for whose authority he was making an appeal.

This text is of necessity, and whether Hale knows it or not, a kind of education of the reader into a particular sense of these things, a sense for which my word has been "rhetorical" or "literary." By this I mean that his understanding of the limits of human thought and knowledge is such that there can be no certainty of knowledge respecting the matters he discusses, and that therefore what matters most is the attitude one takes: recognizing limits, respecting the judgments of others, and incorporating so far as possible the contradictory pressures at work in our minds and the world. It is a way of thinking and being that is a way of living as well, living with the sense of boundedness and imperfection. Truth is not to be found in one voice, one line of argument or another, but in the art of integration and composition which brings them together, for the moment at least, in the mind and in the text.

## Performed Authority

The quality of Hale's mind, working as it does by internal oppositions, might be called "medieval," as Shakespeare's similar habits have been called, or perhaps, as I have done, "literary" or "rhetorical," by which I mean that he does not think of reason as a logical progression from proposition to proposition, cast in languages thought to be adequate to their truth, but as a kind of coming to terms with the inadequacy of such a mode of thought and such a view of language. A train of thought, however true, can often be opposed by another, equally true; the best truth we can achieve is therefore one that comprises both. And as Hale makes plain, each train of thought entails not only perceptions and ideas but attitudes and feelings; the opposition is ethical as well as intellectual.

It may help define this quality more clearly to compare Hale briefly with his near contemporary, John Locke, the great theorist of the Revolution of 1688, who contributed of course to the thought of the American Revolution as well.[23] In publishing his *Two Treatises of Civil Government* in 1690 Locke's main aim was to defend the Revolution of 1688, especially against claims that absolute monarchy was the form of government established by God and Nature alike.[24] The *First Treatise* is a devastating

23. Exactly how much is disputed. See, for example, Garry Wills, *Inventing America: Jefferson's Declaration of Independence* (Garden City, N.Y.: Doubleday, 1978), pages 169–75.

24. They were, however, written earlier and were thus originally more radical in impulse than they appeared to be in 1690. References here are to John Locke, *Two Treatises of Civil Government*, edited by W. S. Carpenter (London and New York: J. M. Dent [Everyman], 1924).

rebuttal of the arguments of Sir Robert Filmer's *Patriarchia,* which roots all government in the power held by Adam over his wife, his children, and the world of nature; this means, according to Filmer, that people are all born into subjection and not "naturally free." Locke's response is a fine piece of lawyering, using the Bible as the relevant text, by which he shows, again and again, that Filmer's position cannot stand on the basis of that text and that it is riddled by internal contradictions.

It is in the *Second Treatise* that Locke sets forth his own affirmative case, explaining his influential view of the origin and nature of civil authority, which is in essence that the legitimacy of government rests upon the consent of the governed. What interests me here is not so much his substantive position, so defined, as the terms in which he articulates and defends it. These have been no less influential, I think, than his political ideas, though to my mind they enact a very different politics from the one they recommend.

Consider, for example, the first two sentences in his chapter 2, with which his argument really begins:

> To understand political power aright, and derive it from its original, we must consider what estate all men are naturally in, and that is, a state of perfect freedom to order their actions, and dispose of their possessions and persons as they think fit, within the bounds of the law of Nature, without asking leave or depending upon the will of any other man.
>
> A state also of equality, wherein all the power and jurisdiction is reciprocal, no one having more than another, there being nothing more evident than that creatures of the same species and rank, promiscuously born to all the same advantages of Nature, and the use of the same faculties, should also be equal one amongst another, without subordination or subjection, unless the lord and master of them all should, by any manifest declaration of his will, set one above another, and confer on him, by an evident and clear appointment, an undoubted right to dominion and sovereignty.

This is the voice of certainty, telling his readers how things are. There is no sense of any limitation in the speaker's mind or in his knowledge, no sense that the train of thought entails ways of imagining that could be countered by others, no sense that his language is in the least problematic or defective. This is the mind that will tell you its first principles, then show you what flows from them, all as though this were an automatic process. This is the conception of rational discourse that has dominated Anglo-American political philosophy and analysis from that time to the present moment—with the signal and surprisingly uninfluential exception of the later Wittgenstein, for whom much of philosophy lay in the investigation of the inadequacy of the view of mind and language entailed in this confident propositional style.

This "state of Nature" is not unregulated but "has a law of Nature to govern it, which obliges [governs] everyone." This law is "reason," which "teaches all mankind" that "no one ought to harm another in his life, health, liberty or possessions." The execution of the law of nature is in that state "put into every man's hands": each person can thus punish transgression, and an injured person may compel reparation by self-help. Such a state of nature is not as it may seem, a fiction, for "all princes and rulers" of independent governments "are in that state"; indeed, Locke affirms "that all men are naturally in that state, and remain so till, by their own consents, they make themselves members of some politic society. . . ."

From this point the argument proceeds in a highly familiar way: in nature each person has property in his own person and also in whatever resources of nature he appropriates by his labor. Nature is given us in common but not to be left uncultivated: God "gave it to the use of the industrious and rational (and labor was to be his title to it); not to the fancy or covetousness of the quarrelsome and contentious."

It is by the consent of people so situated that government comes into existence and upon which it depends. The legislature so established is not free to do anything it wishes, however, for one cannot subject oneself to the arbitrary power of another, and because the "law of Nature stands as an eternal rule to all men, legislators as well as others." This law is expressed in terms of fundamental principles: the legislature must work through "standing laws and known authorized judges" and not "extemporary arbitrary decrees"; it may not "take from any man any part of his property without his consent"; it cannot delegate its authority to others; and the right to dissolve the government for violation of its trust remains in the people.

These doctrines are so embedded in our culture as to seem to us a part of nature; they appear self-evidently true, and far be it from me to argue for what Locke is arguing against, the absolute authority of an inherited crown. But there remains the question what kind of intellectual life this text stimulates. Its claim is to assert in satisfactory language propositions that are true; in reading it we can see how metaphorical its language really is, but nowhere is this acknowledged. And in relation to its reader the text is an authoritarian performance. The task of the reader is to submit, not only to the "ideas" but to the voice and language; and if you argue, to do so in just such a style.

Locke in this way helps establish the mode and style that dominates political philosophy today. But Hooker and Hale and Plato too teach us that there is another tradition, more literary or rhetorical in character, which is interested in the articulation of competing claims, competing voices, and that roots its texts in particularity. This is the tradition we see in Burke, and beyond him in much American constitutional thought— not the Jefferson of the Declaration of Independence, or perhaps even Chief Justice Marshall, but in the work of John Harlan—a rhetorical tradition, rooted in political and legal practice, running counter to the theoretical tradition of Locke, Paine, Jefferson, and others.

The question that divides Hale and Coke, whether to speak as if the tradition of the law were fixed and unchanging, as Coke would say, or fluid, a process of self-transformation, as Hale maintains, is present as well in modern constitutional adjudication. Should the effort of the Court be to determine a modern case as nearly as possible in the same way that the framers of the Constitution would do? The assumption here would be Coke's, that the law is an unchanging grid and the task of the Court to uncover its preexisting requirements. Or should the Court conceive of itself as engaged in transforming its tradition, through cases that work over time to reflect fundamental shifts in culture and value? This is Hale's image—and that of most contemporary American and English lawyers— of the way in which common law works. And not just law: other sources of authority rooted in the past, for us in the West at least, have the feature of self-transformation: language, for example, which is always changing; artistic and musical traditions as well; and for some, particularly at the Catholic end of the Christian spectrum, religious tradition works this way too. But the strain of fundamentalism among some Protestants and Muslims works the other way, to define an unchanging and original authority; and some artistic conventions value not innovation but continuity—one thinks of the Siennese School, for example, with its chain of very similar Maestas running over the centuries, or of Chinese flower painting, in which the effort of each artist is to approximate the same ideal.

The absolute extremes are impossible for anyone. Some change is inevitable, and change always takes place on the basis of what is familiar and inherited. It is better, then, to think of this tension not as a choice between alternatives but as a true tension that animates thought; and it is present with special clarity in American constitutional adjudication concerning the "due process" clause of the Fourteenth Amendment, which provides that "no state shall deprive any person of life, liberty, or property without due process of law." In giving meaning to this language, should the Court consider itself frozen by law and practice in the latter part of the nineteenth century when the amendment was adopted? Or, especially given the vagueness of these standards, should it regard this as a term open to wider signification? If the latter, how is this exercise of power by the Court to be justified, especially when the justices are appointed for life in a system that in general works by democratic majority principles?

The next chapter will consider these questions in connection with the Supreme Court's struggles to determine the constitutionality of state laws restricting a woman's right to have an abortion.

• • •

*Hooker and Hale will perhaps be thought by modern readers to be voices of conservatism, and so in a sense they are. But they are "conservative" in the original, not the modern sense: they believe in the conservation of culture, of the past, both for its own value and as a force for educating the necessary partialities of the present—any present—into a fuller recognition of its own limits. This is the sort of "conservatism" that has been at work in the study of the arts and the humanities from the beginning, and in the law too: a sense that we should make the effort to learn from what others have preserved as valuable, even if at first it seems not so. Not with the object of yielding to the dead hand of the past but with that of educating our own judgment, including our capacities to criticize and reform. The movement is towards a cultural dialectic, of which reform and change is as much a part as preservation.*

*But there is still the question, to which Hooker and Hale may be thought to respond inadequately, How is one to behave and talk in the face of a social evil that is at once radical and fundamental? Sometimes, despite what Hale says and Hooker implies, government itself should be changed, perhaps even a war fought to do it. How might people talk well on such occasions?*

*We shall turn to this question at the end of the book, for it is the subject of the two speeches there, one by Nelson Mandela and the other by Abraham Lincoln.*

FIVE

# PLANNED PARENTHOOD
# V. CASEY: LEGAL JUDGMENT
# AS AN ETHICAL AND
# CULTURAL ART

I N CONTEMPORARY AMERICA VERY FEW PEOPLE would find themselves talking, as Hale did, about the authority of the common law,
or of earlier statute law, as if they were constraints on a legislature
wishing to change them. At most, one would speak of the imprudence of
changing settled forms, of the danger of unforeseen consequences, and
the like, not of the true authority of what was done in the past. One
reason has to do with our understanding of popular sovereignty, expressed in the right of universal adult suffrage: within constitutional limits, at least, whatever the legislature chooses to do it has the right to do,
for it is the voice of the people who elected it, and they are sovereign. At
its extreme this view reduces law, as Rousseau foresaw, to a matter of
human will or preference; it has lost its connections to an imagined order
in the universe and owes the past no duty of respect.[1] For Hooker, by
contrast, a human law, however promulgated, was valid only if it did not
contravene one of the various bodies of law superior to it. The criterion
of its authority was not purely procedural or institutional, as it often is
thought to be today, but its concord with fundamental principles of justice and the nature of the world. These were to a large degree established
by prior practice, for human experience reveals the law that is accessible
to human reason.

Another reason why we do not seem to regard the old law as binding
on a legislature is that we tend to think of ourselves as knowing more
than the past, not less; our sense of history as progress, our sense of
knowledge as cumulative, requires it. The tendency of our time is not to

1. "That which a whole Nation chooses to do, it has a right to do." Thomas Paine, *The
Rights of Man* (London: J. M. Dent [Everyman], 1969), page 13.

imagine a cultural process—like Hale's "Time" or Burke's "inheritance"—that works to our benefit in ways that we do not understand, that is wiser than we are, but to think of the social world rather as a kind of machine that can be understood in terms of cause and effect and, when appropriate, redesigned on the same basis.

The image of law as justified by the will of its author—it is what the people want or the king desires—fits rather well with one contemporary way of thinking about the social world and the economy in particular. Following Locke, a powerful ideology of our day imagines a world of individuals, each with a set of desires or wants that he or she pursues through the facilities provided by the culture, especially the market. The best arrangement is the one that permits the maximum satisfaction of human desires, whatever they may be. The analyst is normally careful to claim his own neutrality on the question, which desires are valuable, which not. Limitations on individual action are to be found not in substantive values, or "natural law," but in neutral principles—for example, that no one should be prevented from doing anything he wishes unless it harms another.[2]

In America the legislative will is of course subject to certain constraints, especially those found in the Constitution. But this document also rests upon the authority and will of the People—though in a somewhat different way from legislation, for it is the genius of our Constitution that the same sovereign speaks in different voices. The Constitution is supreme, subject to no limits of value or justice; it could, if "the People" so chose to amend it, provide for inherited titles, a caste system, genocide, an electoral system that disenfranchised one gender, or human slavery. Within constitutional limits the legislature is in turn supreme: unless it contravenes a constitutional principle, it may do what it wishes. And argument within the legislature is not often premised, I imagine, on the authority of existing arrangements. Their jurisdiction is like their property; they can do what they want with it.

The Constitution itself is notoriously not a self-interpreting docu-

---

2. In fact such a principle calls for many independent judgments—for example, on what counts as "harm"—of a kind that the formulation tends to obscure, in this case by representing them as essentially factual. Harm, for example, cannot simply be what the putative victim thinks is harm, because some people are incompetent to protect their interests. This then requires official judgments of competence and of the meaning of harm itself.

There are of course other strains in our culture, especially in the work of those who imagine humanity with an ecological relation to nature. But this is not the language in which most of our public discourse is carried on.

ment but requires our repeated engagement with it, both as lawyers and as a people. The vast bulk of its enduring and authoritative readings are judicial, taking the form of opinions issued in the decision of particular cases over nearly two hundred years. This is a point at which the authority of the past becomes a real question for us, for we must repeatedly ask to what weight an earlier decision is entitled.[3] Is the present Supreme Court bound by a prior case, even if it thinks the judgment wrong or undesirable? Or is it to be read simply as advisory: here is what some people have thought, after putting their minds to the question; you should take it seriously so far as you respect the quality of their work but no more seriously than any other thought on the subject, say by a professor or journalist or a politician? On this view, precedent would simply be another source of information about ways to think about the case. Or is there a different view?

I want to explore this matter in connection with the abortion issue, which raises it in a stark and public form. One way to put the question is by asking whether *Roe v. Wade,* the 1973 case establishing a woman's constitutional right to decide whether to continue a pregnancy, should be regarded as authoritative and hence binding on the present Court—I write in 1992—which has a large majority that would apparently have voted the other way in *Roe.* It is not simply that these justices disapprove of abortion as a moral matter; they believe that *Roe* represented a serious misreading of the Constitution. What attitude should they then have towards *Roe v. Wade?* It is significant that one cannot really begin to think about this question without thinking as well about the cases that precede *Roe,* with an eye both to their meaning and to their authority.

## PRIOR LAW

As the Constitution was originally adopted, virtually no argument could have been made that it prohibited the states from adopting "antiabortion" laws. The reason is that, with the exception of a small number of provisions in Articles I and IV, the Constitution did not limit the power of a state over its citizens at all. It was primarily meant to allocate governmental power among the three branches of the national government and between the national government on the one hand and the states on the

---

3. This is also an issue in common law adjudication. In this chapter I discuss the constitutional form of the question.

other. The Bill of Rights, adopted in 1791, did not change this as far as the states were concerned, for these provisions—guaranteeing freedom of speech and religion, protecting against unreasonable searches and sei-zures, providing for jury trial, and so forth—were limitations only on the federal government. The states were free to violate them as much as they wished, as was indeed necessary if some of them were to maintain the institution of human slavery, which denied all rights to a large class of human beings.

Only after the Civil War was the Constitution amended to regulate the relation between the citizen and the state, as it had earlier regulated the relation between the citizen and the federal government. The method chosen was not, however, simply to apply the Bill of Rights to the states; rather, the new amendments focused on the rights of the newly freed slaves and other African Americans. The Thirteenth Amendment prohib-ited slavery; the Fifteenth provided that the vote should not be withheld on the grounds of race; the Fourteenth, for our purposes the most im-portant one, spoke in more general language, providing that no state should deprive any person of "life, liberty, or property without due pro-cess of law" or deny any person "equal protection of the laws." What is this language to mean? In answering this question, the Supreme Court created a jurisprudence deeply affecting many aspects of the relation be-tween the citizen and the state.

## Lochner

At first, this jurisprudence was fashioned by a conservative Court, hostile to social legislation and in particular to state laws regulating the economy. In a case that has become symbolic of the era, *Lochner v. New York* (1905), it struck down New York laws that prohibited bakers from work-ing more than ten hours a day or sixty hours a week, on the grounds that this was an impermissible interference with the liberty of the workmen to contract for their labor. Other welfare laws were invalidated for similar reasons. The idea of "due process" that these laws were held to violate was substantive, not merely procedural: however correct its processes of lawmaking, the state could not interfere with an economy working by the principles of the market without a clear need articulated on recognized grounds.[4] As powers of the federal government were limited by their enu-meration and by the Bill of Rights, state governments were limited too,

---

4. David Currie has pointed out that "although *Lochner* was on its facts a notable break with tradition, in the larger sense it was the predictable outgrowth of a long and

by the Civil War Amendments, including the Fourteenth Amendment, which in the Court's view constitutionalized a certain view of the nature of government: the states could not exceed what were called "police powers," that is, those designed to protect the public health, safety, and in some cases morals.

This image of the world was rooted in a tradition, for which Locke is the major spokesman, based on the view that the state existed to secure "property," originally conceived of as whatever one could produce from nature by one's labor. One mixes labor with the earth and water to produce corn, with the wool of the sheep to produce cloth, and so forth; what makes it yours is the admixture of labor. In the industrial economy of the later nineteenth century, as indeed in much political rhetoric today, this reasoning was applied to sanctify what one obtained not from nature by one's labor but from other people, and the institutions of society, by one's superior wealth, power, or skill. The workings of the economy were imagined as analogous to the workings of nature in another way as well, for it was thought that any attempt to ameliorate the harshness of the consequences of the market would only backfire, in the long run harming the very people one was trying to protect.[5]

On this point, the position of the Court was gradually overturned. The legislative program of the New Deal was based on very different premises: that our economy and society were partly made by human beings, properly subject to reform and transformation, and that the health of the economy required a prosperous working class to serve as its customers. This was a stage in the development of our contemporary consumer economy. Through changes of mind and personnel the Court came to support legislation based on these views, at the state and national levels alike.

In the process, the authority of *Lochner* and its kin was thoroughly

---

consistent development." David Currie, *The Constitution in the Supreme Court: The Second Century, 1888–1986* (Chicago: University of Chicago Press, 1990), page 49. He also observes that even after *Lochner* the Court "continued to uphold most challenged regulations." (Page 50.)

For another approach to *Lochner*, see Cass Sunstein, "Lochner's Legacy," 87 *Columbia Law Review* 873 (1987).

5. This argument was partly based on an apparently erroneous view of the work of Malthus. See Gertrude Himmelfarb, *Victorian Minds* (New York: Knopf, 1968), chapter 3, showing that Malthus himself believed in the possibility of effective reform. It is still a staple of economic argument, for example with respect to minimum wage laws, said to hurt the poor more than they help them. See generally Albert Hirschman, *The Rhetoric of Reaction: Perversity, Futility, Jeopardy* (Cambridge, Mass.: Harvard University Press, 1991).

repudiated, the Court insisting that these decisions represented an inappropriate form of judicial legislation, involving the imposition of partisan political or economic values on the legislatures to whom our democratic system assigned authority for resolving those questions. The Court's task, it was said, was not to impose its view of the economy or society but to confine itself to interpreting the limitations found in the Constitution.

During the twenties, while the conservatives were still in power, the Court decided a case of enormous significance for the future development of the law relating to abortion, though at first glance it would seem to have a wholly different subject. This case, *Olmstead v. United States* (1927), held that wiretapping by federal officials was not a "search" within the meaning of that word in the Fourth Amendment to the Constitution, defining the term, as though it were obvious, in terms of a physical invasion or trespass.[6] The main significance of the case lay not in its holding, however, but in the dissents of Holmes and Brandeis, especially the latter, who thought the majority's view unduly narrow and technical. Brandeis believed that the Constitution should be regarded not simply as a set of commands to be read in an unimaginative and literal way but as a text meant to govern our polity for generations, composed on the understanding that its language should be read not restrictively but generously, whether one speaks of grants of power to the national or state legislatures or of definitions of the rights of citizens. A particular provision, such as the regulation of "searches," should be read not only in light of the particular kinds of abuse with which the framers were familiar, and which animated the provision in the first place, but in light of principles defining the abuse in its more general form. For Brandeis the basic principle of the amendment was the protection of privacy. It is not to protect property that the provision was adopted but to protect the right of people to be let alone. When that right is violated as effectively by technology unknown to the framers as it would be by a physical search, it should be held within the constitutional prohibition.[7]

6. For an extended discussion of this case, see my *Justice as Translation: An Essay in Cultural and Legal Criticism* (Chicago: University of Chicago Press, 1990), chapter 6.

7. For a proposed analysis of this case that is neither so literal minded as the majority nor so expansive as Brandeis, see Clark Cunningham, "A Linguistic Analysis of 'Search' in the Fourth Amendment: A Search for Common Sense," 73 *Iowa Law Review* 541 (1988).

## Griswold

In the 1950s and after the Court became activist once more, but in quite a different way from the Lochner Court. Again the "due process" language of the Fourteenth Amendment was read expansively, and "equal protection" was too, but this time mainly to protect not economic rights but civil rights and liberties. To a large extent the provisions of the Bill of Rights were read into the due process clause, or considered "incorporated" by it, especially those that protected the freedom of press and religion and those that governed the rights of those suspected of crime. The most important single case was *Brown v. Board of Education* (1954), holding state-enforced racial segregation in public schools to be a violation of the equal protection clause.

Much of this was opposed as shocking judicial activism, the conversion of neutral constitutional law into value-based politics, but often by those who would have supported *Lochner;* and defended, often in self-righteous terms, by those who would have regarded *Lochner* as a low point of judicial irresponsibility, indeed as a subversion of the constitutional process. Insofar as these two sides were defined by their affiliation with one Court or another, both of them were presented with the same problem: how to disapprove of *Lochner* without also disapproving of the Warren Court, or vice versa.

One of the crucial cases of this era, from the point of view of theory and consequence alike, was *Griswold v. Connecticut* (1965), which held unconstitutional a Connecticut law prohibiting the use of birth control devices, even by married couples. This was obviously, to most of the Court, an undesirable, bad, even "silly" law—but how was it unconstitutional? Speaking for the majority, Justice Douglas explicitly refused to be guided by the analogy to *Lochner*, a case he loathed, but instead looked to the Bill of Rights, most of which had by now been incorporated in the Fourteenth Amendment. None of these provisions, it is true, spoke of birth control or reproductive freedom, or of privacy, but many of them, taken together, could be seen to serve the fundamental value of human privacy. This is an extension of the kind of reading Brandeis gave the Fourth Amendment in *Olmstead.* To make up for the want of helpful language, Douglas spoke of "penumbras" formed by "emanations" from these provisions, for which he was widely ridiculed.

Others, notably Justice Harlan, found in the due process clause itself an injunction to the Court to insist upon the protection of those rights that have been fundamental to our society.[8] To determine these, it is not enough to look within the self, at one's own values; one must look without, at our history and culture. The Constitution chose to protect these rights under such vague language because in the nature of things they cannot be spelled out more precisely. Their definition and elaboration is entrusted to the Court because the way the Court works—by the decision of particular cases, carefully argued on both sides; by the refusal to decide more than is actually before it; by the resulting particularity of the judgment, informed as it is by the ways in which conflicting values present themselves in real cases—entitles it to a trust, and an authority, that a more political, or less disciplined, branch of government would not have. On Harlan's view, the idea that the Constitution should be regarded as speaking in plain English and saying just what it means is dispensed with, just as it was by Brandeis, and for much the same reason: that the Constitution is meant to serve the highest purposes of government and collective life and that these cannot be reduced to a code. Instead, the Court must accept responsibility for judgment, which for Harlan means a responsibility to educate itself at the hands of its own past. His image of the cultural process that is wiser than any person, yet entails principles of its own transformation, is familiar to us from Hale; and as Harlan himself sees, the extraordinary duty and privilege of the judge is to reconstitute this source of authority in his own prose. The line between self and world is in this way blurred, as the mind of the judge is partly made by the very material it transforms.

But this was only his view. There were six judges in the majority in *Griswold*, each of them writing a separate opinion, on a different theory, leaving the law, to say the least, unsettled.

### Roe

Such, in extremely reduced outline, was the state of affairs at the time *Roe v. Wade* was decided in 1973. As everyone knows, this case held that a woman has the right to terminate her pregnancy during its early stages. But the opinion of the Court, written by Justice Blackmun, focused rather less on the nature of her right than on the nature of the interests that the state asserted as the ground for limiting it. In this its method was reminiscent of *Lochner* itself, for the idea of both is that state interference with individual freedoms is invalid unless based on good reasons, spoken of

8. His views are best expressed in his famous opinion in an earlier stage of the *Griswold* case, *Poe v. Ullman* (1961).

by the *Lochner* Court in terms of the public health, safety, and morals, by the *Roe* Court in terms of legitimate, substantial, or compelling state interests.[9]

In *Roe* the Court held that during the first trimester, before the fetus quickened, the decision about abortion was solely for the woman and her doctor; after that the state had a sufficient interest to justify regulation in the interests of the woman's health, for now abortion presented greater dangers to the woman than childbirth did; in the third trimester, when the fetus became independently viable, the state could act to protect that future human life by prohibiting abortion, except in the case of danger to the woman's life or health. The whole process was thus seen in largely medical terms, with a substantial role envisaged for medical advice and judgment. This was to find a source of authority external to the Court, but different from the legislature, in a profession which it was perhaps especially easy for Justice Blackmun to trust, since he had long lived in Rochester, the home of the Mayo Clinic and had, indeed, served as its counsel.

This opinion was widely criticized, not only by those who simply opposed abortion but on institutional grounds. *Roe* was felt by many to be an unwarranted interference with the rights of the people of the states to decide such questions for themselves through the political process. While the Court can invalidate state legislation inconsistent with the Constitution, here there is no constitutional language justifying such action—nothing about "abortion" or "privacy"—and no earlier precedent sup-

---

9. By the language of "interests" here and elsewhere the Court does not merely mean the economic interests of the public fisc: the state has an interest in protecting its citizens, and residents, from various sorts of harm. This language is really a way of talking about the propriety of the state's ends and the rationality of the means it has chosen to pursue them.

One difference between the modern and the older formulation, based on the "police power," is that interests, like rights, can be ranked or graded—as the terms "legitimate," "substantial," and "compelling" all suggest—thus arguably permitting finer analysis. But the language of interests also has a kind of false factual sound, as though the Court is simply asking what is there—"Does the state have an interest?" "Oh yes. I see one."—rather than making important judgments of value; and it is less meaningfully tied to precedent than the "police power" language, which invoked an enormous body of earlier cases, state as well as federal. See the magisterial treatise by Ernst Freund, *The Police Power: Public Policy and Constitutional Rights* (Chicago: Callaghan, 1904).

Justice White's opinion in *Griswold* was based on such grounds: he said that the Connecticut birth control law advanced no legitimate state interest. But thought and argument cast in such terms is likely to be highly conclusory: Why, for example, is there not a moral interest in preventing sexual relations that are not tied to the possibility of human generation?

porting it, except maybe *Griswold*, which was felt to be an unwarranted piece of judicial activism, and one or two cases building upon it. Nor is it supported by the prior practice of the states, which was nearly uniformly to regard abortion as subject to their prohibition or regulation, at least in recent decades. Finally—and for some most important—the form of the opinion was legislative rather than judicial, in that it consisted not of the decision of a particular case, in all its complexity, under general constitutional standards, but the decision of an abstract issue by the articulation of a regulatory code of the sort we normally associate with legislation. Whatever the Constitution may be thought to say about the principles of privacy or reproductive rights, it is ludicrous to think that it speaks in terms of trimesters.[10] And to make rules of this sort, the argument goes, is peculiarly the task of the legislature, because by their nature such rules work as approximations that rest on estimates of factual probability which the legislature is in a far better position than the judiciary to make.[11] My own judgment at the time, for what it is worth, was that

10. Is there authority for such a "legislative" approach in a case like *Miranda v. Arizona* (1966), requiring police to give the famous warnings? Perhaps, but that case can be described, as *Roe* cannot, as a true due process case, in which the Court is charged with the obligation of determining the adequacy of the procedures by which a person is tried. These rules are not "substantive," for they do not say what conduct may or may not be punished, but "procedural," for they establish the conditions on which the substantive issues are to be decided. In *Miranda* they define the conditions on which a confession can be received into evidence. Once the Court has determined that fairness requires a particular procedural protection—say the jury, or the assistance of counsel, or the *Miranda* warnings—it cannot normally decide whether a violation is harmful without supplying the right in question. You can only know what an attorney would have done for a defendant, for example, by giving her one, and the same can be said for the warnings.

11. As Aristotle put it, every legal category will, when measured by its ultimate purposes, in some cases include what it ought not to include, in others fail to include what it should include. This circumstance, caused by the fact that the rule is cast not in terms of its ultimate purposes but at an intermediate degree of generality, calls for what Aristotle calls "epieikeia," usually translated "equity," or the art of tailoring the rules to a particular case in light of their larger purposes. Equitable justice corrects legal justice. This art is by nature judicial, for it is an art of application and interpretation: it has received institutional expression in English law in the development of equity itself, which worked by principles framed with great generality, and in our own constitutional practice, which has a similar intellectual structure. See Aristotle, *Nicomachean Ethics*, 1137b. For further discussion of the relation between equity and constitutional law, see my *The Legal Imagination: Studies in the Nature of Legal Thought and Expression* (Boston: Little, Brown, 1973), chapter 5.

A related point: one way to justify judicial review in a democratic system is to say that the Court is in a better position than the legislature to make certain judgments. It can see how different rules work out in practice, in cases the legislature may not have imagined, or thought marginal to its concerns. It is not, however, in a better position to make rules of general application, based upon assessments of general or social facts and probabili-

the Court was wrong as a matter of constitutional law, though on the underlying moral issue of abortion I was unsure what was right.

More can of course be said about *Roe*, but for our purposes this is enough to suggest that the situation of the Court in 1992, faced with a challenge to that case, was a complex and difficult one. *Roe* established both a general principle, that the right to control reproduction lay within the right to privacy, and a set of quasi-legislative rules, which may be entitled to significantly less authority than its central holding. And the status of the principle itself can be questioned, to say the least: the case was controversial when it was decided, and on institutional as well as substantive grounds; it depended on *Griswold*, itself a case that many people felt to be wrong in principle and method alike. To what, then, should authority be given in deciding *Casey*, and why?

## POLITICAL AND CULTURAL CONTEXT

The context was more complicated, in at least three ways, than I have so far suggested. First, it is significant that the history of the common law, and state legislation, did not do much to help clarify the question. At the time of the founding of the nation abortion was prohibited at common law, but only after "quickening," roughly the point at which *Roe* held that the balance of interests shifted to permit state regulation in the interest of protecting the mother.

Second, there was at work in *Griswold*, and to a lesser extent in *Roe* too, another element, some sense that the legislation was the work of sectarian religious politics. The Connecticut statute was only the most extreme of several pieces of legislation, in many states, that sought to bring birth control to an end, including the federal "Comstock Law," which prohibited the use of the mails to transport birth control devices as "obscene." The roots of this movement were in fundamentalist protestantism, but by the time of *Griswold* the Roman Catholic Church was the major political force opposing birth control. During this era, the Catholic church was powerful in southern New England: the mainly Catholic Italian and Irish communities had begun to come into their own, not only in the cities where these populations were concentrated but in the state legislatures as well. It was widely thought that the prohibition on birth

---

ties. (For an argument in favor of judicial rule making as a form, see Antonin Scalia, "The Rule of Law as a Law of Rules," 56 *University of Chicago Law Review* 1175 [1989].)

control would not have been supported by a majority of the people of Connecticut in the 1950s and that the Catholic opposition made it a crucial issue. To oppose the birth control legislation was to oppose the church, and who would do that? It was thought, in sum, that a well organized and dedicated minority, like the National Rifle Association today, had imposed its view in a way inconsistent with majoritarian politics.

The church's opposition rested on religious doctrine as articulated by the pope, and it was felt by some to be illegitimate on that ground as well: as a kind of partial establishment of religion, or perhaps even as a kind of foreign intrusion into American affairs. Recall that in 1960 John Kennedy's Catholicism was a great political liability; the issue of papal control over the presidency was raised with sufficient energy to require Kennedy to answer it formally.[12] Behind the language of *Griswold*, then, was another current of feeling and opinion, which might be characterized either as anti-Catholic bigotry or as resistance to a law that was felt to impose what are at the center religious views. Today, of course, it is not just Catholics who oppose abortion with vehemence, and not all Catholics either, but there is still some sense that the opposition to abortion is fundamentally a religious movement.[13]

Third, and perhaps most significant, is the issue of gender politics. In *Griswold* contraception is seen as an aspect of married life (sensibly enough since the prohibition in question reached marriage); but the Court spoke as though the marriage was by nature a happy unit, without its own internal political struggles, to which contraception might be relevant. In fact, contraception not only permitted harmonious couples to plan their reproductive lives more consciously and coherently (though, it must be remembered, always imperfectly); it also marked an enormous shift in the status and role of women within marriage and, of course, outside it as well. Contraception was a way in which a wife might protect herself, at least to some degree, against at least some of the consequences of sexual imposition in marriage. For many women, then and now, it is not really an option to leave an abusive husband, as might seem to others to be the natural course, for she may have no way of supporting herself or her ex-

---

12. See *"Let the Word Go Forth": The Speeches, Statements, and Writings of John F. Kennedy*, edited by Theodore Sorensen (New York: Delacorte Press, 1988), pages 124–40.

13. For a view of *Roe* as involving religious issues, see Laurence H. Tribe, "The Supreme Court 1972 Term, Foreword: Toward a Model of Roles in the Due Process of Life and Law," 87 *Harvard Law Review* 1, 18–25 (1973).

isting children, may fear losing the children she has, or may fear for her own physical safety if she withdraws from an abusive spouse. Psychologically she may be conditioned to accept abuse as normal, or in some cases even to like it, in the sense that she associates it with the closest thing to love she has known. In speaking of abusive husbands, I do not mean to refer only to men who beat their wives but to husbands or men of every class and background who believe that marriage gives them the right to their wives', or women's, sexual services on demand. This may be a very large number indeed. It may in fact be that a great deal of "normal" sexual relations, among the married and unmarried alike, are not really consensual on the woman's part, especially if by "consent" one means a choice that is truly free and unconstrained.[14] Contraception and abortion do not prevent imposition or rape, but they do protect against some of their consequences.

This aspect of the social context in which *Griswold* was decided, and in which it operated, was wholly unrecognized in that case. It was unrecognized in *Roe* as well, except insofar as this case spoke of the rights of the woman, not of the married couple or the wife. But the "woman" was imagined as a kind of rights-bearing integer—like the man in the "state of nature" from whose arrangements with other men all political and civil rights, according to Locke and the theory of our Framers, derive—rather than as a person existing in a set of relations that are themselves political in character, relations of power and powerlessness.

In *Roe* the key relation the woman was imagined as having was in fact with her doctor, himself imagined as a male but also as having her best interests at heart; and it was partly to protect that relation that the case was decided as it was. Perhaps unwittingly, but certainly silently, *Roe* replaced one relation with a male, that by which the conception occurred, with another. This relation was, of course, as every patient knows, loaded with issues of power, but of a different kind: it could be with a female, in the atypical case of a woman doctor; and, if it was professionally correct, it was not a sexual relation. To this extent, and perhaps unconsciously, *Roe* did acknowledge something of the unseen political reality it addressed. Whether the Court knew what it was doing or not, however, some women did, and some men too, and this adds enormously to the significance of any case deciding whether *Roe* continues to be the law.

---

14. For discussion of this point see Christina Whitman, "Law and Sex," 86 *Michigan Law Review* 1388, 1392–93 (1988).

FOR SOME PEOPLE THE ISSUE IN A CASE considering the continued vitality of *Roe* is whether the Constitution prohibits the state from passing laws protecting unborn human life. Since the Constitution says nothing on the matter in explicit terms, since this is an issue over which reasonable people can and do disagree, since our traditions permit the prohibition, and since there is no clear way to articulate standards governing the matter that are judicial rather than legislative in form, from this perspective the question looks relatively easy. But from another perspective, abortion laws, like contraception laws, seem to involve the official imposition of religious views, which makes them deeply questionable; and from still another, they represent a continuing effort by men—men in the legislature, in the courts, in the presidency—to see to it that the continuation of pregnancy, in every case caused by a man, is subject to male control. On this view, the idea that women should themselves decide when and whether to have children is deeply threatening to a widespread, if unconscious, feeling that the female should be subject to the control of the male, especially with respect to sex and reproduction.

In *Casey*, this issue shows up with special clarity in a provision of the Pennsylvania statute that requires a woman seeking an abortion to notify her husband. While this provision can be justified in appealing ways—by speaking of the father's natural interest in his potential offspring and the importance of common family judgment—from another perspective this can be seen as a legislative requirement that the woman submit herself to the very regime of private power from which her capacity to choose to have an abortion promises, or threatens, to release her.

The reader need not of course accept my account of the forces at work on this issue, but I think it is plain that abortion arouses very deep feelings and that the reasons for this have been imperfectly articulated in the law or other public forums. Both political parties thought that it might be the deciding issue in the presidential campaign of 1992; in the campaign of 1984 Cardinal O'Connor said that he did not "see how a Catholic in good conscience can vote for a candidate who explicitly supports abortion."[15] This issue often serves as a litmus test of political acceptability, in both directions, and is correspondingly marked by severe distortions and denials. The "pro-life" position is often associated with those who favor capital punishment, for example, the "pro-choice" with

15. *Washington Post,* August 7, 1984 (Final Edition), first section, column by Mary McGrory; *New York Times,* September 7, 1988 (Late City Final Edition), Section A, page 29, column 1.

those who on moral grounds oppose the infliction of the death penalty—and the ironies on both sides are instantly apparent. The "pro-life" position rests upon sympathetic identification with the unborn child but is often—with some honorable and compelling exceptions—associated as well with political positions that resist "welfare programs" of the kind that might make these children's lives more endurable after they are born. The "pro-choice" side speaks of freedom to choose as though abortion were entirely nonproblematic, like choosing some other consumer good, rather than the tragic decision it surely is for almost every woman who faces it. On both sides there is thus significant denial; if each side could admit just this much of what is problematic in its position one could imagine a conversation—unsatisfactory, no doubt—beginning to occur.[16] But often they cannot; abortion is not an issue on which public and shared thought of a high quality seems possible in our political world but one that divides us into opposed camps, creating a political situation having many of the features of a civil war. One question for the Court, then, is how far it should seek to understand the larger currents of feeling and attitude that are at work here, and how far it should restrict itself to familiar conceptions of the issue and to familiar ways of talking about it. Is it possible, or proper, for the Court to shift the ways we talk about this issue to include what is now left out, on both sides?

One other piece of background, of a more traditionally legal sort: *Roe* had been controversial from the day it was decided, on substantive and procedural grounds. It was the object of excoriation by the Republican party in particular, with both Reagan and Bush seeking to appoint justices who would overrule it. Of those on the *Roe* Court only Blackmun, who wrote the opinion, and White and Rehnquist, who dissented, were left on the Court at the time of *Casey*. All but White had been appointed by Republican presidents, four of them by Reagan or Bush. In a series of inconclusive cases, the Court had avoided either reaffirming or overruling *Roe*, though Rehnquist and Scalia repeatedly called for its rejection.[17] *Casey* presented the issue of *Roe's* continued vitality, not so

16. For efforts to civilize the discourse, see Mary Ann Glendon, *Abortion and Divorce in Western Law: American Failures, European Challenges* (Cambridge, Mass.: Harvard University Press, 1987); Faye D. Ginsburg, *Contested Lives: The Abortion Debate in an American Community* (Berkeley: University of California Press, 1989); and Laurence H. Tribe, *Abortion: The Clash of Absolutes* (New York: Norton, 1990).

17. See, for example, *Webster v. Reproductive Health Services*, 492 U. S. 490 (1989); *Thornburgh v. American College of Obstetricians & Gynecologists*, 476 U. S. 747 (1986); *Akron v. Akron Center for Reproductive Health*, 462 U. S. 416 (1983); *Maher v. Roe*, 432

much because its facts required the judgment as because the recent appointment of Clarence Thomas was thought to give the overrulers the majority they needed. It was widely believed that the Court would face and resolve it, but no one could confidently predict how the Court would vote, largely because it was uncertain what Justices O'Connor and Souter would do.

## CASEY

The legislature in *Casey* did not attempt to prohibit abortion entirely but instead regulated it, with a series of requirements: that the doctor give the woman certain information about abortion itself and about the availability of adoption agencies and others who would support a decision to carry the fetus to term; that minors obtain the consent of their parents, except in certain cases; that a woman wait twenty-four hours after first coming to the clinic or hospital before actually having the abortion; and that a married woman inform her husband of her plans to have an abortion. It would have been possible to determine the validity of the regulations, especially in their favor, without addressing the underlying issue, whether *Roe* was still good law. But no one on the Court favored that; all wanted to face the central question.

There are two relatively easy ways to think about it: that *Roe* was right and therefore still is the law, and that it was wrong, and therefore is not. Justice Blackmun, and to some degree Stevens, adopted the first approach, Justices Scalia and Rehnquist—Thomas and White voting with them—the second. Justices Kennedy, O'Connor, and Souter wrote an opinion for the Court, taking a different approach, and one that is remarkable in several respects. It was jointly written and signed, a rare event in the history of the Court;[18] it was largely written, I think, by the justices themselves and not by their clerks;[19] it was without a single footnote; and it addressed not just the "rightness" or "wrongness" of *Roe* abstractly

---

U. S. 464 (1977); *Planned Parenthood of Central Mo. v. Danforth*, 428 U. S. 52 (1976); *Doe v. Bolton*, 410 U. S. 179 (1973).

18. This happened also in *Cooper v. Aaron*, 358 U. S. 1 (1958) and *Regents of the University of California v. Bakke*, 438 U. S. 265 (1978).

19. I have no inside knowledge, but think this is likely for several reasons: the importance of the case, the delicacy of the negotiations required to keep all three together, and the fact that parts of it seem written in distinct voices. It does not read like a bland committee report, nor is it written in the law review-ese that has become standard in judicial writ-

considered but the kind of weight and respect it should be accorded, even by those who disagree with it, under the doctrine of *stare decisis*—"let the decision stand."

## The Authority of the Past

The Court reaffirms what it calls the "essential holding" of *Roe,* that prior to viability it is the woman alone who should decide whether to terminate the pregnancy. Other parts of the holding of that case, in the view of these justices less essential, are discarded: the idea that the state has no interest at all in protecting the future of a fetus before quickening, for example, and the rigid "trimester" structure. Rather, for them the critical line is viability: prior to that point the state may regulate abortion, including in most of the ways Pennsylvania has chosen to do, but it may not take away the woman's right to choose or subject that choice to "undue burdens." In this way they reaffirm the central core of *Roe.* But they do so less because they personally agree with *Roe* as an original proposition than because they believe respect for the Court's own past requires it.

This is itself a remarkable fact. Appeals to the authority of the past in constitutional law are often make-weight arguments, used to reinforce arguments on the merits rather than themselves decisive. To a certain degree this makes good sense, both because the judge will naturally tend to imagine that other sensible people see the question as she does, and because the ingrained habits of the lawyer are to claim that all sources of authority coincide. Thus the judge, like the lawyer, will argue that the result she reaches is supported, or even compelled, by the statute in question, by the Constitution, by earlier cases, by the history of our traditions, and by sound policy. The tension that gives life to the law is to be found, then, not so often within an opinion as between opinions, for the text that sees all these sources of authority as lining up one way will often be met by one that sees them lining up the other way. Thus it is that one often hears arguments based on the authority of the past, or other forms of institutional restraint, by both the right and left, each accusing the other of following their personal philosophies rather than the law; but in hard cases one is hard-pressed (except in the case of John Harlan) to see much evidence of restraint in action. A judge may piously say that, although the result she lets stand is one that she might question on the

---

ing, but has the feel of a text written by three minds, with some of the cracks and chinks still showing.

merits, she is compelled by other sources of the law to affirm it; but one seldom feels that she is much frustrated by this situation.

As a general matter this is not a bad thing. It is a deep part of our understanding of the law that the results in particular cases should not only be legal but just, and this naturally leads judges and lawyers alike to see harmony in the various sources of authority that bear on a case. This shows up in legal argument: a lawyer will virtually never admit that the position he is arguing for is compelled by the law but unjust. To be complete and effective the legal argument must claim that law and justice coincide; and so must the judicial opinion. On the other hand, if law is to perform its function it is essential that it not be infinitely malleable; it must bite somewhere, and compel a result, in an important case, against the judge's preferences, even against his educated judgment.

*Casey* is such a case. Given what we know of their attitudes, there is little likelihood that any of the three authors of the Joint Opinion would have voted for *Roe* in the first instance, yet they now feel compelled to reaffirm its essential holding as the law. They do this, however, not by simply knuckling under to what they regard as an unavoidable command, not as cogs in an authoritarian intellectual machine, but by virtue of a complex conception both of this case and of the Court that it is their object in this opinion to make real and comprehensible to their audience—a conception that bears an interesting resemblance to the views of Hale. This is not a reluctant or joyless opinion; its writers find in their understanding of their role and situation under our Constitution a way of thinking and talking about this issue that, in my view at least, dignifies both it and them. Indeed, it is partly because they would not originally have voted for *Roe* that the conception they have both of themselves and of that case, which leads them to affirm it, has such force and gravity.

What this opinion says and does cannot be reduced to the taking of sides on one or another false question—for or against legal change, for example—but, like Hale's "Considerations," is a complex creation that requires detailed attention. To start with the merits of *Roe:* the authors describe this case in a way that does not commit them to the view that, taking everything into account, it was "right" when decided, but rather explains why, on the merits, the case is entitled to a high degree of respect. They define *Roe,* that is, not as an unjustified or bizarre decision, which they might be entitled to disregard, but as an important effort by the Court to speak to a crucial issue that is entitled to real respect—certainly not deserving the derisory sneers of the chief justice and of Justice Scalia. Here is what they say:

Our law affords constitutional protection to personal decisions relating to marriage, procreation, contraception, family relationships, child rearing, and education. *Carey v. Population Services International*, 431 U. S., at 685. Our cases recognize "the right of the *individual*, married or single, to be free from unwarranted governmental intrusion into matters so fundamentally affecting a person as the decision whether to bear or beget a child." *Eisenstadt v. Baird*, 405 U. S. 438, at 453 [emphasis in original]. Our precedents "have respected the private realm of family life which the state cannot enter." *Prince v. Massachusetts*, 321 U. S. 158, 166 (1944). These matters, involving the most intimate and personal choices a person may make in a lifetime, choices central to personal dignity and autonomy, are central to the liberty protected by the Fourteenth Amendment. At the heart of liberty is the right to define one's own concept of existence, of meaning, of the universe, and of the mystery of human life. Beliefs about these matters could not define the attributes of personhood were they formed under compulsion of the State.

This is idealistic language, and it exposes its authors to the contempt of those who cannot stand that way of talking, but it catches an essential point about *Roe* and *Griswold* raised above, the connection between the law and religion. Not that they see the Pennsylvania or Connecticut laws as simply sectarian; rather, their position is that for the state to prohibit abortion is to take a position on an essentially religious topic, the nature of human life, which it is the aim of our Constitution to leave in private hands. While an antiabortion law may not be a full-fledged establishment of religion in violation of the First Amendment, it has overtones of that kind, for its effect is to preclude an individual woman from addressing this essentially religious issue on her own. The effect of this in turn is to dwarf or limit her capacity for maturation and responsibility as a full human being. On this view, it is natural to see the issue as the Court frames it, not in terms of a specific right to abortion—which is open to the objection that it cannot be found in the Constitution—but as an aspect of the "liberty" explicitly protected by the Fourteenth Amendment. The point of liberty, so conceived, is not simply freedom from constraint, but the creation of conditions in which the possibilities for human life and flourishing can be most fully achieved. Without themselves using invidious sectarian language, then, the Court here finds a way to define what is at stake that connects it with the issue I raised above, about the religious character of the laws prohibiting abortion, and their possible incompatibility with our commitments against establishment of religion.

To conceive of what a legislature intrudes upon when it prohibits abortion not as a "right" but as an aspect of "liberty" not only ties the holding more firmly to the language of the Constitution, it connects its two aspects, the affirmance of *Roe* on the merits and the institutional obligation to protect the liberties defined by the Constitution in a consistent and coherent way. As the first sentence of the opinion, in a sense organizing the whole, puts it: "Liberty finds no refuge in a jurisprudence of doubt." This sentence calls on the Court to determine whether liberty includes a woman's right to make her own decisions with respect to abortion, not in the abstract, as if the issue were wholly new, but in light of their obligation as a Court to preserve the liberties established by prior decisions. This in turn calls for a process of "reasoned judgment," a phrase that the Court will define for us in the rest of what it says. What it tells us now, in the first sentence, is that it will not proceed in the quasi-scientific manner that characterizes so much legal analysis, as though the issues before it could be separated into wholly discrete entities, but with the acknowledgment that for them the judgment on *Roe* is necessarily at the same time a judgment about the authority of the past. These issues are interdependent; the Court thus establishes a mode of proceeding that is comprehensive and integrative in character, or what I earlier called "literary" rather than linear and abstract.

### Liberty

They first focus on the "liberty" aspect of the case, summarizing cases establishing that the liberty protected by the Fourteenth Amendment is not merely procedural but substantive, that it includes many of the Bill of Rights (articulated in the first ten amendments) but is not limited to them, and that it is not to be defined by the specific protections that existed at the time of the ratification of the Fourteenth Amendment. For them the central modern text is not the majority opinion in *Griswold,* upon which *Roe* is usually thought to depend, but Harlan's earlier opinion in *Poe v. Ullman* (1961), in which he urged that the Court strike down the same Connecticut statute. This opinion is perhaps the classic definition of a certain view of "due process": Harlan refused to reduce it to a code, or to specific rules or practices of the past—for the essence of liberty cannot be protected that way—yet at the same time refused to see it simply as the imposition of contemporary or evolving political values. The task of the judge, as Harlan defined it, is to engage with the traditions of the law and of our country in a responsive and responsible way; to defer in all reasonable ways to the judgments of others; to educate, and thus transform, his own mind by full consideration of what others have said and done; and, in a case which calls for it, to make his judgment whether the state has interfered with a liberty defined by that tradition. As Hale did too, he sees an essential part of the tradition in its principles of self-transformation. Conservation requires change.

The very fact that the power the Constitution has given the Court cannot be reduced to rules, but rests on principles and understandings necessarily broad and indeterminate, means that great restraint is essential to its exercise, indeed to its continued existence, for such power will be tolerated in unelected officials only when used sparingly and well. Likewise, the act of judgment must be reasoned, and in this sense justify itself: it is not simply the past that decides, as if you could take any modern issue and see how others dealt with it, nor simply the present, as if the meaning of the case could adequately be cast in terms of contemporary political debate; the task of the judge is to educate himself, to modify his own sensibilities by engagement with our tradition, so that in the end it is neither he alone, nor the past alone, that decides, but he as formed and educated by engagement with the past, for which the Court's term here is "reasoned judgment." The idea of tradition with which Justice Harlan works is not as a set of discrete decisions that are entitled to authority but as a process of development and change, to which it is the judge's task to contribute in an intelligent and responsible way. In invoking the shade of Harlan as their guide, the writers of the Joint Opinion ask to be tested by his standards of intelligence, responsibility, and humility. What sort of education in the law, and our own traditions, does this text reflect? What sort of education does it offer its reader?

They begin, as I said above, by describing the kind of "liberty" that the abortion laws invade, but in so doing they are careful not to speak as though it could be abstracted from the context in which they in fact face it, that defined by the existence of *Roe* itself. As I said above, it is not the case for them, as it is for more abstract thinkers, that legal questions should be decided as questions of theory, as it were out of time and place, but the opposite of that: the case before them cannot be separated into the "merits of *Roe*" and the "obligation to follow the law." Both aspects are before them, and they interact: "The reservations any of us may have in reaffirming the central holding of *Roe* are outweighed by the explication of individual liberty we have given combined with the force of *stare decisis*." This insistence upon the actual context, and upon the interrelatedness of the decisions before them, like their earlier invocation of Justice Harlan at his greatest, enacts a kind of conservatism very different from radical dogmatism of our era: it is a cultural conservatism, reminiscent of Burke's, of which an important element is the location of authority outside one's own dispositions, and outside one's own ratiocinations, in the culture, as this is reconstituted by an attentive mind.

## Stare Decisis

Their explicit discussion of *stare decisis,* to which they next turn, proceeds from the double assumption that some obligation to follow the past is necessary both to the idea of law and to the legitimacy of the Court, yet that the past cannot in the nature of things be followed slavishly. The Court thus explicitly resists the temptation to collapse a complicated inquiry into a slogan, either way, but recognizes that the twin necessities they describe define a field for what they have called "reasoned judgment" and will now undertake to exemplify.

They begin their performance by looking to the other cases in which the Court has been faced with the issue of *stare decisis,* in order to see how this matter has been dealt with. In considering the degree of authority to be given the past, that is, they proceed by first considering the past itself. What they claim to discover is that this judgment has been guided by several factors: whether the case in question has proved unworkable; whether its continuance is supported by reliance of a kind that would make its overruling especially burdensome or inequitable; whether doctrine in related fields has developed to such a degree that the case in question is merely a "remnant" of an abandoned view; and whether the factual perceptions that supported the original decision have changed in such a way as to undermine it. Asking of *Roe* the questions that these criteria suggest, they not unsurprisingly find that it has not proven unworkable, that doctrine has not developed in such a way as to leave it behind—quite the reverse in fact—and that while the factual context has changed, owing to medical advances, it has done so in ways that affect only the trimester scheme of *Roe,* not its essential holding.

With respect to reliance, their argument is more complex, difficult, and important: first, they acknowledge that this is not a case in which people have advanced sums of money in reliance upon a rule of property or contract, in such a way as to make it unfair to change it on them. But this should not exhaust the meaning of reliance:

> To eliminate the issue of reliance that easily, however, one would need to limit cognizable reliance to specific instances of sexual activity. But to do this would be simply to refuse to face the fact that for two decades of economic and social developments, people have organized intimate relation-

ships and made choices that define their views of themselves and their places in society, in reliance on the availability of abortion in the event that contraception should fail. The ability of women to participate equally in the economic and social life of the Nation has been facilitated by their ability to control their reproductive lives. See, e.g., R. Petchesky, Abortion and Woman's Choice 109, 133, n. 7 (rev. ed. 1990). The Constitution serves human values, and while the effect of reliance on Roe cannot be exactly measured, neither can the certain cost of overruling Roe for people who have ordered their thinking and living around that case be dismissed.

This passage connects the issue of reliance, which itself bears on the analysis of *stare decisis,* with a larger sense of the nature and importance of a judicial decision of this character. Such an opinion becomes a part of the culture, they say: it affects the ways in which people conceive of themselves and their possibilities for life; insofar as it is not to be repudiated on one of the grounds suggested, this is a large and deep reason for its continuance.[20] In Burke's terms, the significant decisions of the Supreme Court help shape our "prejudices," the attitudes and feelings, the ways of imagining our world and affiliating ourselves with it, that makes us what we are.

## Overrulings

The Court could, as it in fact says, stop here, but it goes on to consider the two instances of overruling that cut most powerfully against what it has said: the rejection of *Lochner* in the 1930s and the repudiation of the "separate but equal" doctrine in *Brown v. Board of Education.*

With respect to the *Lochner* tradition, the key case was *West Coast Hotel v. Parish* (1937), overruling *Adkins v. Children's Hospital of D.C.* (1923), which had struck down a statute requiring employers of adult women to pay a minimum wage. This case was properly overruled, the Court says, and on the grounds that do not reach *Roe,* for *Adkins* unlike *Roe* rested on "fundamentally false factual assumptions about the capacity of a relatively unregulated market to satisfy minimum levels of human welfare." Even if one does not oneself believe these assumptions false, that does not blunt the force of the Court's point, for it is still the case that to the overruling Court in *West Coast Hotel* the assumptions were plainly false in a way for which there is no analogue in *Roe.*

---

20. Compare the famous remark of Brandeis in *Olmstead v. United States,* 277 U. S. 438, 485 (1927), that "the Government is the potent, the omnipresent teacher."

With respect to *Brown* the Court has a harder time, for if there ever was a case on which people relied in the generous sense defined above, it was *Plessy v. Ferguson* (1896), the case that legitimized the entire structure of racist laws that were adopted throughout the South. The Court in *Casey* focuses on language in *Plessy* which denies, as a factual matter, that the mere separation of the races, in this case on railroad trains, stamps one of them with inferiority. Admitting that the justices may not in fact have believed this—How could they?—the Court says that it is nonetheless the "stated justification" for their opinion, and by the time of *Brown* this factual assumption was seen as plainly wrong. *Brown* in fact addressed that issue head on, resting its result in large part on findings that segregated education injured African-American children. Assimilating *Brown* to the model of *West Coast Hotel* in this way the Court sees it as an overruling that rests on changed understandings of fundamental and relevant facts, a ground that does not exist with respect to *Roe*.[21]

In a final section of its opinion, before reaching the particular provis-

21. I would myself read the language in *Plessy* very differently, as a direct expression, in half-ironic form, of exactly the kind of racial domination the statute in question exemplified and was meant to promote. This is especially evident at the point where the Court speaks of the way the "white race" would respond if by some chance the "colored race" were in power and imposed such separation by law:

We consider the underlying fallacy of the plaintiff's argument to consist in the assumption that the enforced separation of the two races stamps the colored race with a badge of inferiority. If this be so, it is not by reason of anything found in the act, but solely because the colored race chooses to put that construction upon it. The argument necessarily assumes that if, as has been more than once the case, and is not unlikely to be so again, the colored race should become the dominant power in the state legislature, and should enact a law in precisely similar terms, it would thereby relegate the white race to an inferior position. We imagine that the white race, at least, would not acquiesce in this assumption. The argument also assumes that social prejudices may be overcome by legislation, and that equal rights cannot be secured to the negro except by an enforced commingling of the two races. We cannot accept this proposition. If the two races are to meet upon terms of social equality, it must be the result of natural affinities, a mutual appreciation of each other's merits, and a voluntary consent of individuals. . . . If one race be inferior to the other socially, the Constitution of the United States cannot put them upon the same plane. [*Plessy v. Ferguson*, 163 U. S. 537, 551–52 (1896).]

*Brown* did rest, formally speaking at least, on factual claims about the damage done by segregation, but this too was somewhat misleading: this ground enabled the Court to benefit from the prestige of social science, such as it was, and to avoid, to some degree, the charge that it was imposing its "values," for in the rhetoric of the day a bright line was drawn between fact and value. But my own reading is that the opinion rested not so much on

ions of the Pennsylvania statute before it, the Court expands on what it thinks is at stake in its decision: the legitimacy of the Court itself, and its capacity to perform its essential and unique role in our democracy. To discharge its responsibilities and maintain its position the Court must seek to decide cases on the ground of principle, or what it earlier called "reasoned judgment," and it must be seen to do so. "The Court must take care to speak and act in ways that allow people to accept its decisions on the terms the Court claims for them, as grounded truly in principle, not as compromises with social and political pressures having, as such, no bearing on the principled choices that the Court is obliged to make." Essential to this goal is respect for the decisions of the past; frequent overruling of its own decisions would be a statement by the Court itself that they were not entitled to respect.

Where, as here, the Court decides a matter intensely divisive of our polity, it is especially important to respect the choices that have been made by the past. "Only the most convincing justifications" could demonstrate that an overruling in such a case was "anything but a surrender to political pressure." Once the decision is made, it is essential to live with it unless it is plainly wrong. This is the point where the Court comes closest to acknowledging the existence of the enormous forces at work in our country on this subject, referred to above, making it a focus of opposition that has some of the characteristics of a civil war itself. The extraordinary character of the issue makes principled judgment, and adherence to prior authority, all the more important. To reverse oneself under pressure will give the impression, perhaps correctly, that the Court is nothing but another vehicle for political life—and that, though they do not say so, the appointment of new justices can properly rest on purely political and result-oriented judgments rather than on qualities of mind and character traditionally thought essential to the judicial role.

There follows now an extraordinary moment in the history of American law. The Court turns its mind to the way citizens respond to its decisions, especially to those they disagree with. Of course it is easy to support the Court when it comes out your way, and of course many people who disagree respond with simple and continuing opposition or resis-

---

factual grounds of that sort as the sense that this kind of imposed separation was itself directly opposed to the aim and spirit of the Civil War amendments.

I would agree with the Joint Opinion that *Plessy* was rightly overruled but not on the grounds that it rested on incorrect factual assumptions; rather that in it the Court represented and reinforced the specific evil against which the relevant amendments had been aimed, and to some degree for which the Civil War had been fought.

tance. It is not with either of these groups that the Court concerns itself but with those who disagree with the result, yet "struggle to accept it, because they respect the rule of law." To them the Court must keep its promise; for if it does not, but reverses itself too easily, in the end "a price [will] be paid for nothing." The Court does not explicate this point further, but what they mean, I think, is this: they are imagining the moral drama that occurs when a person is opposed to a law yet respects it, a drama in ordinary life that is in fact the parallel of the one they are experiencing as judges. This drama is seen as a painful but also as a good thing, good especially for the character of the person in question and for any community of such people. The reason it is good is that only at such moments is the commitment to the rule of law a meaningful one: when you agree with the law, there is no problem; when you resist and oppose, you are refusing to accord the law respect. Only when you disagree on an important matter are you given the opportunity to learn what respect for the law means and to engage in the moral practice of respecting it. Such a moment is a stage in the development of an essential ingredient of civic character; it is a part of an education, not purely practical or intellectual or a matter of training but an education of the whole self. In this it would be recognizable by Plato and Aristotle, both of whom saw education as the development of the character through testing and the development of habit. A person who has been through the struggle the Court describes will know, as no one else really can, the importance of the rule of law itself; and having respected it against his own inclination, he will be in a position to insist that others respect it against theirs.[22]

On such a view of civic life in general, and of the activity of the Court as well—for as I say, the Court is talking about itself here—the Court is resisting many tendencies of our culture: the attitude stimulated by the consumer economy, and given theoretical standing by certain schools of economics, that reduces all choices to preferences and treats them all as equal; the comparable view in the political arena, that democracy means the collective preference of the majority, however uneducated or biased it

---

22. Compare here the argument of Lee C. Bollinger, *The Tolerant Society: Freedom of Speech and Extremist Speech in America* (New York: Oxford University Press, 1986), that the best reason for the special protection afforded to speech under our Constitution is that it creates a space in which the majority is forced to confront and to tolerate not merely "views" but a kind of social action it finds odious. This is beneficial not for its own sake but because it tests our collective capacity to tolerate, thus contributing to the formation of the national character.

may be; the way in which certain political candidates, especially for the presidency, address the voting public by trying to stimulate whatever feelings will move it to vote for them, however impossibly simplistic the language in which they do so; and, when we come to the Court, the view that it is really just another political agency, to be staffed by those who will carry out the president's political agenda, and that all its opinions are really just the rationalization of the exercise of power. The Joint Opinion resists all of those assumptions, seeing in the citizen a capacity for responsible tension and growth, in the process of law—especially in the work of the Court—a source of education for itself and the polity. It defines the life of the citizen as an ethical drama, and its own life as one too, providing a basis on which one can find possibilities for meaning in our shared life that are worthy of humanity. So read, this opinion enhances the dignity of the Court and the nation alike.

In another pair of laconic sentences the Court puts its central point another way: "If the Court's legitimacy should be undermined, then, so would the country be in its very ability to see itself through its constitutional ideals. The Court's concern with legitimacy is not for the sake of the Court but for the sake of the Nation to which it is responsible." This is the core of the case: to the Joint Opinion the Constitution provides a set of ideals against which the action of government can be tested; these must continue to be seen as ideals, not simply as the political process in another form, or they will die. We should be left in a world that had no way to idealize itself.

The Court thus commits itself to a vision of law as a process of culture that works across time. As they say at the end of the opinion:

> Our Constitution is a covenant running from the first generation of Americans to us and then to future generations. It is a coherent succession. Each generation must learn anew that the Constitution's written terms embody ideas and aspirations that must survive more ages than one. We accept our responsibility not to retreat from interpreting the full meaning of the covenant in light of all our precedents.

When properly engaged in, the law works, as they have said, as a process of communal education, both of mind and character, an essential part of which is the continuance of a conversation based upon ideals. The nature of law is to idealize. The conversation to which the Joint Opinion is committed is the direct descendant of that to which Socrates was committed, which he would rather die than damage, the conversation that assumes that Athens, or America, is a moral actor with a moral career, capable of justice or injustice.[23]

Against this vision of the Joint Opinion is a double argument, based in part on its own sense of the authority of the past and the judicial role. First, it can be argued that the Opinion should not treat *Roe* with the respect it does because *Roe* itself does not respect its own past. *Roe*, the argument goes, was an unjustified piece of judicial legislation that intruded into an existing discourse a set of rules, and a way of talking, that had no place in it. Not itself respectful of its tradition, nor an integral part of it, *Roe* should not now be entitled to the kind of respect it failed to give others. Important reasons why these justices would have dissented in that case—assuming that to be so—are thus still in force: its reaching out in ways not justified by prior cases, the legislative form of its rules, its own disregard of history, and so on. *Roe* is a bad case that does not deserve to have the authority the Court grants it.

This is the argument the Court is trying to meet when the justices speak of the merits of *Roe*, by asking not whether they agree with it but to what degree *Roe* is to be regarded as entitled to respect. Their conclusion is that even though they might have dissented, they regard it as a serious and worthy effort. Of course the reader may not be persuaded by this, or any other argument; but it does seem to me that the Court has addressed it and done so well.

There is also this to say: that *Roe*'s defects, if you regard it as defective, may be to a large degree cured by the transformation of that case in this opinion. It is after all the nature of cultural processes, including the law, to transform the material with which they work. A block of stone becomes a statue, a palette of colors a painting, and, in the law, the trial

23. The Court's treatment of the specific provisions of the Pennsylvania law are for the most part of a piece with what they have already said. Looking to essentials and not to details, for them the central holding of *Roe* is the right of the woman to choose whether to continue or terminate a pregnancy, prior to viability. The choice must be hers; but the state may rationally seek to inform and condition that choice. The provisions requiring that she be informed of alternatives, that she wait 24 hours after first coming to the clinic before having the abortion, and that, if a minor, she obtain parental consent or be excused from doing so by a judge, are accordingly held valid; the requirement that she notify her husband is struck down.

of a bootlegger the occasion for a great constitutional case, as in *Olmstead*. So too, a case one does not admire can become an important and healthy part of the law, as it is reconceived to acquire new meaning.

The second argument against *Casey* is this: one could concede that this process of transformation is part of the law, yet say that it is appropriate only when the case has worked its way deeply into the fabric of the law and our collective life. Otherwise the case should be abandoned. To establish that *Roe* has become part of the fabric of our life and consciousness is the point of the opinion's passage on reliance, reproduced above. Once more, the reader might of course disagree, but to me at least the argument is persuasive.

All this assumes, as I imagine these justices to believe, that *Roe* was originally wrong. From the opposite side it can be argued that *Casey* fails to give *Roe* the respect it is due. *Roe* is a major case that carries the *Olmstead* dissent and *Griswold* to a proper conclusion, protecting the privacy of the reproductive process from state interference and control. From this point of view *Casey* can be seen as insufficiently respectful. In particular, on this view the statutory waiting period should be invalidated as an "undue burden": just imagine what it might mean for a woman who has to drive a hundred or more miles to the clinic, who must arrange for leave from her job and perhaps care for her children, who may wish to keep her visit private, and so on, to have to do all these things twice. And the rationale upon which the requirement rests is deeply patronizing, for it assumes that women cannot make up their own minds in mature and responsible ways, on this of all issues. The part of the opinion approving this requirement seems written by an altogether different hand from the portion striking down the requirement that the husband be notified, where the Court seems to recognize with some fullness both the plight of the woman and what it would mean for the law to tell her what to do in this case. On these grounds in particular, as well perhaps out of exasperation with the very aspects of the opinion I most admire, some critics have been infuriated with the opinion. But this argument does not address the central moral fact of *Casey*, which is that the writers of the Joint Opinion would presumably not have supported *Roe* when it was first decided—a position to which they are surely entitled—yet are compelled by a combination of its merits, as they now see and define them, with their sense of obligation to the past, to uphold it. It is their definition of this drama, with themselves as central actors, that gives such remarkable meaning to the opinion and judgment. The rule of law they describe is enacted in the process in which they engage both themselves and their reader; it is in this mode of thought and life, not in mere statements or commands, that they imagine the law's authority.

. . .

*The trouble with my reading of* Casey, *a critic writes, is that it obscures the fact that law is a product of power:*

> The joint opinion exhibits precisely the mix of respect, care, and critical distance from legal precedent that one would hope to find from judges mindful of their custodial duty to preserve the legal traditions and culture of the past but equally mindful of their right, as well as obligation, to critically appraise and reform it when need be. The result is a judicial opinion that gets high marks from you as a communitarian, neo-Burkean, but liberal-minded rhetorician.
>
> But none of that amounts to a hill of beans if one is of the opinion that a fetus is human life and abortion is murder. If that is the case, Casey, like Roe before it, is simply condoning murder, regardless of whether it is admirable in its moral stance towards past authority. The important questions are not the ones that you pursue, but more familiar staples of legal argument: What are the consequences of this decision? Who is hurt, who is helped, and by how much? Who suffers, and to what end?

*Of course the question of consequences is important, and I have my own views as to how I wish the question of abortion should be treated, based on my sense of exactly those things. It would be open to me to argue for those views, as I have occasionally done on other matters.*

*But here I assume, what I think to be the case, that this is an issue that divides people irremediably; nothing I could say would persuade the bulk of those who judge differently, or vice versa. The central question we face, then, is not how to reach a shared view of the merits of the case—to some abortion is murder; to others, the criminalization of abortion is slavery—but how to reach a shared view of the way in which we can hope these differences can be lived with and addressed. Here too I cannot hope to persuade everybody: there are plenty of people for whom the merits of this issue are so salient that they are simply not interested in any other question than whether the Court came out their way. But it seems to me essential to ask what forms of thought and argument we should respect even in those who disagree with us.*

*With respect to* Casey *I am arguing that however strong our feelings about abortion may be—however sure we are that we are right—we should be interested in another question, or another set of questions, namely, how the Court goes about thinking and talking about the issue; who it makes itself, and its various audiences in the process; how it defines the intellectual and conversational process that is the law to which it asks that authority be given. The more bitterly we disagree, the more important these questions are. It is exactly here, where the divisions among us are so strong and irreconcilable, as the Court points out, that fidelity to the law becomes an important ethical possibility. How the Court, and the rest of us, face up to that challenge should in my view indeed amount to a hill of beans, and a great deal more—especially to those who think the decision on the merits wrong.*

# III

THE AUTHORITY OF THE SELF

# Six

# Austen's *Mansfield Park:* Making the Self Out of — and Against — the Culture

In making vivid the tense and problematic relation between citizen and city, self and world, the *Crito* raises two lines of thought, one public, the other private. The first focuses on the Athens to which Socrates feels such loyalty, and on the character of this loyalty itself, which is in part at least to the idea that the city can be a moral actor in the world—like a person—and that its central aim can be the attainment of justice. This naturally leads one to ask what such a city would be like, and how to understand and define the justice that is its characteristic virtue, questions that Plato addresses at length in the *Republic* and the *Laws*, but to which he suggests answers here as well.

The texts we have subsequently read—*Richard II*, Hooker's *Lawes*, Hale's "Considerations," and the Joint Opinion in *Casey*—all, in different ways, pursue the construction of a public world. While none of them proceeds on the dialectical terms favored by Socrates, to say the least, all present variations on his central idea, that the polity can be a moral actor, and most of them think of its central mission and quality—perhaps what Socrates would call its *arete*, or specific virtue—in terms of justice. Authority is located in public practices and institutions—the crown, the church, the law—as these are defined, descriptively and performatively, in these texts. The person who relies wholly upon his private experience, in Hooker at least, is seen as insane; and in Hale and *Casey* we have minds working in institutional contexts, eschewing the merely private. In *Casey* this is all the more obvious because the effort of the Court is to recognize and validate an experience—deciding what to do about an unwanted pregnancy—that is as private as anything could be.

To make claims of the sort these texts do about the public worlds they define is necessarily to idealize, for no actual society is truly just, or

187

capable of being so. When we pursue the lines of thought laid down by Socrates and Plato, then, we face the terrible tension, made explicit in the *Crito,* between our insistence that our laws—our constitution, our institutional arrangements, our exercises of power—be just ones, and our knowledge that the public world that actually exists necessarily fails to live up to its own ideals (or any other ones either). The problem is like that faced by the historian, who knows that any story he tells will be incomplete, and in that sense false, whether it is couched in terms, say, of the spread of Western civilization or of the colonial system of oppression. History is an idealizing simplification with respect to the past; claims for the justice or wisdom of the result in a particular case, or of a rule of law, or of a political program or regime, are similar simplifications with respect to the present and future.

General formulations—"We are a democracy based on equality of persons"—can function as ideals, and thus as ways of defining and locating ourselves and our motives. As such they are essential to human life. But they are all radically imperfect. Think of the world of America from the point of view of a hungry and homeless person, for example; make his experience—and not our forms of public talk—the center, and see how different things look. The split between the two versions of Athens in the *Crito,* the one run by "the many," which unjustly convicts Socrates, and the Athens that might be, the possibility to which Socrates commits his life, is thus a split in every polity, between its reduced idealizations and the particular and manifold realities that are unreflected in that language. This tension is structural to American constitutional adjudication, where the validity of governmental action, taken by the authority of our own "many," is challenged by comparison with an ideal, the Constitution; yet when we examine this Constitution we find that it too can fail to meet the most elementary standards of justice and fairness, indeed, that in some sense it must. Our Constitution once permitted slavery and laws disempowering women, contrary to what we now think of as our most fundamental values; and there is right now a horrible contrast between the ideal of equal citizens exercising their vote in responsible ways and the reality that a huge number of our fellow citizens have not the material and cultural resources essential to the life our talk assumes they have. Our world, like every human world, is riddled with injustice and cruelty, just as it has its moments of justice or kindness too.

In the progression from the *Crito* to *Casey* we have moved from the margins of the public world towards its center, from the outside in. In this section we shall reverse direction and return to the experience of the self, the experience upon which Socrates paradoxically relies in submitting to the judgment of the city. What are the proper claims of the individual voice, of individual experience, against the authority of law, or any other form of public talk? After all, Socrates' own argument ultimately rests on the meaning to him of the death he foresees; and he repeatedly asserts his own commitment to philosophy, which is his own special activity, against the wishes or commands of the city.

Throughout his career Socrates makes plain that he is at odds with his city and his culture in a way that forces on the reader the question, How is one to think of such a relation? What weight is one to give one's own views, one's own experience, when these run contrary to those of one's world? No thoughtful person would say that everyone's values are just as good as everyone else's, or that you should simply try to gratify your various wishes as fully as possible to the extent you can do so; likewise, no one, except certain tyrants, would say that you are simply to do what you are told and to give no weight to your own thought and judgment. What is one to do, then, about the sense that there is an imperfect fit between what one is told and what one sees, between what one is supposed to think and what one actually thinks? When, and how, does one see this as calling for submission or education on one's own part, and when, and how, as calling for resistance and the assertion of the self? How, in particular, is one to address such questions with a lively sense of the fact that what we call our "selves" are not independent integers but are given much of their identity and form by the very language and culture we hope to criticize?

The whole career of the Platonic Socrates is a sustained answer to these questions, and we have already seen some of its parts. One is the double idea that human beings know different things and that knowledge should be respected. By its nature, he says, knowledge belongs to the one or the few, against the mistaken views of the many. Knowledge in this way becomes a principle of cultural criticism: if one has knowledge, one should insist on it against the mere opinions of others. But what counts as knowledge? Socrates himself knows little or nothing, or so he says, and knowledge as an actual ground of present judgment or action, though not as an ideal, thus drops away. This in turn brings into play the other central ingredient of the solution, the Socratic conception of dialectic. This is a kind of conversation, between two people, that begins in acknowledged ignorance and seeks refutation of one's own false beliefs. This mode of thought and life is a way of recognizing that we are ourselves made by the very cultures we wish to criticize, and that there is therefore no place outside the world from which to examine it—for the world is within us. Dialectic works by establishing a community of two, to which all our loyalties extend; its very function is to counter the larger world; it is thus a kind of groping in the dark, an activity in which both of us try, together, to come to a clearer understanding of what is right, knowing that the instruments by which we do so, our minds, are radically flawed.

One way to address the tension between self and world is to focus on the world, and ask whether it might be changed to incorporate what it now leaves out or suppresses, and if so how this might be done. What voices, what experiences, what truths and values, are excluded from our public discourse? In the context of the abortion case, for example, much has been built on this ground by scholars who argue that the discourse of the law imperfectly represents the experience of women in pregnancy, childbirth, and motherhood.[1]

But the question can be asked not about the world but about the individual, which is how Socrates presents it, and it is this version of the issue I wish to pursue here. To do so I shall turn to a text, Jane Austen's *Mansfield Park,* that has little to do with the law but much to do with our concerns, for it is at its center about the authority of the culture, of the family—especially the father—and of the self.

## A First Reading

I shall begin by telling the story of the novel as I first understood it. This is a summary not so much of "the novel" as of one, rather severely limited, understanding of it. While it may be of use to the reader in recalling her own reading of the novel, or in giving her a sketch of it if she has not read it, it may also appear, like most such summaries, flat and dull. This has its own significance; it can be taken as pointing to what is not flat and dull in the experience the novel offers.

Mansfield Park is the name of a grand country estate belonging to Sir Thomas Bertram, a wealthy man who represents the county in Parlia-

---

1. See, for example, Marie Ashe, "Zig-Zag Stitching and the Seamless Web: Thoughts on 'Reproduction' and the Law," 13 *Nova Law Review* 355 (1989); Teresa Godwin Phelps,

ment. His wife, Lady Bertram, has two sisters: Mrs. Norris, at first the wife and then the widow of the local clergyman—to whom Sir Thomas had given a clerical living—and Mrs. Price, who married a lieutenant in the navy who has since had little success in the world. Mrs. Price has many children and few resources; at the suggestion of Mrs. Norris, Sir Thomas and Lady Bertram agree that one of the Price children shall be brought to Mansfield Park, to be raised by them. Fanny, our heroine, is chosen, and at the age of nine she leaves her family for this strange and grand world.

She has four cousins: Tom, the eldest, who will become Sir Thomas himself one day; Edmund, the second, who is destined for the clergy, a far more modest position in the world; and two daughters, Maria and Julia, only two or three years older than Fanny. Like all women in this class and world, they will determine their station in life mainly by their marriages.

Fanny is timid and frightened. At Mansfield her uncle is a remote and imperious presence; her Aunt Bertram is wholly indolent and uninterested in anything beyond her own comfort; her Aunt Norris is a perpetual scold; Tom teases or ignores her; the girls treat her with disrespect and contempt; only Edmund shows her kindness, whenever he is home from Eton and Oxford, but this is hardly enough to give her a sense of confidence in her own value.

The main action of the novel begins a few years after Fanny's arrival, when Maria and Julia are of an age to be looking for husbands, and Edmund is about to take orders as a clergyman. It is not emphasized, and hardly recognized by anyone, but this is the moment at which the family—which is in this book always represented as stable and immutable, as it would naturally appear to a child—will undergo great transformation, as the children variously depart to other lives. Just at this moment two more people are added to the neighborhood, Mary and Henry Crawford. They are the brother and sister of Mrs. Grant, the wife of the clergyman who has taken the place of Mr. Norris. These two are charming, energetic, and manipulative, and cause considerable excitement and distress.

The main theme of the novel is Fanny's growth to maturity. She is by disposition timid and quiet, apparently the weakest person in the family, but she gradually develops the strength to make judgments of her own

---

"The Sound of Silence Breaking: Catholic Women, Abortion, and the Law," 59 *Tennessee Law Review* 547 (1992); and Mary F. White, "Choice," 59 *Tennessee Law Review* 571 (1992).

and stand by them. There are three major stages in her progress, the first occurring when all the young people visit the estate of Sotherton, held by a Mr. Rushworth to whom Maria has just become engaged. Though Fanny tires quickly and must spend much of the day resting on a bench, she can see what no one else clearly can, that Henry Crawford is flirting successfully—in this world a serious matter, for flirting can arouse expectations so strong as to amount to commitment—not only with Julia but Maria, and that bitter envy is developing between the two sisters; that Mr. Rushworth is a fool; and that Edmund is attracted to Mary Crawford, despite her lapses of taste and occasional coarseness of mind. Fanny can do nothing; but she can observe.

The second stage begins when Sir Thomas has to go to the West Indies to look after some property he has there, incurring an absence of a year. While he is gone the young people decide to put on a play, over the objections of Edmund, who thinks the project at best indecorous and, in his father's absence, wrong. Lady Bertram makes no objection, so long as the young people do "nothing improper," and Mrs. Norris favors the idea, for it both enables her to manage things and because she has hopes that this will further Julia's chances of captivating Henry.

The play chosen, *Lovers' Vows,* presents serious issues of decorum, for in it one of the young women (the role taken by Mary) must be more than decently forward in attracting the attentions of a young man (the role reluctantly taken by Edmund); one knows that Sir Thomas would never approve. More seriously than this, the roles of two other lovers are played by Henry and Maria, who is of course engaged to Mr. Rushworth. In the course of their rehearsals, Henry continues his flirtation to the point of raising her hopes that he will ask her to break her engagement and marry him. But he has no such idea. He is merely trifling with her feelings to gratify his own. Fanny alone refuses to take a part in the play, even when importuned by others. She does this partly out of timidity, but partly as well out of her sense that the whole thing is deeply wrong. Just as the final rehearsals are beginning, Sir Thomas comes home unexpectedly; the instant they hear the news that he is among them once more, everyone knows they have done badly. Fanny's judgment is thus confirmed by that of Sir Thomas, the moral authority of the house; and now, for the first time, he begins to take an interest in her, protecting her from Mrs. Norris and promoting her social life.

The last half of the book consists of Edmund's efforts to persuade Mary to marry him, and Henry's attempts on Fanny. At first Henry means only to trifle—as he tells his sister, "to make Fanny Price fall in love with me"; later, however, he means to marry her, and offers her his hand. Fanny, who is all this time secretly in love with Edmund, to everyone's astonishment and disappointment refuses. Sir Thomas turns the full force of his will and anger on her, accusing her of ingratitude in failing to accept such an offer; even Edmund tries to win her over, at the same time making clear that his heart belongs to Mary Crawford. At the critical moment Fanny returns to her original home, in Portsmouth, which is crowded, noisy, ill-mannered, and, to one of her sensibilities, unendurable. Crawford comes to Portsmouth and presses his suit still further, but she resists again, at least for the moment.

Back in London, while waiting for Fanny to soften, Henry takes up his flirtation with Maria once more, even though she is now married, and this time with more startling effects. In an impulse of crazed infatuation she leaves her husband, joining Crawford and creating a public scandal. In her letters to Fanny Mary tries to make light of what he has done, revealing her character in a way that breaks her hold on Edmund.

At the end Fanny is wholly justified. Sir Thomas is apologetic and remorseful, understanding that he has raised none of his children well, and sees Fanny's value as never before; Edmund too sees her with new eyes and marries her. She returns to Mansfield, not to the great house, but to the handsome home that belongs to Edmund's living, and to a future of her own making. Having begun as weak and frail, Fanny ends by being the only strong person in the family, almost the only healthy one; she becomes the center on which all the others depend.

THERE ARE SEVERAL DIFFICULTIES with the novel so construed that have led many readers to think less of it than of Austen's other work. To begin with the heroine: Fanny is at once too mousy and too perfect to interest a modern reader. She seems never to be wrong on any question of morals or manners, which makes her boring;[2] worse, she is to the end a person of reduced vitality and energy, the soul of timidity in fact. Mary Crawford

2. This is not quite true: She is wrong in calling Mary Crawford "cruel" (page 442), for example. (All references are to Jane Austen, Mansfield Park, edited by Tony Tanner [London: Penguin Books, 1966].)

is by contrast much more promising as a heroine: full of charm and wit and fun, all of which Fanny entirely lacks, and with the interesting addition that she has flaws both of perception and attitude. The novel could tell the story of her life and correction, which would be far more interesting than Fanny's moral vindication.

One way to understand Jane Austen's choice of Fanny as her heroine is to see her as one of a series of protagonists. Austen begins with Lizzie in *Pride and Prejudice,* full of wit and charm and sprightliness, perhaps the most pleasing of all Austen's characters. Yet as that novel itself makes plain—especially in recognizing that the witty and amusing Mr. Bennett is in fact an isolated and irresponsible man, a deep failure both as a father and a person, and in showing Lizzie to have tendencies that way herself— there is a danger in wittiness and charm itself, if these are unconnected with other qualities. *Mansfield Park* can be read as an exploration of this moral and psychological problem, only hinted at in the earlier book; indeed, as something of an exercise in self-correction. One can imagine Austen wondering whether she had not misled her reader and herself into too uncritical a pleasure in Lizzie's wit. Now it is Mary who has the charming qualities of Lizzie, Fanny none of them. By this I think Austen is telling herself, and her reader, not to be captivated by mere vivacity and energy, for unless they are connected with what Austen might call virtue or "principle"—and what we, more psychologically, might call a central and guiding self—these qualities amount to nothing.[3] The book can be read, then, as testing both Austen's and the reader's susceptibility to a certain sort of charm. On this reading the feeling that Fanny is too dull and that Mary would be a more pleasing and fun companion—a better date, as my male students occasionally have put it—is not an accidental

---

3. In *Emma* the series continues, for here we do have a charming, beautiful, witty heroine, yet deeply flawed by selfishness, who is corrected by her experience. This is the book one imagines being written about Mary Crawford; but *Mansfield Park* raises the bleak possibility that Mary simply cannot be corrected.

Another parallel exists, with *Persuasion.* There Anne Elliot is asked by a young navy lieutenant, whom she loves, to marry him, but on the advice of an older friend she refuses, since he has no money and most uncertain prospects. As it happens, he later has a successful career: the marriage would have been fine, and Anne is left to regret her choice in solitude until chance brings the two together somewhat later in life. In *Mansfield Park* Fanny's mother faced a similar choice and decided the other way, but with opposite consequences: her husband never advanced, and she paid the price of what is now defined as her rashness. Again, *Mansfield Park* presents the bleak version of a theme at work in another, more optimistic, story.

defect but part of the aesthetic and moral structure of the book. Austen means to stimulate just that attitude, so that it may be corrected.

This leaves open the question whether it is corrected or not, and judging by their comments many readers find that it is not. Fanny for them is just as unsatisfactory at the end as she was at the beginning, too much of a goody-goody.[4] In fact her marriage to Edmund confirms this view, for he is revealed to be a bit of a dullard himself. He is helpful and kind to Fanny at the beginning and thus a source of much that is good in her; but as a mature figure, he is stupid in his reading of Mary Crawford and quite without wit or charm. He does of course come to see both Mary and Fanny more nearly as the reader does, but there remains something unsatisfactory about the ending. We do not enter as wholly and happily into this marriage as we do, say, the one between Lizzie and Darcy, or Emma and Mr. Knightley. There is an element of distance, or misfocus, which still needs an explanation.

A related problem is presented by the narrator's observation about Henry Crawford, towards the end, that "could he have been satisfied with the conquest of one amiable woman's affections," there would have been "every probability of success and felicity" for him. "Would he have persevered, and uprightly, Fanny must have been his reward—and a reward very voluntarily bestowed—within a reasonable period from Edmund's marrying Mary." (Page 451.) These remarks seem to undo the whole basis on which Fanny, and the reader, have proceeded, namely, that both Henry and Mary are simply too selfish and empty to be capable of the kind of feeling and action that a marriage with either Fanny or Edmund would require. We have been led to think Fanny right in regarding a marriage with Henry as wholly impossible. And the narrator's attitude is troubling for an additional reason, for here she seems to look only from Crawford's point of view and to erase the sense of what marriage with such a person

---

4. The strongest statement of this position I know of appears in Kingsley Amis, "What Became of Jane Austen?" the opening essay in a book of that name. For him Sir Thomas is a "humane and high principled man whose defects of egotism and a kind of laziness . . . betray him into inhumanity"; Henry and Mary are "good fun," especially compared to Edmund and Fanny, who are "morally detestable"; Edmund is guilty of a "narrow and unreflecting pomposity," especially with respect to the theatricals; Fanny, lacking "self-knowledge, generosity, and humility," is a "monster of complacency and pride, who, under a cloak of cringing self-abasement, dominates and gives meaning to the novel." Kingsley Amis, *What Became of Jane Austen? and Other Questions* (London: Cape, 1970), pages 14–16.

would mean to Fanny. Are we really to take it that we are being told, against virtually everything else in the book, that Crawford was capable of deep amendment? Or, on the other hand, that a marriage with him would nonetheless have been a good thing for Fanny? Or is the narrator asking us to regard Fanny simply as an object that Crawford succeeds or fails to get?

One final puzzle: when she is at Portsmouth, visiting her family, Fanny is overwhelmed by the lack of order and decorum, by what she feels to be the noise and slovenliness of the place. It is easy to read her response as fastidious disdain, or perhaps as simply undue sensitivity to bustle. She is like the princess and the pea, unable to bear what others have to face all the time. And Fanny's reflections do not help:

> [S]he could think of nothing but Mansfield, its beloved inmates, its happy ways. Every thing where she now was was in full contrast to it. The elegance, propriety, regularity, harmony—and perhaps, above all, the peace and tranquillity of Mansfield, were brought to her remembrance every hour of the day. . . . At Mansfield, no sounds of contention, no raised voice, no abrupt bursts, no tread of violence was ever heard; all proceeded in a regular course of cheerful orderliness; every body had their due importance; every body's feelings were consulted. [Page 384.]

What stands out on first reading, is Fanny's undue sensitivity to what after all are not differences of morals but only of manners: surely she should be able to put up with this, one thinks, and, more important, to attend to what is really happening among these people, psychologically and morally, and not just to the noise and disorder. She is really a bit of a neurotic. On second reading the puzzle is increased, for how can she possibly talk about Mansfield, where she was ignored and abused, in such terms? *Her* feelings were almost never consulted; So how can she talk this way? And how are we to read it?

## Rereadings

Before presenting a more complicated sense of the way the novel develops I want to draw attention to the fact that the series of puzzles given above—having to do with the ending of the book, the narrator's prediction as to Crawford's success, and Fanny's reflections on Mansfield— could all be thought of in terms of our larger subject, authority: the authority, in each case, of a speaker and a position. Are we to regard Fanny as authoritative on the character of life at Mansfield and Portsmouth? If not, to what can we turn? Similarly, are we to regard the narrator as our authority on the probable success of Crawford, and on the happiness of the marriage between Fanny and Edmund? Again, if not, to what can we turn?

Authority in a different sense can be seen as a theme of the novel as a whole: During the theatricals, for example, to what extent should the young people be guided by the wishes of Sir Thomas? by the authority of other, unstated principles of manners or of morals? And at its central crisis, what is the authority of Sir Thomas's wish or command that Fanny accept Mr. Crawford? She resists it on the basis of her own experience and judgment. But how and why is *that* to be granted authority? Who is she to oppose herself and her judgment to that of all her family and friends? Behind these events, from the beginning of the book, is the question of what might be called the authority of the language of morals and manners by which every person in the novel, or at least at Mansfield, purports to regulate his or her conduct. How is this language to be understood? To what degree are "propriety" and "decorum" to guide our judgments? And how are such conclusory terms of value to be defined?

A great part of the power of the novel arises from the fact that the issue it takes as its explicit subject in the world it imagines—authority in the life of Mansfield Park and Fanny—is directly paralleled in the other dimension of the text's meaning, in its relation to its reader. That is, just as the novel presents in its imagined world the question of the authority of Sir Thomas, or of the conventions of decorum, so it forces on us in reading the book the question of the authority of its narrator. The novel in this way brings the reader to face the problem of authority both in its imagined world and in its performed relation with the reader himself, at one and the same time. One result is a kind of complexity of structure, suggesting the possibility of an art combining different dimensions of meaning at once. Another is that it suggests one reason why the plot summary given above is wholly inadequate to the novel, for its events are not just put before us, as if they could simply be seen, but are constantly mediated in these twin ways, as they present the question of authority both in the text and in its imagined world.

## The Language of Status

The first sentence of the book presents the double issue of authority I define:

About thirty years ago, Miss Maria Ward of Huntingdon, with only seven thousand pounds, had the good luck to captivate Sir Thomas Bertram, of Mansfield Park, in the county of Northampton, and to be thereby raised to the rank of a baronet's lady, with all the comforts and consequences of an handsome house and large income. [Page 41.]

To the speaker defined by this sentence, the values of life are plain: money and rank, "comforts and consequences." The object of marriage is to promote one or both of these goals, especially on the part of women, who have no other field for their ambition or energy. Its art, at least on the part of the person of lower status, is "captivation," but success depends as well upon "good luck." It is too obvious for words that in all this we are concerned only with people of a certain degree of wealth and gentility, as the beginning of the next sentence makes plain: "All Huntingdon exclaimed on the greatness of the match, and her uncle, the lawyer, himself, allowed her to be at least three thousand pounds short of any equitable claim to it." It is not just the speaker who sees things this way, then; everyone does, sometimes to the point of measuring the amount of money that a particular match should require. There is here a hint of another perspective on the matter, in the evident silliness of measuring things as finely as "her uncle, the lawyer" does. This can be read to imply a kind of distance, as can the element of irony in "all Huntingdon" as well.

But the rest of the paragraph continues, for the most part, in its original vein, reporting the widespread hopes that the two remaining sisters would marry "with almost equal advantage," observing that "there certainly are not so many men of large fortune in the world, as there are pretty women to deserve them," and describing the subsequent marriages of the two sisters, the one to Mr. Norris, "with scarcely any private fortune"—but whom Sir Thomas could aid with a clergyman's living—the other to the lieutenant, Mr. Price, whom he was unable to assist.

In all of this the speaker is in a sense simply setting the stage of the novel, and as readers we typically accord her that right. We need the characters and setting to be defined, so that the story may begin, and it is too early to challenge the language in which she does this. (In the summary I made of the book above I in fact told the story in similar terms.) The effect is that we accept this language, this whole way of defining people and their relations in terms of status and money, almost without knowing it, and certainly without yet seeing the dangers it presents. In this sense we submit to the narrator's authority as naturally as a child submits to that of a parent, and for much the same reason, that in the world made in this book things are like this from the beginning.[5]

For the reader the question will come to be, How authoritative is this language in the life of the book as a whole? Very much the same question is presented to the imagined characters, Fanny and Edmund and the rest: Is this the right way to think of marriage? There is enormous social support for it in the story: this is how Maria thinks of her marriage with Mr. Rushworth, the wealthy dolt, and how those around her, especially Mrs. Norris, do too, including Sir Thomas himself. (At one point, it is true, he observes how little Maria loves her future husband and offers to secure her release from her engagement if she wishes; but he is so pleased by the value of the connection that he does not pursue this as much as he should.) And when Fanny refuses Crawford, the whole situation is seen in very much the terms established in the opening paragraph: Lady Bertram, for example, gives Fanny almost the only advice she has received from her during her nine years with the Bertrams, saying: "[Y]ou must be aware, Fanny, that it is every young woman's duty to accept such a very unexceptionable offer as this." (Page 331.) Sir Thomas is almost as blunt: "Here is a young man of sense, of character, of temper, of manners, and of fortune, exceedingly attached to you, and seeking your hand in the most handsome and disinterested way; and let me tell you, Fanny, that you may live eighteen years longer in the world, without being addressed by a man of half Mr. Crawford's estate, or a tenth part of his merits." (Page 319.) It is true that Sir Thomas does not see the matter purely in terms of status and money, but he largely does so, and he has nothing but contempt for Fanny's statement that she does not and cannot love Crawford.[6] And behind the general social conventions to which he appeals he puts his own authority as uncle and master, claiming in fact the right to participate in this decision with her.

---

5. Of course sometimes the writer can make the language she is employing overtly problematic: "Emma Woodhouse, handsome, clever, and rich, with a comfortable home and a happy disposition, seemed to unite some of the best blessings of existence; and had lived nearly twenty-one years in the world with very little to distress or vex her." The "seemed" and "some" put us on notice that what is asserted is also doubted, though it would be a quick reader who noticed it the first time through.

6. Notice how differently he treats Maria, whom he offers to extricate from her engagement. Is this because Maria's distaste is so obvious and rude, as Fanny's would never be, or because he extends to the one consideration he withholds from the other? Or because he can see that Rushworth is an idiot and cannot see the problem with Henry? If so, the two cases would be similar: he can act on what he sees but cannot credit what another tells him.

Her duty is not simply to marry Mr. Crawford but to consult Sir Thomas; and it is all too obvious what such consultation would mean:[7]

"I should have been very much surprised had either of my daughters, on receiving a proposal of marriage at any time, which might carry with it only *half* of the eligibility of *this,* immediately and peremptorily, and without paying my opinion or my regard the compliment of any consultation, put a decided negative on it. . . . I should have thought it a gross violation of duty and respect. *You* are not to be judged by the same rule. You do not owe me the duty of a child. But, Fanny, if your heart can acquit you of *ingratitude*—"[8] [Page 319.]

When Fanny persists, Sir Thomas does not give up but supports Crawford's continued assaults upon her and sends Edmund to persuade her. In all of this, Sir Thomas and his wife, and others too who see marriage in this way, speak with the unacknowledged if partial authority of the narrator, who at the beginning of the book established this mode of talk and thought, the authority of which is in turn a problem simultaneously for Fanny and for the reader.

ANOTHER NOTE IS STRUCK IN THE OPENING PARAGRAPH—it has to be, or one might not read on—in the remark about "pretty women" and "men of large fortune." This does distance the reader from the language of status and money, at least to the point of saying something about the world in which these motives have their field of action, and in its muted but real wit. It may even remind one of the beginning of *Pride and Prejudice:* "It is a truth universally acknowledged that a single man in possession of a large fortune must be in want of a wife." But in that book wit of this sort is largely seen as a good thing, especially in Lizzie, and its dangers understated, while in this one, as I said earlier, it will be seen in its less pleasing and more dangerous versions, especially in Mary Craw-

7. As is said earlier in the book, when he advises Fanny to retire from the ball: "'Advise' was his word, but it was the advice of absolute power." (Page 285.)

8. Earlier: "[Y]ou have now shewn me that you can be wilful and perverse, that you can and will decide for yourself, without any consideration or deference for those who have surely some right to guide you—without even asking their advice. You have shewn yourself very, very different from any thing that I had imagined." (Page 318.)

ford, who will say, with cheerfulness, things like this: "I look upon the Frasers to be about as unhappy as most other married people."[9] (Page 356.) The authority of the voice that opens the first paragraph is thus subject to the challenge of a kind of wit (as we also saw in the remark about "all Huntingdon" and Lady Bertram's "uncle, the lawyer"); but this turns out to be the cynical kind of wit later to be found in Mary Crawford, not the generous and amusing wit of a Lizzie Bennett. The way it works on the reader of this paragraph, however, is as a kind of relief, and we are drawn to it without being able to question it. The two possibilities to which the opening paragraph thus introduces us, and invites us to take as authoritative, are thus versions of the voices, respectively, of Sir Thomas and Mary Crawford. There is no place for Fanny; and our experience, like hers, is distorted from the beginning by our natural acceptance of the way things are in this book.

But at the end of the first chapter—after we have heard Sir Thomas tell Mrs. Norris that it will be important to maintain the "distinction proper" between Fanny and her cousins, by which he carelessly licenses Mrs. Norris's subsequent sadism—a note of a wholly different kind is struck. The narrator tells us that Mrs. Price was willing to part with Fanny, "a very well-disposed, good-humoured girl," whom she thought might be "materially better for change of air." The narrator then says: "Poor woman! she probably thought change of air might agree with many of her children." (Page 48.) This is a gesture of human sympathy, wholly missing from the first paragraph and quite different indeed from anything we see in any of the characters except Fanny and Edmund; it thus defines an unresolved tension that will serve as a source of life and attention.

## Mansfield as Heaven

When Mrs. Norris and Sir Thomas discuss the idea of giving Fanny a home, both of them naturally think of the change as an incredible piece of good fortune to Fanny. Mansfield is, after all, just what anyone would want, and, as we have seen, Fanny at the end looks back on it as a kind of heaven. But what is the reality of it? This question has two possible versions: the reality as the narrator presents it to us, and the reality as we

---

9. Of this marriage, confirming in herself the other attitudes of the opening paragraph, she says: "She could not do otherwise than accept him, for he was rich, and she had nothing." (Page 356.) Compare her remark to Fanny: "Selfishness must always be forgiven you know, because there is no hope of a cure" (page 98), or her comments on marriage on page 79.

come to see it ourselves, especially when we look back on it from the perspective afforded by the end.

Of course there is in a sense not one single narrator in this or any other Austen novel, for Austen is a genius at what is known as the *style indirect libre,* by which, sometimes in a single sentence, she speaks in a series of voices, as we have in fact begun to see. Still, one does have an overall impression of life at Mansfield as one reads the book through, and we may speak as though this were the work of a single mind or voice. This voice tends to affirm the essential view that Mansfield holds about itself as a most superior place and family, excusing the various deprivations and injuries that Fanny suffers as minor, or at least endurable. The narrator never for a moment suggests that Fanny might have been better off left where she was.

If we attend to what the narrator reveals but slides over, however, we shall see that the truth is that, far from being a heaven, the house is in fact a kind of hell. Lady Bertram offers nothing to anyone, including her own daughters, and although we are invited by the narrator to regard her indolence as amiable and harmless, it is in fact far worse than that, as the consequent selfishness and mindlessness of her daughters attests. Sir Thomas is remote, opinionated, and insistent mainly on his own power and convenience. He offers very little except a sense of terrifying power, which is, in the event, without much effect. (For example, when he has to sell one of the two livings held for Edmund in order to pay Tom's gambling debts, his remonstrances to Tom are weak and ineffectual.) The two Bertram sisters, flattered as they constantly are by Mrs. Norris and unregulated by anyone, are selfish and vain. And Mrs. Norris! She is a crab, bitter and unpleasant towards Fanny; but this is presented as being no worse than her other bad qualities, her stinginess and her tendency to manage and intermeddle. All her vices are seen as the objects of mockery and, to that extent, a source of pleasure. The narrator seems to invite us to adopt a forgiving attitude, or at least an accepting one, towards her. But in fact, from Fanny's point of view—though she lacks the language to say so—Mrs. Norris is a monster, perpetually subjecting her to what would in our day be called child abuse. She is not only a crab: she is perpetually angry and means to humiliate and degrade Fanny whenever she can. She arranges that Fanny has to sleep in a cramped and cold attic room, with no fireplace; and in the nursery, which is given her to sit in when it is no longer needed, there is by the order of Mrs. Norris never to be a fire for her, no small matter in an English winter. She tries to subordinate Fanny to her sisters at every turn—to keep her from Sotherton, to keep her from the Grants, to deny her a carriage—and she perpetually attacks and undermines her.

As the narrator presents it, this relation is not the center of the book but rather to the side; yet its character is made plain throughout, if one will only attend to what one is told. For example, when Fanny is at last invited to dine at the Grants, Mrs. Norris gives Fanny this advice on how to behave herself:

> "I do beseech and intreat you not to be putting yourself forward, and talking and giving your opinion as if you were one of your cousins—as if you were dear Mrs. Rushworth or Julia. *That* will never do, believe me. Remember, wherever you are, you must be the lowest and last." [Page 232.]

Certainly it is her effort to see that such is the case; and no one could need the particular advice she gives less than the retiring and bashful Fanny. When Sir Thomas asks when Fanny would like the carriage brought round, this ensues:

> "My dear Sir Thomas!" cried Mrs. Norris, red with anger, "Fanny can walk." [Page 233.]

To his credit, Sir Thomas resists it, but in characteristically self-referential terms: "My niece walk to a dinner engagement at this time of year!"

As I say, the narrator's eye is not on this aspect of Fanny's life, but Austen gives us enough to see what it is like. As a child of nine Fanny is taken from her home and sent to live, with no prospect of return, at a house where no one, with the exception of Edmund, treats her with respect or kindness, and where some, especially Mrs. Norris, systematically abuse her. It is no wonder that she is timid and mousy, afraid to assert herself; no wonder too that she is forever seeking quiet and repose, for that is the best that life offers. One moment speaks with special poignancy, at least to me: when there is to be a dance at Mansfield, in honor of William and indeed of Fanny, she tries out one or two of the dancing steps in pleasurable anticipation.

> Her cousins' former gaiety on the day of a ball was no longer surprising to her; she felt it to be indeed very charming, and was actually practising her steps about the drawing-room as long as she could be safe from the notice of her aunt Norris, who was entirely taken up at first in fresh arranging and injuring the noble fire which the butler had prepared. [Pages 278–79.]

We have never before seen such a moment of relaxed playfulness in her, and by now we should know why.

All this colors the sense we have that Fanny is timid and mousy, for we can see its cause. Of course she is these things: the forces that make her so render all the more remarkable her capacity to assert herself and her judgment as she increasingly does. We can think of her timidity, then, not as a quality held forth as a virtue, for it is not, but as a kind of limitation or injury. She would rather have high spirits too, but these have been taken from her. The story of her growth into relative health, out of this condition, is in fact also a story of self-correction, like that of Emma, but of a different kind: it is the correction of an improper want of self-esteem.

FANNY HAS A TRULY GOOD AND UNCONFLICTED RELATIONSHIP only with her brother William, with whom she corresponds but whom she scarcely ever sees. Between them is confidence and trust and love. As for her own mother, Fanny reveals at the end that she feels that she was not loved by her; she was sent away, after all, and she thinks, as children always think, that it was for her own fault: "She had probably alienated Love by the helplessness and fretfulness of a fearful temper, or been unreasonable in wanting a larger share than any one among so many could deserve." (Page 366.) We can see in a flash that this is of course how she feels, and has been feeling throughout her life at Mansfield, though our attention has never been directed at this question before. Any child who had been sent away would feel something like this: the fact of exile must be explained somehow; it is in our nature to attribute goodness to our parents, so the fault must be with us—all the worse because it is never named. At the same time we see the utter injustice of Fanny's self-accusation, for we know Fanny and know that these particular qualities can never have been hers. (They are like Mrs. Norris's accusations, which, we can now see, have redoubled power for they confirm Fanny's own sense of herself). It would in fact have been better for Fanny had she been capable of the kind of self-regard that in its extreme form becomes the selfishness of which she accuses herself, for in its proper form self-valuation is essential to the making of a healthy person.

How far Fanny's sense of guilt extends is suggested by this remark: "Fanny's disposition was such that she could never even think of her aunt Norris in the meagreness and cheerlessness of her own small house, without reproaching herself for some little want of attention to her when they had been last together. . . ." (Page 287.)

Out of Edmund's genuine but sporadic kindness—most of the time
he is at Eton or Oxford, and when he is with Mary Crawford his concern
is converted to forgetfulness—Fanny does create a person to love, and by
whom to feel cared for, but the fragments with which she does this are
small. I am reminded here of a point made by Alice Miller, the Swiss
psychotherapist who studies people whose early lives are dreadfully damaged: despite terrible circumstances a child will sometimes manage to become healthy and even strong if she has someone good in her life—a
teacher or an aunt or the parent of a friend—who treats her with respect.[10] Some people at least can make an adequate sense of self out of
the tiniest pieces of confirmation, and something like this seems to be true
of Fanny.

### Fanny's Mystification

Fanny is perpetually abused by Mrs. Norris, ignored by almost everyone
else, and starved for what a child needs most, respect and affection, but
she seems not to know this. Why does she not recognize that Mansfield
is no heaven to her but a kind of hell? Partly because, like many such hells
on earth, Mansfield represents itself in completely opposite terms, as a
wonderful place, the sum of human felicity and achievement. Again I
think of Alice Miller, who says that worse for the child even than abuse
and emotional starvation itself is the fraudulent representation of the
state of affairs by members of the family, and others: the truth that the
child knows then has no language and is never uttered.[11] Far better is it
when someone finally makes explicit what the child has in one sense

---

10. See, for example, Alice Miller, *For Your Own Good: Hidden Cruelty in Child-
Rearing and the Roots of Violence* (New York: Farrar, Straus, Giroux, 1983), pages viii and
284; and Alice Miller, *The Drama of the Gifted Child: How Narcissistic Parents Form and
Deform the Emotional Lives of Their Talented Children* (New York: Basic Books, 1981),
pages 32–33.

11. See Miller, *For Your Own Good*, pages 247–51, 261–64, 274–75. Compare the
abused child who is told that Daddy loves him, as he indeed must of necessity love Daddy;
for him love and abuse become permanently entwined.

The need for children to think well of their parents, and those who act as parents, is so
deep that it is quite normal not to be able to see, or say, what would to an outsider be
plainly true. Here is a brief example I recently came across, from an article by Cal McCrystal
in *The Independent on Sunday*, [London] September 20, 1992, page 26:

I was eight when sent to a prep boarding school. It was by no means a vile place,
and I do not think it scarred me horribly. . . .

What I recall most from my (Irish) prep boarding days was the incontinence of
small boys who could neither control their bladders at night nor their tears in the
morning when caned for it. Punishment was applied to buttocks, over pyjamas or

known, but in another not—for without language there is no real knowledge—say, that her mother does not love her, or that her older brother,
though always spoken of as a hero, is emotionally disturbed and sadistic.
To Fanny this kind of clarification never happens in the course of the
entire book, though at the end Sir Thomas does realize something of his
own fault as a parent, and even Mrs. Norris no longer regards the "ideal
cousins" as ideal in any way. This must make some impression on Fanny,
but she never sees what the reader does.

Fanny's want of knowledge is also the consequence of her most en-
dearing and valuable quality, namely, her readiness to love others. When,
after she has lived with the Bertrams a few years, it is suggested that it is
time for her to go to live with Mrs. Norris, Fanny says to Edmund: "I
love this house and every thing in it." (Page 60.) And Edmund's real but
somewhat casual kindnesses are repeatedly met with deep gratitude and
devotion. It is in fact mainly through the eyes of Fanny's capacity to love
that we are offered Mansfield and Edmund throughout, and she idealizes
both. But by the end of the book we have seen enough to give us a perspective different from hers.[12]

There is still a third reason for Fanny's mystification, relating to the
character of the language of value—of morals and manners—by which
this world is constituted and regulated. Every single character in the novel
uses the same ultimate terms of commendation and blame. Everyone is
for propriety and manners and good taste and elegance and consideration

---

nightshirts (pink flannel in my case). Those who refused to cry received extra strokes
for defiance.

My younger brother, hardly seven, was harshly beaten in this fashion (by a
*priest!*) while I watched, trembling, not so much at his pain as in fear of him bubbling
dishonourably. A nine-year-old stoic called Greene fainted outright at the twelfth
vicious stroke without having shed a tear for the gratification of the man belabouring
him. My older brother was persecuted by pupils and teachers alike because of his
shyness. . . .

At night, muffled sobs would break out across the dormitory; by day, the cubicles
of school laboratories resounded to heartrending cries from *les enfants perdus,* while
in the junior study hall of an evening, secret monodies dripped into letters home.
This is what McCrystal calls "by no means a vile place"!

12. Even Fanny's capacity to love has its limits. When Fanny is told that she is to move
to Mrs. Norris's house, the narrator says: "The news was as disagreeable to Fanny as it had
been unexpected. She had never received kindness from her aunt Norris, and could not love
her." (Page 59.) Later, when Sir Thomas departs for the West Indies, the narrator says of
Maria and Julia that "their father was no object of love to them . . . and his absence was
unhappily most welcome." Fanny was also relieved, but "a more tender nature suggested
that her feelings were ungrateful, and she really grieved because she could not grieve."
(Page 66.)

of others and decorum and respect for the family, and against the opposite of these things. There is no revolutionary here who speaks in favor of breaking the trammels of convention or liberating the self from the structures of meaningless morality. When put to it, everyone, including the Crawfords—though perhaps not their uncle—and Mrs. Norris would affirm, at a certain level of generality, exactly the same values. But what they actually mean by these terms of course varies enormously. As Hume says in his essay, "On the Standard of Taste," there is far more apparent than real unanimity on moral and aesthetic matters; the gap arises from the fact that while human behavior varies greatly, certain terms claim everyone's approval, others everyone's disapproval. Who argues for rudeness, or selfishness, or ugliness, or ill-manners, or thoughtlessness, or cruelty? Yet the fact that these things are subject to universal disapproval has never meant that they do not exist, or are not strongly defended in practice.

From the point of view of one growing up in this world, or reading one's way into it, this is a source of confusion and mystification. To hear Sir Thomas spoken of as if he were the model of all virtue, or Maria as if she were just what a young lady ought to be, or Mrs. Norris as though she truly loved her niece, is to present the self with serious problems of understanding. Is one simply to accept these judgments as authoritative? If not, how is one to examine them? The question for Fanny is in this way like the question for Socrates, who was also mystified by the language that dominated his culture and unclear how to think about it, especially when that language was itself his only instrument of thought. Fanny has no dialectical partner, but she does have one instructor, Edmund, with whom she discusses her experience in ways that sometimes clarify her language. Here is one example of what I mean: in speaking of Mary Crawford's loose remark about her uncle the Admiral—"Of *Rears,* and *Vices,* I saw enough. Now, do not be suspecting me of a pun, I entreat" (page 91)—Fanny says she "ought not to have spoken" that way; Edmund agrees and calls it "indecorous"; Fanny adds, "And very ungrateful I think," which Edmund takes up: "Ungrateful is a strong word. I do not know that her uncle has any claim to her *gratitude.* . . . I do not censure her *opinions;* but there certainly *is* impropriety in making them public." (Page 94.) In this he is acting like Mr. Knightley in *Emma,* or Samuel Johnson in his *Essays,* helping to clarify language and thought, and for the most part in sensible ways.[13]

---

13. This continues to the end of the book: see his remarks about Mary's supposed cruelty, on page 442.

But notice how quick both of them are to say that the admiral should be treated with respect; in fact, he is a corrupter of the Crawfords' minds and it would be far better for Mary and Henry if they were allowed to know and say this. Both Fanny and Edmund thus unconsciously mirror and reinforce the authoritarian principles of Mansfield, based as they are ultimately on submission to the Father. And Edmund is by no means always even this reliable as a guide. Soon after the conversation about Mary Crawford, for example, we find Fanny saying to herself: "She was a little surprised that [Edmund] could spend so many hours with Miss Crawford, and not see more of the sort of fault which he had already observed, and of which *she* was almost always reminded by a something of the same nature whenever she was in her company; but so it was." (Page 96.)

In all of this Austen places the reader in a situation that directly parallels Fanny's: as she grows up in the world, trying to make sense of it, so we are introduced as readers to the same world and with the same task of understanding before us. The narrator misleads us, just as the family misleads Fanny, not into thinking the Mansfield family perfect, as it claims, but into regarding the indolence of Lady Bertram, the self-centeredness of Sir Thomas, and the cruelty and perpetual anger of Mrs. Norris as far less serious than they are. Our attention is diverted from the reality before us to its construction by the various characters, especially Fanny, who is always ready to think the best of anyone, especially at Mansfield, and to blame herself—her own weakness and timidity—for everything that goes wrong. Her self-protection is limited to trying to avoid Mrs. Norris, though without ever having an adequate language in which to explain to herself why she is doing this. For example, in resisting the proposed move to her house, the most she can say to Edmund is: "I shall love nothing there. You know how uncomfortable I feel with her" (page 60)—as if this feeling were her fault, not Mrs. Norris's.[14]

When Edmund tries to reconcile her to the proposed move—which is in fact, owing to the stinginess of Mrs. Norris, in no danger of realization—he exemplifies the kind of confusion in which Fanny lives by sliding over Mrs. Norris's true qualities with no doubt sincere euphemisms: "I can say nothing for her manner to you as a child; but it was the same with us all, or nearly so. She never knew how to be pleasant to children. But you are now of an age to be treated better; I think she *is* behaving better already; and when you are her only companion, you *must* be im-

---

14. Compare the passage where she reproaches herself for her treatment of Mrs. Norris, quoted above page 204.

portant to her." (Page 60.) That Edmund's perceptions are confused with respect to Mary Crawford, Fanny will be able to see; that they are confused with respect to Mrs. Norris, and herself, she cannot. Edmund's guidance thus has its limits, to say the least; instead of resisting the proposed change of home, as he should, he tries to talk Fanny into it, and in doing so deeply misrepresents what it would mean for Fanny: sending her to live with Mrs. Norris!

Fanny, in response, reveals the diminished sense of her own value that is the natural consequence of her experience: "I can never be important to any one." A few moments later she defines perfectly her want of confidence in her own judgment: "I cannot see things as you do; but I ought to believe you to be right rather than myself, and I am very much obliged to you for trying to reconcile me to what must be." (Page 61.)

CREATING THE AUTHORITY OF THE SELF

The question presented to the reader by these sources of confusion—Mansfield's misrepresentation, Fanny's loving and compliant nature, the mystifying use of the same terms for opposite purposes, Edmund's defects as an advisor, and Fanny's own impaired vision, especially of herself—is this: How is it that Fanny is able to lead herself out of this condition to any sort of clarity of vision and solidity of judgment? To this question we now turn.

### To Observe and Remember: The Visit to Sotherton

After Maria has become engaged to Mr. Rushworth, a visit is organized for all the young people—even Fanny, despite Mrs. Norris's best efforts—to visit Sotherton, the Rushworth estate, partly for the simple pleasure of the trip, partly to permit Crawford, who is at the moment taken with such things, to offer his opinion as to the best way in which the estate might be "improved." The issue here brought to the front of our attention by the narrator is Crawford's simultaneous flirtation with the two sisters, Maria and Julia, the one improper because trifling, the other really wrong, for he is alienating the affections of a woman engaged to another, with no serious romantic interest of his own.[15]

15. The process by which young men and women communicated their interest to each other was almost entirely public and highly regulated. To give a misleading impression was thought seriously wrong, for it was likely to arouse serious hopes; particularly if the impression extended beyond the young woman, to her family, as it was likely to do, it could

The young people divide into groups and walk the grounds, some entering a wood called the "wilderness," barred by an iron gate at the end, others wandering through paths. In the course of this, Edmund and Mary spend time alone together, as do Maria and Henry, notwithstanding Rushworth. Fanny tires quickly and sits on a bench: before her, as on a stage, comes first one group, then another, then the isolated and angry Rushworth, then the first group again. The whole thing has a surrealistic effect, a bit like the madness and magic of the woods in *Midsummer Night's Dream*. But part of what we see is that Fanny, who does not act (in either sense of the term), observes, watches, remembers: she alone performs the function of trying to make sense of who people are and what they are doing. As Stuart Tave has suggested, one way to read this passage, and others like it, is to think of Fanny as here engaged in the first processes of self-creation and self-identification.[16] It is true that she is here supposed to be nearly eighteen years old, but the functions she is performing are those that belong to an earlier stage of life: she simply observes, accurately so far as she can, and remembers. This is in a sense her equivalent to dialectic, necessarily solitary for she has no partner beyond the imperfect Edmund. It is only from observation and memory that experience can become a source of education, for if you observe incorrectly, or forget what you observe, your experience is of little value. These tasks, as Tave says, are prior to those of action; and the first action is itself likely to be passive, a refusal to act, as is the case with Fanny both at the theatricals and, later, in refusing Mr. Crawford.

Observation and memory become central to the rest of the novel, for Fanny sees, as most of the others do not, that the behavior of Henry and Mary makes them both untrustworthy. Edmund, who alone observes some of what Fanny does, and in some respects a bit more, forgets what

---

amount to a commitment of honor. The appropriate analogy in our world would not be in sexual relations but in business ones: to give someone the impression that you are serious about a transaction when you are not is felt as a real wrong, with continuing social consequences and sometimes legal ones as well.

When Mary warns Henry that Maria is engaged, he says: "Yes, and I like her the better for it. An engaged woman is always more agreeable than a disengaged. She is satisfied with herself. Her cares are over, and she feels that she may exert all her powers of pleasing without suspicion. All is safe with a lady engaged; no harm can be done." (Page 78.)

As for the flirtation itself, it is to say the least heavy-handed: when they are in the Church, for example, Henry whispers to Maria, "I do not like to see Miss Bertram so near the altar." (Page 116.)

16. In his beautiful book, *Some Words of Jane Austen* (Chicago: University of Chicago Press, 1973), to which my own reading is much indebted.

he knows, coloring Mary's conduct very differently as he falls in love with her. At the end, he expresses his restoration to understanding in visual terms, saying that now he sees what he had almost willfully obscured before.

The emphasis on observation, memory, and judgment in Fanny's experience at Sotherton and elsewhere—she alone really sees what is happening at the theatricals; she alone remembers what she sees—is of significance to the reader of this book in still another way, for it is exactly the capacities we observe Fanny develop that are required for an understanding of this book itself. The narrator clouds things, and misdirects attention, in the ways I have suggested, and more; it is ultimately up to us to see and remember and judge. To take one clear example, think of Fanny's apostrophe to Mansfield, where "every body's feelings were consulted"; we know that this is not true, but we are not reminded of it by the narrator. To read this remark we must either become supine and ignore the difficulty, or become active and address it; in that task what is required of us is observation, memory, and judgment, just what is needed on Fanny's part to survive in this world. Only when we have these things will we see what is actually before our noses, the kind of emotional starvation and abuse to which Fanny has been subjected, and which in turn explains much of her psychology, including her timidity, her need for tranquility and repose, the place Edmund has in her heart, and her love for Mansfield.

## Distinguishing Manners and Morals

In the Sotherton episode we experience a partial clarification of the language of value at work in this world, as we are invited both by the narrator and by Edmund to distinguish between the domain of manners and that of morals.[17] This is significant because both are governed by the more general standard of "propriety," and because both—of equal importance to this book—are taught and learned by example in the family. One cannot reduce morals to a set of rules, after all, or manners either; one learns to behave as the people one admires behave, being guided as well by their praise and blame of others. Even though we Americans may think of our-

---

17. For elaboration of this distinction, and for development of Austen's use of the word "principles," see David Lodge, "The Vocabulary of 'Mansfield Park,'" in *The Language of Fiction: Essays in Criticism and Verbal Analysis of the English Novel,* (New York: Columbia University Press, 1966), pages 94–113. My discussion of these points is much indebted to this fine piece.

selves as so frank and open and honest that we in a sense have no manners, of course we do, and our children learn from us, just as Fanny and her cousins learned from their family, what is acceptable and what is not; and, like them, our children learn not so much from our pronouncements as from our behavior, sometimes to our own chagrin or shame.

The narrator draws this distinction when speaking of Julia, who is unable to join the other young people for she has found herself walking with Mrs. Rushworth, whom she cannot abandon: "The politeness which she had been brought up to practise as a duty, made it impossible for her to escape; while the want of that higher species of self-command, that just consideration of others, that knowledge of her own heart, that principle of right which had not formed any essential part of her education, made her miserable under it."[18] (Page 119.)

Elsewhere in the chapter the distinction between manners and morals (or principles) is presented in a different form. When he is reproached by Mary Crawford for his plans to be ordained, Edmund says that he "cannot call that situation nothing, which has the charge of all that is of the first importance to mankind, individually or collectively considered, temporally and eternally—which has the guardianship of religion and morals, and consequently of the manners which result from their influence." (Page 120.) Miss Crawford, not really understanding, says that she thinks a clergyman cannot much affect the manners of the people, and Edmund responds: "Miss Crawford must not misunderstand me, or suppose I mean to call them the arbiters of good breeding, the regulators of refinement and courtesy, the masters of the ceremonies of life. The *manners* I speak of, might rather be called *conduct*, perhaps, the result of good principles."[19] (Page 121.)

"Principles" then becomes a key term in the text: we are told of Julia

18. Sir Thomas of course insisted that his daughters be well mannered, especially in showing respect to their elders—thus even at the moment when he discovers that Mrs. Norris has prevented Fanny from having a fire in her room, he insists, at great length, that Fanny must not cease to pay her all the respect she is due as her aunt—but he failed to attend to more important matters. As the narrator told us earlier, "In every thing but disposition, they were admirably taught." (Page 55.) Compare the comment at the end of the book: "He had meant them to be good, but his cares had been directed to the understanding and manners, not the disposition." (Page 448.)

19. Page 119. Earlier, when Tom Bertram told of a Miss Anderson, whose manner changed enormously when she became "out," Mary Crawford thinks of the matter in terms of the ill-management of manners, Edmund in its moral aspect: "[T]here is no more real modesty in their behaviour *before* they appear in public than afterwards." (Page 82.)

and Maria, when they fall into envious and bitter competition over Crawford: "With no material fault of temper, or difference of opinion, to prevent their being very good friends while their interests were the same, the
sisters, under such a trial as this, had not affection or principle enough to
make them merciful or just, to give them honour or compassion." (Page
183.) And when, at the end, Fanny complains of Mary's "cruelty" to Edmund in speaking so lightly of what Henry and Maria have now done,
Edmund, in a new version of his old role as teacher, responds: "Cruelty,
do you call it?—We differ there. No, her's is not a cruel nature. . . . Her's
are not faults of temper. . . . Her's are faults of principle, Fanny, of
blunted delicacy and a corrupted, vitiated mind." (Page 442.) And Sir
Thomas, reflecting on his failures as a father, "feared that principle, active
principle, had been wanting, that [his daughters] had never been properly
taught to govern their inclinations and tempers, by that sense of duty
which can alone suffice." (Page 448.)

Despite the rather heavy implications of the term "duty" in the last
sentence, what Austen means by "principle" is not obedience to a set of
commands but responsiveness to the feelings and situations of others. In
*Mansfield Park* the term is associated not so much with rules of conduct
as with feelings that will lead to conduct that is right not only externally
but internally.[20] Mary Crawford, for example, simply had not the kinds of
feelings she should have about the adulterous elopement, which brought
shame to all involved. "She was speaking only, as she had been used to
hear others speak, as she imagined every body else would speak." (Page
442.) Earlier, Fanny says to herself about Henry Crawford, "No, he can
feel nothing as he ought." (Page 238.) It is not really that he is a bad
person, cruel or rapacious, but that he is a trivial one, with his considerable capacities never organized or mobilized in a coherent way. What he
lacks is less a sense of what is expected by others on various occasions—
he is a superlative actor, after all—than a central self, capable of attachment, feeling, and judgment. He lacks reality and depth as a person; this,
not compliance with rules, is what Austen means by "principle."

Crawford shows that he can see some of this, when the narrator reports him as observing, rightly, of Fanny that "she had feeling, genuine
feeling." And he reveals much of his own nature too when he adds, "It

---

20. I am reminded here of Samuel Johnson's use of the term in *Rambler* no. 32, where
speaking of the capacity to bear pain and suffering he says that "a soul well principled"
may sometimes be able to endure pain to the death without complaint.

would be something to be loved by such a girl, to excite the first ardours of her young, unsophisticated mind!" (Page 245.) But his essential triviality leads him to misunderstand the very capacity he can dimly see:

"No, I will not do her any harm, dear little soul! I only want her to look kindly on me, to give me smiles as well as blushes, to keep a chair for me by herself wherever we are, and be all animation when I take it and talk to her; to think as I think, be interested in all my possessions and pleasures, try to keep me longer at Mansfield, and feel when I go away that she shall be never happy again. I want nothing more." [Pages 240–41.]

It is this absence of emotional capacity that enables him, in the middle of his assiduous courtship of Fanny Price, to renew on a whim the dangerous relation with Maria, which is to destroy them both. And, to return to one of our puzzles, when we are told that if Crawford had been "satisfied with the conquest of one amiable woman's affections" and if he had accordingly "persevered, and uprightly" Fanny would have married him, the narrator is describing what could never have been. Such perseverance, and satisfaction, are simply not possible for a character so thin and unformed.

To return to Fanny: this novel is the story of the development of her character as a principled one, capable of seeing and remembering and judging for itself, and capable of "genuine feeling" too—the development of what we might speak of as an identity. There remain two stages of this process to discuss, both involving the authority of Sir Thomas: her response to the theatricals and her resistance to the suit of Henry Crawford.

### The Theatricals: Fanny's Judgment Confirmed

Austen's achievement in these wonderful pages is to make the reader feel that the decision to put on this play, at such a time, and to assign these parts to these actors, is momentous. Take it as a writing assignment, and you will see what I mean, for it seems on the face of it to be utterly inconsequential. But, as Austen develops it, it is not: we are told by the narrator that to put on the play inherently involves want of respect for Sir Thomas, away on a dangerous mission, as he so acutely feels when he returns, and there is truth in this; but not as much as Sir Thomas feels, for there is also a sense, unmarked by the narrator, that this is just another case in which he is conscious of the claims of his own dignity and feelings over all others. After all, he was gone a year. Was the household to hold itself in semi-mourning that whole time? But the building of a stage in the billiard room and the changes made in Sir Thomas's own study so that it could be used as a changing room are genuine invasions, though not of the largest magnitude. There is, too, by the standards we have been made to share real indecorousness: Mary Crawford asks, "Who is to be Anhalt? What gentleman among you am I to have the pleasure of making love to?" (Page 167.)

But all this is minor—a matter of "manners" in the less significant sense—compared to the real evil, which is Crawford's flirtation with Maria. She is all eagerness, so seduction is hardly the term, but what happens is not merely unseemly, it is truly destructive. For Maria it is a bad way to express her unhappiness with her choice of Rushworth, the dolt, partly because it is so indirect: instead of thinking, "This is a mistake," she thinks, "Crawford would be better." When he disappoints her by making no declaration and leaving Mansfield for a time, her father offers to secure her release from her engagement to Rushworth—the best thing he does in the course of the book. She should certainly have taken him up, for she has only contempt for her future husband, but she does not, and the reason reveals another evil of the flirtation: she will not give Crawford the satisfaction of seeing her suffer for him in this way. And, at the end of the book, it is the revival of the relation with Maria that destroys Henry's chances with Fanny. The evil is not abstract but real, and it does not consist merely in the violation of a rule of propriety but in its deeply destructive consequences for the happiness of more than one person.

At the beginning of the rehearsals, Edmund sees, though rather vaguely, that what is happening is wrong both with respect to Sir Thomas and in light of Maria's situation, but he is prevailed upon to join the others on the grounds that if he does not join them they will choose an actor from elsewhere in the neighborhood. This would give the proceedings a publicity that would make them worse than anything. Edmund sees the offense to his father, and some of the impropriety of the play, but not what Crawford and Maria are actually doing, partly for the understandable reason that he is playing a love scene with Mary Crawford that embarrasses and compels them both. But the major quality of his objection is in the end its vagueness: he is sure the play is improper, but he does not really know why. His is a mind for which it is enough to know, rightly, that his father would disapprove, thus demonstrating the way that one's basic character is formed, and deformed, by one's parents. Fanny, who is on the margin, looking in from outside just as the reader is, can alone see what is really happening, but she cannot prevent it.

What is striking about Fanny here, seemingly so meek, is her capacity to stand out against the combined forces of all the others, except Edmund but including Mrs. Norris: "I am quite ashamed of you, Fanny, to make such a difficulty of obliging your cousins in a trifle of this sort,—So kind as they are to you—Take the part with a good grace, and let us hear no more of the matter, I entreat." (Page 169.) When Edmund intervenes, asking her not to urge Fanny in this way: "'I am not going to urge her,'— replied Mrs. Norris sharply, 'but I shall think her a very obstinate, ungrateful girl, if she does not do what her aunt and cousins wish her—very ungrateful indeed, considering who and what she is.'" (Page 169–70.) This is sheer insult, and felt so by the others, a public revelation of private abuse. For Mrs. Norris this behavior has become so habitual that she cannot see how it will be taken by others, just as, in her enthusiasm for promoting the match between Julia and Henry, she fails to see how Sir Thomas will regard the whole enterprise of the theatricals. But Fanny, supported by Edmund and her own natural timidity, resists them all.

Though Edmund aids her here, his own resolve soon after wavers, and he comes to Fanny to seek, as he terms it, her advice. This is a lovely scene: it shows his real sense of her moral ascendancy—he is not "comfortable" without her approbation—yet his manner makes plain that he seeks not advice but confirmation of his decision to act in the play, and he misreads her diplomatic but firm reiteration of what they both know in such a way as to claim her acquiescence. This is a performance of the capacity of one mind to remember what it has known and observed, and the other to forget it.

OVER THE WHOLE EXPERIENCE broods the imagined and dreadful presence of the absent father. When he returns, all instantly know that he will disapprove, as he of course does; Fanny is in this sense justified, and feels it, as we do too. Sir Thomas, the ultimate moral authority as always, is in the right.

But in fact he is not. He knows nothing of what Fanny has seen; his whole disapproval, forceful as it is, is directed at the social impropriety, the violation of manners rather than principle, and at the want of respect shown to him, especially in the invasion of his room. Moreover, despite his appearance as a titanic figure of judgment, he demonstrates that he is actually a rather weak father, for he speaks about it only to Edmund; to the others, whom he knows to be the principal movers, he says nothing at all: "[H]e was more willing to believe they felt their error, than to run the risk of investigation." (Page 203.)

The reader will not notice this the first time through, however, and is likely to experience what Fanny does, a false sense of alliance between Sir Thomas and her. He confirms that she judged right, though on very different grounds from hers; and to the extent that Fanny's own objection was based on the claims of Sir Thomas to a kind of perpetual somberness in honor of his absence, her judgment is itself awry, shaped in part by his insistence upon his own importance and power. The apparent alliance by which her weakness is at last supported by his strength is reaffirmed when Sir Thomas insists upon treating her with respect, effectively resisting Mrs. Norris for the first time. Fanny is grateful and feels valued. But all of this will only make the ultimate crisis more intolerable, when Sir Thomas insists on her marrying Crawford. She has leaned on him, and the reader has too, only to have the prop thrown away; far from a moral authority in this book, he will reveal himself to be a blind and authoritarian figure.

### Resisting Henry Crawford: The Authority of the Self

The great crisis of the book is presented by Henry's courtship of Fanny, reinforced as it is by everyone else at Mansfield Park, and by Fanny's experience of life at Portsmouth as well. Henry's initial plan was simply to make her love him. What he meant by that we have already seen, but part of the significance of his impulse is what gives rise to it. Henry's interest in Fanny is first stimulated by her refusal to acquiesce in his wit and humor. He is speaking of the theatricals as a wonderful time in his life— "I was never happier"—and suggesting that the return of Sir Thomas ruined everything:

> "[I]f Mansfield Park had had the government of the winds just for a week or two about the equinox, there would have been a difference. Not that we would have endangered his safety by any tremendous weather—but only by a steady contrary wind, or a calm. I think, Miss Price, we would have indulged ourselves with a week's calm in the Atlantic at that season."
> [Page 236.]

She responds stiffly, the narrator tells us "angrily": "As far as *I* am concerned, sir, I would not have delayed his return for a day. My uncle disapproved it all so entirely when he did arrive, that in my opinion, every thing had gone quite far enough."²¹ As Mary puts it to Henry later: "And so that is her attraction after all! This it is—her not caring about you— which gives her such a soft skin and makes her so much taller, and produces all these charms and graces!" (Page 240.)

Just as Mary changes in her feelings about Edmund as she comes to know him better, almost to the point of encouraging him to propose, Henry moves towards seeing and valuing Fanny more accurately. He announces to Mary that he is "quite determined to marry Fanny Price." (Page 295.) Of course this phrase leaves little room for Fanny's choice in the matter, but neither person expects her to cause difficulty: "Lucky, lucky girl!" says Mary; and, later, "Does she know her own happiness?" (Pages 296–97.)

When Henry says he will "marry" Fanny, what does he mean by the term? Partly, of course, a legal change of status; that is the kind of "marriage" with which everyone in the book has been concerned from the beginning, and it is seen largely as a matter of "captivation" and "luck," with the men entitled to choose, the women entitled to use their arts to see that they choose well. But this is the marriage of "manners"; What of the marriage of "morals," or what we might call psychological and emotional life? We get a glimpse at least of what Mary thinks when she says, "You will have a sweet little wife; all gratitude and devotion. Exactly what you deserve." (Page 296.) And, echoing the language with which the narrator began the book, "What an amazing match for her!"²²

Henry's own confused moral condition is made plain enough when we are told, within two pages, first that he "had too much sense not to feel the worth of good principles in a wife, though he was too little accustomed to serious reflection to know them by their proper name" (page 298); then, that he imagines his future with Fanny in these appealing terms, that "I could so wholly and absolutely confide in her"; then, that he says of his earlier "wicked project upon her peace," as Mary terms it, that it was "very bad in me," but with the qualification "against such a creature"; and then, that he praises the admiral in these terms: "The Ad-

---

21. This shows that she is capable of anger on behalf of Sir Thomas, as she was earlier on behalf of Edmund, but not yet on behalf of herself. It is a sign of health when she can finally feel that emotion on her own account, as she does in response to Crawford's ceaseless importunities: "Now she was angry." (Page 327.)

22. Earlier, Mary said of marriage that it is "of all transactions, the one in which people expect most from others, and are least honest themselves." She calls it "a manoeuvring business," which often results in a "take in." (Page 79.)

miral has his faults, but he is a very good man, and has been more than a father to me. Few fathers would have let me have my own way half so much." (Page 299.) This state of confusion is almost worthy of an Emma Woodhouse, and this novel, like that one, could well have been written from such a point of view. The central question of the book would then have been whether Henry could work out of such a condition into something like emotional clarity and health, as Emma does. But this book is not that one; here Jane Austen is examining a less promising candidate than Emma, one more damaged by indulgence and want of education, for whom the answer might well be "no."[23]

Fanny's opposition to him is not disheartening to Crawford but the reverse: "He rather derived spirits from it." (Page 326.) Her affection appeared "of greater consequence, because it was withheld, and determined him to have the glory, as well as the felicity, of forcing her to love him." (Page 325.) This last phrase, presented as natural both to Crawford and the narrator, says it all. His insistence, which she calls a "perseverance so selfish and ungenerous," makes Fanny "angry," the first time in the book she feels that emotion on her own behalf. (Page 327.) And he does pursue her relentlessly:

> "What did that shake of the head mean?" said he. "What was it meant to express? Disapprobation, I fear. But of what?—What had I been saying to displease you?—Did you think me speaking improperly?—lightly, irreverently on the subject?—Only tell me if I was. Only tell me if I was wrong. I want to be set right. Nay, nay, I entreat you; for one moment put down your work. What did that shake of the head mean?" [Page 339.]

THE CENTER OF THE BOOK is chapter 35, in which Edmund too seeks to persuade her to accept Crawford. At first, Fanny is anxious, afraid that Edmund is there to work on her. When he says, "How could you imagine me an advocate for marriage without love?" she feels enormous relief: "Fanny had not felt so comfortable for days and days." (Pages 343–44.)

---

23. One more word for Henry Crawford. He alone sees that Fanny has been maltreated by everyone: "I will make her very happy, Mary, happier than she has ever yet been herself, or ever seen any body else." (Page 298.) And he sees something else as well: "Edmund—True, I believe he is (generally speaking) kind to her; and so is Sir Thomas in his way, but it is the way of a rich, superior, longworded, arbitrary uncle." (Page 301.)

But her comfort is short-lived: Edmund goes on to say that Crawford "perseveres, with the hope of creating that regard which had not been created before. This, we know, must be a work of time. But (with an affectionate smile), let him succeed at last, Fanny, let him succeed at last." When she says that "he never will succeed with me," Edmund reproves: "Never, Fanny, so very determined and positive! This is not like yourself, your rational self." And he goes on to replicate the language of conquest and possession at work in Crawford's own mind: "[B]efore he can get your heart for his own use, he has to unfasten it from all the holds upon things animate and inanimate, which so many years growth have confirmed. . . ." (Page 344.) Edmund's language, like Crawford's "forcing her to love him," speaks volumes.

With Edmund, unlike Sir Thomas, Fanny can say what she thinks, which is that she disapproves of Crawford's character, referring especially to the theatricals. Edmund, however, "scarcely hearing her to the end," simply says, "let us not, any of us, be judged by what we appeared at that period of general folly." And when Fanny says, "I am persuaded that he does not think as he ought, on serious subjects," Edmund responds:

> "Say rather, that he has not thought at all upon serious subjects, which I believe to be a good deal the case. How could it be otherwise, with such an education and adviser? Under the disadvantages, indeed, which both have had, is it not wonderful that they should be what they are? Crawford's *feelings*, I am ready to acknowledge, have hitherto been too much his guides. Happily, those feelings have generally been good. You will supply the rest; and a most fortunate man he is to attach himself to such a creature—to a woman, who firm as a rock in her own principles, has a gentleness of character so well adapted to recommend them. He has chosen his partner, indeed, with rare felicity. He will make you happy, Fanny, I know he will make you happy; but you will make him every thing." [Page 347.]

This is a marvelous paragraph, for in it Edmund, Fanny's most trusted friend and adviser, recommends Crawford on exactly the ground upon which he should do the reverse: that "he has not thought at all upon serious subjects." And as for his "feelings," we know enough by now to recognize that "genuine feeling" is a function of character and identity, just what Crawford has been shown to lack. As his subsequent conduct with Maria will show, he is incapable of real feeling.

Fanny remains resolute, even when the authority of Mrs. Grant and

Miss Crawford is called upon.[24] "I *should* have thought . . . that every woman must have felt the possibility of a man's not being approved, not being loved by some one of her sex, at least, let him be ever so generally agreeable. . . . His sisters should consider me as well as him." (Page 349.) As with Fanny's anger on her own behalf at Crawford, Edmund's assault upon her stimulates a kind of self-protective capacity that we have not yet seen in this novel. But all this is wasted on Edmund, who is able to read what Fanny says after his own inclination, seeing her as open to further persuasion. Edmund does notice that she is wearied and distressed, and changes the subject. The chapter concludes this way, its final phrase showing how Edmund conceives of his own role:

> Still, however, Fanny was oppressed and wearied; he saw it in her looks, it could not be talked away, and attempting it no more, he led her directly with the kind authority of a privileged guardian into the house. [Page 351.]

The reader's task is to see that phrase in the context of what we have just read and thus to reject the claims of "kind authority" entirely. In doing that, the reader will be exercising his own capacities to observe, to remember, and to judge, just those by which Fanny learns to give authority to her own experience.

FANNY IS RELIEVED FROM THESE PRESSURES only by events: Tom's illness—at which Mary revives her interest in Edmund in an obvious and crude way—and subsequent recovery; Henry's flirtation with Maria, which leads her to abandon her husband and throw herself upon Henry in such a way as to make her return impossible; and Mary's response to his behavior, which at last makes her character plain to Edmund.

It is important to see in what respect Mary and Henry have defective characters: it is not that they are wholly evil or coarse, or incapable of appreciating moral and emotional quality; it is rather that they have never been organized into wholes, with a center, never become capable of forming a self. In a deep sense they have no experience because they have no selves. This is the defect of character from which they suffer, and it is far more frightening than simple vice would be.

---

24. As for Mrs. Norris, we are told: "Angry she was, bitterly angry; but she was more angry with Fanny for having received such an offer, than for refusing it." (Page 330.)

ONE STORY OF *MANSFIELD PARK* is that of Fanny Price, telling of her development into a person capable of seeing, remembering, judging—as having a self that is capable of real experience. She grows up in a world dominated by authority of many kinds: of Sir Thomas, Mrs. Norris, her aunt Bertram, her cousins; of the languages of manners and morals; of wealth and power. As she proceeds, she grants increasing authority to her own experience, to her own judgment, at the end standing entirely alone against her world in her knowledge of the character of Henry Crawford. She, alone of all the characters in the book, has learned to use the languages of manners and morals at work in this world to assist her observations, memory, and judgment, and thus to render her capable of "genuine feeling." It is not the mere impulses of her being but the experience of what could be called a formed and educated self upon which she knows she has to rely in the end.

The other story is the reader's, which parallels hers. As we observe what she does, and remember it with her, and judge as she does, we feel an alliance between her and us, just as she does with Sir Thomas; but just as that alliance is undone, so is this one, when at the end she says the things she does about Mansfield's perfection. At the very close of the book the parsonage at Mansfield, into which Fanny and Edmund finally move, is said to be "as thoroughly perfect in her eyes, as every thing else, within the view and patronage of Mansfield Park, had long been." And our alliance with the narrator, who has at key moments told us just what to think, is undone too, when she talks about Henry Crawford's chances of success.

The effect of these undoings is deeply disturbing: it is to distance the reader both from the heroine of the book and from its narrator; to force us to attend to our own experience, educated as it may have been by this book, just as Fanny is forced to rely on her own judgment too. This may look like a very old fashioned book indeed, but in fact its conception of the human personality, and its predicament, is remarkably modern. As Fanny must finally act on her own, so the book requires us to act on ours. Authority in the end lies not in fathers, or mothers or aunts, or cousins, not in rules of manners or morals, not in the culture as it is interpreted for us by others, but in our own experience of life and of the culture; and not in just any experience—Austen is as far from that kind of moral nihilism as it is possible to imagine—but in the experience of an education, in relation at once to the culture and to other people—the kind of education it is the object of this novel to offer us.

• • •

*In* Mansfield Park *we see at work the authority not of a formal institution, such as the law or the church or the crown, but that of certain social and intellectual practices, and the claim of authority on their behalf is not so much argued for as performed. In the household of Mansfield Park itself you must at least pretend to think and talk like Sir Thomas, and act in the ways this thinking entails, at the risk of a kind of banishment. Similarly, the narrator's opening invites the reader to think about marriage in a certain way, presented without argument, as if it were the only way. As you acquiesce in this language, you are carried into a community of expectation and value that includes nearly everyone in the story, and from which you will be excluded if you reject its premises—though it is one purpose of the novel in the end to lead you to exactly that.*

*Does something similar happen in explicit argument about public institutions? In seeking to define the kind of authority that the law should have, for example, Hale enacts in his language a set of ways of thinking and talking, for which he does not argue—in what language could he do so?—but for which he claims authority by performance. And the same could be said, as I have suggested above, of the Joint Opinion in Casey, of Hooker's arguments for the church, of Richard's speeches on behalf of the crown, of Plato's definition of philosophy: in each case the institution whose authority is in question is not only described in the text, as the object of explicit argument and analysis; it is enacted in it, and it is thus for its own language, for its own procedures, that the text most deeply argues. If these are mirrored in the actual practices of the institution, the argument supports that too; if not, the performance suffers from an incoherence between surface claims and enacted meanings.*

*Are we then to think of our institutions not as social or cultural or political objects, as we usually do, but as themselves systems of language? For their claims of authority in the end work like the claims made by a language: they offer us ways of thinking and talking not otherwise available, through which we can express ourselves and establish relations with others; one must comply, however, with the sets of expectations by which they work, on pain of exclusion from the community they define; and our acquiescence in them may lead by stages to consequences we cannot imagine. If so, the education in autonomy offered by* Mansfield Park *can be seen to reach deep to the center of human social and cultural life, where we manage the claims made on us by the very languages we speak, and seek to discover the art by which those languages can in turn be transformed, and used to make claims of our own on the world.*

# SEVEN

# DICKINSON'S POETRY:
# TRANSFORMING THE AUTHORITY
# OF LANGUAGE

THROUGHOUT HER LIFE AS A POET Emily Dickinson struggled with the authority of the conventions and expectations that defined what poetry was in her world, and thus the possibilities for her own poetic speech. To count as "poetry," for example, a text had to be regular in both meter and rhyme, as was the verse of Elizabeth Barrett Browning, whose work Dickinson greatly admired, or, closer to home, that of Longfellow, the lion of American poetry. But Dickinson's work is famous for her irregularities in both dimensions, perhaps especially for the half-rhymes or part-rhymes that jarred the contemporary ear. In these respects—and others too: its voices, its subject matter, its extraordinary violations of grammatical expectation—her poetry was by the standards of her day regarded not as innovative, as we think of it, but as defective.

Her struggle with the authority of poetic convention is of interest not only for its own sake, for the beauty and strength of her achievement, but because, as I suggested in the Preface, this is a special case of a struggle in which all human beings must engage, a struggle with their language. Each of us must face the fact that our language exists outside of us—it preexists us—and if we are to function in our world we must learn to speak it as it is. We cannot simply make up a language and hope to be understood—indeed, as every child who has fantasized about a secret spy-language knows, we cannot even imagine making a really new language, for the very terms in which we try to do so have their origin in the languages we know.

Whenever we speak, those who listen to us have expectations as to how we shall do so. While we need not confirm these in every respect, we do need to respond to them: "please" is normally a way of being polite;

"dog" usually refers to the kind of animal that barks, sometimes meaning man's best friend, but in other contexts, especially as applied to human beings, an insult; "all-y, all-y in free" is a cry made as part of a game; and so forth. Language is continuous with manners: the meaning of what we say with words is as dependent upon external convention as the meaning of what we say with our clothes, our faces, or our hands. To speak ungrammatically, or overgrammatically, has social meanings that are as clear as those of clothes—the Hawaiian shirt at the Boston symphony, the three-piece suit at the barbecue. In becoming competent at our languages, each of us must find a way, actually a set of ways, to address the expectations that are in some sense the most important material with which we work.

Sometimes, of course, there is no problem: there are moves in our discourse that seem adequate to the occasion on which we wish to use them. Casual greetings and well-wishing are normally in this category. But if all of our talk were of this kind it would be nothing but reiterated cliché; it, and we, would be impossibly dull, as a perusal of Swift's "Polite Conversation"—a dialogue consisting of nothing but stereotyped remarks[1]—or Flaubert's collection of *Idées Reçues* suggest. Instead, in the course of life we find ourselves again and again confronting the inadequacy of our languages, both on small and large occasions. Our experience ranges from the frustration we commonly feel in trying to write a letter of sympathy to a friend who has lost a parent or a spouse, to the kind of major challenge mounted against a whole culture by Plato, of which we saw a small piece in Chapter 1.

Dickinson faced the question whether her expressions would count as poetry, and be taken seriously as such, or whether they would be classified some other way—and since they obviously aspired to be poetry, not prose or some other established form, this would mean their being entirely erased. The same issue comes up today, not so much with poetry as with the other arts: Is John Cage's composition of silence actually music and hence entitled to a certain kind of attention, or is it "not music" and, therefore, properly disregarded? In the professions, too, the ultimate sanction is exclusion from the discourse and the community of power: acupuncture is "not medicine," this scholar's study of the way people live with each other and with nature is "not economics," an appeal to intuition is "not a legal argument," and so forth.

---

1. Jonathan Swift, *A Complete Collection of Genteel and Ingenious Conversation* (London: Printed for B. Motte, and C. Bathurst, 1738).

In our negotiations of the sometimes easy, sometimes enormously difficult relation between the mind and its languages, a part of our difficulty—as the career of Fanny in *Mansfield Park* in fact demonstrates—is that we are partly made by the very languages with which we struggle. Thus the idea of "poetry" with which Dickinson had to come to terms was not simply "out there" in the culture, to be confronted, but in her own mind too: she had been raised to think, like other people, that poetry must be regular, have certain subjects and voices, employ standard grammatical usages, and so on. The struggle is not between two wholly different things, the self and the culture, then; the struggle is to make an identity, a voice and a language, out of the materials one inherits, in a process by which the authority of the expectations that govern the meaning of what one says is being repeatedly established, conceded, eroded, destroyed, and transformed.

But as we are partly made by our languages we are makers of them too, and this is true not only of great artists and thinkers, like Dickinson and Plato, but of all of us. All of us transform our languages all the time— no one speaks in pure clichés—and in so doing we make new claims for the rightness and authority of what we have done. In an art that is deeply reciprocal we modify the expectations that shape our minds. Our life with language is in this sense a life of creation, and at the most ordinary as well as at the most elevated level. Consider, for example, this experiment, often performed by the linguist A. L. Becker. He asks a room full of students to describe in a single sentence the event they are about to witness; he then walks to the side of the room, and back, and drops his book on the podium. The sentences composed by the students become the subject of the class or lecture. For our purposes, what is of special interest is that he reports that never, of the hundreds of people writing sentences about what is nearly the same simple event, have any two sentences been identical. Deep in the simplest practices are the springs of creation. So many choices must be made in the framing of any sentence that we cannot simply speak in clichés, even if we wanted to; each of us lives the life of the poet and philosopher, whether we know it or not. When an artist like Dickinson struggles with the resources of her language, and the authority of the expectations that determine the status and the meaning of what she does, she acts not only for herself but for all of us.

IDEAS OF POETRY

Dickinson's situation in the world can be defined in many different ways. To begin as the narrator of *Mansfield Park* might have done, we can say that she was born in 1830 as the second child and eldest daughter of Edward Dickinson, an Amherst lawyer who was one of the first citizens of the town. She was educated partly at a local school, partly at Mount Holyoke Seminary, which she attended but from which she did not graduate. She lived all her life in her father's house, much of it as a recluse, seeing only members of her family. She traveled little and had only a small circle of friends.

She wrote poetry apparently from early womanhood on, often giving poems to her family or friends as gifts. She came to the attention of Samuel Bowles, editor of the *Springfield Republican,* but he could see little merit in her verse. In 1862 she read an article in the *Atlantic Monthly* by Thomas Wentworth Higginson, giving advice and encouragement to aspiring young writers, and wrote to him, enclosing a few of her poems and asking his opinion of them. He could see merit in her verse but thought it formally flawed. With his help and that of Bowles, and after some "correcting," a few of her poems were later published, but to rather little notice, after which she seems to have given up the idea of publication entirely. After her death, her poems were published by members of her family, in versions that were heavily revised to make them more congenial to the taste of the day. Only in 1955 was a serious attempt made to publish all her poems in the form in which she wrote them, and so far as possible in chronological order. But even this edition is imperfect, as the recent publication of photographic copies of her manuscript books enables us to see.[2]

2. The standard one-volume edition is *The Complete Poems of Emily Dickinson,* edited by Thomas H. Johnson (Boston: Little, Brown and Company, 1955). Compare *The Manuscript Books of Emily Dickinson,* edited by R. W. Franklin (Cambridge, Mass.: Harvard University Press, 1981). Quotations are from: (1) *The Complete Poems of Emily Dickinson,* edited by Thomas H. Johnson. Copyright 1929, 1935 by Martha Dickinson Bianchi; Copyright © renewed 1957, 1963 by Mary L. Hampson. By permission of Little, Brown and Company. (2) *The Poems of Emily Dickinson,* edited by Thomas H. Johnson (Cambridge, Mass.: The Belknap Press of Harvard University Press). Copyright © 1951, 1955, 1983 by the President and Fellows of Harvard College. Reprinted by permission of the publishers and the Trustees of Amherst College.

A note on bibliography. The book and article I have found most useful on Dickinson's verse are, respectively, (1) Cristanne Miller, *Emily Dickinson: A Poet's Grammar* (Cam-

What was so odd and disturbing about her verse? This is in a sense the subject of this whole chapter, but it may be helpful to say that her innovations go far beyond obvious irregularities of meter and rhyme: she feels free to write in ways that are explicitly "ungrammatical," for example, using a plural noun and a singular verb, or making a noun out of any part of speech ("Acres of Perhaps" [696] or "knows not an Until" [779]) or a verb out of a noun. She uses pronouns, especially "it," with no clear reference; she sometimes slides from what looks like a realistic poem, with a speaker situated in a context and a narrative we can follow, to a kind of imagism that resists translation into such terms. Even so good a judge as the poet Conrad Aiken could say in his introduction to a selection of her verse published in 1924 that her genius was "as erratic as it was brilliant. Her disregard for accepted forms or for regularities was incorrigible. Grammar, rhyme, meter—anything went by the board if it stood in the way of thought or freedom of utterance. Sometimes this arrogance was justified; sometimes not."[3] It may be, as Alice Fulton has recently argued, that Dickinson's poetry is so profoundly novel that it is only now, after we have become thoroughly accustomed to modernist verse and prose, from Eliot and Stein and Pound to the present day, that we can begin to see Dickinson's accomplishment in a more appropriate context.[4] Although she is often thought of as eccentric, a kind of genetic sport of poetry with no progeny—or in her terms no "dower"—she may in fact have been influential in ways still unrecognized.[5]

---

bridge, Mass.: Harvard University Press, 1987); and (2) Alice Fulton, "Her Moment of Brocade: The Reconstruction of Emily Dickinson," Parnassus 15 (1989): 9–44. Other useful books include Sharon Cameron, Lyric Time: Dickinson and the Limits of Genre (Baltimore: Johns Hopkins University Press, 1979); Jane Donahue Eberwein, Dickinson: Strategies of Limitation (Amherst, Mass.: University of Massachusetts Press, 1985); Susan Howe, My Emily Dickinson (Berkeley: North Atlantic Books, 1985); and Robert Weisbuch, Emily Dickinson's Poetry (Chicago: University of Chicago Press, 1972). For biography, see Thomas H. Johnson, Emily Dickinson: An Interpretive Biography (Cambridge, Mass.: Harvard University Press, 1955) and Cynthia Griffin Wolff, Emily Dickinson (New York: Alfred A. Knopf, 1986).

3. Selected Poems of Emily Dickinson, edited by Conrad Aiken (New York: Random House [Modern Library], n.d.), page xv.

4. Fulton, "Her Moment of Brocade," page 18. Aiken's comment makes it sound as though Dickinson, a kind of natural free spirit, did not value form at all. Nothing could be farther from the truth: form is essential to meaning in her poetry; though she resists certain established forms, she creates others. Compare Alice Fulton, "Of Formal, Free, and Fractal Verse: Singing the Body Eclectic," Poetry East (Fall 1986): 200–13.

5. "Dower" is a rich term for Dickinson, meaning at once the process of transmission by inheritance and her own participation in it. See Fulton, "Her Moment of Brocade"; and

If she seems difficult to us, as she does, one can imagine how she must have read to one whose sensibility was formed by the conventions of poetic discourse out of which, and against which, she wrote. To define these would be the subject of a book in itself, but perhaps a slight sense of her world can be conveyed by some instances. Consider, for example, the *Atlantic Monthly,* in which the essay by Higginson appeared. This was the leading literary magazine of New England; it normally published a mix of stories, essays, and poems, and the Dickinsons subscribed to it. Here are the beginnings of some poems it published between January and June of 1863, at the height of Dickinson's productive period. None of them is worth reproducing in full, but these glances at them will give some sense of the demands of the contemporary ear for rhythm, rhyme, voice, and diction:

A

O mourner by the ever-mourning deep,
Full as the sea of tears! Imperial heart,
King in sorrow over all who weep! [Page 176.]

B

The Word of the Lord by night
To the watching Pilgrims came
As they sat by the sea-side,
And filled their hearts with flame. [Page 227.]

C

Yes, tyrants, you hate us, and meanwhile you hate
The self-ruling, chain-breaking, throne-shaking state!
The night-birds dread morning,—your instinct is true,—
The day-star of Freedom brings midnight for you! [Page 288.]

D

We are two travellers, Roger and I.
Roger's my dog.—Come here, you scamp! [Page 321.]

---

Dickinson's poem 505: "What would the Dower be, / Had I the Art to stun myself / With Bolts of Melody!"

E

One year ago, this dreary night,
This house, that in my way,
Checks the swift pulses of delight,
Was cordial glad, and gay. [Page 372.]

F

There's a flag hangs over my threshold,
      whose folds are more dear to me
Than the blood that thrills in my bosom,
      its earnest of liberty:
And dear are the stars it harbors
      in its sunny field of blue
As the hope of a further heaven
      that lights all our dim lives through. [Page 443.]

G

Over the wooded northern ridge
      Between its houses brown,
To the dark tunnel over the bridge
      The street comes straggling down. [Page 626.]

Of course these writers cannot have much influenced Dickinson through her admiration for them, but they do help define the context of approved verse within which she wrote. In one of her letters Dickinson speaks of Keats and Barrett Browning as poets she loved, and presumably she read other well-known poets too: Longfellow and Emerson, Browning and Tennyson. But all of these, while working at a different level of accomplishment from those excerpted above, usually followed the contemporary standard requirements of form.[6] What they wrote was recognizable as poetry; what Dickinson wrote was not always recognizable, by others, as literate. To take an example closer to Dickinson's home, consider her childhood friend, Helen Hunt, later Helen Hunt Jackson, who

6. Whitman was, of course, resisting these same conventions at much the same time, but probably had little influence on Dickinson, both because his work was not well-known until after the best of hers was done and because his resistance took such utterly different forms.

Emerson was a different case: while more conventional in his verse than Dickinson, he was given to a density and intenseness something like hers, and his highly poetic prose did much to undermine the conventional tone in that literary form as well.

became a highly successful and widely published poet.[7] Here is a poem on April, not her best but not wholly atypical either:

> Robins call robins in tops of trees;
> Doves follow doves, with scarlet feet;
> Frolicking babies, sweeter than these,
> Crowd green corners where highways meet.
>
> Violets stir and arbutus wakes,
> Claytonia's rosy bells unfold;
> Dandelion through the meadow makes
> A royal road, with seals of gold.
>
> Golden and snowy and red the flowers,
> Golden, snowy, and red in vain;
> Robins call robins through sad showers;
> The white dove's feet are wet with rain.
>
> For April sobs while these are so glad,
> April weeps while these are so gay,—
> Weeps like a tired child who had,
> Playing with flowers, lost its way.[8]

Hunt was connected with Dickinson by more than time and location; they became friends, and Hunt appreciated Dickinson's verse and urged her to publish it.[9] In a sense, Hunt's work represents what was required to succeed, establishing the standards by which Dickinson's poetry was a failure.

Sometimes Dickinson herself wrote in something of the sentimental vein I am trying to indicate, including in poems that have become famous:

7. She was born as Helen Fiske in Amherst in 1831. She moved away when still a child and lived in many places, including Colorado Springs, where she married William Jackson, a banker. Her verse was praised by Emerson in his introduction to *Parnassus* (1875), his anthology of poetry, and became very popular. Emerson says that her poems "have rare merit of thought and expression, and will reward the reader for the careful attention which they require." *Parnassus,* edited by Ralph Waldo Emerson (Boston: Osgood, 1875), page x. Her book, *A Century of Dishonor* (New York: Harper, 1881), was an indictment of the treatment of Indians by the United States, as was her far more famous novel, *Ramona: A Story* (Boston: Roberts, 1884). She died in 1885. For a brief account, see Rosemary Whitaker, *Helen Hunt Jackson* (Boise, Idaho: Boise State University, 1987).

8. H[elen] H[unt], *Verses* (Boston: Roberts Brothers, 1888), page 150.

9. See Wolff, *Emily Dickinson,* pages 509, 528–29. Wolff tells us that Thomas Wentworth Higginson, upon whose judgment Dickinson at one time counted so much, declared Jackson to be America's finest woman poet. (Page 528.)

## 1

I never saw a Moor—
I never saw the Sea—
Yet know I how the Heather looks
And what a Billow be.[10]

I never spoke with God
Nor visited in Heaven—
Yet certain am I of the spot
As if the Checks were given— [1052.]

## 2

If I can stop one Heart from breaking
I shall not live in vain
If I can ease one Life the Aching
Or cool one Pain

Or help one fainting Robin
Unto his Nest again
I shall not live in Vain. [919.]

## 3

How the Waters closed above Him
We shall never know—
How He stretched His Anguish to us
That—is covered too—

Spreads the Pond Her Base of Lilies
Bold above the Boy
Whose unclaimed Hat and Jacket
Sum the History— [923.][11]

10. Notice this "be," in place of "is": Is this simply bad grammar, compelled by necessity of rhyme? Or has the "be" a larger function? See below pages 238–39.

11. The sentimental poem on the death of a child was a well-established genre. Compare Helen Hunt, "When the Baby died," in *Verses*, page 100; and Dickinson's own "The Beggar Lad—dies early—" [717].

IN ADDITION TO THE GENERAL REQUIREMENTS for "poetry" a set of special conventions applied to would-be poets who were also women, or "poetesses." They were expected to be creatures of feeling, not thought; sentimental; preoccupied with death and sorrow; and pious to the point of simplemindedness.[12]

> In the overwhelming mass of nineteenth century female poetry, the setting is either "the sacred retirement of home" or the inspirational world of nature in which every brook laughs, every mountain is lofty, every sunset-cloud is angel-hued. Love and death are favorite themes, but love excludes sexuality, and death scenes are vague on bodily details beyond a fevered or pale cheek, preferring to concentrate on the sorrow or despair of the mourners and the consolations of faith. . . . Since the typical poem is contemplative and its real subject is the state of the poet's ardent yet submissive soul, it usually contains little action, much aspiration.[13]

Yet as Cheryl Walker says, Dickinson in fact shared some of the preoccupations of the genre: "the concern with intense feeling, the ambivalence towards power, the fascination with death, the forbidden lover and secret sorrow."[14] It would be possible, for example, to read her meeting with

---

12. See Cheryl Walker, *The Nightingale's Burden: Women Poets and American Culture before 1900* (Bloomington: Indiana University Press, 1982), pages 21–57; and Laura Wendorff, "'The Vivid Dreamings of an Unsatisfied Heart': Gender Ideologies, Literary Aesthetics, and the Construction of 'The Poetess,'" which is chapter 1 of a dissertation entitled "Race, Ethnicity, and the Voice of the 'Poetess' in the Lives and Works of Four Late-Nineteenth-Century Women Poets" (1992), on file at the University of Michigan.

13. Alicia Suskin Ostriker, *Stealing the Language: The Emergence of Women's Poetry in America* (Boston: Beacon Press, 1986), page 32. This book has a fine introduction on the kinds of condescension to which women's poetry has traditionally been subjected.

14. Walker, *The Nightingale's Burden*, page 116. As this tradition developed there grew up beside it another, that of the critical notice ironically praising the poetess (or poet) for excruciatingly bad verse. Julia A. Moore, for example, was subjected to such treatment for passages like this:

> If I went to school half the time,
> It was all that I could do;
> It seems very strange to me sometimes,
> And it may seem strange to you.
> It was natural for me to compose,
> And put words into rhyme,
> And the success of my first work
> Is this little song book of mine.
> [*The Sweet Singer of Michigan,* edited
> by Walter Blair (Chicago: Pascal
> Covici, 1928), page 7.]

In his preface Blair objects to the mockery, and sensibly enough: it is ugly to ridicule

Higginson, described by him in a letter to his wife, as having an element of staged posing, meant to establish her as a "poetess":

> A step like a pattering child's in entry & in glided a little plain woman with two smooth bands of reddish hair & a face a little like Belle Dove's; not plainer—with no good feature—in a very plain and exquisitely clean white pique & a blue net worsted shawl. She came to me with two day lilies which she put in a sort of childlike way into my hand & said "These are my introduction" in a soft frightened breathless childlike voice—& added under her breath Forgive me if I am frightened: I never see strangers & hardly know what I say—but she talked soon & thenceforward continuously—& deferentially—sometimes stopping to ask me to talk instead of her—but readily recommencing.[15]

The combination of "continuously" and "deferentially" catches something of what Dickinson's situation must have been, enacting what Alicia Ostriker calls the "conflict in a woman writer between the assertion required of her as a writer and the submission required of her as a woman."[16]

Dickinson's relation to the contemporary sense of what counted as poetry was thus necessarily a complex one. She was not after all a Martian, dropped into western Massachusetts with a sensibility somehow all her own, but a person trained and educated into her culture. The forms of poetry as it existed around her, and its themes too, were her starting point, as they had to be. Yet she transformed her medium beyond recognition, in this sense denying the authority of convention and claiming authority for her own voice and style, perhaps as completely and effectively as anyone ever has.

---

the efforts of such a wholly self-taught woman to write poetry, and doubly so when one encourages her by seeming praise.

Perhaps the ultimate of this type is a man, J. Gordon Coogler, whose immortal couplet— "Alas, for the South! Her books have grown fewer—She never was much given to literature"—was the centerpiece of Mencken's attack on southern culture in "The Sahara of the Bozart." See J. Gordon Coogler, *Purely Original Verse,* edited by Claude Neuffer and Rene Laborde (Columbia, S.C.: Vogue Press, 1974); and H. L. Mencken, *Prejudices: Second Series* (New York: A. A. Knopf, 1920), pages 136–54. I am grateful to Professor Stanley Gwynne of the University of Chicago for introducing me to Coogler.

15. *Emily Dickinson: Selected Letters,* edited by Thomas H. Johnson (Cambridge, Mass.: Harvard University Press, 1971), pages 207–8. Alice Fulton suggested this reading in conversation.

16. Ostriker, *Stealing the Language,* page 34.

THE CONSTRAINTS WITHIN WHICH she was raised were not merely formal ones. What mattered was not merely that people expected poetry to rhyme and scan, but why they did so, and this raises the question what they thought poetry was for in the first place. From the examples given above we can see that poetry was meant as a kind of elevated expression, as indeed the prose of the time was too. The *Atlantic,* for example, is full of stuffily cultivated writing, one function of which was no doubt to reassure the reader that he too was a cultivated person, in touch with the best sort of people. This was the creation of a world of tone and taste in which the reader could feel comfortably secure; and it established manners that would enable one to carry this sense over to the social world as well, in a tradition of English prose that goes back at least to Addison and Steele. Emerson played off this style, using it, for example, in the famous opening of "Nature": "To go into solitude a man needs to retire as much from his chamber as from society." Here he assumes, as natural, a way of talking that generalizes confidently about what "a man" needs to do—a certain sort of man, of course—and takes for granted a division of the world into one's "chamber" and something called "society." (As I shall in fact briefly suggest later in this chapter, however, he rather quickly moves from this into very different ways of talking indeed.)

Poetry was elevated expression of a somewhat different kind. To characterize this tradition in a phrase would be impossible, but I do have a sense that part of its point was a kind of transportation to another level of life from the usual, one that is sentimental and hence pure, or purified: to a plane of higher feeling.[17] One can imagine readers treating this kind of poetry a bit like a drug, to be taken regularly, or perhaps using it as a kind of cultural icon, to be referred to with admiration and even reverence.

Both the poetry and the prose that Dickinson is likely to have read were written to affirm solidarity rather than distinctiveness of sentiment. Any expression, that is, must choose a point on the spectrum from usual to unique, for a wholly original linguistic gesture is as impossible as a wholly reiterated one. Our sentences are new, but they cannot be too new

---

17. As Wendorff tells us in "'The Vivid Dreamings of an Unsatisfied Heart,'" page 35, "A critic for the North American Review . . . wrote that 'the true and only worthy object of literary effort . . . is to purify the heart while . . . enlarg[ing] the mind, and thus to render both, according to their humble measure, worthy of the Source to which they owe their powers." The critic is unnamed. The article is "Mrs. Sigourney and Miss Gould," *North American Review* (1835):442.

or they will be wholly unintelligible. In certain social and cultural contexts it seems to be important to affirm the ways in which we are different, in others the ways in which we are the same—for contemporary instances of the latter one can think, for example, of political rallies or alumni magazines. These are forms easy to disparage, but great art can have this function too, as we shall later see in connection with Lincoln's Second Inaugural Address, and as perhaps tragic drama by its nature demonstrates, to the extent it touches human universals. And, of course, there is nothing about the assertion of individual uniqueness that guarantees that it will be great art; it can be irresponsible, self-indulgent, and boring. The point, then, is not that one kind of literature is good, the other bad, but to suggest that in Dickinson's world the literature that defined high culture tended to confirm sameness of attitude, sentiment, and manners. Perhaps this was driven by the fear that America was, compared with Europe, nowhere;[18] but, whatever the reason, in reading the *Atlantic* and the verse of such people as Holmes and Lowell and Channing, one feels in the presence of those who are constantly asserting the meaning and value of a shared way of life, all in the service of a kind of gentility.

This may begin to suggest why Dickinson did not, or could not, compose verse that met the standards of her day. One might ask, after all, "If she was so good a poet, why couldn't she work within these constraints? Keats at least met the formal requirements of verse, if not the social ones just referred to, and so did Barrett Browning—two of her favorite poets. So why couldn't she?" The short answer is that the constraints were, as I say, not merely formal but substantive, deeply affecting the meaning of what she did, conflicting with what she thought her poetry "was for." She strenuously resisted the sentimental, for example, including her own tendencies that way. As for a longer answer, it is my aim in the rest of this chapter to provide one, by sketching out what poetry might have meant

18. Here is what Henry James in a famous paragraph says about America:

[O]ne might enumerate the items of high civilization, as it exists in other countries, which are absent from the texture of American life, until it should become a wonder to know what was left. No State, in the European sense of the word, and indeed barely a specific national name. No sovereign, no court, no personal loyalty, no aristocracy, no church, no clergy, no army, no diplomatic service, no country gentlemen, no palaces, no castles, nor manors, nor old country-houses, nor parsonages, nor thatched cottages, nor ivied ruins; no cathedrals, nor abbeys, nor little Norman churches; no great Universities nor public schools—no Oxford, nor Eton, nor Harrow; no literature, no novels, no museums, no pictures, no political society, no sporting class—No Epsom nor Ascot! [Henry James, *Hawthorne* (1879: Ithaca, N.Y.: Cornell University Press, 1956), page 34.]

to her and why it could not, without intolerable loss, be cast in ways that met the expectations of her time.[19] This was a central issue for her in every way, since poetry was central to her life. Not a profession, not even an art, it seems to have been the essence of her existence: she withdrew from the world and from the family to a private space in which she wrote out her experience in poetry, as an alternative way of being that she chose over engagement with the social and external world of Amherst. Yet poetry for her was not escape; it is where she focused her energy and ambition, placing the bet of her life here.

## DICKINSON'S WAY OF MAKING POEMS

Dickinson's achievement lies not so much in the composition of a few discrete works of art that are undeniable masterpieces, like Keats's Odes,

---

19. Consider the very article by Higginson to which Dickinson responded so strongly, "Letter to a Young Contributor," *Atlantic Monthly* 9 (April 1862):401–11. In tone this article is formal, smug, and stuffy; it must have felt patronizing to Dickinson, especially as a woman. Here is how it began: "My dear young gentleman or young lady,—for many are the Cecil Dreemes of literature who superscribe their offered manuscripts with very masculine names and in very feminine handwriting,—it seems wrong not to meet your accumulated and urgent entreaties with one comprehensive reply, thus condensing many private letters into a printed one."

This speaker lives in a world in which the standard of excellence in writing is perfectly plain and, he assumes, universally shared. "No editor can ever afford the rejection of a good thing, and no author the publication of a bad one. The only difficulty lies in drawing the line." The extremes are easy to identify; the trouble lies in the "vast range of mediocrity which perplexes: the majority are too bad for blessing and too good for banning." When an editor does make an error, he is unlikely to confess it but to "stand up stoutly for the surpassing merits of the misshapen thing, as a mother for her deformed child." All this presupposes that the author knows, that "everyone" knows, what good literature is; just the suppositions that Dickinson must have felt herself obliged to write against.

Why then was she so excited by this piece? His remarks on style strike a different note, one that may have encouraged her enormously. "An unexceptionable style is merely a matter of culture and good models," he says; true enough and true, to my ear at least, of him. But he calls for something else entirely, a kind of condensed and vital writing, different from his own and from the run of material he published and evidently thought so good. "Often times a word shall speak what accumulated volumes have labored in vain to utter: there may be years of crowded passion in a word, and half a life in a sentence." This acknowledgment of the value of intense and concentrated writing is odd, for he certainly does not meet his own standards, and who knows what he meant by these phrases; but this language does describe Dickinson's poetry, and she must have been thrilled to read it. "Literature is attar of roses, one distilled drop from a million blossoms." To see what she made of the same image, compare "Essential Oils—are wrung—" (675) and "This was a Poet—" (448).

This note, however, is the only one of its kind in an essay that for the most part repro-

say, as in the definition of a new way of making poetry. Not that she does not write wonderful poems that can stand well alone, but they mean much more when they are read together, as part of a larger effort and in each other's light. Like Stein or Picasso, she defined a new style or method of expression; as with their work too, the whole of her poetry is much more than the sum of the parts.

One way to think of it is to say that in the course of her poems she made a language of her own, running against the poetic conventions of her day. Part of this is a matter of particular words—"noon" and "circumference," for example, take on quite remarkable meanings of their own—but this is not all: part of it lies in her habits of punctuation and capitalization, part in her transformed grammar, part in her mixtures of diction, part in her voice, part simply in the intensity and density of her expression. She feels perfectly free to make new words, or use them in new ways: "plummetless" (271), "stirless" (780), "contenteder" (639), "miles of Stare" (243), "to fail—is Infidel" (387), "Because I see—New Englandly" (285), "countless Butterfly" (100), "The Adequate of Hell" (744), and so on. She especially likes to make her verbs tenseless or modal, by dropping the "s" that a singular subject calls for, just as she drops the plural in "countless Butterfly." One effect of this is to break the comfortable connection language has with the mind and thus to make the language itself the object of attention; another is to create a world that is unspecified and abstract.

Consider the following:

> Essentials Oils—are wrung—
> The Attar from the Rose
> Be not expressed by Suns—alone—
> It is the gift of Screws—
>
> The General Rose—decay—
> But this—in Lady's Drawer
> Make Summer—When the Lady lie
> In Ceaseless Rosemary— [675.]

A paraphrase might go like this: "Perfume is not created by a purely natural process (by 'Suns—alone': which is also 'Sons—alone,' so it is not

---

duces conventional ideas in conventional language: "The first demand made by the public upon every composition is, of course, that it should be attractive." Or: "Be neither too lax nor too precise in your use of language: the one fault ends in stiffness, the other in slang."

created by a purely male process either), but requires human and mechanical effort, pressing by 'Screws' (which may, depending upon the state of slang when Dickinson wrote, reintroduce the male); when this is done, the perfume will continue its force long past a human life, though the ordinary or untransformed rose decays." This poem is not only about perfume, of course, but art; both its cost, and its claim to immortality.

This poem, like many others, puts several of its verbs in an apparently ungrammatical or at least odd form, in which a singular subject takes a plural, or perhaps subjunctive, or perhaps just unmarked verb. In *A Poet's Grammar*, Cristanne Miller says this:

> In ordinary prose the sentence would read: Attar *is* not expressed by suns: "Be" is the infinitive or subjunctive or the uninflected form of the expected, standard "is." Three other uninflected verbs occur in the poem's remaining five lines: "the Rose *decay*," "This *Make*," and "the Lady *lie*." Leaving these verbs unmarked for person, function, or tense suggests that they represent essential or primary process and activity.[20]

Another feature of "Essential Oils—are wrung" is its sheer difficulty, largely created by the extraordinary density and compactness of language, so different from the poetic convention of the day, which was to spell things out at sometimes tiresome length. As Miller says, one result of this condensed style is a sense of power withheld, if only the power to explain, and with it often an implied sense of profundity as well. Dickinson's words are delphic or lapidary—each one counts for many words— and this gives them a weight and richness lacking in ordinary prose and most poetry too. The grammatical dislocations—like the dashes and capitals—also focus attention on the words as they appear in the poem, one by one, related not by prose logic but by poetic association. Likewise Dickinson's pronouns, especially "it," are often unspecified, again leaving us with a deep uncertainty: there is either no reference to a specific person, or thing, or experience, or there is a secret one, and in either case one has the sense of poetry disconnected from the material and social world.[21]

---

20. Cristanne Miller, *Emily Dickinson*, pages 64–65, and compare *ibid.*, pages 4–5. Much of Miller's book, to which I am greatly indebted, is given to an explication of the way Dickinson makes a new language that is far more complete than the one sketched here. Her reading of "Essential Oils—are wrung" is especially helpful.

21. *Ibid.*, pages 27, 81. Compare "It's like the Light" (297), where the "it" is never specified at all, and "Many a phrase has the English language— / I have heard but one" (276), where the speaker never identifies the phrase she speaks of.

To give a more particular sense of the way Dickinson makes poetry, I reproduce below a series of poems, mostly well-known, followed by comments or explications. These will of necessity be somewhat skeletal, tending to slide over alternative readings.[22] In each poem, I shall focus attention mainly on the way Dickinson addressed and transformed the poetic expectations of her world. See, for example, how conventionally she begins this one:

*"Success is counted sweetest"*

Success is counted sweetest
By those who ne'er succeed.
To comprehend a nectar
Requires sorest need.

Not one of all the purple Host
Who took the Flag today
Can tell the definition
So clear of Victory

As he defeated—dying—
On whose forbidden ear
The distant strains of triumph
Burst agonized and clear! [67.]

The tone of the first two lines seems utterly standard: it is an assured pronouncement of accepted truths and values, almost a kind of preaching, having as its function the sort of authoritative reassurance that I ascribed to the prose of the *Atlantic*. One thinks, unfairly, of Matthew Arnold, perhaps more fairly of Arthur Hugh Clough or one of the lesser Victorians. But the next two lines use quite a different diction and style: Why think of "nectar" here, with implications of bees and honey, or, if of nectar, why not in a formula like "the nectar of Victory"? And what of this word "comprehend," which seems vague and out of place: why not "desire" or "taste" or "appreciate" (which would even scan if the "to" were elided, thus: "T'appreciate a nectar . . .")? There is a shift here from one language to another, an unexplained break in the surface of assurance established by the opening lines. Similarly, "Requires" must be read as three syllables to scan, which is either a real awkwardness or the

22. For a fine demonstration of the openness of Dickinson's verse to multiple readings, see Fulton, "Her Moment of Brocade," pages 27–42.

incorporation of the rhythms of colloquial speech, either of which undermines the sedate cultural confidence of the initial voice.

The poem has the familiar metrical structure of the hymn, "eights
and sixes," that is, with four iambic feet in one line, followed by a line
with three. This, along with other hymn-forms, will be a dominant form
throughout Dickinson's verse, marking her religious themes, her pretense
of simplicity, and her willingness to use established forms. She transforms
what she touches; but what she touches is a set of verse forms as conservative as any in the language.[23]

In this poem Dickinson moves from a conventional, almost pietistic
opening to a disturbing application of the truism about success: it is not
just in games and war that the loser "comprehends" what the winner
misses but in the great struggle for salvation, in which she imagines not
the triumph described in the hymn but a kind of essential defeat, claiming
that it is compensated for by an increase in knowledge. The dead and
dying can "tell the definition" of victory better than anyone; as applied
to salvation, it means that the lost and the damned are in this respect
better situated than the saved. This is to give particular value to a certain
kind of failure, which can then be seen to bring with it the possibility of
another kind of success, based on knowledge. What seems to be a sermon
propounding established and sentimental truths becomes on this reading
a thinly veiled expression of the poet's own situation in life, an early definition of the dramatic relation between her withdrawal from life, with all
its victories, and the even greater success she hopes for.

*"I like a look of Agony"*

I like a look of Agony,
Because I know it's true—

23. In this poem she also uses a language of martial victory that is common in hymns.
Compare the images here, for example:
    And when the strife is fierce, the warfare long,
    Steals on the ear the distant triumph song,
    And hearts are brave again, and arms are strong.
    [William Walsham How, 1864. Hymn 287 in
    the Episcopal Church Hymn Book, 1982.]
Dickinson may not have known this hymn, but in the collection of hymns by Isaac Watts
that the Dickinsons owned there was plenty of talk about "battles" and "victory" and
"triumph." (I mention the How hymn here because it so closely matches the "distant strains
of triumph" in the poem.)

Much of Dickinson's early verse is emotionally simple, some of it sentimental, but there
are occasional touches of the bleakness that will follow. Think, for example, of Poem 136,
beginning as a pure piece of sentimental nature poetry—"Have you got a Brook in your

Men do not sham Convulsion,
Nor simulate, a Throe—

The Eyes glaze once—and that is Death—
Impossible to feign
The Beads upon the Forehead
By homely Anguish strung. [241.]

The voice at work here is as far from the sentimental and cozy as one could easily imagine. It first admits that it "likes" the agony of others— as is no doubt true of much of the lugubrious death poetry of the day, a fact usually masked or denied—and then explains why, in terms completely inconsistent with the sentimentality of ordinary funereal verse: because it is "true." This is the expression of a mind haunted by mistrust of her experience of what other people say, or what they claim to feel, to the point of finding affirmative satisfaction in the suffering of others. The satisfaction comes not from sadism—there is no pleasure of that kind here—but because, for once, the central obsession with "truth" is satisfied. This poem thus catches an essential ingredient of Dickinson's own psychology, and one that helps explain her need to speak in her own forms and voices, to assert herself against the literary authorities of her world: authenticity is the first test of value for the voice at work here; yet the conventional verse of her day repeatedly asserted the adequacy of a language that blurred or occluded individual experience. To a voice like Helen Hunt Jackson's, what mattered was not the self but the culture. Dickinson reverses the hierarchy built into the idea of poetry at work in her world.

As I suggested earlier, and as this poem makes plain, Dickinson's punctuation and capitalization are distinctive. Cristanne Miller has shown that this aspect of form in Dickinson's work is not incidental to its meaning, or simply fey or quirky, but of great importance.[24] See what happens, for example, when this poem is regularized in these respects, as it is in the Aiken edition of the poems referred to earlier:

I like a look of agony,
Because I know it's true;

---

little heart, / Where bashful flowers blow . . ."—and continuing in this vein until the end— "Beware, lest this little brook of life, / Some burning noon go dry!"—where she introduces a different and more ominous note.

24. See Cristanne Miller, *Emily Dickinson,* pages 58–59.

Men do not sham convulsion,
Nor simulate a throe.

The eyes glaze once, and that is death.
Impossible to feign
The beads upon the forehead
By homely anguish strung.

In this instance the changes are rather few, but they deeply affect the way the whole is read. In Dickinson's first line, for example, the capitalization emphasizes "Agony," leading the reader to pause upon it. The Aiken version reduces this effect, leading the reader to run on quickly to the next line, as though the speaker's emphasis were on the explanation, not the fact explained. Dickinson's typography invites an equal balance: first, unconnected to anything else, comes "I like a look of Agony," with its sense of shock; second, the reason, which is that it is "true."

The semicolon at the end of line two in the Aiken edition defines the speaker as a rationalist, moving now to a subsidiary argument the relation of which to the main point requires exactly this marker. In Dickinson the dash leaves all suspended. In this, as in her use of capitalization, Dickinson moves from syntactical structures that are meant to clarify by subordination, as standard English prose does, to a kind of parataxis, a placing side-by-side without marking the relation. "Men do not sham Convulsion, / Nor simulate, a Throe—" thus looks forward as well as backward, surrounded as it is by dashes; we slide naturally from this image of agony to the next one, when "The Eyes glaze once." In the Aiken version, the period breaks this connection and forces the lines about "Throe" and "Convulsion" into a single status, as explanatory of line two, breaking its forward-looking impetus. Likewise, Dickinson's line "Impossible to feign" looks both back to the eyes glazing and forward to the beads, while in Aiken the only connection is forward. This means that the reader does not experience the moment of uncertainty about the placement of this line, whether it connects forward or back; this is to damage the poem badly, for an essential part of its meaning lies precisely in this moment of glide, of uncertain attachment and detachment. To rewrite this poem to emphasize logical structure and connection is to undo just what the poem does so well. Similarly, in the Aiken version the regularity of the rhythm becomes overwhelming, turning this bleak poem into just the kind of singsong from which Dickinson's punctuation, her capitals and dashes, were all a way of escaping.

*"There's a certain Slant of light"*

There's a certain Slant of light,
Winter Afternoons—
That oppresses, like the Heft
Of Cathedral Tunes—

Heavenly Hurt, it gives us—
We can find no scar,
But internal difference,
Where the Meanings, are—

None may teach it—Any—
'Tis the Seal Despair—
An imperial affliction
Sent us of the Air—

When it comes, the Landscape listens—
Shadows—hold their breath—
When it goes, 'tis like the Distance
On the look of Death— [258.]

   To begin with the matters of form just discussed, one can see how the capitals here serve to mark emphasis, the dashes and commas to indicate pauses and shifts of voice. The punctuation is to be read, that is, not as it is in most modern prose, as an index of logical relations, but, as it was originally used in English, and Latin too, as a set of directions to one reading it aloud. Hence, for example, the comma after "Meanings" in line eight works as a pause, and the dash after "Shadows" tells the reader, like the shadows, to hold her breath.

   But there is a gap even between the version reproduced above and the poem as originally composed. While Dickinson did at one stage seek publication, and a handful of her poems were published during her lifetime—mainly in the *Springfield Republican,* as I said earlier, and in versions reflecting the editing of others—the form in which she preserved her poems was in manuscript leaves and books (now partly available in facsimile form) and in letters to her friends and family.[25] It would have been possible for her to print the poems privately, as others—including Walt Whitman—did, but she seems gradually to have given up the desire

<hr>

25. For the history of the publication of her poems, see Wolff, *Emily Dickinson,* pages 238–59.

for publication at all.[26] "Publication—is the Auction / Of the Mind of Man," she later said with contempt (709).

When we focus on the poems she actually wrote, as she left them behind her, we discover that they cannot be translated to print without loss. For one thing, the dashes are not the regular and straight em-dashes of the print shop but gestures, in ink, of varying lengths and directions: some are long, some very short, almost periods; some are lightly drawn with the pen, others dark and heavy; some are horizontal, some angle up or down. Likewise the letters do not fall into two rigid classes, majuscule and minuscule, but range in size from the small to the large. In the manuscript book version of this poem, for example, the word "Can" in line six looks like a capital to me, but it is not registered that way by the editor, presumably because it is a verb and he assumes that Dickinson's aim, following standard eighteenth-century style, is to capitalize only nouns. But in this he may miss an important element of Dickinson's improvisatory resistance to convention.

The biggest difference in reading the manuscript is the sense one has that this poem was written, actually written by a person with pen on paper, at a moment in time, and meant to exist in this form, not another. Her manuscript books were not texts to be later converted into print but careful compilations to be preserved as written. Reading the facsimile manuscript is thus like reading a photocopy of a letter, itself no accident since so many of her poems were included in letters or were themselves letters. ("This is my letter to the World / That never wrote to Me" [441].) All this contributes to the sense that the poem is not a public performance but a part of a person's life. It still speaks with her voice, and we want to hear her say these words; they are still marked as hers, and have not yet become merged with the voice of the *Atlantic Monthly* or with the other poets declaiming on its pages.

"A certain Slant of light" seems at first thoroughly accessible. The only difficulties of surface meaning are the "Any" in line nine, which translates rather quickly into "Anything," (or maybe a reiteration of "None" in a different key), and "the Seal Despair," which is actually plain enough: she speaks here of a seal like one used to mark the wax on an envelope, a seal that reads "Despair" or belongs to a personified Despair. And, to judge by my own response at least, the initial appeal of the poem is to familiarity: "There's a certain Slant of light, Winter Afternoons"

---

26. Ibid., pages 240–41.

invites the reader to say, "Yes of course, I know exactly what you mean," an invitation reinforced by the colloquial "There's" and the cadencing omission of the preposition "on" before "Winter Afternoons."

But what are we in fact told of this "Slant of light"? Is it the kind of dim luminescence that casts just the slightest shadow on the brown lawn but pains the eyes with brightness, or perhaps the slightly yellowing sunshine of the late afternoon—here's the "Slant"—falling on snow that has melted and frozen again during the day, or the cast of heavy grayness through a window into a room whose inhabitant depends upon the outside light to read by until the time to light the lamps has come? All these and many more would do; an infinity of possibilities. We are told nothing, however, of the physical particulars. The quality of the light is defined rather by its effect on the speaker, generalized to include all of us: it oppresses, and hurts, and leaves us looking as if upon death. The manner of oppression is defined—it is "like the Heft / Of Cathedral Tunes"—reminding one perhaps of a glumly wheezing church organ, or of being made to go to church in the first place, especially on Sunday "Afternoons." This tells us nothing of the physical qualities of the light, but it does define the speaker as resistant to the institutions of religion.

The next two stanzas define "it"—the light, the oppression—by its source: "it" does not happen randomly but comes from Heaven, as a "Hurt," and is irresistible, an affliction sent from the "imperial" power of the universe. "None may teach it": And what would one seek to teach it? Presumably, the pain it causes; like the father who does not listen to the child, it gives us hurt, without attending or caring. (Notice how the word "it" starts to shift reference from the "Slant of light" to its imperial author.)

All this takes place in a universe that is itself alive and sentient, like a person—the landscape "listens" and shadows "hold their breath"—a universe that is subject to the same source of oppression, the same authority, that converts the world into a death-like state.

The "Slant of light" is specified not in terms of its appearance, then, as it might be in Frost or Keats, but solely by its effect on the speaker's inner life: "internal difference, / Where the Meanings, are—" The poem works out of an experience for which the poet has no words, no images, one that does not, despite its claim, begin in the common world that we observe and share, but within.[27] In describing this feeling, the poet creates

---

27. The word "Slant" itself expresses this obliqueness. Compare: "Tell all the Truth but tell it slant" (1129). Not surprisingly, the word "within" plays a powerful role in her verse.

a world of significance, moving almost instantly from a shared world of observation to what is in fact private and inexpressible: a movement from what can be said in language to what cannot. This is a direct reversal of the premise of the poetic against which she was writing, that everything was mutually understood, everything sayable in this language, the function of which was to affirm the tones and values of a cultured life.

The transformation I describe, from the known to the unknown, or unknowable, is common in Dickinson's poetry, especially in many of her most familiar poems, which have become familiar, I think, partly by the appearance they give of ready intelligibility. Here is another example:

> A Bird came down the Walk—
> He did not know I saw—
> He bit an Angleworm in halves
> And ate the fellow, raw,
>
> And then he drank a Dew
> From a convenient Grass—
> And then hopped sidewise to the Wall
> To let a Beetle pass—
>
> He glanced with rapid eyes
> That hurried all around—
> They looked like frightened Beads, I thought—
> He stirred his Velvet Head
>
> Like one in danger, Cautious,
> I offered him a Crumb
> And he unrolled his feathers
> And rowed him softer home—
>
> Than Oars divide the Ocean,
> Too silver for a seam—
> Or Butterflies, off Banks of Noon
> Leap, plashless as they swim. [328.]

---

"To hear an Oriole sing / May be a common thing— / Or only a divine"; it depends on the hearer, or what she calls "The Fashion of the Ear":

> So whether it be Rune, [meaningful]
> Or whether it be none
> Is of within. [526.]

Compare: "Gethsemane— / Is but a Province—in the Being's Centre—" (553); "Growth of Man—like Growth of Nature— / Gravitates within—" (750); "The Outer—from the Inner / Derives its Magnitude" (451).

The poet begins with a way of talking in which she has complete confidence, and we do too: the bird is like us—like a reader of the *Atlantic,* in fact—for he has manners (he lets the beetle pass) and familiar equipment too (he drinks from a "grass," as we from a glass), though he does have a touch of the uncivilized, even the cannibal: he "ate the fellow, raw." The overt shift in the poet's feelings begins at "frightened beads," where she imagines the bird not so much as another human being but as a cross between us and the inanimate and unfeeling world, as an object with feelings. Perhaps out of anxiety created by the collapse of her effort to humanize and socialize the bird, she reaches out to it; but it, in response, becomes something else altogether, a blur of images—oars on a silver sea, butterflies swimming in air. The bird cannot be appropriated in our language of social familiarity after all; to speak of what it is and does the poet uses a language that we might call surreal.[28]

*"Nature—sometimes sears a Sapling"*

Nature—sometimes sears a Sapling—
Sometimes—scalps a Tree—
Her Green People recollect it
When they do not die—

Fainter Leaves—to Further Seasons—
Dumbly testify—
We—who have the Souls—
Die oftener—Not so vitally— [314.]

Like "There's a certain Slant of light" and "Success is counted sweetest," this poem takes the form of declamation, a version of the voice of the philosopher or theologian or moralist, telling us how the world is. In speaking of "Nature," which is one of the great categories of transcendental thought and of romanticism more generally, Dickinson gives rise to the expectation that this will be a poem of uplift, speaking of the force of good that rolls through all things, like Emerson perhaps. This hope is quickly dashed: to begin with, the "sometimes" creates a sense of vari-

---

28. The same structure is at work in another familiar poem, "A narrow Fellow in the Grass" (986), where the speaker at first tries to appropriate with ordinary social discourse a snake seen in the grass—"You may have met Him, did you not? / His notice sudden is"— but cannot maintain this and is forced at the end to admit its alienness: "Several of Nature's People / I know, and they know me— / I feel for them a transport / Of cordiality— / But never met this Fellow / Attended, or alone / Without a tighter breathing / And Zero at the Bone—"

ability, maybe whimsicality, that is inconsistent with it; and then "sears a Sapling" is an image of hostile and, so far as we can see, motiveless destruction. "Nature" is known by this action, this sibilant-laden injury, which is reinforced by the next: the "Sometimes" in line two at first suggests an alternation from the destructive to the constructive, but what we get instead is an intensification: "scalps a Tree."

"Her Green People"? At first it sounds like elves, as though this will break into a kind of cute nature poem; but then we realize that it is the injured trees themselves that recollect, when they are not killed by the operation. This possibility adds another dimension of bleakness, on either assumption: either it kills them or the pain is with them forever.

"Fainter Leaves—to Further Seasons— / Dumbly testify" is to me obscure, yet in a generative way. Does it mean: The leaves are fainter because of the scalping, but their continued existence promises that the tree will continue to grow? Or are the "Fainter Leaves" not on the tree, growing, but on the ground, where they become fainter as they decay, testifying not to future but to earlier "Further" seasons, when the tree was alive? Both of these readings assume that *although* the leaves are fainter they testify to "Further Seasons," but the syntax suggests that these two words are in some way parallel: the fact that they are "Fainter" is exactly what implies the "Further," though I see no way to make that work in the world of trees and leaves. In this, as in so much of her work, Dickinson carries us from an imaginable to an unimaginable world.

One suggestion is that with the trees there will be something further, in contrast with "us," who die even though we "have the souls" and are supposedly immortal. And how do we die? From the contrast we expect something like "more quickly," "more permanently," without a "further" stage; but what we get is "oftener," which presents a puzzle. How can we die "oftener"? If people are aggregated it would work, so that it meant: the death of a person is commoner than the storm-caused death of a tree. But it could also refer to each of us: each of us dies frequently, in which case death has to mean not the single unique termination of life but the kind of death-in-life we sometimes suffer when it seems that all has died within us—the sort of death described in fact in "A certain Slant of light."

All the energy of the poem is now focused: we die "—Not so vitally—" What can this mean? That our deaths are less energetic than scalping and searing, a kind of mild passing away? That when we are dead we are less vital than the trees, when they are dead? That while their "Fainter Leaves—to Further Seasons— / Dumbly testify," we do not continue on as they do but perish completely? "Vital death" is a radical paradox, an intense and dislocating compression that leaves us, so far as explicit prose sense goes, nowhere at all; but in the experience of the poem, we end in a flash of energy, created by the paradox itself and by the emphasis given the terminal trisyllabic word by the rhyme and meter, an emphasis so common as almost to amount to a signature for Dickinson.[29]

The poem Dickinson's editor places next in the series picks up some of the key terms of the preceding, showing us, in slow motion as it were, how Dickinson creates a vocabulary of her own as she works through her poems:

*"He fumbles at your Soul"*

> He fumbles at your Soul
> As Players at the Keys
> Before they drop full Music on—
> He stuns you by degrees—
> Prepares your brittle Nature
> For the Ethereal Blow
> By fainter Hammers—further heard—
> Then nearer—Then so slow
> Your Breath has time to straighten—
> Your Brain—to bubble Cool—
> Deals—One—imperial—Thunderbolt—
> That scalps your naked Soul—
> When Winds take Forests in their Paws—
> The Universe—is still— [315.]

Here "scalps" is made the central moment of the whole poem, intensified not only by its placement at the climax but because it is "you"—not a tree—that is scalped. Again we have "fainter-further" but this time it refers to the hammers of the piano, fainter than those that will strike the great fortissimo blow, now heard as it were from a distance. These "Hammers" will themselves come back in "The Morning after Woe" (364), when the grieving speaker feels of the bird songs that surround her that "The Birds declaim their Tunes— / Pronouncing every word / Like Hammers"—that is, the bird song is not song at all but declamation, and

---

29. Compare the ending of "Because I could not stop for Death," in which the "Immortality" of the opening carriage ride becomes something very different indeed: "Eternity." A modern poet could not end a poem with a word like this without evoking memories of Dickinson's work.

it hits like hammers. The "imperial—Thunderbolt" recalls the "imperial affliction" of "There's a certain Slant of light"; and it too will come back in another form, still associated with "stuns," in the famous Poem 505, also about art, which concludes: "What would the Dower be, / Had I the Art to stun myself / With Bolts of Melody!"

In both "He fumbles at your Soul" and Poem 505 art is seen as a form of aggression or violence, in the latter absolutely, in the former as a term of comparison: it is the unspecified "He" who acts on you, not through art but like it. The verbs that describe what he does, as opposed to what the piano player does, are "scalps" and the erotically laden "fumbles." The whole image is of a hostile, intelligent male force acting against "you" but with some of the qualities of art. The emphasis has shifted from the quality of the death—"Not so vitally"—to the quality of action, the scalping, and the nature of its nonresistant victim. The final couplet catches the moment before it happens, when the predator has the other in his paws, a moment of "pause" in the temporal sense, before the act of destruction. To return to typography, see how essential the dashes are to the central line—"Deals—One—imperial—Thunderbolt"—and how comparatively vapid it would be without them.

THESE POEMS MAINTAIN SOME OF THE regularities that the conventions of the day demanded, but they also transform them. "I like a look of Agony" is metrically quite regular until Dickinson acts upon the rhythm with dashes and capitals. And its rhymes are overtly partial—"true" and "Throe," "feign" and "strung"—in ways that affirm the minor key in which the poem is composed. "A certain Slant of light" is regular in rhyme throughout, but "Nature—sometimes sears a Sapling" puts "Tree" with "die," "testify" with "vitally," moving in the direction of whole rhymes without ever quite getting there. "A narrow Fellow in the Grass" moves from off-rhymes to whole rhymes, but in a context that makes these threatening, not reassuring: "But never met this Fellow / Attended, or alone / Without a tighter breathing / And Zero at the Bone—." And "A Bird came down the Walk" reverses this direction, from comfortable and familiar rhymes at the beginning—"saw"/"raw," "Grass"/"pass,"—to patterns that enact the sort of dissociation the end of the poem brings: "Crumb"/"home," "seam"/"swim." The point is that Dickinson does not simply abandon rhyme as a constraint, or meter either, but employs both in newly expressive ways. Her art lies not in rejection but in refinement of form.

Her substantive attitudes likewise transform those with which she was surrounded. She writes about "Nature," it is true, but not in accord with usual romantic assumptions. It is sometimes an implacably hostile force, sometimes—as in "A certain Slant of light"—it witnesses or suffers as we do at the hands of an even greater force. Art is one of her subjects, as it is for others, but for her art is not reassuring, civilized, and tame—not genteel—but aggressive, violent, and erotic, and the erotic is not sweet and virginal but itself violent. In expressing these attitudes she is herself in a sense violent with her reader and her language alike, upsetting the expectations of one by attacking the surface coherence of the other. She deals in problem and paradox, not ready intelligibility and cultural reassurance.

One last poem:

*"Because I could not stop for
Death"*

Because I could not stop for Death—
He kindly stopped for me—
The Carriage held but just Ourselves—
And Immortality.

We slowly drove—He knew no haste
And I had put away
My labor and my leisure too,
For His Civility—

We passed the School, where Children strove
At Recess—in the Ring—
We passed the Fields of Gazing Grain—
We passed the Setting Sun—

Or rather—He passed Us—
The Dews grew quivering and chill—
For only Gossamer, my Gown—
My Tippet—only Tulle—

We paused before a House that seemed
A Swelling of the Ground—
The Roof was scarcely visible—
The Cornice—in the Ground—

Since then—'tis Centuries—and yet
Feels shorter than the Day
I first surmised the Horses' Heads
Were toward Eternity— [712.]

The speaker here begins by asserting the adequacy of a social language that will later be found inadequate, just as we saw in "A Bird came
down the Walk." She seems to think that she can neutralize the threat of
death by defining herself, him, and their relation in genteel terms—"He
kindly stopped for me." There is too a faint touch of the genteelly erotic,
when the speaker says that the "Carriage held but just Ourselves," though
this is modified by the addition of "Immortality" as a kind of benign
chaperone. I say benign, for it neutralizes the threat of death: immortal
life is the great promise of Christianity, after all. And like "vitally" in
"Nature—sometimes sears a Sapling," the word "Immortality" is here
emphasized by its terminal location, by the meter, and by the Saxon diction of the rest of the stanza. The language of simple narrative is combined with that of abstract theological reflection, as often in Dickinson,
who is at once one of the most particular and homely of poets, and one
of the most philosophical.

In the stanzas that follow, time itself is transformed: first we are told
that the carriage went slowly, and that the speaker was part of the slow-
ness: she had put away her labor, hence was not anxious about wasting
time; and, more threateningly, she had put away her "leisure too" and is
thus moving into the trance-like state that travel often brings. "We passed
. . . we passed . . . we passed. . . ." The repetition of phrase expresses the
sense of sameness within the carriage, but the stages of the journey are
different: the school, with the young people active in their contained
place, different from ours; the undifferentiated and hence endless fields
of grain, which we now come to see as alive (the fields are "Gazing":
alive, but inactive, in a state not bounded by time); and, finally the "Setting Sun," at which point the narrative starts to become surreal, like a
Greek legend or a fairy tale in which people can pass to the land beyond
the sun. But this is instantly reversed: "Or rather—He passed Us."

Movement has gradually slowed to the point where it becomes stasis:
with the passing of the sun comes cold, an awareness that the speaker is
unprepared for it, the recognition that where she is going is the grave—
described defensively as a "House," but a puzzling and unappealing
one—and finally the shift to: "Since then—'tis Centuries." This phrase
works as the casual incorporation of immense time into the now familiar

voice and rhythms, extending the stasis forward without limit and establishing a new scale of time—forever—for which her word is "Eternity." This word, having the familiar signature emphasis of the closing latinate polysyllable, contrasts directly with "Immortality": those two terms indeed mark the points between which the poem moves, from the claim of immortal life that neutralizes death to the recognition that death itself goes on forever; a movement from promise to despair. From this eschatological perspective the signal event that changes time—in this sense parallel to the incarnation in history—is the moment of recognition, when she first "surmised"—Keats's word—what was to come; a moment that was at once a flash of understanding and longer than centuries.[30] In thus moving from one term to the other—from "Immortality" to "Eternity"—she redefines both, remaking these central terms of her language.

## The Need to Speak Her Own Way

In such ways as these Dickinson transformed the language of poetry, not only in the peculiarity of her diction and her resistance to overly regular meters and rhymes but, more deeply, in her invented syntax, her deliberate opacities, her insistence on the primacy of inexpressible interior life, and her mixture of the philosophic and the ordinary, thus indeed making "amazing sense" of "ordinary Meanings" (448).[31] One is especially struck by the strength of her resistance to the authority of the forms of speech she was given to use as a poet, especially as a "poetess"—by her insistence on speaking her own way. This was not the result of modesty or want of ambition—she wanted to be a poet, and to count as one, and at times her grandiosity is breathtaking—but of a kind of integrity of

30. There is a similar transformation of time in Poem 692:
> The Sun kept setting—setting—still
> No Hue of Afternoon—
> Upon the Village I perceived—
> From House to House 'twas Noon—

The sun seems frozen perpetually in the setting position, or actually in the process of setting; yet the effect of this is not crepuscular but universal "Noon," a physical impossibility that marks Dickinson's familiar movement from the external to the internal world. Compare also, "I'll tell you how the Sun rose—" (318) which has a gradual slowing down that produces a conversion of morning into evening with overtones of death.

31. This phrase evokes the well known hymn, "Amazing Grace," and thus claims a kind of sacramental function for her art.

mind, an insistence, as she says in "I like a look of Agony," on what is "true."

One of the subjects of her poetry is, I think, the drama of this very insistence. To trace out this line of meaning may make her poetry somewhat more accessible and also give some sense of the forces at work within her that drove her to confront and transform her world.

## Moments of Meaning and Instability of Experience

I begin with the observation that her poetry often focuses upon the transforming but impermanent quality of a moment in time. This was true of "A certain Slant of light," in which the world is converted by the "light" into a kind of death, and of "Because I could not stop for Death" too, where the moment of recognition expands to fill eternity.[32] I think that Dickinson often experienced, in a strong form, what people commonly feel in a weaker way, the sense that this, right now, is a moment of intense reality—this moment, as we sit on the river bank, looking at the dappled light fall through the leaves on the water; or as we stand by the fireplace at home, in the evening; or as we glance out the bus window, through the gray afternoon, at the child and the mother, both in red jackets, bending towards each other in symmetry—a moment that is at once timeless and transitory. One thinks of Emerson's well-known account of an extreme version of this kind of experience in "Nature":

> Crossing a bare common, in snow puddles, at twilight, under a clouded sky, without having in my thoughts any occurrence of special good fortune, I have enjoyed perfect exhilaration. I am glad to the brink of fear. . . . Standing on the bare ground,—my head bathed by the blithe air, and uplifted into infinite space,—all mean egotism vanishes. I become a transparent eyeball; I am nothing; I see all; the currents of the Universal Being circulate through me; I am part or parcel of God.

---

32. See also "A Light exists in Spring," which similarly tells of a moment that comes, and passes:

> A quality of loss
> Affecting our Content
> As Trade had suddenly encroached
> Upon a Sacrament. [812.]

"It would never be Common—more—I said" speaks of a momentary sense of great artistic power: "I dealt a word of Gold / To every Creature—that I met— / And Dowered—all the World—" (430). But the moment passes, leaving her shrunk and questioning. "I am ashamed—I hide—" has a similar structure (472).

Such a moment has the quality of transcendence, which means, among other things, that it seems at once momentary and eternal. It can be a moment of perfection, but it can also be, as Emerson hints, a moment of fear or horror.

I think Dickinson had this kind of experience often and intensely.[33] Consider, for example, the following:

> Did Our Best Moment last—
> 'Twould supersede the Heaven—
> A few—and they by Risk—procure—
> So this Sort—are not given—
>
> Except as stimulants—in
> Cases of Despair—
> Or Stupor—The Reserve—
> These Heavenly Moments are—
>
> A Grant of the Divine—
> That Certain as it Comes—
> Withdraws—and leaves the dazzled Soul
> In her unfurnished Rooms [393.]

Here ordinary life is transformed for the moment, this time in a good way, a miraculous way, after which comes the despair of deprivation: "in her unfurnished Rooms." The presence—if it was a presence—made everything wonderful: it goes, and all is worse than before. (Compare: "The Moments of Dominion / That happen on the Soul / And leave it with a Discontent / Too exquisite—to tell—" [627].)

The reader's experience parallels the narrator's, for the poem moves us first from the plainly comprehensible language of the first two lines into an experience of dense and allusive verse that does not easily shake clear into any kind of explicit prose sense, then back into the readily accessible. At the end we know that a visitation has occurred and is now gone, leaving the soul alone in an unfurnished world, but the nature of the visitation is uncertain. The relatively difficult middle section thus in-

---

33. In using her poems as evidence of her own condition I do not mean to regard them as simply and directly autobiographical. Of course she spoke in different voices, tried out different genres, and so forth. Yet her imagined experiences and personae are imagined by her, and it is fair to ask what they mean, especially when we see patterns emerge. Here I will trace out some lines of significance, but without any claim that this is the whole story.

duces in the reader an experience of loss of sure contact with ordinary reality, a kind of transcendence like that of which the poem speaks.[34]
    More disturbing is the following:

> The Soul has Bandaged moments—
> When too appalled to stir—
> She feels some ghastly Fright come up
> And stop to look at her—
>
> Salute her—with long fingers—
> Caress her freezing hair—
> Sip, Goblin, from the very lips
> The Lover—hovered—o'er—
> Unworthy, that a thought so mean
> Accost a Theme—so—fair—
>
> The soul has moments of Escape—
> When bursting all the doors—
> She dances like a Bomb, abroad,
> And swings upon the Hours,
>
> As do the Bee—delirious borne—
> Long Dungeoned from his Rose—
> Touch Liberty—then know no more,
> But Noon, and Paradise—
>
> The Soul's retaken moments—
> When, Felon led along,
> With shackles on the plumed feet,
> And staples, in the Song,
>
> The Horror welcomes her, again,
> These, are not brayed of Tongue— [512.]

Here life is represented as a series of moments: bandaged, escaped, retaken. The collapse at the end is not accidental but explicitly punitive:

---

34. Not that these lines are purely imagistic or unintelligible. One possible reading is this: "Only a few people ever attain this kind of experience, and that at great risk; because these moments are so dangerous they are not made available to those not energetic and daring enough to procure them for themselves, except as a kind of medicine: 'as stimulants—in / Cases of Despair— / Or Stupor.'" I don't quite know how to read "The Reserve," but after this point the poem flows readily enough if you see that the last sentence begins with "These Heavenly Moments."

the achieved freedom and bliss—the experience of "Noon, and Paradise"—is defined as a felony. The use of "Noon" to describe the state of freedom has deep resonance in the rest of Dickinson: this is a word used over and over to express a certain kind of perfection of being. "Noon," as she defines it, is a moment, for it passes and in a sense you know it will, yet it is also timeless, for it feels like forever.[35] "Noon" is paradise, the moment that promises to last for ever—"Degreeless Noon," Dickinson says in Poem 287—though it will not do so. It is marked by heightened consciousness, the sense of the self being itself in a full way. When not in such a state, the self feels unstable, impoverished, maybe doubting its own existence:

> A Custom of the Soul
> Far after suffering
> Identity to question
> For evidence 't has been— [957.]

These items begin to sketch a part of Dickinson's inner life: the sense that it comes in moments, good and bad; that the good moments—"Our Best Moment," "The Moments of Dominion," and "The Soul's Superior instants" (306)—do not last, although they feel as if they are going to go on forever; that their departure is felt as deprivation of life, a collapse into another state, perhaps a form of punishment. In these poems I often hear the voice of a person who is constantly uncertain as to her own existence and identity; whose sense of herself is momentary at best and always vulnerable to dismantling, perhaps to be achieved again, perhaps not.

Virginia Woolf described something of what I mean in her essay, *A Sketch of the Past*.[36] She begins with an account of her two earliest memories, of colors on a dress and a window shade blowing in the breeze, of

---

35. Compare:

> There is a Zone whose even Years
> No Solstice interrupt—
> Whose Sun constructs perpetual Noon
> Whose perfect Seasons wait—
>
> Whose Summer set in Summer, till
> The Centuries of June
> And Centuries of August cease
> And Consciousness—is Noon. [1056.]

And Poem 624: "Forever—is composed of Nows—."

36. In *Moments of Being: Unpublished Autobiographical Writings,* edited by Jeanne Schulkind (New York: Harcourt Brace Jovanovitch, 1976), pages 61–138.

which she says that "each was very simple. I am hardly aware of myself, but only the sensation. I am only the container of the feeling of ecstasy, of the feeling of rapture." (Page 67.) She then goes on to distinguish such "moments of being" from the context of "non-being" in which they occur: "[E]very day contains much more non-being than being." For her, like Dickinson, some moments of being are ecstatic, others full of fear and dread; but in each case she feels they are intense, as the rest of life is not. Her moments of being conclude, she says, either in despair or satisfaction; when the latter, it is because she can find a way to make sense of it in writing. "I make it real by putting it into words. It is only by putting it into words that I make it whole: this wholeness means that it has lost its power to hurt me; it gives me, perhaps because by doing so I take away the pain, a great delight to put the severed parts together. Perhaps this is the strongest pleasure known to me. It is the rapture I get when in writing I seem to be discovering what belongs to what; making a scene come right; making a character come together." (Page 72.) For Woolf, the sense that life consists mainly of "cotton-wool," interrupted by transforming moments of being, is part of what makes her a writer: she can endure the intensity of those moments by connecting them with the rest of life, and the rest of herself, in language. It may be that writing is literally what enabled her to keep her self and mind together.[37]

I do not mean by this to claim that Dickinson was just like Woolf, but to point to features of Dickinson's poetry that suggest that she had a somewhat similar structure of experience, a life of alternating moments, hard to connect, threatening, by their intensity and alternation, the very coherence of the self, and that her writing was, in part at least, a way of dealing with this difficulty.

Notice, for example, that the "moments of Escape" of which she speaks in "The Soul has Bandaged moments" are expressed in language that connects them with her life of art and writing. The soul "dances," we are told—recalling her poem about writing, "I cannot dance upon my Toes" (326)—and "Swings upon the hours," making of time itself an element of art rather than constraint. She experiences a kind of deliriousness, a transformation of the world, somewhat similar to that described in the famous lines "Inebriate of Air—am I— / And Debauchee of Dew— /

37. For a development of this theme, see Ernest S. Wolf and Ina Wolf, "We Perished Each Alone: A Psychoanalytic Commentary on Virginia Woolf's *To The Lighthouse*," *International Review of Psychoanalysis* 6 (1979): 37–47. My own reading is much indebted to this piece.

Reeling—thro endless summer days— / From inns of Molten Blue—"
(214). But the most surprising and powerful image of this "Liberty," this
moment of self-expression and coherence, is the "Bomb": "She dances
like a Bomb, abroad. . . ."

This language connects this poem with another:

> I tie my Hat—I crease my Shawl—
> Life's little duties do—precisely—
> As the very least [as if ]
> Were infinite—to me—
>
> I put new Blossoms in the Glass—
> And throw the old—away—
> I push a petal from my Gown
> That anchored there—I weigh
> The time 'twill be till six o'clock
> I have so much to do—
> And yet—Existence—some way back—
> Stopped—struck—my ticking—through—
> We cannot put Ourself away
> As a completed Man
> Or Woman—When the Errand's done
> We came to Flesh—upon—
> There may be—Miles on Miles of Nought—
> Of Action—sicker far—
> To simulate—is stinging work—
> To cover what we are
> From Science—and from Surgery—
> Too Telescopic Eyes
> To bear on us unshaded—
> For their—sake—not for Ours—
> 'Twould start them—
> We—could tremble—
> But since we got a Bomb—
> And held it in our Bosom—
> Nay—Hold it—it is calm—
>
> Therefore—we do life's labor—
> Though life's Reward—be done—
> With scrupulous exactness—
> To hold our Senses—on— [443.]

The forces of repression so well presented here—"I tie my Hat—I crease my Shawl"—are resisted by the bomb, the same bomb that dances in "The Soul has Bandaged moments." To express the self is felt not as a source of coherence and sense but as violence.[38] The poet has a need to speak and to exist in language—perhaps it is essential to her very sense of self and coherence—yet this act of expression is repressed or prohibited with such force that to assert this need (or right) requires cosmic ambition and cosmic force—a bomb—which in turn makes both repression and punishment natural. This sense of incredible force is related as well to the grandiosity of her imagined achievements: "Did Our Best Moment last— / 'Twould supersede the Heaven—" (393).

## The Writing Self

With this series of poems I would like to put another that seem to me to catch a related aspect of Dickinson's mind. These are poems that might be thought of as coming from memories of childhood, poems that tell of smallness and erasure, of the tentativeness of the grasp on reality, and the like. Not that any of these are simply autobiographical,[39] but as I said earlier it is her mind from which these poems come, and the voices in which they are composed are of necessity in some sense hers, as is the story they tell. Here is the way Poem 486 begins, for example:

> I was the slightest in the House—
> I took the smallest Room—
> At night, my little Lamp, and Book,
> And one Geranium—

Childhood deprivation is imagined in even more extreme terms in this poem:

> It would have starved a Gnat—
> To live so small as I—
> And yet I was a living Child—
> With Food's necessity
>
> Upon me—like a Claw—
> I could no more remove

38. Compare Dickinson's occasional use of the images of the volcano (for example, Poems 175, 601, 1677, and 1705) and of the gun in "My Life had stood—a Loaded Gun—" (754).

39. As she said in one of her letters, "When I state myself, as the Representative of the Verse—it does not mean—me—but a supposed person." (*Selected Letters,* page 176.)

Than I could coax a Leech away—
Or make a Dragon—move—

Nor like the Gnat—had I—
The privilege to fly
And seek a Dinner for myself—
How mightier He—than I—

Nor like Himself—the Art
Upon the Window Pane
To gad my little Being out—
And not begin—again— [612.]

The "Food" of which she speaks may at some stage have been actual physical nourishment, for children are sometimes left hungry by unaware parents as well as by sadistic ones, but here it is representative of nourishment and support more generally. The poem is like a dream in which she imagines herself as small as an insect or, rather, sustained at a level so minuscule that it would have starved one, yet grasped by the giant claw of necessity, pinned by it into immobility: unable to search abroad for what she needed, unable even to smash herself to death against her transparent prison walls. This is an image of repression and containment even more severe than in "I tie my Hat—I crease my Shawl," and the force repressed is different too, one more purely of self-destruction, without the element of self-expression except as the existence of the poem itself adds it. The situation is imagined in childhood, but it has parallels later in life as well, for it was true that as Dickinson grew up she had no way to "go abroad" into the world, other than by marrying, which would after all have been to go from one man's house to another.[40] In this respect the gnat, most insignificant of visible creatures, was indeed "mightier" than she.[41]

Consider the following, which continues the theme but with a more explicit emphasis upon writing, and the life of the imagination, which are now seen as means of escape and sources of power:

They shut me up in Prose—
As when a little Girl

40. There were, of course, more adventuresome women. See, for example, Isabella L. Bird, *A Lady's Life in the Rocky Mountains,* edited by Daniel Boorstin (New York: Ballantine Books, 1971).

41. It is not surprising that she says "I never felt at Home—Below—" (413).

They put me in the Closet—
Because they liked me "still"—

Still! Could themself have peeped          [themselves]
And seen my Brain—go round—
They might as wise have lodged a Bird      [wisely]
For Treason—in the Pound—

Himself has but to will
And easy as a Star
Abolish his Captivity—
And laugh—No more have I— [613.]

This is more than a fantasy of escape, it is a specification in the imagination of what there is to be escaped from: "They," meaning her parents or the other grown-ups who put her in the closet. (Not "a" closet: the definite article points to a specific place and gives a sense of repeated threat and action: "I'll put you in the closet!") The reason they did this is that they wanted her spirits, her nature, contained. This is not starvation but its correlative, repression. But she has her escape, her "Brain" and her "will," the one giving her a life anywhere, under any circumstances, the other announcing the intention to claim this power for herself. But of course, despite what she says, a bird can be effectively imprisoned, though not in the "Pound" where the dogs and cats are restrained by fences alone, and escape is "easy" for the star in a way neither bird nor girl can imitate, for the star is already independent and distant. And the closing phrase, "No more have I," which on one reading means "I have to do no more than he does to will myself to freedom," also means simply: "I have no more," that is, my analogy has run out.

The primary restraint spoken of here is not actually of the girl in the closet but of the writer in the woman, for which the former is an analogy. The mode of restraint is the same, a shutting up, but the location is different: "Prose." This is a clear statement of her sense that the forms in which she was told to speak were impossible for her, inauthentic and false; to speak them would not be liberty but captivity. Opposed to prose, of course, is poetry, but by this she does not mean, I think, just any versification but the specific kind of poetry she writes.[42]

---

42. Compare: "I dwell in Possibility— / A fairer House than Prose— / More numerous of Windows— / Superior—for Doors—" (657). She later transvalues these terms: "Impossibility, like Wine / Exhilarates the Man / Who tastes it; Possibility / Is flavorless . . ." (838).

She was not entirely joking, then—who could be in using such words?—when she said, in a famous early poem: "I'm Nobody! Who are you?" (288). She felt, or a part of her did, insignificant, perhaps her very existence in doubt, her liberty denied her; to all of this her solution was writing, but not writing that perpetuated the imprisonment—that would be worse than anything—but writing that freed her. ("Captivity is Consciousness— / So's Liberty" [384].) In Poem 262 she speaks of "The lonesome for they know not What," those whose sense of need or deprivation is so primal that it can have no words; part of her career as a writer was to fill in that blank, to identify what she was "lonesome for" and give it definition and meaning.[43] It is no wonder that the question she put in her first letter to Higginson was whether her poems were "alive": "Should you think it breathed—and had you the leisure to tell me, I should feel quick gratitude—".[44]

---

43. She sometimes felt herself to be a soul facing the universe itself: "What Duplicate— exist— / What Parallel can be— / Of the Significance of This— / To Universe—and Me?" (515).

44. *Selected Letters,* page 171.

It is striking that the line of poetry I have been discussing is almost entirely without self-pity. From a literary point of view that is a virtue, of course, for with us self-pity is an outlawed emotion, but from the point of view of Dickinson as a person, to the extent she is revealed in these poems, the same fact can have another significance. Why can she not feel sympathy with her own experience?

> I tried to think a lonelier Thing
> Than any I had seen—
> Some Polar Expiation—An Omen in the Bone
> Of Death's tremendous nearness—
>
> I probed Retrieveless things
> My Duplicate—to borrow—
> A Haggard Comfort springs
>
> From the belief that Somewhere—
> Within the Clutch of Thought—
> There dwells one other Creature
> Of Heavenly Love—forgot—
>
> I plucked at our Partition
> As One should pry the Walls—
> Between himself—and Horror's Twin—
> Within Opposing Cells—
>
> I almost strove to clasp his Hand,
> Such Luxury—it grew—
> That as Myself—could pity Him—
> Perhaps he—pitied me— [532.]

In this poem the speaker is able to bring herself to feel sympathy with her own situation

Of her own actual early experience we of course know little or nothing, but Higginson, in a letter to his wife, does report her as saying to him, when they finally met:

"Could you tell me what home is"

"I never had a mother. I suppose a mother is one to whom you hurry when you are troubled."

"I never knew how to tell time by the clock until I was 15. My father thought he had taught me but I did not understand and I was afraid to say I did not and afraid to ask anyone else lest he should know." [45]

Of course these may not be exactly her words. But later in a letter to Higginson she said: "I always ran home to Awe when a child, if anything befell me. He was an awful Mother, but I liked him better than none." [46] Even if one makes allowances for momentary feelings, or for her desire to present herself in a particular way to Higginson, these are extraordinary statements. And earlier, in her first letter to him, she said: "I have a Brother and Sister—My Mother does not care for thought—and Father, too busy with his Briefs—to notice what we do."

FOR THE MIND THAT IS UNSURE of its own existence, that lives from moment of meaning—good or bad—to moment of meaning, there are likely to be occasions when the self seems to shrivel to nothing, perhaps to disappear. But there are also moments in which the self expands to include the universe. It is one of the functions of her key term "circumference" to point to this possibility. (Dickinson said in a letter to Higginson, "My Business is Circumference.")[47] As Jane Donahue Eberwein puts it:

---

only by imagining another, who shares it, whom she can pity; this performance persuades her of the possibility that she could be the object of imaginative identification as well.

45. *Selected Letters*, page 210.

46. *The Letters of Emily Dickinson*, edited by Thomas H. Johnson (Cambridge, Mass: The Belknap Press of Harvard University Press, 1958), volume 2, pages 515–16.

47. *Selected Letters*, page 176. "Circumference" is a central word in her poetry. See, for example, "I fear me this Circumference / Engross my finity—" (802); "And Place was where the Presence was / Circumference between" (1084); "'Twixt Firmament above / And Firmament below / The Billows of Circumference / Were sweeping him away—" (1343) (of a bee); and:

When Bells stop ringing—Church—begins—
The Positive—of Bells—

The design of her life was a process of movement from her smallness, a haunting sense of primal inadequacy, to circumference or the point of ultimate boundary between the finite and the infinite, the known and the mysterious, the human and the divine. . . . It is as if she drew tightly in upon herself until the very energy of her contraction exploded her, like a poetic atomic bomb, toward the margins of the universe.[48]

The feeling of expansion of the self can take a variety of forms, one of which is to attribute one's feelings to "the landscape," as we have seen Dickinson do, or to its various parts. One may either feel harmony with the universe, or that it is hostile, alien; in either case, the attribution of feeling is an act of the mind, not of the universe. To feel that nature is out of harmony with one's feelings and that it should change, but will not, expresses the need to have one's feelings mirrored, or responded to, by the universe itself; it is thus a mild, and normal, form of grandiosity. But the same impulse can have more extreme versions as well and may result—as we have seen in such poems as "Because I could not stop for Death"—in imagined transformations of the world and of time itself. In Poem 471, for example, the speaker imagines a night so complete and overwhelming that "The Day that was Before— / And Day that was Behind—were one—," merging past time and future into the not-now and not-night.[49]

To be able to imagine the world transformed is an enormous act of power, and a dangerous one. It can even threaten madness:

> Much Madness is divinest Sense—
> To a discerning Eye—
> Much Sense—the starkest Madness—
> 'Tis the Majority

---

> When Cogs—stop—that's Circumference—
> The Ultimate—of Wheels. [633.]

As these examples suggest, her use of this word is nearly always partly mystifying; like "Noon," "Circumference" acquires much of its meaning from her use of it.

48. Eberwein, *Dickinson*, pages 16, 19.

49. Compare:
"And whether it was noon at night— / Or only Heaven—at Noon— / For very Lunacy of Light / I had not power to tell—" (593).

"Behind Me—dips Eternity— / Before Me—Immortality— / Myself—the Term between—" [721].

"One and One—are One—" (769).

In this, as All, prevail—
Assent—and you are sane—
Demur—you're straightway dangerous—
And handled with a Chain— [435.][50]

MY SUGGESTION IS THIS: that it was essential for Dickinson to resist the poetic molds and forms of her time and insist instead upon casting things in her own language, her own shapes, because this is how she managed to give her life a center and a coherence against overwhelming pressure. This is how she negotiated the shifting senses she had both of herself—now shrinking to nothing, now expanding to fill the universe—and of the universe too, that it was uncaring or caring, hostile or responsive. Her experience was unique, she felt, and it did not connect readily with that of others. "All this—and more—if I should tell— / Would never be believed" (416). To speak in the highly conventional verse forms and voices of her culture would have meant exactly the opposite, for the function of that literature was less the expression of a sense of uniqueness of the poet's experience than the articulation of sentiments and attitudes that were assumed to be widely shared and shareable. I think of the prose of the *Atlantic,* for example, as being a bit like a suit of clothes, put on to give a certain definition and quality to one's life, in affirmation of solidarity with other like-minded people of goodwill and proper taste—a little like attending a genteel church. One way to think of Dickinson's role, in fact, may be to imagine someone in such a church, to which people generally resort in order to hear the same comfortable language, who is by contrast full of the burning experience of the gospel, alive in her heart. Such a one would feel that it was above all the supposedly religious forms of life that were most false to her experience. Hence both Dickinson's insistence on her own forms of speech, including their often mysterious and untranslat-

---

50. The threat is acute not only because the boundaries between the self and the universe—between what one imagines and what is really there—are sometimes blurred or lost, but because the inner experience of the self is discontinuous. At the end of Poem 410, for example, telling of the shock of grief, the poet says:
And Something's odd—within—
That person that I was—
And this One—do not feel the same—
Could this be Madness—this?

able quality, and her sense that to write poetry was to threaten violence—
recall the images of bombs and volcanoes discussed above, or the opening
of her poem "She dealt her pretty words like Blades" (479). More than
that indeed: though she gradually turned away from publication, she saw
poetry-making as a kind of substitute self, a self that would continue even
when the poet had died:

> The Poets light but Lamps—
> Themselves—go out—
> The Wicks they stimulate—
> If vital Light
>
> Inhere as do the Suns—
> Each Age a Lens
> Disseminating their
> Circumference—[51] [883.]

ONE COULD THINK OF EMILY DICKINSON, then, as something like a
real-life Fanny Price, a woman who manages to make her own voice, and
self, against the forces of her world. Both had domineering father figures;
Dickinson's older brother Austin was admired and indulged in much the
same way as Tom Bertram; no one in Dickinson's house shared her qualities of mind, and this was true of Fanny too; and the claims of neither
Fanny nor Dickinson seem to have been taken seriously by anybody, in
part no doubt because they were women. Both were subject to incredible
pressures, represented in Fanny's case by Sir Thomas, whom ultimately

---

51. It may help to understand how fully form was meaning for Dickinson to try to
translate this into "proper verse" with a "proper grammar." It is as impossible as translating
Picasso into the forms of Watteau or Renoir:

> Poets light lamps of beauty
> That burn when they are gone;
> If true light, they glorify
> The world as does the sun.
>
> For each burning light
> Each age provides a lens
> To disseminate its patterns
> In wide circumference.

everyone else joined, and in Dickinson's case by the cultural and social forces against which she felt that her own act of self-expression was a volcano or a bomb. Both found their own ways of being, through acts of great courage, and both transformed what they inherited, discovering a way to make true talk in a world of false talk. Fanny's achievement is often erroneously represented as a mild one, especially since at the end she seems to fold into the image of Mansfield we have had from the beginning; it takes attentive reading to see that this image is hers, not theirs, just as it takes attentive reading to see her as strong, not weak.

For Dickinson to express herself was at once a necessity of life and a "felony." Her achievement was an act of courage and art not only on her own behalf but on behalf of all those, perhaps especially women, who feel that the language they have been given by their world to use is impossible: that it says all the wrong things, in the wrong way; that the self it invites or compels one to become is false, or wrong; that in it truth is not expressed but occluded. She was not a rebel for the sake of rebellion but because the forms in which she was asked to speak were not authentic to her and because authenticity was essential to her life. Her rebellion did not take the form of mere destruction but of transformation, a movement not away from discipline but towards an invented one. What she created was a new way of making poetry, beautiful and original, a new way of living with language. Against the conventional authorities she created new possibilities for poetry and for life and for these, as Plato does for dialectic, she claims an authority of her own.

Not the kind of authority that consists of a command, of course, nor even the authority of "reasons" supporting a particular course of action, but, as with the other writers we have read, the authority of a certain way of thinking, talking, and being. Plato, for example, is really saying to his reader, "Engage in dialectic, and go where it takes you," even though that place cannot be predicted ahead of time: "Live this sort of life, not another." Dickinson is less imperative, but nonetheless opens up possibilities that had not existed before, as Plato did, and makes a claim for their value: "Don't talk that way, like the *Atlantic;* make your own language, as I do." Just as Plato says that the full life is that of the philosopher, as he defines it, so Dickinson says the full life is that of the poet, as she defines it. "If you would speak the truth," she says, with Shakespeare, "be a poet."

For her that meant, above all, authenticity and originality of expression; extraordinary concentration and density of meaning; the striking combination of particularity and generality, which is really a mode of philosophy; the incorporation of contraries in everything she wrote. (As she said, "'Tis Opposites—entice" [355].) Her aim was to reverse the force of poetry as it existed in her time: instead of functioning as a source of assurance and comfort, it was to worry and disturb. In all this she transformed her language from the bottom up.

In doing so she established an authority of another kind, perhaps a little like that of legal precedent. Since this has now been done, other things are possible, and Dickinson legitimates them. Think, for example, of Wallace Stevens, at such moments as this: "Among twenty snowy mountains, / The only moving thing / Was the eye of the blackbird." Does not Dickinson make this kind of poetry both more intelligible and more acceptable? Compare the joint opinion in *Casey,* where the Court is really saying: "This is how we should talk, and be, in the law; this is the process in which we should engage; and we should go where it takes us." This kind of authority is not that of command but of performance. When authorities of a simpler kind are challenged, this is the only kind of authority that exists; it depends upon the acquiescence of its audience, and it works by the rhetorical construction of a world and a way of life.

There is a sense in which Dickinson's verse, despite its domestic and theological cast, can be seen as deeply political in character. When we turn from it to our own world of public talk, we hear a great deal that sounds, with appropriate adjustments, like the language of the *Atlantic,* full of cliché, pomposity, and false assurance, or resting on theories as unquestioningly propounded as any article of dogma. In writing against these things in her world, she writes against them in ours as well. In doing so she defines honesty of mind and truthfulness of speech in ways that may still be helpful to us. Is it imaginable that a public figure could meet her criteria for excellence in thought and speech, or others like them? It is with such a question in mind that we now turn to two explicitly political writers: Nelson Mandela and Abraham Lincoln.

. . .

*While I hope this book can be read with interest by those who are expert in the various fields it touches, and while I have benefited enormously from the work of others, it should be obvious that it is not mainly addressed to a community of specialists. If it were, it would not cohere as a book, because the various chapters belong to different scholarly fields.*

*One chapter would be addressed to one audience, another to another, each written in its own language, to its own community, and excluding others, like a series of articles taken from different professional journals. In this book, as in much of my other work, I am trying to work out a set of questions that will connect texts, and their readers, across the lines of professionalism.*

*In doing this I mean to resist the view that texts such as these are the property of one group or another, or that it is necessary to speak the language of the specialist in order to speak well about them. In fact, I do not think of myself as writing out of a profession, but out of my own experience of these texts, to which I have turned for the life they offer. I would do this, if I could, no matter what my job was, for their importance to me as a person and mind. Likewise I write to my reader not as a Dickinson specialist, or a classicist, or a lawyer, but as the person who is these things and many other things as well, and I do this in part with the object of claiming these texts as an inheritance that is common to us all.*

*My first book was Thoreau's* Walden, *which I heard about as a boy, ordered from the bookstore, and then read and reread. Part of the appeal for me was the image of the person as a discrete self, looking out on the world, participating in it, trying to make sense of it. The test for Thoreau is always his own experience. It is out of a similar sense of the individuality in myself, and in my reader, that I write.*

IV

RECONSTITUTING SELF
AND WORLD:
THE CREATION OF AUTHORITY
AS AN ACT OF HOPE

# MANDELA'S SPEECH FROM THE DOCK AND LINCOLN'S SECOND INAUGURAL ADDRESS: GIVING MEANING TO LIFE IN AN UNJUST WORLD

IT IS NOT ONLY AT DRAMATIC MOMENTS like that described in the *Crito,* where a person sentenced to death is given the opportunity to escape, or in *Richard II,* where one man overthrows a government, that we face the tension between the authority of the world and the claims of the self, but all of the time, whenever we speak in fact, for, as Dickinson's poetry demonstrates, our very language is a system of authority. We speak grammatically or ungrammatically, in established or novel forms, and in so doing acknowledge the authority of our world, or resist it. At some point a refusal to use accepted forms of speech will lead to exclusion from a universe of discourse, whether in the law, the classroom, or somewhere else. "You can't talk that way to a jury," one may be told, or "I am sorry, this book is not history." This is true even in the private side of life, for a part of a friendship or a marriage is the set of expectations that the parties build over time; and although these are in a perpetual process of transformation, they have an authority of their own that cannot be simply disregarded: it is part of the stuff of life.

There is thus a continuity that runs from our every remark, our every response to the remarks of others, to the most serious decisions about whether to yield to or resist the power of the state: whether to refuse conscription, for example, or to take up arms against an evil government. One idea of this book is that we can read any text from this point of view, asking how it defines the external world for which an authority is claimed, how it defines the self, and what relation it creates between them. Managing this tension is a constant feature of human expression, and the hope on which this book has been working is that we may be able to learn something about it from texts that address it in especially intelligent or powerful ways. I would not want to say that this is the only way to think about questions of authority, for it is obviously possible to proceed in an abstract way as well, but it is one that seems to me useful. In my view the most important differences in our positions are marked not so much by the generalities we propound as by the particular enactments we perform.

I am saying that authority is a subject of art, and in more than one way. To start with, authority is created by an act of art. The authority of the law, or the church, or the language of poetic convention, or whatever institution the writer addresses, does not simply exist in unproblematic form in the external world, to be observed or described, obeyed or resisted, but is constituted in one's writing. It is not just "the church" or "the law" that I ask you to obey, or disobey, it is the church or the law as made in my text: it is because it is like this, or, more properly, because we can make it be like this, that one should resist, or yield to, its influence. Of course there are limits on our power to make things what we say they are, but the history of the world shows that these are not so great as is commonly believed—think of the history of human slavery in our own country, for example, which was justified by an insane language of racial difference that is in milder form still with us, or of Nazism, or of the various ways in which gender has been constructed as a "natural" system of meaning in virtually every human culture. Since culture is a collective human artefact, the line between the imagined and the real—as Shakespeare especially shows us—cannot be a bright one.

Similarly, the line between the self and the world, though often felt as stark or vivid, is always blurred, partly because we help make our worlds, partly because we are ourselves shaped by our culture, and not just in superficial ways. To a large degree, the ways in which we think and feel and imagine the world have their origin outside of us. The poetic conventions with which Dickinson struggled, for example, had a life within her, as well as on the pages of the *Atlantic;* and though the differences we think we see by means of our racial classifications are in fact not there at all, we continue to see them and to make them real.

In reading a text about authority, then, we should look not merely at arguments one way or the other, for or against a particular institution, but at the ways in which the particular institution or set of practices is constituted in the writing, and the same is true of the self as well. It is a mistake, as I said earlier, to think of "arguments" about authority as if they could be reproduced as a set of culture-free propositional assertions. What a text offers us is as a whole way of thinking and talking and being, a way of acting in relation to one's language and one's audience; it is this for which authority is ultimately claimed, and it is upon this that I have been trying to focus attention in this book.

Authority is the subject of art in another dimension as well, for it is an aspect of the relation that a writer creates with her or his reader. In reading, after all, one finds oneself yielding to or resisting the writer's way of thinking, granting or refusing its authority. The writer's stance can range from authoritarian and dictatorial to the open and dialogic. Thus the Nomoi in the *Crito* not only characterize the laws of Athens as authoritarian, they give themselves an authoritarian character in the way they talk. This creates a kind of harmony between their performance and their vision, for both are dictatorial and formalistic. In Hooker there is a similar if imperfect harmony, between his image of the church as a discursive entity and his own discourse, for both are open to argument on all matters except those upon which reasoning English Christians (as he sees it) cannot differ. In other cases—we can all imagine them—there will be radical incoherence between message and performance, for example where a text hostile to hierarchy is itself hierarchical in relation to its reader. As readers too we are engaged in an ethical and constitutive practice: we can be generous or envious, resentful or grateful; our minds can be open to the experience a text offers or closed to it; there is an art here too, that of making the judgments necessary to a grant or denial of authority.

The sequence of texts we have so far read in this book is meant to have a shape or movement, from the *Crito,* where there seems to be, but in Socrates' view is not, a direct conflict between self and city, through a series of texts about law, which in various ways constitute the public world as a source of authority—an authority that can in every case be recast as belonging to a way of thinking and talking—to the texts of Austen and Dickinson, which show individual minds asserting themselves in different ways against their world by remaking its resources. Now, at the end, we shift to two other texts, written from very different positions but both addressing the authority of human institutions and practices, in one case the racist laws of South Africa and the underground organization, Umkonto We Sizwe (Spear of the Nation), formed to resist them, in the other the Union of the United States of America for which our own Civil War was fought. Nelson Mandela denies the authority of the sabotage law under which he is convicted, and in doing so creates another vision of the world and himself, in his own text, for which he claims an authority that will justify the acts of sabotage he admits he has committed; Lincoln, faced with the claim that the war in which he has been leading the nation is itself unconstitutional and wrong—a violation of the fundamental right of self-determination for which the nation was established in the first place—creates an image of the Union that, if accepted, will justify what he, and we, have done. Both people live in an unjust world, dominated by hatred and war; both evoke a standard of civilized life that defines other and better possibilities. For each the constitution of authority is an act of hope.

## Mandela's Speech from the Dock

Nelson Mandela, the famous leader of the African opposition to the government of South Africa, and now its president, was born into a family of chiefs. After his father died, he was raised by a relative and sent first to school and then to university, where he studied law. As a lawyer in Johannesburg he became active in resisting the racialist laws passed by the government, particularly after 1948, when the Nationalist party came into power and established the principles of apartheid. He was one of the leaders of the African National Congress, which was committed to fundamental democratic change first through wholly legal means, then through nonviolent protests.

In 1952 he helped organize the Defiance of Unjust Laws campaign, a protest movement, as a result of which he was banned. Four years later he was one of 156 defendants brought to trial in a drawn-out and ultimately unsuccessful treason trial. After the massacre of sixty-nine unarmed Africans at Sharpeville in 1960 he helped to organize Umkonto We Sizwe (Spear of the Nation), which, unlike the A.N.C., made it a policy to engage in acts of sabotage, especially in connection with the government's proposed secession from the British Commonwealth. In 1962 he was convicted of leaving the country without a passport, which he had in fact done on his visits to other African nations, and of inciting to strike, again an offense of which he was guilty. He was sentenced to five years imprisonment.

The next year he was tried again, while still in prison, this time for sabotage and attempted overthrow of the government, and once more convicted. The maximum penalty for these offenses was death; as it turned out he was sentenced to life imprisonment, which under South African law involved no possibility of release except by pardon. As all the world knows, he was imprisoned for the next twenty-five years, most of it on Robben Island, until his astonishing release and reestablishment as an active political figure of even greater importance than before.

It is his speech before sentencing given at his sabotage trial that I shall discuss below. When he made it he of course did not know what sentence he would receive. It could well have been death; if not, his sentence was likely to mean that he would be removed from the public world, and silenced, for the rest of his life. An essential part of the meaning of this speech, like the speeches of Socrates to the jury, is its refusal to seek clemency. There is no apology here in the modern sense of the term, but in an older sense the speech is indeed an apology: it is a justification of his life, an insistence on saying the truth about his motives and his methods, on this last occasion on which he could expect to speak in public in his lifetime. His object is not to get off with a light sentence but to present South Africa and the world with the problem he defines, a critical part of which is that an African can talk this way to a court and dares to do so.[1]

This is how he begins.

## The Voice of the Accused

I am the First Accused.

I hold a Bachelor's Degree in Arts and practised as an attorney in Johannesburg for a number of years in partnership with Oliver Tambo. I am a convicted prisoner serving five years for leaving the country without a permit and for inciting people to go on strike at the end of May, 1961.

At the outset, I want to say that the suggestion made by the State in its opening that the struggle in South Africa is under the influence of foreigners or communists is wholly incorrect. I have done whatever I did, both as an individual and as a leader of my people, because of my experience in South Africa and my own proudly-felt African background, and not because of what any outsider might have said.

In my youth in the Transkei I listened to the elders of my tribe telling stories of the old days. Amongst the tales they related to me were those of wars fought by our ancestors in defence of the fatherland. The names of Dingane and Bambata, Hintsa and Makana, Squngthi and Dalasile, Mo-

---

1. Since, like Hale's "Considerations," this speech is not widely available, I have reproduced more of it than I otherwise might. My reading of it is particularly indebted to John Comaroff, who first brought it to my attention, and to Teresa Scassa.

On Mandela's expectation of the death penalty see *From Protest to Challenge: A Documentary History of African Politics in South Africa 1882–1964*, edited by Thomas Karis and Gwendolen M. Carter, volume 3 (Stanford, Calif.: Hoover Institution Press, 1977), pages 679–83. But see Fatima Meer, *Higher Than Hope: A Biography of Nelson Mandela* (London: Hamish Hamilton, 1988), page 259.

shoeshoe and Sekhukhuni, were praised as the glory of the entire African nation. I hoped then that life might offer me the opportunity to serve my people and make my own humble contribution to their freedom struggle. This is what has motivated me in all that I have done in relation to the charges made against me in this case.[2]

This opening is a striking act of self-definition. Mandela is a lawyer and speaks with the confidence of one. He belongs in court and knows that he is entitled to be heard. In his respectful and objective tone, muted in feeling and focused on the facts, he seems almost to be speaking about a client, not himself. His legal training and manner, like his earlier degree in arts, mark him as "one of us," as a member of the community defined by law—English law—and reason. This is not the voice of a hotheaded revolutionary or saboteur but of an educated lawyer.

He then tells us that he is not only "accused"—which would after all be consistent with innocence—but one "convicted" of crime, thus establishing his central paradox: How is it possible to be at once a lawyer, committed to civilization and reason, as both his training and his voice declare him to be, and a convicted criminal, the enemy of law and the people? As we shall see, this paradox runs through the speech as a whole, generating much of its energy.

But he is not only a lawyer and a convict, he is an African, claiming allegiance to his people and to Africa, and rejecting the influence of "foreigners" and "outsiders." This claim makes it an issue how "Africa" and its "people" are to be defined, which is again a topic that will run throughout the speech. He makes clear part of his own position when he speaks of listening to the elders of his tribe, of the wars fought in defense of the fatherland, and of "the glory of the entire African nation." His nation, then, is not the Union of South Africa but Africa itself; his people are the native Africans, not the Europeans; he is an African patriot engaged in a defensive war. Such are his commitments and his motives: but they are expressed in English, and in a manner and tone that enact a

---

2. In reproducing this speech I have used three sources: the documentary history of the African political struggle in South Africa, *From Protest to Challenge*, volume 3, pages 771–96; Nelson Mandela, *The Struggle Is My Life* (London: International Defence Aid Fund for Southern Africa, 1978), pages 155–75; Meer, *Higher than Hope*, pages 233–58. These versions vary slightly, mainly by omissions. I have included any passage that is included in any of the sources; where there are differences, I have followed Karis and Carter.

commitment to certain aspects of European culture as well, thus continuing in milder form the paradox of the opening sentences.[3]

## Violence

His next step is a remarkable one, namely, to admit that he is responsible for sabotage.

> Having said this, I must deal immediately and at some length with the question of violence. Some of the things so far told to the Court are true and some are untrue. I do not, however, deny that I planned sabotage. I did not plan it in a spirit of recklessness, nor because I have any love of violence. I planned it as a result of a calm and sober assessment of the political situation that had arisen after many years of tyranny, exploitation and oppression of my people by the Whites.
>
> I admit immediately that I was one of the persons who helped to form Umkonto We Sizwe, and that I played a prominent role in its affairs until I was arrested in August, 1962.

This seems like a crazy thing for a defendant to say, unless he is going to express contrition for it, which Mandela obviously will not do. He thus sharpens the tension between his persona and his conduct—he is "one of us"; but "we" do not commit sabotage, which undermines law and civilization—and this in turn defines his task in the speech as a whole, which will be to show that the kind of sabotage he planned is not only consistent with a commitment to civilization, it is in fact expressive of it.

In this passage Mandela speaks in a way that is continuous with the persona of the objective lawyer with which he began—correcting misstatements in the interest of truth—but what he says is also a bit frightening, not only in its affirmation of sabotage but in its calculating nature. He planned sabotage, he says, upon "a calm and sober assessment of the situation," the essence of which was the oppression of "my people" by the "Whites." The dissonance between his persona as lawyer and his conduct as saboteur will ring differently in different ears: the black South African will presumably say, "He is one of us, but he can talk like them"; the white South African, "He sounds like one of us, but is really one of

---

3. In a speech at his trial for passport and strike law violations Mandela made a much fuller, and in some ways more interesting, reference to listening to the elders of his tribe. See Karis and Carter, eds., *From Protest to Challenge*, page 734; Mandela, *The Struggle Is My Life*, pages 141–42; below page 286, note 5.

them." What will the world of nations outside South Africa say: that he is a terrorist and saboteur, using violence for political ends, or that he is a representative of the values of our common civilization?[4]

Here is the first stage of his explanation:

> Firstly, we believed that as a result of Government policy, violence by the African people had become inevitable, and that unless responsible leadership was given to canalise and control the feelings of our people, there would be outbreaks of terrorism which would produce an intensity of bitterness and hostility between the various races of this country which is not produced even by war. Secondly, we felt that without violence there would be no way open to the African people to succeed in their struggle against the principle of White supremacy. All lawful modes of expressing opposition to this principle had been closed by legislation, and we were placed in a position in which we had either to accept a permanent state of inferiority, or to defy the Government. We chose to defy the law. We first broke the law in a way which avoided any recourse to violence; when this form was legislated against, and when the Government resorted to a show of force to crush opposition to its policies, only then did we decide to answer violence with violence.

Notice that there are two distinct justifications: first, that violence was in fact inevitable, and that it had to be managed by responsible leaders or it would result in something far worse; second, that violence was a good and necessary thing, for without it his people would suffer oppression forever. The first represents him as seeking to minimize the evil of violence; the second affirms violence as a proper instrument of liberation, at least in the circumstances he describes, in which lawful means of protest and action had been prohibited. The difference in feeling and consequence carries forward the dissonance at the heart of this speech: in the first he seems to speak for civilization against the common enemy of violence, in the second to represent that very enemy. Both are threatening,

---

4. Mandela makes especially prominent the conflict of his identities by his "admission"—a technical term of legal art—that he is one of the founders of Umkonto, a gesture in which he at once performs like a lawyer and concedes much of his responsibility for the criminal conduct with which he is charged. This locates the responsibility squarely on his shoulders, which under the terms of the paradox already established is at once a manly and dignified claim of power and a confession that it is he, not others, who made the decisions found to be criminal. And in saying that he is "prominent in its affairs," he speaks of Umkonto, in the government's view a criminal and terrorist organization, as if it were a business corporation or social club, of undoubted legitimacy and propriety.

the first in its factual predicate, that violence will happen, the second in his willingness to use it.

But this willingness is conditioned on the fact that the state had prohibited all other forms of political action, leaving the Africans with the stark choice of permanent slavery or violent resistance. Here Mandela starts to make his case that the true enemy of civilization is not the saboteurs but the government against which they act.

His next sentence strikes a middle point between submission and revolt, showing that even here Mandela can distinguish one form from another and that he makes the more civilized choice: "But the violence which we chose to adopt was not terrorism."

## History

It is easy to say that your violence is really the fault of those you oppose, for they leave you no other choice, and easy as well to say that you are less violent than you might be. The force of Mandela's speech, then, will not be so much in the position he takes as in the way he gives these terms meaning in his speech as a whole and in the context in which he speaks. His next effort is to describe that context in such a way as to make credible his claims for his movement: its hostility to violence, its reluctance to authorize it, and its insistence on minimizing its worst effects—in short, its role as the protector, not the destroyer, of civilization. He does this by retelling this history of his movement.

The A.N.C. was founded in 1912 to defend the rights of "the African people" then being curtailed by legislation. Until 1949, when the policy of apartheid was adopted, "it adhered strictly to a constitutional struggle," lawfully presenting demands and resolutions and arguments. After 1949, it engaged in "peaceful, but unlawful" demonstrations against the new laws; but "it remained determined to avoid violence." This is demonstrated by the facts that during the entire Defiance campaign there was no act of violence at all and that the court at the treason trial expressly found that the A.N.C. "did not have a policy of violence."

The next stage of the escalation, as with the introduction of the apartheid laws in 1949, was precipitated by government action: "In 1960, there was the shooting at Sharpeville, which resulted in the proclamation of a State of Emergency and the declaration of the A.N.C. as an unlawful organization. My colleagues and I, after careful consideration, decided that we would not obey this decree." Once again, it is the government who forces the next step towards violence through its repressive legislation. Equally important, though here unemphasized—and perhaps the more forceful for that—is the contrast between the government, shooting the unarmed in Sharpeville, and the A.N.C. leaders, who are defined as "colleagues" engaged in an essential task of civilized government, here called "careful consideration." As an explicit justification for disobeying the decree, he invokes the nearly universal test of governmental legitimacy: "The African people were not part of the Government and did not make the laws by which they were governed." To accept the state of outlawry would be to accept "the silencing of the Africans for all time." The A.N.C. refused to disband, but went underground: "We believed it was our duty to preserve this organization which had been built up with almost fifty years of unremitting toil." Here Mandela invokes an image of the A.N.C. not as an outlaw band but as an institution, one of the essential elements of a social system, and in doing so he uses a term whose meaning is drawn from religion and law alike—"duty." In similarly conservative language he soon invokes the moral ideals of equality and self-respect: "I have no doubt that no self-respecting White political organization would disband itself if declared illegal by a Government in which it had no say."

"In 1960 the Government held a Referendum which led to the establishment of the Republic." Africans were of course not entitled to vote, nor were they "consulted about the proposed constitutional change." They decided in protest to organize a national strike, or "stay-at-home," which was in accordance with A.N.C. policy to be entirely peaceful.

> The Government's answer was to introduce new and harsher laws, to mobilise its armed forces, and to send saracens, armed vehicles and soldiers into the townships in a massive show of force designed to intimidate the people. This was an indication that the Government had decided to rule by force alone, and this decision was a milestone on the road to Umkonto.

Once again, as he tells it, the peaceful Africans are opposed by a government founded on the principle of force and violence. Civilization is not on the side of law and order but with those who resist.

What are the leaders to do? They could not tolerate "abject surrender," but how should they "continue the fight"? "When some of us discussed this in May and June of 1961, it could not be denied that our policy to achieve a non-racial state by non-violence had achieved nothing, and that our followers were beginning to lose confidence in this policy and were developing disturbing ideas of terrorism." Here he separates the Africans into leaders and followers, defining the latter as having learned the lesson the government had taught, that violence is the only way, and the former as interested in containing and controlling this destructive force. "I, and some colleagues, came to the conclusion that as violence in this country was inevitable, it would be unrealistic and wrong for African leaders to continue preaching peace and non-violence at a time when the Government met our peaceful demands with force." But because the A.N.C. was historically committed to nonviolence, Mandela tells us, this had to be through a new organization. In thus respecting the aims of the A.N.C., and the expectations of those who had joined it on the understanding that it was nonviolent, Mandela is demonstrating his own desire and capacity to control violence, in this case by a commitment to the integrity both of people and of institutions.

Moreover, as he suggested earlier in his references to "terrorism," violence is not an undifferentiated unity. Now he says: "Four forms of violence are possible. There is sabotage, there is guerrilla warfare, there is terrorism and there is open revolution." Umkonto chose the least violent form, which did "not involve loss of life, and . . . offered the best hope for future race relations." The plan was to destroy power plants, railways, and telephone communications systems, with the object of scaring capital away from the country and draining its resources, "thus compelling the voters of the country to reconsider their position," and to attack government buildings and other symbols of apartheid, both inspiring the African people and providing an outlet for their need for violence. The hope was that the outside world would also put pressure on the government. Umkonto began with attacks on government buildings, which did indeed encourage the Africans and frighten the Europeans, who began talking of punishing sabotage with death. "If this was so how could we continue to keep Africans away from terrorism?"

The possibility of guerrilla warfare became more likely, and to prepare for that Mandela and others underwent military training in friendly countries elsewhere in Africa. As part of this he wrote the summaries of books on "guerrilla warfare and military strategy" which had been introduced in evidence against him.

### Communist Conspiracy
Mandela next deals with certain specific allegations, denying that the Umkonto was responsible for certain bombings of private houses, as the prosecution charged; that the A.N.C. was part of a general conspiracy to commit sabotage; and that the A.N.C. had the same "aims and objects" as the Communist party.

This last charge occupies him at length. The A.N.C. Charter is "by no means a blueprint for a socialist State." It calls for redistribution, not nationalization, of land. It does provide for nationalization of mines, banks, and monopoly industry but "because big monopolies are owned by one race only, and without such nationalization racial domination would be perpetuated despite the spread of political power." The A.N.C. admits only African members, and its object is for "the African people to win unity and full political rights." The Communist aim is to destroy capitalism and replace it with a working-class government. They are for class division, we for class harmony; they are for the abolition of the bourgeoisie, we for its development. Of course there has been cooperation between A.N.C. and the Communists, as there has been cooperation with liberation struggles elsewhere in the world, for "the short-term objects of Communism would always correspond with the long-term objects of freedom movements."

> Theoretical differences amongst those fighting against oppression is a luxury we cannot afford at this stage. What is more, for many decades Communists were the only political group in South Africa who were prepared to treat Africans as human beings and their equals; who were prepared to eat with us; talk with us, live with us and work with us. They were the only political group which was prepared to work with the Africans for the attainment of political rights and a stake in society. Because of this, there are many Africans who, today, tend to equate freedom with Communism. They are supported in this belief by a legislature which brands all exponents of democratic government and African freedom as Communists and bans many of them (who are not Communists) under the Suppression of Communism Act. . . .
>
> I have always regarded myself, in the first place, as an African patriot. After all, I was born in Umtata, forty-six years ago. My guardian was my cousin, who was the acting paramount chief of Tembuland, and I am related both to the present paramount chief of Tembuland, Sabata Dalinyebo, and to Kaizer Matanzima, the Chief Minister of the Transkei.
>
> Today I am attracted by the idea of a classless society, an attraction which springs in part from Marxist reading and, in part, from my admiration of the structure and organization of early African societies in this country. The land, then the main means of production, belonged to the tribe. There were no rich or poor and there was no exploitation.[5]

5. Compare what he said at his trial in 1962:
Many years ago, when I was a boy brought up in my village in the Transkei, I listened to the elders of the tribe telling stories about the good old days, before the arrival of the white man. Then our people lived peacefully, under the democratic rule

Of course he has been influenced by Marxism; but far from opposing the institutions of the Western European state, he favors them: "I regard the British Parliament as the most democratic institution in the world."

In the course of this speech Mandela stops two or three times to consider particular evidence against him: once the evidence of "X," an insider who turned state's evidence, which Mandela dissects, admitting some portions, denying others; once to explain—perhaps not very persuasively—how certain lectures, composed for use in the Communist party, came to be found written in his hand; once, more persuasively, to explain the existence of copies, again admittedly in his hand, of passages from certain military manuals. Here he defines himself as one who can take a mass of evidence, distinguish various parts, concede, deny, ex-

---

of their Kings and their "amapakati," and moved freely and confidently up and down the country without let or hindrance. Then the country was our own, in name and right. We occupied the land, the forests, the rivers; we extracted the mineral wealth beneath the soil and all the riches of this beautiful country. We set up and operated our own Government, we controlled our own armies and we organised our own trade and commerce. The elders would tell tales of the wars fought by our ancestors in defense of the fatherland, as well as the acts of valour by generals and soldiers during those epic days. The names of Dingane and Bambata, among the Zulus, of Hintsa, Makana, Ndlambe of the Ama-Xhosa, of Sekhukhuni and others in the North, were mentioned as the pride and glory of the entire African nation.

The structure and organisation of early African societies in this country fascinated me very much and greatly influenced the evolution of my political outlook. The land, then the main means of production, belonged to the whole tribe and there was no individual ownership whatsoever. There were no classes, no rich or poor and no exploitation of man by man. All men were free and equal and this was the foundation of government. Recognition of this general principle found expression in the constitution of the council, variously called "Imbizo" or "Pitso" or "Kgotla" which governs the affairs of the tribe. The council was so completely democratic that all members of the tribe could participate in its deliberations. Chief and subject, warrior and medicine man, all took part and endeavoured to influence its decisions. It was so weighty and influential a body that no step of any importance could ever be taken by the tribe without reference to it.

There was much in such a society that was primitive and insecure and it certainly could never measure up to the demands of the present epoch. But in such a society are contained the seeds of revolutionary democracy in which none will be held in slavery or servitude, and in which poverty, want and insecurity shall be no more. This is the inspiration which, even today, inspires me and my colleagues in our political struggle. [From Protest to Challenge, edited by Karis and Carter, page 734.]

plain—in other words, function as a competent lawyer, with all that that means about his capacity for reason and his commitment to it.

In describing his trips abroad to learn about military strategy and rebuild support for his movement, he gives a list of those outside his country who welcomed him, ranging from Gaitskell and Grimond in England to Haile Selassie in Ethiopia to Presidents Bourguiba, Senghor, and Obote of other African states. This is a way of defining himself as a member of the international community; his opponent, the South African state, as a kind of pariah.

Finally, in answer to the charge that the A.N.C.'s claims to be fighting for African freedom are in fact a cover for the truth, which is that it wants to establish a Communist state, he explains what their motives are: to fight against "real, and not imaginary" hardships, especially "two features which are the hallmarks of African life" in South Africa. "These features are poverty and lack of human dignity, and we do not need Communists or so-called 'agitators' to teach us about these things."

### The Moral and Economic Condition of South Africa
There follows now, at the heart of his speech, a statement of the factual premises upon which the movement, including both the A.N.C. and Umkonto, rests.

This is how he begins:

> South Africa is the richest country in Africa, and could be one of the richest countries in the world. But it is a land of extremes and remarkable contrasts. The Whites enjoy what may well be the highest standard of living in the world, whilst Africans live in poverty and misery.

Mandela begins in a voice like that of a person telling a travelogue or of a social studies teacher, neutrally describing this interesting country, full of "extremes" and "contrasts." But these factual terms are quickly converted into terms of value—"poverty and misery"—that are not neutral but call for action or response. This in fact seems to be the aim of this long section of his speech: to describe conditions in such a way as to justify what he has done, including sabotage, to change them. He goes on:

> Forty per cent of the Africans live in hopelessly over-crowded and, in some cases, drought-stricken reserves, where soil erosion and the overworking of the soil make it impossible for them to live properly off the land. Thirty per cent are labourers, labour tenants and squatters on White farms and work and live under conditions similar to those of the serfs of the Middle Ages. The other thirty per cent live in towns where they have developed economic

and social habits which bring them closer in many respects to White standards. Yet most Africans, even in this group, are impoverished by low incomes and high cost of living.

The evil of poverty extends beyond deprivation of material goods, for "poverty goes hand in hand with malnutrition and disease." He lists the diseases: "tuberculosis, pellagra, kwashiorkor, gastro-enteritis and scurvy," and says that "the incidence of infant mortality is one of the highest in the world." Here he speaks with the voice of a statistician or social scientist: "According to the Medical Officer of Health for Pretoria, tuberculosis kills forty people a day (almost all Africans), and in 1961 there were 58,491 new cases reported. These diseases not only destroy the vital organs of the body, but they result in retarded mental conditions and lack of initiative, and reduce powers of concentration."

But the real issue is not material, even in this sense, but ethical or moral: "The complaint of Africans, however, is not only that they are poor and the Whites are rich, but that the laws which are made by the Whites are designed to preserve this situation," both by denying them the possibility of education and by preventing a worker from "acquiring a greater skill at his work and thus higher wages."

He quotes the remarks of the present prime minister made during the debate on the Bantu Education Bill in 1953:

> "When I have control of Native education I will reform it so that Natives will be taught from childhood to realise that equality with Europeans is not for them. . . . People who believe in equality are not desirable teachers for Natives."

As Mandela earlier said, "[T]he other main obstacle to the economic advancement of the African is the industrial colour bar under which all the better jobs of industry are reserved for Whites only," coupled with the prohibition of African unions, which denies to Africans "the right of collective bargaining which is permitted to the better-paid White workers."

This is how he concludes:

> The Government often answers its critics by saying that Africans in South Africa are economically better off than the inhabitants of the other countries in Africa. I do not know whether this statement is true and doubt whether any comparison can be made without having regard to the cost of living index in such countries. But even if it is true, as far as the African people are concerned it is irrelevant. Our complaint is not that we are poor by comparison with people in other countries, but that we are poor by

comparison with the White people in our own country, and that we are prevented by legislation from altering this imbalance.

The lack of human dignity experienced by Africans is the direct result of the policy of White supremacy. White supremacy implies Black inferiority. Legislation designed to preserve White supremacy entrenches this notion. Menial tasks in South Africa are invariably performed by Africans. When anything has to be carried or cleaned the White man will look around for an African to do it for him, whether the African is employed by him or not. Because of this sort of attitude, Whites tend to regard Africans as a separate breed. They do not look upon them as people with families of their own; they do not realise that they have emotions—that they fall in love like White people do; that they want to be with their wives and children like White people want to be with theirs; that they want to earn enough money to support their families properly, to feed and clothe them and send them to school. And what "house-boy" or "garden-boy" or labourer can ever hope to do this?

Pass Laws, which to the Africans are among the most hated bits of legislation in South Africa, render any African liable to police surveillance at any time. I doubt whether there is a single African male in South Africa who has not at some stage had a brush with the police over his pass. Hundreds and thousands of Africans are thrown into gaol each year under pass laws. Even worse than this is the fact that pass laws keep husband and wife apart and lead to the breakdown of family life.

Poverty and the breakdown of family life have secondary effects. Children wander about the streets of the Townships because they have no schools to go to, or no money to enable them to go to school, or no parents at home to see that they go to school, because both parents (if there be two) have to work to keep the family alive. This leads to a breakdown in moral standards, to an alarming rise in illegitimacy and to growing violence which erupts, not only politically, but everywhere. Life in the townships is dangerous. There is not a day that goes by without somebody being stabbed or assaulted. And violence is carried out of the townships in the White living areas. People are afraid to walk alone in the streets after dark. Housebreakings and robberies are increasing, despite the fact that the death sentence can now be imposed for such offences. Death sentences cannot cure the festering sore.

Africans want to be paid a living wage. Africans want to perform work which they are capable of doing, and not work which the Government declares them to be capable of. Africans want to be allowed to live where they obtain work, and not be endorsed out of an area because they were not born there. Africans want to be allowed to own land in places where they work, and not to be obliged to live in rented houses which they can never call their own. Africans want to be part of the general population, and not confined to living in their own ghettos. African men want to have their wives and children to live with them where they work, and not be forced into an unnatural existence in men's hostels. African women want to be with their men folk and not be left permanently widowed in the reserves. Africans want to be allowed out after 11 o'clock at night and not to be confined to their rooms like little children. Africans want to be allowed to travel in their own country and to seek work where they want to and not where the Labour Bureau tells them to. Africans want a just share in the whole of South Africa; they want security and a stake in society.

Above all, we want equal political rights, because without them our disabilities will be permanent. I know this sounds revolutionary to the Whites in this country, because the majority of voters will be Africans. This makes the White man fear democracy.

But this fear cannot be allowed to stand in the way of the only solution which will guarantee racial harmony and freedom for all. It is not true that the enfranchisement of all will result in racial domination. Political division, based on colour, is entirely artificial and, when it disappears, so will the domination of one colour group by another. The A.N.C. has spent half a century fighting against racialism. When it triumphs it will not change that policy.

This then is what the A.N.C. is fighting. Their struggle is a truly national one. It is a struggle of the African people, inspired by their own suffering and their own experience. It is a struggle for the right to live.

During my lifetime I have dedicated myself to this struggle of the African people. I have fought against White domination, and I have fought against Black domination. I have cherished the ideal of a democratic and free society in which all persons live together in harmony and with equal opportunities. It is an ideal which I hope to live for and to achieve. But if needs be, it is an ideal for which I am prepared to die.

MANDELA'S TASK IN THIS SPEECH as a whole is to justify the acts of violence engaged in by Umkonto and approved by him. He does this, as we have seen, by a process of transformation so profound as to become an inversion: he describes the history and motivations of the A.N.C. and

Umkonto, and the responses of the government, in a way that both strips the government of the claim to be a supporter of civilization, which normally goes with an appeal against violence, and transfers it to the A.N.C. and Umkonto. The government is not on the side of the law, or justice, or order, or civilization, or democracy; it is lawless, violent, barbaric; it rules by terror, with no claim whatever to the sort of moral standing usually assumed by those who oppose violence. On the other side, Mandela and Umkonto are the embodiment of civilization—including a large element of Western European civilization—defending itself against barbarism. Sabotage is thus not an instrument of terrorism, as one might at first be inclined to think, threatening the dissolution of civilization; it is a sensible and moderate step taken to prevent a further slide into moral and political degeneration. The state has become the criminal: the criminal the statesman.

In the section of the speech reproduced above Mandela builds upon this foundation in a compelling way. The tone is a bit like that of a government report, or an encyclopedia article, or perhaps a summary of a social science survey: he tells us the facts, sometimes in detail, upon which the activities of the A.N.C. and Umkonto are both based. His tone defines him as rational, objective, grounded in factuality. And the facts define the government too: not only does it act like a barbarian when it uses force to put down the Africans, it does this also in denying them the most basic positive elements of communal life. The Africans live in brutal poverty, from which they are prevented by legislation from escaping either through education or employment. The poverty is thus intended to be perpetual. This is a degradation that denies them the dignity to which all people are entitled, and which it is the purpose of Mandela, and the movement of which he is a leader, to claim. Mandela's own performance reinforces this claim wonderfully, for it is marked throughout by nothing so much as dignity.

It is in a sense odd that this material should come at the end of the speech, for it is the factual predicate for the whole. A more ordinary mind would have put it first, as a way of explaining the grounds upon which the A.N.C. and Umkonto acted, then go into the details of the history of those organizations and their relation to the government. But Mandela reverses the order. The first part could stand on its own, well enough, but it is now reinforced, shifted as it were into a higher key; more important, the speech's ending makes the most powerful appeal of all, when it works, which is to self-evidence. Mandela presents the facts as telling a story with a meaning that cannot be denied. Contradicting the kind of positivism that claims, "You cannot get an ought from an is," Mandela tells a narrative that itself becomes a claim of value, a ground of motivation and action. Perhaps this is the only way you can get an "ought" that really counts.

In all of this Mandela creates his own ground of authority, both in the nature of the situation he describes and in the character he gives to the government and to the movements that resist it. It is upon the narrative—the "facts"—and the characters, as he defined them, on his own creation of a self for the African people, that true judgment and action can be based.

It is striking that throughout the speech Mandela claims the authority of Western European civilization. He does not—as he might have done—oppose Africa to Europe, rejecting the latter and affirming the former. Quite the reverse: he claims Western civilization for himself and his movement; these are the central terms in which he defines the government as barbaric. This is of course a way of making his movement vastly more acceptable to the international community, which is an essential part of his audience, as well as to educated Europeans, and Africans too, in South Africa itself. He separates himself from Europe only in two places: in a passage in which he says that he studies all modes of political thought, Eastern and Western, on the assumption that Africa can choose from these what most meets its needs, and in the sentence, reproduced above, where he describes the kind of polity Africa once had, without rich or poor and without racial division. In this he displays an extraordinary capacity to appropriate from the colonizing culture without embarrassment what is most valuable in it.[6] This is not merely a matter of the reasons given but of identity and character; it is after all Mandela's training as a lawyer upon which he draws in making this speech.

The cultural force of the ideals of democracy and law to which he appeals is demonstrated in another way, by the government's own reluctance to be seen to abandon them entirely. The condition of Mandela's speech is a public trial, presided over by a judge and attended by journalists. The government could simply have murdered him, or tried him in private, or turned the proceedings into a show trial. But they did not, and their decision had consequences against their immediate interest, for it enabled Mandela to speak and be heard. The trial created a moment of rhetorical equality between state and accused, and as such enacted a po-

6. For a wonderful study of this process as a general matter, see C. L. R. James, *Beyond a Boundary* (London: Hutchinson, 1963).

litical value inconsistent with the regime of oppression of which it was a part. To admit such a hearing into one's system is to scatter seeds of possibility whose growth the government cannot entirely control.

As with Socrates' *Apology*, the fact that this speech is made by a person threatened with the death penalty, justifying his life against unjust charges, gives it an extraordinary standing and power. When I first read this speech, many years ago, Mandela was in prison, presumably for the rest of his life. Almost as much as if he had in fact been killed—as Socrates was and he expected to be—these were indeed his last words. In them the justification of his life depends, as he says, ultimately upon a vision or an ideal, a sense of what South Africa could and should be like: certainly not upon what it is. It is for an imagined possibility that he risks death, just as Socrates did, for the city or the country as it might become; for a sense of possibility that he creates in his writing, which can be made real only in the lives of others. In this sense the creation of authority here is indeed an act of hope.

## Lincoln's Second Inaugural Address

In his Second Inaugural Address, Lincoln's task was to justify not a campaign of sabotage but a civil war, which by 1865, when he spoke, had proved much more costly in every way than anyone had expected. This war was fought to preserve the Union; the task then became how to explain what that Union was, and why it was worth killing and dying for. To do this was Lincoln's main aim.

But he had other objectives as well. By the time he spoke victory could be foreseen, and he had the task of defining what that might mean. He had been elected only by the states that remained loyal, but of course he wished to see the entire Union reestablished, including in the rebellious South. To do this he had to speak in such a way as to confirm the North's sense of the rightness of its cause and the justice of its impending victory, yet at the same time to speak to, and about, the people of the White South not as beasts or monsters deserving only death and humiliation but, as he had asserted all along, as fellow citizens, as those who will soon share again in the process of government and in the fate of the nation. "Our" victory is good and right, he must say to the North; yet to the vanquished South he must say you are of "us" too; at the same time he must persuade the North to accept this view of the South. How can he possibly do these inconsistent things?

And how is he to speak to, and about, the African-American people whose enslavement was one of the causes of the war? If he speaks to them as future citizens and equals, the White South will regard anything he says as hostile. If he does not, a large part of the moral basis of the war disappears. And behind all this is a large question of principle, perhaps the deepest issue of the Civil War: why it is proper in the first place for a democratic state, itself based on the right of the people to choose their own forms of government, to use arms to resist secession?

What Lincoln said was characteristically very short, short enough in fact for me to include each sentence in the analysis that follows.[7]

### North and South

Lincoln's words of salutation, usual enough in addresses of this sort, are in this context highly problematic: *"Fellow countrymen."* For who should count as a "fellow countryman" is exactly the issue he addresses: Does he really speak only to the loyal North, or to the rebellious White South as well? If to the latter, in what possible terms? And to what degree will he imply, or acknowledge, that African Americans are his fellow countrymen too?

*"At this second appearing to take the oath of the presidential office, there is less occasion for an extended address than there was at the first."*—The reader may well feel that this is not a rousing start, to say the least. The awkward and official-sounding sentence reads like prose issuing from a typical bureaucratic office. The attention is all on the official occasion; the speaker is entirely erased by the impersonal construction and the absence of pronouns. The promise of this sentence is that the speech as a whole will be one of unutterable dullness. *"Then a statement, some what in detail, of a course to be pursued seemed fitting and proper."* Seemed to whom? To be pursued by whom? One might think that this sounds more like an annual report to shareholders than a presidential inaugural address. This is a sentence, indeed this is a paragraph, that any secondary school–writing teacher would criticize roundly for its passive constructions, its awkwardness, its impersonality. In an obvious sense it is very bad writing indeed, and this from the pen of perhaps the greatest master of American prose.

But in another sense it is not bad writing after all, for the rigorously

---

7. For an extended analysis of another of Lincoln's speeches, see Garry Wills, *Lincoln at Gettysburg: The Words That Remade America* (New York: Simon & Schuster, 1992). He also discusses in briefer terms the Second Inaugural, at pages 177–89.

depopulated universe of the opening paragraph has the effect of creating, as it were, a blank space, free of people, against which the terms that do define the human actors in his drama—"me," "us," "all," "north," "south," "nation," and so forth—will be marked with greater clarity and emphasis when they emerge. It is a way of making plain that he is constructing his social universe in this text, in a kind of creation story: starting with nothing.

> *Now, at the expiration of four years, during which public declarations have been constantly called forth on every point and phase of the great contest which still absorbs the attention and engrosses the energies of the nation, little that is new could be presented.*

We still have the passive voice ("have been called forth," "could be presented"), but we also have an actor and action as well: "the great contest" is the actor, and it "absorbs" and "engrosses" another person, defined here as "the nation." But this is still to think of both the contest and the nation in ambivalent terms: Is the "nation" on one side of the "contest," at war with another side? Or does the "nation" somehow appear on both sides of it? Upon the answer to this question much, including the success of any effort to speak to the South, will depend.

In the next sentence he seems to answer it: *"The progress of our arms, upon which all else chiefly depends, is as well known to the public as to myself; and it is, I trust, reasonably satisfactory and encouraging to all."* The pronouns here identify the speaker, and the audience, with the North; the "all" to whom the progress of arms is encouraging cannot possibly include the White South. But he still insists upon the impersonal and the passive, again to the point of awkwardness: *"With high hope for the future, no prediction in regard to it is ventured."*

Lincoln next repeats in somewhat different terms his earlier invocation of the difference between the present inauguration and his first: *"On the occasion corresponding to this four years ago, all thoughts were anxiously directed to an impending civil war. All dreaded it—all sought to avert it."* Who are these "alls," the reader asks: The North? Or North and South? What of the slaves: Are they included or not? *"While the inaugural address was being delivered from this place, devoted altogether to saving the Union without war, insurgent agents were in the city seeking to destroy it without war—seeking to dissolve the Union and divide effects, by negotiation."* Here we learn that "all" no longer refers to the North alone, but now includes the White South, for the anxiety and dread of civil war includes both sides. But that does not mean there is no moral difference between them: *"Both parties deprecated war; but one of them would make war rather than let the nation survive; and the other would accept war rather than let it perish."* One side is devoted to union and the "nation," the other to secession; one side makes war, the other accepts it. Both North and South are now included in the "all," but there remains an acute moral difference between them. Lincoln closes this paragraph with an allusion to the rains that flooded the earth in Noah's time: "And the war came."

He has thus implicitly raised, and left us with, a question which perhaps he will not answer, namely why maintaining the "nation" in its unified form is something worth fighting for, something indeed that entitles him to adopt his position of moral superiority to the "insurgent agents." We want to know what kind of response this speech will make to this, perhaps the central question about the war; but perhaps the answer is none, we learn, for the next paragraph treats another subject, the human beings held in slavery. Here we begin to see what place they have in the "we" or "all" constituted by this speech.

> *One-eighth of the whole population were colored slaves, not distributed generally over the Union, but localized in the Southern part of it. These slaves constituted a peculiar and powerful interest. All knew that this interest was, somehow, the cause of the war. To strengthen, perpetuate, and extend this interest was the object for which the insurgents would rend the Union, even by war; while the government claimed no right to do more than to restrict the territorial enlargement of it.*

A lukewarm statement to say the least: in this paragraph the slaves are hardly defined as human beings at all. They do make up a certain percentage of the "population" but are more significantly defined as "constitut[ing] a peculiar and powerful interest," a phrase that analogizes them to other interests, such as timber or mining. Lincoln here uses the term by which white Southerners were accustomed to speak of their "peculiar institution." This part of the paragraph indeed looks at slaves very much as the white Southerners would wish; to this extent it tends to include the Southern whites within the circle of its "we" and "all," and to exclude the African Americans.

Notice too that for Lincoln the difference between North and South is not couched in terms of support of slavery versus opposition to it. So far at least, slavery is not seen itself as an evil but simply as an issue over which the parties divide; the difference between North and South, then, lies not in their attitudes towards slavery, but in Southern extremism versus Northern moderation in pursuing this difference. The radical South insisted on extending "this interest" even by war; the moderate North wished only to confine it to its present boundaries. This, not slavery itself, is the moral difference between the "insurgents" and the "government."

All this works as a kind of implicit history that at once explains the war and justifies, perhaps even ennobles, the North's role in it: the North seeks only to preserve union; the South by contrast wishes to impose a kind of tyranny upon the North. So far as these things can be known, this is the "somehow" by which slavery was the cause of the war; not that one side thought it right and the other wrong but that they had different ideas of what to do about that difference itself, one consistent with the premises of constitutional life and union, the other opposed to it.

But the "somehow" does a little more work even than this, for it suggests—as the rest of the speech will amplify—that despite our natural claims to understanding, claims of a kind already made in this address, the actual workings of the universe are to a large degree beyond our comprehension.

### Creating the Union
The speech has been moving towards a sense that in many respects the South and North are on an equal footing. This sense is more firmly established, with heavy emphasis, in what follows, as the syntax—"Neither . . . neither . . . each . . . both . . . each . . ."—drums it home:

> Neither party expected for the war the magnitude or the duration which it has already attained. Neither anticipated that the cause of the conflict might cease with, or even before, the conflict itself should cease. Each looked for an easier triumph, and a result less fundamental and astounding. Both read the same Bible, and pray to the same God; and each invokes his aid against the other.

This is an equality, however, of ignorance, folly, and presumption: both sides expected a shorter and easier war, neither was prepared for a result "so fundamental and astounding," each had the temerity to invoke God's aid against the other. This picks up the note sounded with "somehow" and expands upon it mightily: our common characteristic is our overconfidence, both in our capacity to understand the world and in our moral righteousness. From this perspective the differences of attitude about the Union, and about slavery, slip away; what emerges most is our common plight, not only in this but, by implication, in all circumstances.

Especially dangerous is the last thing that both sides share, a self-righteousness that dares to call on God in aid. To say this is to qualify, perhaps even to purify, the sense of Northern moral superiority—of righteousness—that Lincoln has earlier established, for its tendency is to make the Northerners in the audience feel corrected, the white Southerners feel that they are spoken to as equals.

Now comes a central sentence: *"It may seem strange that any men should dare to ask a just God's assistance in wringing their bread from the sweat of other men's faces; but let us judge not, lest we be judged."* The first clause of the sentence reaffirms the Northern cause, this time grounded not in Union and the Constitution but in opposition to human slavery. We are not equal, after all, he is saying; the moral issue that divides us is a real one, and we in the North are right. And slavery is defined here not merely as an "interest," to be reflected in statistics, but as a deep and radical evil, a denial of the condition of equality with which humankind left Eden, condemned to make our bread by the sweat of our brows. Slavery is an attempt to deny or avoid a scarcity imposed by God on human life and an offense, therefore, not only to the other men, by whose sweat one lives, but to God himself.

Yet the second half of the sentence turns away, not from the particular judgment but from the act of judging, to a position essentially theological in character, as the use of biblical language here and elsewhere also suggests. Lincoln's position here is one that recognizes that our knowledge of our own fault, and of the fault of others, is radically imperfect: "but let us judge not, lest we be judged." This is a point at which South and North can truly meet, space they can openly share. *"The prayers of both could not be answered—that of neither has been answered fully."*

It is to the vacuum of human knowledge thus established that the next line speaks: *"The Almighty has his own purposes."* Although Lincoln has not yet mentioned the "Almighty," the view of human life he has been enacting is a profoundly theological one: an assertion of the limits of knowledge and of the corruption of the human heart, and a concern with the ultimate meaning of things. These are the recognitions that permit him to speak as he does of the Almighty, whose point of view, as represented in the words of Jesus, he then for a moment adopts: *"Woe unto the world because of offences! For it must needs be that offences come; but woe to that man by whom the offence cometh."*

The war here is defined at once as an "offence" in the sight of God and man, as a necessity, and as an occasion of just punishment. Or so it seems; but the next sentence specifies and transforms the "offence" in a surprising way:

*If we shall suppose that American slavery is one of those offenses which, in the providence of God, must needs come, but which, having continued through his appointed time, he now wills to remove, and that he gives to both North and South this terrible war, as the woe due to those by whom the offenses came, shall we discern therein any departure from those divine attributes which the believers in a living God always ascribe to him?*

We see now that it is slavery that is the offense, the war the punishment (or "woe") inflicted for it; and that it is inflicted on both North and South—no longer "government" and "insurgent" but another version of "all" the people—as being both responsible for the offense. This is a far cry indeed from his remarks about slavery as an "interest" that "somehow" "caused" the war, where he spoke as a rather bloodless political scientist. The cause is not of that sort, it turns out, but a moral cause, and slavery is not only an interest, or even an immorality, but an abomination, an "offense."

And his sense of who we are has been transformed as well: we are no longer seen as autonomous individuals or communities in charge of our own conduct, as we were when he spoke of those who sought to "save" or "destroy" the Union without war, but actors in a cosmic drama of which we can only guess at the significance. Our knowledge of everything, everything upon which our judgments of superiority, of unity, of the meaning of our conduct depend, is drawn into question.

But all this is cast less assertively than I have so far indicated, in a conditional sentence, and as a suggestion only. For this is not the voice of a self-certain preacher who has a privileged view of God's will but the voice of one of us, who lives in the universe he describes, one that is and will always be inscrutable.

### Union Achieved

We then get a sentence that could be recast as a poem:

> *Fondly do we hope—*
> *Fervently do we pray—*
> *That this mighty scourge of war*
> *May speedily pass away.*

This is cast in traditional hymn-tune rhymes and almost, but not quite, in traditional hymn-tune rhythms. In this sense its form makes it the kind of prayer it speaks of: the praying, that is, is not merely a practice he is describing but one he is performing, here before us. "Fondly" here has both the modern sense of "affectionately," or perhaps "tenderly," and also

Shakespeare's sense: foolishly, naively. For no hope can be justified in the world he describes except the hope that is an aspect of faith. Prayer is a different matter, and it is not only "they" who do that but we, here and now; and this "we" is all of us, North and South, black and white. The diction, "mighty scourge of war" and "speedily pass away," also establish a continuity between this sentence and the Bible.

> Yet, if God wills that it continue until all the wealth piled by the bondsman's two hundred and fifty years of unrequited toil shall be sunk, and until every drop of blood drawn with the lash shall be paid by another drawn with the sword, as was said three thousand years ago, so still it must be said, "The judgments of the Lord are true and righteous altogether."

By now, slavery has changed its character altogether, from an "interest," to "wringing one's bread from the sweat of other men's faces," to an "offense," to an affirmative crime, both economic and human: the amassing of wealth by "blood drawn with the lash." And it is not only in God's mysterious ways but in our own eyes that we can see the justice of this war that shall sink all that "wealth piled by the bondsman's two hundred and fifty years of unrequited toil" and pay for the blood drawn by the lash with blood drawn by the sword.

IN THIS ADDRESS WE MOVE from a world divided between North and South, with one side righteously victorious over the other, to a vision of a common fate, a common and just suffering that converts the African American—whom he earlier called "colored"—from slave into person. Lincoln never denies the rightness of the Northern cause, nor suggests anything but satisfaction at the progress of its arms. But he has located these motives and feelings in a different context, and transformed them, creating at the end a sense of actual—that is to say imagined—Union, which permits him to close as he does:

> With malice towards none; with charity for all; with firmness in the right, as God gives us to see the right, let us strive on to finish the work we are in; to bind up the nation's wounds; to care for him who shall have borne the battle, and for his widow, and his orphan—to do all which may achieve and cherish a just and lasting peace among ourselves, and with all nations.

Here all sense of triumph over others is gone, all sense of self-righteousness. What is left is a sense of common humanity, common suffering, common decency, a sense that this event in our history is a mark of God's attention to us, giving us a suffering past, and present, like that of the Israelites, and defining us, with divine authority, as one nation—"among ourselves"—in a world of other nations.

This is especially vivid in the pronouns: from talking about "all" in an ambiguous or partisan way, he now plainly uses "none" and "all" in their most inclusive sense. He reaffirms his sense of the right, but equally reaffirms that his sense is necessarily partial. When he speaks directly to his audience and says "let us strive," the "us," like the "all," includes North and South, black and white. And the nation whose wounds he has described is the entire nation for which the war was fought and to define which his speech was given.

# AFTERWORD

IN THIS BOOK I HAVE TRIED TO DEFINE a position from which these texts, highly diverse as they are both in generic type and in cultural context, can be seen to address a common problem, that of managing the relation between the self and the authorities of the world. The suggestion that one could in this way read together Mandela and Dickinson, Plato and Shakespeare, not because they expressed similar ideas but because they are engaged in different versions of the same activity, may have at the beginning of this book been surprising; but I hope it is no longer. Indeed, if this book has done its work, the reader will think, as I do, that all texts can be seen to address this issue, for every text uses language, and language—as Dickinson especially teaches us—is a system of authority. To look for features of life so widely shared is a way of looking for a way to unite what are in our world separate experiences and forms— poetry and law, the private and the public, the past and the present, English and Greek—and in doing so to define an activity of mind and imagination as a ground of human life.

These writers have asked us to grant (or deny) authority to a set of institutions or social practices: the law of Athens, the English crown, the Anglican church, the law of England or America, the manners and morals of Mansfield Park, a certain way of making poetry, Umkonto We Sizwe, and the American Union. Yet to say this is obviously and painfully inadequate to the experience and meaning of these texts, which take positions that are far more complex than a simple "for" or "against" a preexisting institution. In making this list, for example, I have spoken as if the words I used to describe the object of authority—English law, the American Union, etc.—had plain meanings that were shared by everyone, as if they could be used simply as pointers to what we all know, or, as linguists say, indexically. But they cannot. It is one of the lessons of the writers I have discussed, and other good writers too, that we cannot get far in our writing and speaking if we think that our words simply have set meanings, like checkers with labels on them that we can move around at will. Instead, one's words must be defined, and not merely by stipulation—"by the 'Union' I mean . . ."; "by 'dialectic' I mean . . ."; "by 'law' I mean . . ."—but in the whole intellectual and imaginative fabric one creates, the set of distinctions and differences, similarities and analogies, made in one's text, and in the prior texts to which one appeals. The task of the writer is not so much to use words with preexisting meanings as to create a text that gives new meanings to the words within it; this in turn means that a text about authority does not simply point to the authority it invokes or resists but partly creates it. Think, for example, of the way Mandela defines "sabotage"—as an instrument not of terrorism but of civilization, explicitly opposed both to the terrorism of the state and to the terrorist inclinations of the Africans—or of Lincoln's creation of the Union, not merely as a formal arrangement among the States but as a common identity shared by North and South, white and black, given reality by a shared narrative of moral significance.

It is not simply the law of Athens or America or England, then, not simply the crown or a set of manners and morals, to which these writers seek to grant or deny authority, but these things as they are newly imagined and defined in their texts. It is to objects partly of their own creation that they ask that authority be granted.

What is more: in every case the institution in question is imagined not as a thing or a structure but as a process, an intellectual and imaginative activity: as a way of using language, a way of creating an identity for oneself and making a relation to others. Thus in *Richard II* it is not simply "the crown" which Richard invokes but the crown as defined in his poetry—the "crown," really, as a way of imagining the world and acting within it, as the occasion for a certain way of claiming meaning—and much the same is true, in different ways, of Gaunt and York and the others in the play. When people speak of the authority of the crown, what they really mean is the authority of a certain kind of thinking and talking in which the phrase or image, "the crown," has a crucial place. This is what we see in Richard's speeches, for example, and fail to see in Henry's, for he cannot find or make an adequate way to talk about the crown he possesses. Think of the Nomoi, too: Plato represents them not only demanding a particular result but arguing in a certain way for a course of conduct. The real meaning and character of the institution they invoke is found in the practices by which they claim it works, and much the same can be said of Hooker's church, Hale's and *Casey's* law, Lincoln's Union, and Mandela's Umkonto: all these are institutions of which we can speak as objects but which have their real life as systems of thought and discourse. In our own thought too, it is ultimately ways of thinking and talking for which we claim or deny authority. It is not the law as command that is entitled to respect, or not entitled, but the law as a community and culture operating in certain ways. Here is what the law is, and it is here that its authority resides.

This brings me to a third point: each of these texts defines the way of thinking and talking it regards as authoritative in part by exemplifying it. Thus for Hale it is because the law can work as he himself does in his "Considerations" that it is entitled to respect, and to the extent it falls short it loses authority. In a sense, indeed, in all of these texts the highest authority is its own performance. The "law" to which the Court in *Casey* asks that authority be granted, for example, is ultimately the intellectual and cultural activity in which it engages. One cannot simply talk about *"Roe,"* the case that the Court takes as authoritative, as though everyone knew what it meant, any more than one can talk in such a way about the "crown" or the "Union"; in this opinion the object of authority and the Court's relation with it are defined in the process of writing and as a process of writing too. Similarly, it is not the law of Athens to which Socrates asks that authority be given, certainly not to the authoritarian and stupid Nomoi, but to something called philosophy; and this not as if it could be reduced to stipulative or descriptive definition but in the recognition that his term receives its fullest and most precise definition in his performance, in the way in which Socrates works with his language and with his audience. Philosophy, according to Socrates within the dialogue and to Plato in writing it, is not a quest for propositional clarity but a search for a way of life that can be valuable in a world grounded in uncertainty. It is a way of moving from ordinary life into a conversation the aim of which is to enlarge both our sense of what we do not know, and cannot, and our sense that on these terms life can still be lived in a good and satisfactory way.

With Austen and Dickinson the emphasis shifts to the assertion of the value of the individual experience and imagination, but in both writers the key terms are still defined by performances in the text. It makes no sense, for example, to talk about "the manners of Mansfield Park" as if they were the same for everyone; it matters, enormously, whether they are imagined as Mrs. Norris would do, or Mrs. Bertram, or Sir Thomas, or Julia and Maria, or Edmund, or Fanny herself. What Fanny relies on to shape her life is ultimately her own creation—not out of nothing, but her creation nonetheless—and the reader in his turn is led to a position from which he can see that he too imagines his world and makes it real, in ways for which he is responsible. The novel's central authority is its own way of doing these things. With Dickinson the point is even more obvious: she opposes the authority of the sentimental, verbose, genteel, and mechanistic verse of her time with her own poetic performances with language. But their meaning lies not simply in the fact of opposition, or in some general declaration of independence, but in their particular quality: in what she does with language and her reader, and who she becomes in doing so. Likewise, it is Mandela's achievement not merely to defend Umkonto, as though we all knew what it was, but to define it in his prose; and as he does so it too becomes a way of imagining the world and living within it, exemplified in his writing, and much the same thing can be said of Lincoln's Union as well.

In all these instances, then, the object of authority is not an "object" at all but a way of talking and thinking, an activity of mind and imagination and art; it receives its fullest definition not descriptively, but performatively, as the writer finds a way of using language that transforms it, a way of defining himself and others in order to create a new community, a community of discourse, in the world.

Each of these writers thus asks that authority be given to an intellectual and cultural process that is literary, not conceptual in kind. This works in part as a recommendation to us to imitate them, to learn from their example the art they perform. It also invites us to think of the public world itself not as a machine—not as a structure, or an entity with parts regulated by the laws of cause and effect—but as a set of discourses or languages, a set of ways of thinking and talking and acting in the world. That is what the law is, and the Union is, and Umkonto is, and the crown is, and manners are. When they are conceived of as practices it may become possible for us to imagine engaging in them and transforming them and criticizing them in new ways. The art by which one defines oneself and one's relation to authority is not the special province of political philosophy, and its occasions are not limited to moments of dramatic opposition between citizen and state. It is an art essential to full human life; its occasions occur every day; and we have much to learn from the performances of those who can show us how it can be practiced well.

ONE THEME RUNNING THROUGH THESE TEXTS is that of exile or secession and reunion. In this they catch another general feature of human life. Each of us in growing up, in becoming independent, must in a sense secede from the languages we have been taught, resisting and transforming them; yet we can never escape them entirely, and a part of success is a return, though on different terms, an acceptance of what one must accept about oneself, one's world, and the way one has been made. Socrates is an Athenian; he will not deny that by exile but prefers to die, an act with meaning in his world. Mandela likewise refuses exile; he insists on acting in his world, even if it means his death, and doing so on his own terms; yet not his alone, for what he offers South Africa is not a remote ideal but a better version of itself. Lincoln seeks to define a Union that will comprise us all, North and South, black and white, individual and nation, for the theological vision out of which he operates is a narrative in which we all have a common place; and his is a vision that promises to teach us something of our own capacity for charity.

None of these writers thought he lived in a just or perfect world. Everyone saw evil, in himself and in others; everyone saw defects of mind and language, in himself and others. Yet each found a way of living in an unjust world by imagining an ideal into partial reality.

# ADDITIONAL NOTES

## METHOD: LITERARY PARTICULARS

THIS BOOK IS MEANT, AMONG OTHER THINGS, to exemplify a way of thinking not in the abstract but by the use of a series of particular literary and intellectual performances. Thus I do not ask the questions, "What is the nature of authority? To what should authority be granted?" as if they could be answered by a series of propositional declarations, but instead I look at the way in which other people, whose work I admire, have performed responses to such questions in their writing. I am interested in the way authority is created in actual contexts by people embedded in the languages they employ. The idea is not to reach conclusions but to open up possibilities for thought, by drawing attention to ways in which others have responded to, and thus clarified, the aspect of our common experience that consists of our perpetual struggle with the tension between the claims of the self and the claims of the world. In this book I am looking at authority, not as a force in the world, to be described as a social scientist might do, but as a problem, and especially as a problem for the individual mind faced with the difficulty of deciding what to do or to say.

This means that it is a mistake to hope for conclusions that take the form of propositions arranged in a scheme, or even lists of criteria or standards of judgment. In focusing on the way people think and talk about authority, the way in which they constitute themselves and their worlds in their writing in such a way as to claim or concede authority for some part of what they see and say, I am focusing on an art, an art of using language, and we can expect only the sort of conclusions that are possible in such a field. One cannot reduce excellence in painting or music to a grid of criteria or propositions. Even to try to do it is inconsistent with the kind of meaning the works in question have. Instead, one works by drawing attention to details and particulars, to this gesture or that movement, and by thinking comparatively, putting this work beside that one and seeing what similarities and differences emerge. Of course, one speaks in generalities too, but never with the idea that what one says can substitute for the experience of the work of art, as though this generalization were the essential truth; one's generalizations serve rather to focus attention on certain aspects of the work, to connect one with another, to suggest a line of thought that can only be

309

pursued in connection with the experience the work itself offers—putting it in a phrase, one might say that one's generalities serve the function not of explication but of orientation.

In this book my interest is in one sense very general indeed, for I am trying to draw attention to a widely shared aspect of human life, as I imagine it a primary human process: the management of the relation between world and self, mind and language. The impulse is philosophic in character, but the mode of working is not, at least in the modern sense—though perhaps it is in another sense, if the reader accepts my reading of Plato—for it is not propositional in kind. I am not interested in reaching conclusions statable in summary form but in suggesting a way of thinking that is also a way of learning from the performances of others.

The texts I have used are drawn largely from what is now called the Western Canon. This, of course, reflects my own education and tastes—there is no way to avoid that—but also has another point, to show that these texts can be of continuing value in our world, and not simply as aesthetic experiences, or as objects of cultural analysis, but as offering an education that can inform our lives, including our practical and professional lives. Obviously other texts could serve the same purpose, and in choosing these I do not mean to claim that they are the texts most worth attention. I expect my readers to have their own array of texts, their own standards of congeniality and interest, which it is not my aim to supplant. My aim is much more modest: to show how these particular texts can be worth attention.

## THE *CRITO*: RELATED APPROACHES

I said earlier that Chapter 1 is similar in approach to the article on the *Crito* by Ernest Weinrib, "Obedience to Law in Plato's Crito," *American Journal of Jurisprudence* 27 (1982): 85. First, as to general method, his aim like mine is to read the whole text and not just the speech of the Nomoi; he thinks the dream is important (and develops in that connection the thought that Socrates is implicitly comparing himself with Achilles, which had not occurred to me); he sees a paradoxical similarity between the "many" whose views one is to disregard and the laws themselves, whom Socrates seems to be saying one must obey; he thinks that the speech of the Nomoi is directed to the character of Crito and is in fact a response in kind to Crito's earlier speech to him, cast as it is in the terms of the popular Greek morality of the day; and he thinks that this speech is not seriously meant by Socrates, for it is deeply inconsistent with his fundamental principles, as those have been outlined earlier in the dialogue. The function of the speech, then, is an act of friendship; it persuades Crito, the only way Crito is capable of persuasion, to an attitude which, while less to be valued than the philosopher's, is a basically good one for one who cannot meet the demands of philosophy. (He does not say so, but this reading enables one to fit the *Crito* with the authoritarian strain in the *Republic* and other of Plato's political writings.)

In all of this the similarities are obvious and I am sure that while some of them may be accidental, not all of them are, and that much of my own understanding derives from reading his work. On the other hand, there are differences as well: in the reading of the dream, as I suggested above; in my emphasis upon the anxiety of Crito and the repose of Socrates; in my sense of the way in which what I have called the "short course in Socratics" actually works; in my reading of the speech of the Nomoi, which Professor Weinrib sees as a rather unitary presentation, and I as a series of rewritings that move Crito, and the reader, from one topic, and one way of thinking and talking, to another; in our sense, therefore, of the true subject of that part of the dialogue, which for Weinrib remains obedience to the law, for me is the meaning of Socrates' situation, in which the question of obedience to law comes up only hypothetically (if Crito can persuade him that justice requires him to escape); in the kind of friendship Socrates is manifesting, which for Weinrib is to give arguments of a lesser kind to a person of lesser capacity, for me is to move him to the point where the issue disappears; and in my discussion of authority, which has no counterpart in his.

I should also mention here Gary Young, "Socrates and Obedience," *Phronesis* 19 (1974): 1–29, which is far more analytic in style than either Professor Weinrib's piece or my chapter but makes several of the same points. In particular, Young sees the speech of the Nomoi as an act of friendship to an intellectually less able person—he sees Crito as essentially one of "the many"—which offers him the best argument he can accept for the decision to stay. But he reads the *Crito* and *Apology* together as establishing the absolute duty to obey the law, subject only to the exception articulated in the *Apology* in favor of the philosophic life, which is commanded by a god, 19 *Phronesis* at 29.

Finally, I should mention Philip Soper, *Another Look at the Crito* (forthcoming), which roots the authority of law in the good faith with which the state is assumed to act, both in promulgating laws and in listening to arguments against them. This is a development of the theme, which I also see in the *Crito*, that finds the roots of obligation in character and relations.

This chapter was presented as the Robert S. Marx Lecture at the University of Cincinnati Law School and will be published in its law review.

# INDEX

313